ACHIEVING COMPETENCE AND FULFILLMENT

ACHIEVING COMPETENCE AND FULFILLMENT

Arthur G. Nikelly

University of Illinois
at Champaign-Urbana

Brooks/Cole Publishing Company
Monterey, California
A Division of Wadsworth Publishing Company, Inc.

To my parents

Printed in the United States of America

10 9 8 7 6 5 4 3 2 1

Library of Congress Cataloging in Publication Data

Nikelly, Arthur G
    Achieving competence and fulfillment.

    Includes index.
    1. Adjustment (Psychology)   2. Humanistic psychology. I. Title.
BF335.N54   158'.1   76-46477
ISBN 0-8185-0199-5

Manuscript Editor: *Meredith Mullins*
Production Editor: *Fiorella Ljunggren*
Interior and Cover Design: *John Edeen*
Chapter-Opening Photographs: *Shirley Kontos*

Preface

Coping with a rapidly changing, increasingly complex society is a difficult and perplexing task. It is not surprising, then, that an increasing number of lifestyles have come about and have, in turn, created new conflicts. It appears that we are, generally, moving away from the rigid attitudes and behavior of the past and moving toward tolerance of individual differences and greater openness to personal expression in attire, behavior, thought, and living styles. Greater and deeper understanding of ourselves and others, how we came to be what we are, how we can change from what we are into what we want to be, and the constant interplay between the social conditions that shape us and our free choice over our behavior are issues discussed in this book. I have focused on ways to cope effectively with stress, alternate avenues toward fulfillment, where help can be found, if necessary, and what we can expect from such help.

This book is designed for the undergraduate of any age; it focuses on experiences familiar to students and on the student's potential to create his or her own adjustment and actualization. The book is primarily for use in courses on personal adjustment and is particularly helpful to the nonpsychology major. Its study should suggest new possibilities for better living and help students to formulate a positive and viable image of human nature.

I have emphasized an action-oriented, humanistic psychology rather than a medically-oriented concept of maladjustment as illness or disease. Further, I have attempted to view human behavior, whenever possible, as a result of growth and fulfillment rather than as biologically or socially determined. Throughout, I have tried to offer students an optimistic and liberating view of human beings that emphasizes what is positive within us and that stresses our innate ability to find happiness and fulfillment.

I have drawn upon the most recent studies and included areas not extensively covered in other texts. For example, problems of ecology, changing philosophies of education, emerging minorities, alternatives to marriage, life in the cities, the world of work, ways of dealing with our frustrations and anxieties, and ways to find meaning in our lives are topics of current interest given extensive coverage. Also, I have tried to avoid theoretical or abstract discussions and to present instead findings based on research and observational data that arouse interest in the basic issues of living and help to acquaint the student with fundamental concepts of human behavior.

The case histories and other anecdotal material incorporated throughout the book are based on informal conversations with students, on individual and group therapy sessions, and on reports and questionnaires completed by students enrolled in courses on personal adjustment.

I sincerely appreciate the criticisms and comments of Marian L. MacDonald, Theresa Soule, Peter R. Stubing, Robert P. Larson, and James O. White, who read excerpts of the manuscript as it was being written.

I would also like to thank reviewers Norbert Yager of Henry Ford Community College, Ronald Smith of Portland State University, Kay Tudor of California State University at Sacramento, Dale Federer of California Polytechnic State University, Sumner Morris of the University of California at Davis, Robert Osterhouse of the University of Maryland, John Peters of San Diego Mesa College, Donald Tasto of Stanford Research Institute, Alan Dahms of Metropolitan State College, and Richard Hamersma for their helpful criticisms and suggestions.

To Nancy Flom for typing the entire manuscript, Audrey Hodgins for pre-production editing, and Meredith Mullins for final production editing go special thanks for helping me express myself effectively.

I am deeply indebted to Bonnie Fitzwater for her continual encouragement and patience during the critical stages of the organization of the book and to the entire staff of Brooks/Cole, especially Andrea Guillobel and Terry Hendrix, for being cooperative and pleasant during the writing and production of the book.

Arthur G. Nikelly

Contents

I don't want to reach up high
Like the ivy, deceiving and tall,
Tied to strange stakes for support.
Let me grow short and small
Like the tiny grass and weeds,
But as I climb I want to stand
On the strength of my own.

I don't want to shine afar
Like the sea at noon all bright
Only mimicking the dazzling sun.
Let me glow like a candle light
With a soft and humble flame,
As long as the gleam I give is real
And comes from inside me alone.

—Georgios Drossinis, "The Shining Darkness"
(*Collected Poems,* 1914), translated by
A. G. Nikelly

Chapter 1

Personality:
An Evolving Theory

CHAPTER OUTLINE

I. What is the human being?
   A. Becoming truly human
   B. Discovering the human dimension
   C. Are we free and rational?
   D. The meaning of self-actualization

II. Understanding personality
   A. The psychoanalytic view
   B. Adler's theory of social interest
   C. The behavioristic view
   D. Existential psychology
   E. Humanistic psychology
      1. Maslow
      2. Rogers
      3. Fromm
      4. Horney
      5. Allport
      6. White
   F. The eclectic view of personality

III. Application of the four major personality theories
   A. Psychoanalytic approach
   B. Behavioristic approach
   C. Existential approach
   D. Humanistic approach

IV. Combining humanistic psychology and behavior modification

V. Summary

"There are many marvels, but the human being is the greatest of all," wrote Sophocles over 2000 years ago. Humans have traveled in outer space and walked on the moon, smashed the atom and released its energies, and harnessed the vast powers of nature, but we have, for the most part, failed to understand ourselves—our capacity for destruction as well as our ability to create. We continue to ask the questions "Why do we exist?" "What is reality?" "Why are we afraid to love one another?" "Why are our actions so often the opposite of our intentions?" Let us begin here to formulate answers to these perennial questions and to take steps toward self-understanding and fulfillment.

WHAT IS THE HUMAN BEING?

History shows that human beings are complex, diverse creatures with many facets of behavior and many levels of depth involved in their personalities.

When we observe a monkey in his cage, we catch only a glimmer of the freely swinging jungle ape. Similarly, when we study persons who are in mental hospitals or who show unusual behavior, we review only a small population, people who may not really be like the rest of us. In our study of human behavior, it is important to observe ourselves in action: thinking, communicating, planning, creating, working, playing, and relating to others. Only by examining the characteristics of the mature person can we hope to discover how we may cope in reasonable ways with life's problems. Only by studying those who are functioning effectively in their daily lives can we find new possibilities for learning about ourselves and moving toward fulfillment.

The term *fulfillment,* as I used it here, refers not to a state but to a process; that is, we move toward fulfillment, setting out on a course of continued development. Life is not a fixed state of happiness or unhappiness but a condition of flux that holds within it possibilities for change and growth. Fulfilled persons do not look upon the past as an index of how the future is going to be; rather, they reach out toward greater knowledge, new experiences, and deeper insights. They think not only in terms of what we all have in common that binds us together but also in terms of what they want from themselves (Kinget, 1975).

3

Becoming Truly Human

"So graceful and gentle is a person when he behaves like a true human being," wrote the playwright Menander over 2000 years ago. But how can we become "truly human" and what so often prevents us from achieving this goal?

Despite the conflicting views of philosophers, educators, and scientists, "truly human" persons might be defined as those who can accept responsibility for their own behavior. They are willing to make choices and to take risks when they must. They also accept themselves for what they are. Each recognizes that he or she is different from others, but they treasure that uniqueness, acknowledging that individuals must be different from one another. Indeed, one strong reason for loving someone is that the person is, for you, unique and of intrinsic value.

Truly human persons feel at home in the world despite its chaos and inconsistencies because they recognize a part of themselves in every other human being. Because they understand themselves, they understand and treat others as they themselves like to be treated. They are open to the ideas and experiences of others; yet, they want to communicate their own thoughts and feelings as well. They seek love and closeness with others and are not afraid to be spontaneous, to reach out to others, even though sometimes they may not be accepted.

Truly human persons think and act beyond the petty, superficial differences that separate people and make them feel alone, unwanted, or inferior. They believe that every person is capable of responding to common chords—that is, to the shared characteristics that make us human. Sometimes these chords are out of tune or are difficult to reach because an individual has been stifled or mistreated and has withdrawn because of insecurity or fear. In spite of such difficulties, fully human persons search out the mutual inner qualities that sustain us all. Because truly human persons feel a common bond with all people, they give the common good priority over personal advantage. They act, therefore, according to certain ethical principles, even though they may experience personal inconvenience or sacrifice. They believe that, when they work for the benefit of all humankind, they also work for their own betterment.

Discovering the Human Dimension

What makes us act the way we do? One speculation is that our behavior, and the entire course of our lives, is predetermined. Our fate is "written" before we are born, and there is little we can do to control what happens to us. Thus, we may feel inert, futile, or even despairing when we are unable to understand and control the forces of nature or when we are overwhelmed by hostile and threatening living conditions. Historically, we can examine such views of despair during Roman and Medieval times. These pessimistic views were present during these periods probably because people of that time felt unable to prevent wars, pestilence, famine, and other physical forces that plagued society. During the Renaissance and later periods, however, speculations on the origins of behavior became increasingly rationalistic and, thereby, more optimistic. Theories of behavior centered around the idea that if people have the capacity to reason and the ability to use their intelligence, they can do much to control their destiny.

Figure 1-1. When two people express a liking for each other, it can have a profound effect on their attitude toward life. Photo by Shirley Kontos.

Through systematic observation as well as speculation, psychologists have developed four major explanations of the motives for human behavior. The **psychoanalytic** view holds that we are not governed by reason alone and that we are selfish, often giving in to instincts and basic drives of which we are not always fully aware. We desire to attain pleasure and to avoid pain. The bases for this view stem from older, philosophically oriented rather than scientifically oriented thought, but they are still powerful and persuasive. **Behaviorism,** on the other hand, sees us as complex machines governed by our environment. This view rejects the force of inner motives, insisting instead that what we do (output) is a direct result of what happens to us (input). Behavior can therefore be controlled by manipulating external stimuli. Behaviorists rely heavily on laboratory experiments (often with animals) to understand how learning takes place. They believe that if they can understand what causes maladjusted behavior, they can eliminate it through "unlearning" and replace it with "normal" behavior. The learning theory that grew out of behaviorism is called *behavior modification.* This theory aims to teach us how we may, through our own efforts, unlearn unacceptable behavior (such as nervousness, smoking, bad study habits) and relearn desirable behavior (composure, nonsmoking, efficient study habits). Behavior modification will be presented in greater detail in Chapter 10.

A third theory, the **existential** view, is based on literature and philosophy instead of on science. This theory has strong speculative components, but it centers around the experiences we have with ourselves and with other people and the philosophical meaning of those experiences. Existentialism holds that we alone must define our goals and answer such questions as "What is the meaning of my existence?" Although we are capable of rational choice and of self-understanding, we must also learn to accept some frustrations because they are part of the human condition. A fourth view, the **humanistic** view (or, as it is often called, the "Third Force"), does not deny that we strive for meaning, joy, creativity, and fulfillment in our lives. Thus, it espouses many psycho-philosophical principles of existentialism that have existed since ancient times. Humanistic psychology holds further that our behavior is not guided entirely by inner "quirks," and it is not shaped only by outside forces; thus, humanistic psychology encompasses elements of psychoanalytic thought as well as of behaviorism. This "Third Force," however, emphasizes the sense of human isolation; we may be unhappy because we have not actualized ourselves, and we may be frustrated because our interpersonal relationships are not as fulfilling as they might be. This view has several important ramifications, but it tends to focus attention on how we feel *right now* and on how we can go about making decisions that will alter our lives in significant ways. It is a view of the individual as a functioning *whole,* who deals mostly with the *here* and the *now.*

Are We Free and Rational?

Most of us feel that we have a certain amount of freedom, even though many of our actions seem to be determined by the outside environment—on the one hand by our families, our teachers, our peers, and society in general and on the other hand by our impulsive behavior and unthinking reactions. No one is absolutely free, but neither are we automatons, functioning by learned actions alone. What is important is that we come to understand those aspects of behavior that are conditioned and those that are not; it is by recognizing both aspects in ourselves that we can become more free. Even though we may be "programmed" into uniform habits of dress, speech, and eating, most of our behavior involves acting on our own.

Krasner and Ullmann (1973) have clearly shown that we are not only shaped by other persons but that we influence those around us and those with whom we interact. We influence our friends in subtle ways without, of course, fully realizing our impact. As we interact with others, we provide an input for them, which in turn helps to determine their behavior toward us. We, naturally enough, then respond in the light of that behavior. The student protest movement of the 1960s is a good example of this spiraling action through mutual reinforcement. Once we realize that we ourselves have determined the quality of life today, we can act in more productive ways to improve it.

Can you become what you want to become, despite the many obstacles in the environment? Can you follow a path that is truly your own and achieve those things in life that mean the most to you? If you are realistic and free about your choices of career, goals, relationships, and so on, then, in all probability, you can become the person you want to be.

Human beings are capable of self-destruction through restraint and withdrawal. They are also capable of actively inflicting evil and suffering on others. Yet, there appears to be a virtually innate (inborn) potential for benevolence, creativity, and happiness in humans. For example, aggressive behavior is unknown to the Tasaday tribe in the Philippines; they use no weapons, and they share with one another everything they have (Llamson, 1971). It is this area of positive potential that we will explore further in this book; that is, if we do have such innate capabilities, how should we go about realizing them and finding genuine fulfillment?

The Meaning of Self-Actualization

Self-actualization means striving to develop our capabilities to their fullest and discovering our natural selves. Consider the potential for growth in yourself: you have the innate ability to grow and to develop into a well-adjusted, happy, and productive person. But if conditions are not conducive to fulfillment, you may become stifled. Just as we might experiment with different conditions of temperature and sunlight in maximizing the growth of a plant, so can we alter living conditions to determine which are best for individual maturation.

Maslow (1954), a contemporary humanistic psychologist, holds that we have certain needs and abilities that form our essential nature. Ideally, these needs and capabilities are in constant movement toward actualization. In addition, Maslow felt that we must overlook our failures and weaknesses and concentrate on developing our successes and strengths so that we can become what we were meant to be.

To actualize yourself, then, means to liberate the undeveloped possibilities that are present in you. We can more easily understand these possibilities for growth if we consider them as taking place in successive steps—that is, a hierarchy of needs. Maslow's hierarchy of psychological needs begins with physical needs (food, shelter, clothing, safety) and also includes the need to feel accepted and to belong, the need to give and to receive love, the need to be effective with others and to master the environment adequately with skills that others recognize, and, finally, the need to be creative and expressive and to develop potential in an original way.

People in impoverished areas of the world still function at a low level in such a hierarchy, since food and shelter are basic needs that they are unable to satisfy. For these people, the need for esteem (an important need in certain cultures) may have lower priority than the immediate securing of food. Or, for example, consider the temporary upset in the social hierarchy that can occur when you leave the security of home and go off to college. At first, you may feel alienated and unaccepted, and, thus, certain other needs will go unsatisfied until you have reestablished a sense of belonging. Wealthy persons who overvalue material possessions may never reach the higher stages of basic human fulfillment. An unhappy childhood or an unsuccessful marriage, however, does not mean one must remain "stuck" at a certain level of need fulfillment. No one is doomed to be what he or she is at the moment. In fact, handicapping conditions can become a challenge for understanding where we are, how we got there, and where we want to go.

Self-actualization does not occur overnight; it requires experimentation, the acquisition of new skills, and the ability to sometimes forego immediate pleasures for certain long-range and higher goals. Fulfillment can be experienced in a variety of ways—becoming involved, sharing, creating, and, most of all, loving someone—

Figure 1-2. While society encourages us to be aloof and insensitive, self-actualization stresses feeling, joy, and emotional responsiveness to life. Photo by Jody Ellyne.

and it need not be denied us at any period of life. In fact, we never really stop growing in understanding and perception; there is always more to be done, to be learned, to be experienced. Life is fluid, and the more we learn about ourselves, the further along we are on the path toward self-actualization.

UNDERSTANDING PERSONALITY

Each of us adjusts to the environment in different ways because of our individual histories. Adjustment is affected by our relationship with our parents, by their education and social status, by the number of siblings (brothers and sisters) we have, by our ordinal position within the family (first, second, middle, last child), by the quality of our education, by peer relationships, and by career choice. Thus, no two persons ever develop identically, regardless of similarities in background or genetic structure.

Personality reflects many elements—motives, habits, needs, interests, aptitudes, values, even physique, and it is often difficult to separate those characteristics that have been inherited from those that have been learned. Since such categorization is necessarily rather arbitrary, it is sufficient to say that, although a potential ability may be inborn, its development and use will depend on social conditions, cultural opportunities, and many personal factors. While we can never exclude the importance of biologically inherited factors (such as height or endurance), we must also consider the enormous influence of socially inherited (learned) behavior patterns—political views, feelings of social responsibility, moral values, and vocational aspirations. We might note here that the word *growth* is often used to imply the coming into being of the physiological person—through physical growth from within—whereas the word *development* is frequently used to suggest expansion through the influence of social and environmental stimuli— through stimulation from without. Occasionally, however, the terms *growth* and *development* are used interchangeably.

The controversy over whether we are dominated by heredity or social influences or whether we can shape our own destiny cannot be resolved simply. Complex interactions between innate traits and social conditioning have always affected human growth and development (Graham & Crow, 1973). Not only do physical and inherited factors determine growth, but so do social interactions, achievement, the opinion of others, and many other life experiences (the effect of nurture). In addition to nature and nurture—the key words in this almost classic controversy—the way each person perceives and reacts toward these influences is highly significant in determining personality, and that reaction is often difficult to predict. For example, obese or unusually tall persons may have negative feelings about their appearance, however they might hide these feelings behind a facade of jolly, outgoing behavior.

People are always growing; their personalities are never static. Recall the person you were a few years ago. In many ways you are probably a different person now: you may think differently about politics, about marriage; you may feel estranged from old high school friends or suddenly closer to a kid sister with whom you used to quarrel frequently. Yet, there is a core in your personality that has undergone relatively little change—a center that provides a certain consistency in your behavior from one place and time to another. Although all behavior reveals personality, certain behaviors may be more consistent than others and are, therefore, used to characterize a given personality. For example, we may see an individual as *generally* easygoing, moody, cynical, or aloof.

Psychologists are inclined to view personality as an entity, clustering its various elements together as a functioning unit. They also hold that personality is best understood when it is observed in action. For that reason, psychologists tend to be interested in the goals toward which we are striving, because only by understanding our intentions can our actions be fully understood. If we can be helped to recognize our goals and the patterns of behavior they produce (our *lifestyle*), we may be able to predict our behavior in a given situation as well as to change it. Such a chain of events is at the heart of much current psychotherapy. Certainly it is true that part of our behavior is determined by biological factors, genetic factors, and social learning, but part of our behavior can overcome biological and social limitations. It is this independent behavior that can be changed, that *can* be actualized.

How we adjust to life reveals a great deal about our personality. And we judge others' personalities by how they impress us socially—that is, what image they project and how they adjust to particular social situations. Adjustment, however, can also reflect the quality of a person's relationship with the environment; therefore, it is possible to judge an individual's personality "good" but his or her adjustment "poor" or vice versa. Personality and adjustment are, however, intertwined in complex ways and usually cannot be considered separately; rather, they influence and reinforce each other.

The way one personality interacts with other personalities is called the *dynamics* of personality. For example, people considered introverts may avoid emotional closeness because they fear rejection. By maintaining distance from others, they assure themselves that they will be able to control their fears, although their fears—perhaps quite unreasonable ones—thus are controlling their actions. These underlying reasons for certain behavior patterns and the resulting actions and interactions combine to create the dynamics of personality.

Psychologists studying the human personality often talk about the *self,* a term that relates to our total personality, encompassing our unique identity as it has developed through social interaction. When we analyze our own behavior or when we say such things as "This is the real me talking," we are centering in on our selves. However, there may be a contradiction between how we see ourselves and how others see us.

The *ego* is evidenced in the way we act or exhibit certain qualities of personality. The ego can be best described as the conscious and rational side of ourselves that brings our personality together and helps it work as one unit. We may say, for instance, that confident, alert, responsive persons who like themselves and their work and who can postpone the immediate satisfaction of needs without being easily hurt have "strong" egos. From the lack of any of these qualities, we may infer a "weak" ego. In order to defend the self, maintain self-esteem, and cope with life's pressures, the ego uses protective devices. If these devices become too strong or rigid, however, they can distort reality and cripple our ability to cope. Placing the blame on others in order to cover up our own faults is an example of a protective device. We will discuss such protective devices more extensively in Chapter 5. Since protective devices operate on a more or less unconscious level, we normally use them without full knowledge of their existence. As a matter of fact, if we do become conscious of them, their effectiveness may be impaired.

The Psychoanalytic View

Sigmund Freud, a Viennese psychiatrist born in 1856, regarded the self as three separate parts—the *id, superego,* and *ego* (1943). The id, according to Freud, is made up of instincts and pleasure-seeking impulses. The most important of these impulses is sexual drive, or *libido.* The superego is similar to the conscience; it reflects the moral and ethical values of society, values that often conflict with the desires of the id. The ego handles these conflicts by rechanneling the drives into more socially acceptable behavior. Should these conflicts begin to get out of hand, anxiety develops as a warning sign.

The libido consists of sexual energy that expresses itself in different parts of the body at various periods of physical development and that, if hindered, can result in problems of maladjustment during adulthood. In the infant, Freud identified the first phase of the development of sexual energy, the *oral phase*, during which pleasure was associated with the lips and sucking. If oral needs were not met during this period, the person might later eat or drink constantly (perhaps becoming obese or an alcoholic) or become verbally aggressive. The next few years of life marked the *anal phase*, in which bowel control was achieved. Conflicts during this period may be reflected in adult behavior through undue punctuality, inordinate neatness, or other compulsive manifestations. In the 3- to 6-year-old child, Freud identified the *phallic phase*, during which the child expressed curiosity about sexual organs. Frustration at this level may result in selfishness and vanity. From this phase until the child reaches the age of about 11 (or the beginning of puberty), he or she experiences the *latency phase*, during which sexuality is considered to be essentially dormant or in suspension. Finally, Freud defined the *genital phase*, the most mature level of psychosexual development, as that period marked by sexual development and heterosexual attraction. During this phase, drives are given vent through socially acceptable channels and through the fulfilling fusion of love and sex with a special partner.

In Freudian therapy, often referred to as psychoanalysis, the patient is encouraged to associate freely—that is, to express openly whatever thoughts he or she may have at that particular moment. The therapist then interprets these expressions within the framework of psychosexual development. In addition, the patient may experience feelings of *transference*—an emotional reaction to the therapist that is transferred from the relationship the patient had with his or her parents. Together with the therapist, the patient works through these feelings in an effort to resolve conflicts. The therapist attempts to uncover the "unconscious" portion of the patient's personality, enabling that individual to function more effectively through a fuller understanding of his or her self. Such a process, of course, is time consuming and seems too mysterious, speculative, or equivocal for some therapists.

Freud constructed a model of human functioning based on biological instincts or drives and on stages of emotional and sexual development. These stages were dependent on the early interactions of the patient with his or her parents, particularly the mother. On the basis of this model, Freud attempted to explain human behavior.

Freud hit upon a useful resolution from the contemporary therapist's point of view when he balanced the basic drives (sex, aggression, selfishness) against the superego (conscience). He believed that only when there is harmony between these two extremes can we live effectively. It is not surprising, then, that Freud felt that, to fulfill ourselves, not only must we love—by tempering our basic drives with a reasonable superego—but we must also work and create—by using the released energy of the superego in other activities.

In retrospect, it is believed by many psychologists that Freud may have placed too much emphasis on hereditary predispositions and innate instinctual forces. Many therapists today find his idea of personality too deterministic and mechanistic; they contend that it ignores conscious responsibility for action and the ability to organize experiences in a meaningful manner in order to achieve fulfillment. Others question the idea of separate impulses within a personality and whether such impulses, if they do exist, are capable of "playing games" with one another. Freud, they contend, also overlooked the effects of social conditions and the quality of interpersonal relationships that shape human personality. Since Freud's time, there has been a growing trend toward theories, based on clinical evidence, that human beings have an inborn ability to solve their problems and to actualize themselves, if they are free to function effectively.

Certain significant developments that complement or alter Freud's major ideas and that further help us to understand human behavior and the achievement of self-fulfillment will be presented in the following discussion.

Adler's Theory of Social Interest

Alfred Adler, born in Vienna in 1870, disagreed with Freud's theories, maintaining that the child's position in the family, the child's own mistaken interpretation of experiences with parents, peers, and siblings, and parental pampering or domination are the forces that govern adult personality (1927b). Adler provided his clients with a chair instead of a couch and treated them more as equals. He paid less attention to unconscious processes and made every effort to offer his client a viable, constructive human relationship. He lectured to teachers on how to handle the problems of children in the classroom, and he treated the parents of the maladjusted child together with the child. For him, psychotherapy involved the client's relearning through encouragement.

Adler concentrated on the client's immediate problems rather than on his or her past, although he also aimed at uncovering goals and intentions of which clients were often unconscious. He viewed behavior problems as devices "useful" to clients for gaining attention and for controlling others; thus, he attempted to help clients discover what sort of "games" they were playing. His clients were not "sick" persons requiring "treatment." Rather, they needed to see where they had made mistakes along the path of their development; that is, what in the lifestyles they had adopted caused them to fail in life or prevented them from enjoying it.

Adler's theory that we are active beings who are not merely at the mercy of our instincts or the conditioning forces of our environment was later adopted by several other personality theorists, such as Maslow, Fromm, Ellis, and Dreikurs. Adler also believed that heredity and environment, although important, were not the decisive forces his predecessors had felt them to be; rather, they were just stimuli to which each person responded according to his or her unique personal style.

This theory is not as philosophical as it first appears to be. Simply put, we all have inherited traits (intelligence, physique, drives), and we all are affected by society; yet, it remains for us to choose in a self-directing manner what we want from these raw materials. Our decisions, of course, will be influenced by what we value most, by what our goals are. We have the power to originate and to construct out of basic elements many complex creations; we can produce, in a sense, a blueprint of our selves. This force by which we design our own blueprints is known as the "creative self," and it is one of the basic tenets of humanistic psychology today (Ansbacher, 1971). It means that we are governed not by social forces and hereditary factors alone, but also by what use we make of them to our own advantage.

Adler (1927a), unlike Freud, focused attention on the potential of the healthy, functioning personality; he believed that most people want to overcome feelings of inferiority or incompleteness, although they often choose ineffectual means. These inferiority feelings, Adler theorized, are a natural outcome of childhood, a period during which children perceive adults as bigger and stronger. Through peer relationships, however, the child's feelings of inner strength are awakened. These feelings of strength spiral as the personality unfolds and grows, as people extend their efforts of helping from family and friends to the society at large. Thus, people perfect and complete themselves, not at the expense of others, but in the service of improving the human condition.

To eliminate feelings of inferiority, Adler proposed increasing the social feeling or social interest of the individual through encouragement and re-education (Ansbacher, 1968). Social feeling can be described as an innate urge to belong to and to harmonize with society while maintaining individual validity and to live for the good of all. Encouragement and support from other individuals or groups can foster the development of social feeling in persons who feel negatively about themselves and society.

Adler, like so many significant theorists, was not entirely original in his formulations. As far back as the fourth century, Plato (*Republic,* 1945) considered human beings to be a reflection of their society; and, therefore, there could logically be no conflict between individual self-interest and the common good, provided that everyone was equal with respect to rights, privileges, and personal wealth. When people behave on the basis of benefiting others or society first, they cannot avoid benefiting themselves; "self" and "others" exist in harmony within the same person. We are incomplete, then, only when we live in isolation; thus, we must seek fulfillment as an active participant in society. Only through friendship and love for others is actualization possible; that is, self involves an interaction with others who also seek fulfillment.

Adler (1930) saw a parallel between physical growth and psychological striving to fulfill oneself. This impetus from within is necessary for solving problems, for survival, for pleasure, and for self-completion. The urge toward actualization begins in infants as they explore and manipulate the environment. As children grow, they begin to master the academic, athletic, and social arenas. As they enter adolescence, they continue trying to cope with the tasks of living, although they may rely on undesirable and ineffectual means. Unrealistic goals of fulfillment based on mistaken self-images will create anxiety and insecurity and will most likely require compensatory behavior.

An aspect of Adler's views that has been incorporated into the humanistic movement discussed earlier in this chapter is the *subjectivity of experience*—that is, perception and its effect on us. Subjectivity implies that our experiences of feeling, perceiving, doing, and communicating originate from within ourselves and have little to do with the external, objective world. For example, two persons may react quite differently to the same event. Such dissimilar responses stem not only from dissimilar past experiences, but from differences in perception. Each individual's response is unique for that particular moment in time, and it is this uniqueness that differentiates the individual from other persons.

The Behavioristic View

The theories presented so far have been based on the assumption that undesirable behavior springs from an internal state of frustration, tension, guilt, or conflict. An honest exploration of feelings and thoughts can provide a new understanding of why we behave as we do and can thus lessen these undesirable internal states. Behaviorists, on the other hand, hold that what makes us behave as we do stems quite directly from what we have learned in the past. They maintain that we can change our behavior by manipulating the environment and by altering our own responses. Other theories generally hold that it is the perception of self and others that affects or determines actions.

Behaviorists believe that the most reliable way to study human behavior is to observe it objectively—that is, not to become involved with the subjective and unreliable area of thoughts, feelings, and inner awareness. Behaviorists study what they can see and measure (habits, reactions, activity, learning) and bypass everything else, except, perhaps, what might be deduced from a person's report.

Skinner, a leading behaviorist, views behavior as conditioned through interactions with reinforcers in the environment (1971). Any condition that increases the tendency toward a certain response is called a positive reinforcer; hence, if we desire a certain behavior for ourselves, we must present ourselves with positive reinforcers, which will strengthen the behavior we want. Thus, we are responsible for the consequences of our actions—for avoiding the reinforcers that may bring about undesirable behavior as well as for choosing the behaviors that we wish to reinforce. The question of *what* is good for us thus becomes a decision that we all must make for ourselves after taking into account the consequences of our behavior on ourselves and others.

Consider, for example, persons who are passive and shy, dislike themselves for being that way, and want to change. They can discuss with a counselor or therapist how the behavior might have started and why it may continue as it does. By learning more about their inner nature and by evaluating themselves differently, they come to realize why they act as they do. Hopefully, the new insights will be evident in subsequent actions. There is, however, another possibility. We need not "tinker" with our minds; we may, instead, subject ourselves to new situations that reinforce assertive behavior—that is, situations in which it "pays off" for us to take the initiative, in which responding to others provides positive feedback, and in which such behavior can spiral into increasingly outgoing actions. In short, we become the person we want to be by reinforcing behaviors associated with that type of person. More detailed applications of the behavioristic method will be discussed in Chapter 10.

Existential Psychology

It is not surprising that many persons today are unable to find meaning in their own lives simply because they do not find consistency and permanency reflected in society. A rather new movement in psychology—existential psychology—attempts to reduce this dilemma by indicating how we can become actualized through the expansion of self-awareness (May, 1961). Like most other psychological points of view, existentialism maintains that self-awareness is a major step in the search for self-fulfillment. Further, it stresses the importance of meaningful goals and the willingness to accept the consequences of our decisions and actions (Bugental, 1965). Indeed, the existentialist psychologist holds that it is necessary for us to place ourselves in situations in which we must encounter others, in which we will say what we feel without fear, in which we will help one another in difficult situations, and in which we must make decisions and accept responsibility for our actions (Nikelly, 1964). Only through interactions in which we accept ourselves does life gradually take on increased meaning.

Charlotte Bühler (1933) made an extensive investigation of "meaningful" existence by examining the biographies of persons whose lives either had intense personal meaning or significantly lacked it. She found the meaningful life to be characterized in persons who dedicated themselves to valid and socially useful goals. The goals varied (social causes, creative achievement, or more limited personal goals), but, in any case, successful subjects found fulfillment by devoting themselves to an idea or to a person outside themselves. This process was particularly characteristic of creative persons, who never ceased working at something that they valued. The goal outside themselves actually seemed to symbolize their personal identity. When that goal was achieved, it reflected their own development; it was an extension of their self.

Bühler (1959) described four basic human propensities that can bring us closer to self-realization: (1) the natural bent toward finding a suitable, comfortable niche in society where we can enjoy a measure of security; (2) the propensity to look for satisfying experiences in life, especially in the areas of personal recognition and interpersonal relationships; (3) the tendency to express our basic, unique character; and (4) the inclination to find order in life and to develop a feeling of perspective that encompasses where we have been and where we are going. Bühler particularly stressed our innate capacity, based on freedom of choice, to direct our lives; individuals have choices based on their unique values, needs, and perceptions. This ability, she contended, constitutes a major tenet of the humanistic view. Bühler also assigned considerable responsibility to individuals for creating their own lifestyles, despite potentially damaging social influences, such as the family.

Humanistic Psychology

Humanistic psychology is concerned with the purposeful, creative, and productive aspects of individuals whose perceptions are personal and subjective. It deals with human behavior according to purpose (the future) rather than cause (the past)—that is, pull rather than push. The humanist maintains that, once we see the

Figure 1-3. Sometimes it is worthwhile to ponder seriously who we are, what we are here for, and where we are going in life. Photo by Shirley Kontos.

goal and direction of behavior, all else will fall into place (Buhler, 1971). Important characteristics of humanistic psychology include the necessity for interdependency among people, the importance of dealing with the "here and now," the assumption of responsibility for one's actions, and the view of unpleasant emotions (guilt, conflict, loneliness) as a part of life that must be accepted, even valued, rather than denied or repressed.

Hampden-Turner (1970) finds an active conscience and the ability to make valid moral judgments integral to the humanistic model. Specifically, the ideal person by humanistic standards is the individual who can become involved with goals and who believes that the needs of others are of greater importance than mere regulations or convention, a belief that often impedes human actualization rather than promotes it. Further, such a person is able to act on the basis of ethical judgments and is willing to accept the risks involved in defending higher principles. The convictions of such a person, in fact, may be so inspirational that they often elicit willing confirmation from others. Indeed, the ideal person is sometimes seen in the vanguard of a new order. Such an individual may be a Jesus, a Rousseau, or a Martin Luther King, but the humanist is also found among lesser persons, as, for instance, among youthful activists of many persuasions (Nikelly, 1971; Schindler-Rainman & Lippitt, 1971). The humanist, then, finds fulfillment through helping to build a society in which the lives of others are also enriched.

The humanistic view of personality generally overlaps and embraces the existential view. The two views can be distinguished from each other by the fact that humanistic psychology stresses improvement in the quality of social conditions and emphasizes the development of fulfilling interpersonal relationships more than does existential psychology, which tends to explore the meaning of existence and to examine what is most important and worthwhile to the individual—that is, his or her values (Misiak & Sexton, 1973). In general, existential psychology adopts a less optimistic stance and has less hope that science will improve the human condition than does humanistic psychology.

Abraham Maslow. Considered the founder of humanistic psychology, Maslow held an optimistic view of human nature, considering us to be essentially good but likely to encounter experiences that stifle or distort our growth. Instead of studying "sick" people in order to understand human behavior, Maslow studied well-adjusted people to discover a meaningful definition of personality (Maslow, 1954). He believed that, by their very nature, people are basically good and that they gradually mature if nothing interferes with their growth. When they become unhappy or maladjusted it is because the environment has interfered with their maturation.

Maslow described six levels of psychological growth, which he called *hierarchy of needs.* When one level is reached, the next emerges and becomes dominant. In other words, as higher needs emerge, further growth is fostered. However, if lower needs are not met, they may dominate individuals who, in turn, may find their lives to be unfulfilled or "deficient." After satisfying basic biological needs—food, comfort, shelter—human beings, according to Maslow, desire a general sense of well-being and security. When this desire is achieved, humans move to a third level of need—the desire to belong to and be accepted by a group. Reciprocal love and care comprise the fourth stage, and feelings of self-worth, competence, and independence constitute the fifth phase of development. Finally, *self-actualization* represents the summit of emotional and intellectual development through knowledge of self, through an aesthetic appreciation of beauty in the natural world, and through artistic expression. Healthy personality growth requires fulfillment at each progressive level.

Maslow (1971) was able to isolate eight ways of achieving actualization. One way is to experience something (people, situations) selflessly or without self-consciousness—to become totally absorbed without the interference of defenses, personal preoccupation, or situational distractions. Another is to think of life as a process of making retrogressive and progressive choices; the former are reflected in fear, withdrawal, deception, and suspicion, and the latter, in curiosity, empathy, openness, and social interest. A third way is to let yourself "go"—to express your "gut" reaction, your inner voice. A fourth way is to take responsibility for your actions—not only to make a decision but to accept the outcome. Another is to go in your own direction, to feel comfortable even when your feelings or opinions do not agree with those of others. Preparation and persistent work to perfect special abilities is a sixth way of achieving actualization. Not frequently experienced, but nevertheless significant, is a seventh possible way—self-actualization through peak experiences. Peak experiences are characterized by an overwhelming emotion or revelation. Moments of utter surprise, of awe, or of sudden insight or when everything seems "to click" can be referred to as peak experiences. Finally, actualization is achieved by discovering yourself—understanding your defenses as well as your perceptions—so that your life takes on an added purpose and meaning. Recognizing what you want from life, as well as acknowledging the defenses that stand in the way of realizing your goals, involves honest reflection and an objective perspective.

Maslow (1962) characterized fully actualized persons as being (1) realistically oriented toward people and the world around them, (2) respectful of other people as individuals, (3) spontaneous toward others, (4) directed outwardly toward society—not inwardly toward themselves, (5) comfortable living with themselves, (6) reliant on their own inner resources, (7) able to experience people in new, unstereotyped ways, (8) capable of caring for their fellow human beings, (9) able to form sustaining, deep relationships, (10) imbued with a democratic philosophy of living, (11) humorous, (12) creative, and (13) responsive to novel situations.

Maslow did not break personality into isolated, conflicting units; rather, he stressed its "wholeness." We become ill-behaved insofar as the conditions under which we live are not conducive to our psychological growth. If we find ourselves in an inadequate environment that stifles our potential for actualizing ourselves, our personalities will unfold in an unnatural way; we may become destructive or aggressive. Maslow used the term "full humanness" to describe normality and psychological health. Moreover, he considered a society to be healthy only when it promotes humanness in its members.

Carl Rogers. Another clinical psychologist who emphasized the desire for actualization was Carl Rogers. He held that conflicting or ambivalent values often hinder us from saying what we think, from making choices, or from acting (1961). What we experienced and valued in childhood, what our parents taught us, and what society maintains all may confuse us as well as guide us. Within an atmosphere of freedom and encouragement, Rogers maintained, it is possible for us to acknowledge and ultimately to resolve rigid, often inaccurate, pictures of ourselves. As we become more self-accepting, we gain and accept knowledge of ourselves, and we become better able to actualize our capabilities. In short, self-knowledge precedes meaningful action.

Like Maslow, Rogers observed persons who developed their potentialities and fulfilled themselves. They seemed, he noted, to be more interested in seeking the things they wanted rather than in merely accepting what others expected of them. Their lives were not rigidly defined by "shoulds" or "oughts." Such persons, according to Rogers, are not afraid to accept themselves as they are and do not hide their real experiences, thoughts, and desires merely because others find them uncomfortable or undesirable. They are capable of examining their own feelings and accepting those of others without defensiveness.

Rogers adhered to the notion that the directive force of human behavior—that is, its all-embracing motive—is growth and fulfillment. Lesser motives, he maintained, are not separate entities; they fall under the influence of the whole organism and the drive of the organism to actualize itself.

Rogers believed that the process of actualization is characterized by communication, openness, self-acceptance, mutual sharing, and fully experiencing things in the present. He also believed that the greater the discrepancy between what we do and what we feel, the greater the likelihood that we will display maladjusted behavior.

We begin in childhood to differentiate ourselves from others, to form a unique self. By the time we have become adults, this self is based on how we interpret our thoughts, emotions, and actions. The more aware of them we are, the easier the road toward actualization becomes. Yet, because of new experiences, the self must continue to change throughout life. If we fail to respond to new observations and events, we may begin investing energy only in self-preservation and maintenance. But by remaining susceptible to life, we can continue to revise the self through "reshuffling" from within and through new understanding gained from experiences with the outside environment.

Erich Fromm. Contemporary psychoanalyst Erich Fromm insists that, although we create our own problems, we do have the ability to solve them (1955). Like Maslow, Fromm recognized certain basic needs in all of us—the need for identity, meaningful work, a feeling of equality with others, and the need for increasing knowledge about ourselves and the world. Because of the contradictions often found in society, it is sometimes necessary for people to adjust by escaping, fighting back, or by conforming to the contradictions without complaining. But Fromm looked to love as a remedy for loneliness and the discomforts of the mechanisms of escape. Striking a positive note, he envisioned a humanistic, equalitarian, and communal mode of living that might fulfill our basic needs.

Fromm maintained (1947) that we are often afraid to be ourselves. We want freedom, but we become anxious when there is no one on whom to depend. Either we are too willing to conform, or we move to the other extreme by alienating ourselves from others. Instead of becoming what we are, we often play roles, pretending to be someone other than ourselves. Fromm suggests that one answer is to see others as people like ourselves and to put something of ourselves into the milieu in which we live so that it might be reflected back to us, thereby reinforcing our perceptions of ourselves.

Karen Horney. In a similar vein, Karen Horney, a German-born psychoanalyst, pointed out (1945) that a hostile environment may create a "basic anxiety" that causes a child to feel helpless, alienated, and insecure. In addition, disparaging, inconsistent, overprotective, domineering, or indifferent parents often aggravate this basic anxiety. In order to overcome these stifling experiences, the child may develop "neurotic needs"—ineffective and unreasonable coping reactions that are energy draining and that prevent self-fulfillment. Horney classified such coping behavior into three major categories: turning against people in order to survive—that is, becoming strong in order to eliminate threats; turning away from people to avoid demands and conflicts in order to feel safe; and moving toward people to feel accepted, yet dependent. Although these classifications may fall within the normal range of behavior, such responses can become neurotic when they fall into rigid patterns or when their intensity is out of proportion to a particular situation. We note here that maladjustment is a social issue rather than the mere frustration of biological drives and that the exaggeration of normal tendencies may cause us to experience difficulties in fulfilling ourselves as social beings.

Gordon Allport. A theory that behavior is often shaped by motives or personal goals that are quite unrelated to biological or survival needs was presented by Gordon Allport (1955). He maintained that these motives work *autonomously* (without outside control) and are necessary for emotional fulfillment. The medical student, for example, who worked as a cook to earn money for college, may collect recipes and prepare exotic dishes for his guests and family long after he has become a financially successful physician. His original need to cook—to earn money—no longer exists, but he still enjoys cooking. Cooking gives him a sense of fulfillment because it satisfies his need to create something and to provide pleasure for others.

Our behavior is not merely pushed by a bundle of drives; it is also pulled by the need to rise above or beyond the confining limits of life. Allport called this tendency *proprium,* or psychological maturity. According to Allport (1961), *propriate functioning,* or the expression of the self, refers to the way you want to be, the things you want to do. Thus, it defines character and basic personality beyond the immediate satisfaction of biological needs and physical survival. Proprium begins with body awareness, develops into self-consciousness (awareness of the self-image), and culminates in rational coping ability. Proprium is characterized by being in touch with your body and with how you think, by how well you function consistently, and by the way you evaluate yourself as a rational, worthwhile being. Understanding the environment as an extension of the self—as part of our own personality—is another characteristic of proprium.

By its very nature, proprium is generally associated with directing our behavior; that is, it motivates us toward behavior that is guided by values, by a sense of self-worth, and by rational thinking. Such behavior, then, is not merely a reaction to external stress or an effort to restore a biological balance in the human body; rather, it is influenced by ambition, planning, and imagination. Allport insists on the notion of "propriate striving" to explain why individuals persist in certain tasks in spite of formidable obstacles. In summary, the proprium represents conscious choice, realistic coping, rational behavior, and high self-esteem—all characteristics of a competent and effective personality.

R. W. White. White, who extensively analyzed what motivates behavior (1959), pointed out that primary drives (hunger, thirst) are not responsible for the self-motivated desires such as personal autonomy, experimentation, and desires to change the environment. In fact, pleasure often seems to be the end in itself, with no apparent connection to basic drives. By seeking novelty, stimulation, and excitement, we exercise capacities that keep increasing the more the experiences satisfy us. As we become capable of coping with our environment, we find fulfillment and discover that we have the power to produce changes and desired effects. These activities give us a sense of competence—a feeling of efficacy—that enhances our adaptation to the world.

White (1960) maintained that, regardless of our biological makeup, we desire to be and to feel competent. He defined competence as the ability to cope effectively with tasks involving people and environment. Since such competence is measured by its effects, White called it *effectance motivation;* and the sense of awareness of competence he called the "feeling of efficacy." Competence develops from experiences in a variety of situations. Through testing the limits of what we can do, through trial and error, we increase our sense of competence within the social and physical environment.

Spontaneous activity provides us with an opportunity for developing skillfulness and proficiency that is not dependent on external reward or punishment. The satisfaction from these activities alone generates a feeling of competence, independent of reinforcement from the social environment. According to White, this type of spontaneous transaction with the environment becomes an autonomous need that spurs the individual toward growth and fulfillment.

These six psychologists, although they have used different terms, have each presented the basic theme of humanistic psychology; that is, the truly human person is basically good, behaves consistently, strives to change and to grow, is guided by goals, intentions, and values, rather than by only the basic physical drives, is capable of finding meaning and purpose in life, is directed by the future rather than by the past, and is able to make choices and live with the consequences.

While Horney, Allport, and White are not always classified under a humanist label, they are mentioned here because their theories strengthen the humanist position by extending certain humanist concepts of growth, fulfillment, and competence.

The Eclectic View of Personality

It is important to keep in mind that not all psychologists share the humanistic orientation. Many psychologists tend to incorporate several theories of personality and to apply the techniques of various personality theories throughout their professional careers. They are *eclectic;* that is, they do not align themselves exclusively with one theory of personality; they choose the best or most agreeable technique for a given individual. If a person has only one symptom or sign of disturbance (for example, an unreasonable fear of dogs), the psychologist might use techniques of behavior modification. Such techniques may be easier or perhaps less time-consuming for a situation that does not seem to require extensive exploration. If, on the other hand, a person feels generally inadequate and has feelings of low self-esteem, the psychologist might choose one of the "talking" therapies, which encourages clients to take a hard look at themselves and to explore various strategies for change. The eclectic psychologist seeks to meet individual needs with precision and sensitivity. And although he may appear indecisive because he lacks commitment to a particular theory, his consistency lies in always seeking what is best for the individual client—in searching for the most effective route for a client's fulfillment.

There are several other interpretations of human behavior that should also be mentioned. The *biological* view, for example, is based on a reciprocal relationship between the biological organism and its social environment. The *constitutional* perspective holds that behavior is basically determined by physique. The *cognitive* approach is based on the premise that invalid beliefs and erroneous ideas are the basis of ineffectual behavior. The *systems* view maintains that human behavior must be studied at many different levels, ranging from the level of atoms to the level of large groups interacting with one another, because of the multitude of interacting components in the environment that may influence a particular individual.

I might add here that the personality of the psychologist may often be as important as the knowledge he or she possesses. Some practitioners are more effective than others simply because their clients find it easy to respond to them. Trust, humor, and receptivity in the therapist—qualities that are not necessarily learned from books—may be as important for the person seeking help as impressive, theoretical knowledge.

APPLICATION OF THE FOUR MAJOR PERSONALITY THEORIES

In order to consider how these major personality theories might be used by a helper (therapist) to guide a client toward more satisfying interpersonal experiences, let's apply each of the theories to one example. Let us assume that John has difficulty relating well with Mary and wants to develop a more satisfying relationship.

Psychoanalytic Approach

The psychoanalytic (Freudian) helper attempts to discover John's unconscious feelings toward Mary and to make him consciously aware of the emotional significance of these feelings, which he has repressed (hidden). He may begin by exploring John's early relationship with his parents, particularly with the parent of the opposite sex. He may find evidence of strong dependence in that relationship or indications that the parent was domineering or strongly controlling; either of these situations in childhood might prevent John from interacting honestly and satisfactorily with members of the opposite sex. John will need to work through this problem with the helper, openly revealing his feelings about the past and even coming to view the helper as representing one or both of his parents (*transference*).

The helper assumes that John is not fully aware of why he behaves the way he does and that only by increasing this level of awareness can change be effected. In order to discover the repressed, unconscious material, the therapist encourages *free association,* or the uncensored and spontaneous expression of thoughts. If John cannot respond—that is, if he is resisting (holding back)—the therapist must persist in trying to uncover what has happened. Encouraging the individual to remember, perhaps even to relive, a childhood event that may have influenced the current problem may help.

Theoretically, John will react differently with Mary once he has obtained insights into why he has been acting as he has. With this understanding he will have a better chance of changing or of finding alternate and more satisfactory ways of interacting with Mary and with other members of the opposite sex.

Behavioristic Approach

The practitioner of behavior modification tries to precisely determine the problem and under what circumstances it occurred. He or she then attempts to retrain the client by manipulating the conditions that precede or follow the behavior to be changed. The approach is essentially *ahistorical;* that is, no attempt is made to determine how the problem developed, and no assumptions are made regarding its basic cause. Rather, the behaviorist is concerned only with the removal of the unwanted symptoms.

Thus, the therapist might try to desensitize John's negative feelings toward the opposite sex. He or she might begin by introducing relaxing techniques. Together with John, the therapist might work out progressive situations in which the least anxious or least negative feelings about the opposite sex would be dealt with first. After some initial success, the more intense, fear-producing situations would be approached. Further, the therapist would reinforce (through praise, support, and encouragement) any evidence of progress that John makes in improving heterosexual relationships. If John should become anxious before reaching his goal, the therapist will stop progression, beginning again at an earlier level—perhaps a situation relating to older or younger persons of the opposite sex—and then progressing again toward the goal of opposite-sex peer encounters. He or she may begin with a very modest prescription—asking John merely to smile at a girl, then to say "Hello," and then, during a third meeting, to speak at least one sentence. There are several techniques available in applying behaviorist theory; they will be discussed more extensively in Chapter 10.

Existential Approach

The existentialist helper, like the Freudian psychologist, is also interested in exploring John's private world, but the existentialist places particular emphasis on whether or not John is able to find meaning in his existence, a purpose in living. This type of therapist holds that only when an individual understands a reason for his own existence is he able to relate to others and live effectively. The helper may thus try to challenge John's pessimistic views about himself and others or his unwillingness to take risks and responsibility for his actions.

The existential helper insists that John must discover what is of value for himself, since these judgments are not the same for everyone. Further, John must work to destroy the illusion that past experiences control current behavior. He is not as inadequate or as helpless as he thinks he is. Indeed, he can surpass his apparent limitations and avoid or conquer stress by realigning his expectations and by putting more trust in himself, in others, and in life. Often the helper can demonstrate, through his or her own experiences or those of others, how a mental set can shape the outcome of our actions. By adopting an optimistic mental set any problem may become more bearable. Survivors from concentration camps, for example, often had an attitude of fortitude that somehow enabled them to endure what others could not.

Humanistic Approach

The humanistic helper approaches a case quite differently from the Freudian or existentialist psychologist. He or she is interested in exploring what it is about John's current lifestyle that prevents him from relating effectively to members of the opposite sex. The helper examines John's present attitudes and identifies, if possible, faulty beliefs that may be at the basis of his hesitancy or inability to relate. Specific situations are analyzed to see how John reacted to members of the opposite sex, and, in turn, to assess how he interpreted the actions of others toward him. The emphasis is on the present, not the past. For example, the therapist might ask: "What do you make of your behavior last night at the dance? What were you trying to say by acting that way?" The client must be helped to see that he has the capacity to choose his course of action and the ability to go along with whatever consequences occur. The basis for his actions may well rest in a distorted view of himself or in a biased view of others. Talking about these faulty perceptions and their consequent actions within the framework of immediate situations is a common tactic of the humanistic therapist. Only then is it feasible for the client to begin to devise alternate behaviors based on a more accurate perception of the situation.

In addition to analyzing current actions, the therapist may also explore John's immediate feelings. He or she might ask "What goes through your mind when you are with a member of the opposite sex?" The objective here is to make the client more aware of how he creates his own problems from the way he thinks and feels; that is, his actions are governed by his preconceptions.

Finally, the emphasis of the humanistic therapist will be on the capacity for self-direction: we can be the architects of our lives. A practical approach may include placing the client with a therapist of the opposite sex or in group therapy with members of the opposite sex, so that he receives immediate feedback about his conduct.

COMBINING HUMANISTIC PSYCHOLOGY AND BEHAVIOR MODIFICATION

Personality is formed and behavior learned to a large extent from our interactions with parents, peers, and society in general. Obviously, we are shaped by the conditions in which we live. However, we help to create these external conditions. If we genuinely desire to alter our personality or to achieve more desirable behavior, we must work to create the conditions in which these changes can occur. It is at this point that the forces of humanistic psychology and behavior modification can be joined effectively to provide productive insights and feasible, concrete solutions.

Like humanistic psychologists, practitioners of behavior modification do not make judgments about whether a person is good or bad, although they do assume that a great deal of our behavior is governed by forces outside ourselves. Behaviorists do, however, adopt a positive stance; that is, although people may not be responsible by nature, they can learn those things that permit true responsibility. The humanistic psychologist and the behaviorist tend to place considerable weight on our innate capacity to grow, to change, to become what we aspire to be. They assume, generally, that the natural (healthy) personality will develop if obstacles are removed.

Both humanists and behaviorists, then, sound an optimistic note, stressing what we can do for ourselves to change undesirable behavior as well as to modify those aspects of the environment that interfere with our development and change. In short, both hold the view that persons *can* change insofar as they *want* to change. Obviously, there are forces in the environment that are beyond control, but there are areas that we can at least influence. Through these areas, we can spur our own growth and hopefully achieve actualization.

There are other similarities between the technique relied upon by behavior-modification and humanistic therapists: (1) Both hold the client alone responsible for wanting to change and for actually working to effect behavior change. (2) Both refrain from diagnosis—that is, searching for the causes and labeling the nature of a problem or symptoms; rather they tend to examine symptoms in terms of their consequences. (3) Both insist that goals for change be set up by the clients themselves and not by the therapist, parents, or social institutions. (4) Both emphasize reinforcement—strengthening a desirable response by rewarding it. The humanistic therapist may rely on acceptance, encouragement, approval, and warmth, while the behaviorist may associate pleasurable rewards (a candy bar in return for a completed homework assignment) with desirable behavior. By combining these two schools of psychological thought, the helper is in a position of advocating environmental change by fostering personal change, and vice versa. In this double thrust lies flexibility as well as strength.

SUMMARY

In this chapter, we have discussed the trend in the study of human behavior away from the examination of unconscious factors and toward the direct consideration of conscious behavior, away from the analysis of conflicts within the individual and toward the study of the client in action, away from the emphasis on biological, instinctual drives and toward the study of how we determine values and make responsible choices. Since all of us unknowingly "make" ourselves, we must learn how we got that way if we are to attempt to change. The emphasis of this chapter is on those aspects of ourselves over which we have control, taking into consideration, of course, the biological and environmental factors in our lives that have affected us since childhood and that we cannot fully change.

Contemporary therapeutic principles imply that we as human beings are intrinsically good and that our *immediate* experience—how we view things and feel about them—is of the utmost importance. Personal meaning cannot be objectively defined nor can it be "found"; rather, it is created within us. Self-fulfillment, whether it is defined as self-actualization or self-realization, incorporates personal uniqueness, wholeness, goal-directedness, and self-consistency. Such criteria suggest that we can become more competent—that is, more able to cope with life—and that we can achieve self-fulfillment by liberating the creative forces that lie dormant within us.

We have seen that self-actualization is an innate need that can be satisfied in much the same way that social feeling can be nourished and strengthened—that is, by accepting ourselves and others as worthy persons, by understanding the world around us through the eyes of others, and by meeting the needs of others the same way we want our own needs to be met. When we seek help, we are not labeled "sick"; rather, we are seen as having problems that we may be able to overcome with the help of another person. The feeling of personal significance—the sense that we are "somebody"—comes not from isolation but from being with others. And we have the innate potential to realize this personal significance and to change, provided that we have a realistic view of ourselves and of others with whom we interact.

We also examined four major psychological theories in this chapter, both in general terms and in reference to an actual case study. The psychoanalytic theory emphasizes the unconscious urges that control us; the behavioristic theory gives considerable weight to what we learned in the past and to how that learning may now be modified; the existential theory stresses the meaning in life; and the humanistic theory holds that feeling, experiencing, and being aware are of key importance. Finally, a combination of techniques adapted from humanistic and behavioristic theory was discussed as an approach of unusual strength and flexibility.

QUESTIONS TO THINK ABOUT

1. Which of the four approaches to therapy discussed in this chapter would you choose if you needed someone to help you with a problem? Why?
2. Based on your own experience, what do you consider to be our innate characteristics? Does your evidence support or refute the positions stated in this chapter?
3. With which of the experts in the study of personality referred to in this chapter do you agree? Can you give any specific reasons for your preferences? Are there others with whom you disagree? Explain.
4. Can you think of how humanistic psychology might be applied in practical ways to education, to family life, to society? Explain.
5. Do you think that behavior modification could be so extended that whole societies might be conditioned into behaving peacefully and productively? Defend your answer.
6. Do you think that society is "sick" and individuals are "normal," or is it the other way around? Defend your argument.
7. Imagine yourself on a couch talking to a psychoanalyst. Do you think that you will understand yourself better by this process? What might you expect to gain? How do you think this change may come about?

REFERENCES

Adler, A. *Practice and theory of individual psychology.* New York: Harcourt, Brace and World, 1927(a).

Adler, A. *Understanding human nature.* New York: Greenberg, 1927(b).

Adler, A. Individual Psychology. In C. Murchison, (Ed.), *Psychologies of 1930.* Worcester, Mass.: Clark University Press, 1930.

Allport, G. W. *Becoming.* New Haven, Conn.: Yale University Press, 1955.

Allport, G. W. *Pattern and growth in personality.* New York: Holt, Rinehart & Winston, 1961.

Ansbacher, H. L. The concept of social interest. *Journal of Individual Psychology,* 1968, *24*(2), 131-149.

Ansbacher, H. L. Alfred Adler and humanistic psychology. *Journal of Humanistic Psychology,* 1971, *11*(1), 53-63.

Bugental, J. F. T. *The search for authenticity.* New York: Holt, Rinehart & Winston, 1965.

Bühler, C. *The course of human life as a psychological problem.* Leipzig, Germany: S. Hirzel, 1933.

Bühler, C. Theoretical observations about life's basic tendencies. *American Journal of Psychotherapy,* 1959, *13*(3), 561-581.

Bühler, C. Basic theoretical concepts of humanistic psychology. *American Psychologist,* 1971, *26*(4), 378-386.

Freud, S. *A general introduction to psychoanalysis.* New York: Garden City, 1943.

Fromm, E. *Man for himself.* New York: Holt, Rinehart & Winston, 1947.

Fromm, E. *The sane society.* New York: Holt, Rinehart & Winston, 1955.

Graham, T. F., & Crow, L. D. *Human development and adjustment.* Totowa, N.J.: Littlefield, Adams, 1973.

Hampden-Turner, C. *The radical man.* Cambridge, Mass.: Schenkman, 1970.

Horney, K. *Our inner conflicts.* New York: Norton, 1945.

Kinget, G. M. *On being human: A systematic view.* New York: Harcourt, Brace, Jovanovich, 1975.

Krasner, L., & Ullmann, L. P. *Behavior influence and personality: The social matrix of human action.* New York: Holt, Rinehart & Winston, 1973.

Llamson, T. A. The Tasaday language so far. *Philippine Journal of Linguistics,* 1971, *2*(2), 1-30.

Maslow, A. H. *Motivation and personality.* New York: Harper, 1954.

Maslow, A. H. *Toward a psychology of being.* Princeton, N.J.: Van Nostrand (Insight Books), 1962.

Maslow, A. H. *The farther reaches of human nature.* New York: Viking Press, 1971.

May, R. (Ed.). *Existential psychology.* New York: Random House, 1961.

Mead, M. *From the South Seas: Studies of adolescence and sex in primitive societies.* New York: Morrow, 1939.

Misiak, H., & Sexton, V. S. *Phenomenological, existential, and humanistic psychologies.* New York: Grune & Stratton, 1973.

Nikelly, A. G. Existentialism and education for mental health. *Journal of Existentialism,* 1964, *5*(18), 205-212.

Nikelly, A. G. Ethical issues in research on student protest. *American Psychologist,* 1971, *26*(5), 475-478.

Plato. *Republic* (F. M. Cornford, trans.). New York: Oxford University Press, 1945.

Rogers, C. R. *On becoming a person.* Boston: Houghton-Mifflin, 1961.

Schindler-Rainman, E., & Lippitt, R. *The volunteer community.* Washington, D. C.: Center for Voluntary Society (NTL Institute for Applied Behavioral Science), 1971.

Skinner, B. F. *Beyond freedom and dignity.* New York: Knopf, 1971.

Watson, D. L., & Tharp, R. G. *Self-directed behavior: Self-modification for personal adjustment.* Monterey, Calif.: Brooks/Cole, 1972.

White, R. W. Motivation reconsidered: The concept of competence. *Psychological Review,* 1959, *66*(5), 297-333.

White, R. W. Competence and the psychological stages of development. In M. R. Jones (Ed.), *Nebraska Symposium on Motivation.* Lincoln, Neb.: University of Nebraska Press, 1960, *8*, 97-141.

Marching to Our Own Drummer: Actualizing Ourselves

CHAPTER OUTLINE

I. The drive toward fulfillment

II. Paths to fulfillment
- A. Self-realization
- B. Love
- C. Independence
- D. Transcending ourselves
- E. Personal involvement
- F. Self-disclosure
- G. Humanistic identification
- H. Interpersonal competence

III. Summary

There is no such thing as instant adjustment, no prepackaged happiness. Rather, we learn through experience and experimentation. Although we have inherited capabilities, these can be seen only in the context of our interactions with others. Only through doing *can we create a meaningful past and design a future built on reasonable as well as satisfying expectations. Only by daring to become involved will we discover our limitations as well as our possibilities.*

THE DRIVE TOWARD FULFILLMENT

Maddi (1968) rejected the Freudian view that the human personality is composed of conflicting drives that must be kept in an always precarious balance and instead asserted that change in personality is propelled by a single basic force—the need to find fulfillment.

A second corollary of this optimistic view is that the human personality tends to compensate for what it lacks as it moves toward completion. For example, a political activist of lower-class origins may devote his energy to creating optimum social conditions so that others will not experience the difficulties he did. Or, in a less ideal situation, the emotionally deprived girl who feels insecure as a young woman may react by attempting to control, even tyrannize, others through her passive actions. She may have learned to live with her insecurity, but only at the price of manipulating, even enslaving, others.

As many contemporary psychologists move away from emphasizing drives and instincts and toward stressing the importance of self-awareness and values, they are increasingly able to offer specific suggestions as to how we might best proceed toward personal fulfillment. They have successfully challenged the medical model, which viewed emotional problems as if they were a disease, preferring instead to look at such problems as mistaken ways of behaving that may be corrected. Many therapists present the humanistic approach that people make themselves what they are; that is, they create their own problems and therefore can provide their own solutions. Thus, regardless of childhood experiences or biological determinants, every person is able to move optimistically toward positive adjustment and to resolve any conflicts in society that may be inharmonious with personal growth.

We detect here the beginning of an optimistic, liberating movement, a movement initiated by Adler and expanded later by psychologists who maintain that, although the social environment—family, school, society—does not always provide a setting in which people can actualize themselves, people can nevertheless learn to change not only themselves but also their society. The child's mistaken views about himself and society may be challenged and realigned through an emphasis on the logical or natural consequences of inappropriate behavior and through an equal emphasis on the strength of the larger society. Even some adults who exhibit symptoms of antisocial behavior are not always "sick"; rather, their actions declare that they want to change. Acting out behavior such as anger, destruction of property, truancy, or aggressiveness can mask personal unhappiness and can underlie a cry for help. The attempts at adjustment of such people may be invalid or incorrect; only by rediscovering themselves can they fulfill themselves both personally and socially.

PATHS TO FULFILLMENT

Self-Realization

Self-realization refers to knowing and expressing your "real" self—that is, the actual *you*—instead of acting in a way that is not your authentic self or wearing a mask that shows only what others want you to be. Self-realization means that you fulfill all of your capacities and talents as best you can, without using irrational or ineffective means to cope with life. The term *self-realization* is sometimes used synonymously with the term *self-actualization,* though in self-realization there is greater emphasis on first knowing yourself well. Self-realization is not so much thwarted by preventing unpleasant, forbidden, and intolerable thoughts from becoming fully conscious as it is endangered by a lack of basic security, trust, and love (Horney, 1937). When love and trust are missing, people may try to cope with situations in unsatisfactory ways—by aggressive, submissive, or withdrawn behavior that does not release the abilities embedded in the "real self." They may lose their flexibility and spontaneity and become rigid or compulsive in their responses.

When we feel anxious and insecure, we fail to develop feelings of self-worth, thus crippling the development of the "real self." For example, overprotective parents may damage a child's self-esteem; the child may look for security by becoming a "clinging vine," by seeking to control others, or by running toward the "safety" of isolation and solitude. Even reasonably well-adjusted persons often rely on these three behavioral possibilities, but to a lesser extent.

Basic contradictions within society can also work against the self-realization of individuals. Theoretically, all people are created equal and have certain inalienable rights; yet, the exploitation of certain individuals has long been rationalized in the name of material gain, progress, or free enterprise. A similar contradiction occurs in the relationship between self-realization and individual success; in our society, success is often equated with power or material wealth, rather than related to happiness or altruistic (unselfish) behavior. How can we be aggressive competitors—one societal definition of success—while giving of ourselves to others and treating them with respect? Another such conflict is fostered by the advertising industry's creating new consumer needs. Although such products are often shallow and unimportant, they may be tied to genuine psychological needs for security, belonging, esteem, and love. Mass media, then, may offer false or superficial answers to deep and genuine needs: a deodorant, a mouthwash, and a new car do not provide solutions for the insecure person who seeks closeness with others but seems unable to build lasting relationships.

Despite the inconsistencies within our society, fulfillment through self-realization can be found.

Incident

Gail's parents had high expectations for her, their only child. They fussed over her clothes in grade school and pressured her to do the "right" things and to be seen with the "right" people in high school. Her mother insisted that she learn proper etiquette for social situations, become an actress, study French, ballet, and piano, and join a sorority. Gail began to realize there was a big gap between the "inside" her and the "outside" her. When she went away to college she began to realize that her real *self* was a sensitive, delicate, warm, and simple human being who didn't need any social props to feel complete. She wanted to wear blue jeans and sandals, sing, laugh, play with stray dogs, gaze at the moon, and think. She began to do the things she wanted to do and to say what she felt. She changed her major to Social Work when she realized her feeling that "the most precious being in the world is the person who wants to be reached and touched."

Love

Through love we can find paths toward self-actualization and fulfillment. Fromm (1956) describes four types of love: (1) love of self, a form of love that involves respect and knowledge of our self and often reflects the love we have for others; (2) erotic or sexual love; (3) motherly love, a form of love, usually found between people unequal in emotional strength, that ideally works to help the weaker person become independent and equal; and (4) brotherly love, the basic and all-embracing type of love existing between equals. True fulfillment, according to Fromm, is achieved by actualizing the fundamental potential for loving, within a humanistic and humanitarian society.

The bond that comes from feeling close to others offers the potential for ultimate fulfillment. Further, the notion of productivity is not unrelated to love when such work is defined as contributing to society. Using your unique capabilities to establish a continuity between your own interests and those of others leads to a strong identification with the goals of society and to an important sense of fulfillment.

Self-actualization involves the pursuit and fulfillment of one's nature, but the freedom to be creative and productive may alienate people from some aspects of their surroundings. Rather than risk freedom, some people prefer to conform,

Figure 2-1. We need to like ourselves before we can begin to fully like others. Photo by Shirley Kontos.

forfeiting freedom for security and structure and sacrificing in the process their potential individuality and productiveness. Adjustment to society is only an indication of human fulfillment when society fosters the growth of creative and productive lifestyles and full human expression. Unchanging and authoritarian societies stifle human fulfillment and actualization; a rigid social structure suppresses human expression, stunts personal competence, and denies people the freedom to learn and grow (Fromm, 1947). When we live in a stunting and demoralizing society, we cannot actualize ourselves to our fullest capacity, and hence, we cannot love as best and as strong as is possible. Besides authoritarian conditions there are also contradictions of ideas and even values that can stifle our actualization and our capacity to love.

We can reduce or eliminate many of the contradictions in society, for we have helped to create them. To list only a few: we make war but want peace; we desire freedom but cling to security; we value friends and social interchange but often want solitude; we seek political protection but wish to avoid restrictions. These contradictions make us feel isolated and lonely; to overcome them we may (1) submit to those people stronger than us, (2) control and dominate someone so that we will feel being in power, (3) destroy those persons who pose a threat to our sense of powerlessness, and (4) become compliant and conform to things as they are—a common response of many unfulfilled persons in our society.

Incident

Here are one student's thoughts.

I think every person is basically good. But people with problems have been hurt; somebody let them down. And it takes them time to begin trusting people again. In fact, lots of people are suspicious in this world; they've been brought up with a "dog-eat-dog" attitude and think that everybody is out for himself. When a person realizes he cannot change the system, he becomes cynical; he hates being alive. It's no wonder that we haven't been able to relate very well with each other, but I don't think we're doomed to this condition. Things seem to be changing slowly.

Sometimes I feel that love is too often repressed. It seems that we've been conditioned to think that expressing love is foolish, unmanly, or an irrational weakness, and we end up suffering from a feeling of being separate from each other when we have so many things we want to say to each other. It's delightful to see people who just care for each other, without looking for rewards. Think of it this way: if we don't love somebody, who's going to do it? I'm one of the people who loves somebody, and I feel fulfilled because the somebody I love feels good and gives love to others. Love just spreads itself around.

Independence

Democratic societies have always emphasized freedom—freedom from the rule of others, even from their assistance. In frontier times, independence was a virtue for survival, but it is difficult to justify such a stance today when people appear to be suffering deeply from a sense of personal isolation. Indeed, independence has been misunderstood and distorted until it has come to mean self-sufficiency, and even arrogance toward others. Too much stress on independence makes it difficult to acknowledge that we "need" people, and, thus, it is difficult to achieve closeness. However, overdependence prevents us from discovering our own strengths and from making our own contribution.

Independence begins at birth, when the baby leaves the protective womb and the umbilical cord is cut. Rank (1947a, 1947b) finds in the trauma of birth (the "shock" the infant feels when it suddenly leaves the warm, protective environment of the mother) an explanation for much of the anxiety we feel. The individual must somehow master the transition from total passivity in the womb to full independence in adulthood in order to achieve personal fulfillment. The infant is helpless, dependent almost entirely on its parents, but it gradually develops certain physical skills (such as grasping and walking) that increase its independence. When the child is weaned, independent behavior is encouraged. Through positive reinforcement, encouragement and rewards, children gain mastery over their environment and become increasingly self-directed, although they may always rely on others as a means of securing approval or attention. Life becomes a progression of breaking away from secure, dependent relationships and situations in order to achieve greater self-sufficiency and independence. As one takes more steps away from secure and safe situations, there is more stress on self-reliance and independence and on testing one's strength to face up to these stresses. The price is paid in the form of anxiety and uneasiness.

Independence is crucial in developing those capacities that make us effective in work and in personal relationships. Dependent people seem to spend their time getting others to do what they could do by themselves. They allow their potential to remain dormant and undeveloped. Consider, for example, a small plant that remains attached to a larger plant. Two undesirable things happen: the small plant never grows properly; it remains stunted and ancillary. The larger plant, on the other hand, suffers because it must help to feed the small one. Neither is fully matured; neither benefits from dependency as much as it would from independence.

Ideally, a balance can be achieved between "leaning on" and "breaking off" with a person. It is possible to relate to others without being consumed by them. Since independence is learned, it is desirable that we place ourselves in situations in which independence is most likely to be developed. Moving away from home as soon as you are capable of handling the responsibility, taking a trip on your own, enrolling in an independent study course for which you are rewarded for working on your own, choosing a job in which there is little supervision and structure, refusing to be overprotected or coddled, developing skill in a hobby or sport, and assuming care for others who actually need care, such as children or the elderly, are some examples of achieving independence. However, awareness of dependency and dissatisfaction with it are the first steps toward independence.

Incident

I pick up the sexual messages a guy is giving me when I first meet him, but, when I get to liking him, I freeze up. Of course, he can't like me when I'm so tense, so he dumps me. When it's a guy I don't care about, things are easier, because I know I could tell him to go to hell and it wouldn't bother me. This sounds funny, but I have no one to open up to. I'm scared that no one will like me the way I am. The other day I was playing with a little terrier out on the lawn, and I hugged him and he sort of kissed me. It felt so natural, like the real me was coming out. But I guess I knew the dog couldn't hurt me. I just wish I could be that open with a guy. I would really like to know why I am afraid of getting hurt, and what's stopping me from being what I really am.

The desire to get close to someone can often be accompanied by feelings of insecurity and by a fear of being hurt and rejected. Such feelings are likely to produce a situation in which the person, trying to avoid becoming dependent on a desirable other, behaves clumsily and ineffectively. An emotionally independent person is more likely to accept the challenge and take the risk of reaching out toward another rather than be crippled by the need for or fear of becoming dependent on someone else.

Transcending Ourselves

Although people often blame their parents, the schools they attended, and even "society," environment has, for many persons, little to do with their ability to function, to pursue goals, and to succeed. Many people are able to actively manipulate the environment instead of falling victims to "circumstances beyond their control." They accept or challenge when others retreat in frustration, anger, or depression.

We all have the ability to act beyond our perceived limits of operation if we acknowledge that such limits are often self-imposed rather than dictated by environmental conditions. Jourard (1966) observed that when we are particularly interested in or attracted by a particular activity or personal encounter, we operate with full efficiency. Distractions of time and place are obliterated; we focus all our powers of concentration on the moment at hand. Such an experience may occur in reading or writing a poem, seeing a play, creating a piece of art, or engaging in an enlightening conversation.

People may "rise above" their limitations and the confines of their environment by overthrowing habits of social conformity. Instead of playing prescribed roles, they release their bound-up energies, expand their viewpoints and attain a new sense of fulfillment. Children and many artists, writers, scientists, and religious people experience this rewarding "transcendence." They allow their thoughts to move freely rather than focusing them in a certain direction. Their imagination is often unrestrained by societal limits or by the bounds of reality. They hold no fixed or limited opinion of themselves and find novel situations challenging rather than threatening. The fact that some persons undergo such experiences suggests that everyone has such potential; however, many yield to emotional blocks, to interpersonal pressures, and to social conditions. Some persons in our society try to experience a short cut to transcendence by using boundary-eliminating drugs. We will discuss this process in Chapter 7. Others attempt to expand their consciousness by borrowing concepts from various Eastern religions; these techniques will be presented in Chapter 10.

Our society, especially its educational system, often fosters a rather narrow definition of what people can do. Psychologists generally agree that those who are unhappy and unfulfilled have learned rigid and repetitive patterns of living, have adopted values that do not correspond to their authentic needs, and are overly concerned with defending themselves for the sake of security and social approval. Consequently, they are unable to expend energy in creative pursuits and innovative work. In other words, their actions are governed by their belief in their capabilities. We should not be surprised then when persons who have fixed ideas about themselves (for example, "I am stupid," "lonely," "inferior," "a failure") operate within such self-styled rigid limits that their words eventually become a self-fulfilling prophecy. These persons must discover that no one is a static entity. Rather, we are all in the process of becoming, emerging, and developing beyond self-imposed limits.

Self-transcendence may also be promoted by "letting go"—that is, making no conscious effort to direct thoughts, to pursue solutions to problems, or to formulate answers. Letting fantasies, images, and free associations pass through your mind may help to resolve a predicament or solve a problem, especially if your previous deliberate efforts were not productive. What we are discussing here are the several varieties of meditation in which we ponder, reflect, and contemplate on some thing, object, or idea. While meditation for some persons is an effortless activity, it can also mean effort for those who attempt to study something thoughtfully, fix their attention on some idea, and search for something.

Fulfillment may be achieved by dedicating yourself to an objective that has great value for you, regardless of whether or not the results are tangible. Throughout history, persons have persistently fought against great odds in support of what they believed. For example, Galileo and Joan of Arc fought against religious ignorance and political oppression, and Elizabeth Browning fought against poor physical health. The internal personal organization of such dedicated people was strong and well composed; external conditions did not sway or trap them.

Incident

Joel withdrew from his friends and lost interest in his work because his girlfriend abruptly terminated their relationship. He had been strongly dependent on her and now he suddenly found himself all alone. This separation cost him emotional drain and mental confusion.

Joel pampered himself for the first week, allowing himself feelings of self-pity. Then he began to redirect his feelings into more creative things; he read poetry and even tried writing some. He found that his feelings came through in his work and that they weren't so hateful or hostile as he had originally thought. He decided that he needed something or someone else to take up his thoughts and time so he enrolled in summer school. He started making friends again—girls as well as guys—and suddenly realized that other people were finding him a nice person to be with.

"I have become closer to other people," Joel said, "more aware of their feelings, more helpful to them. When I look back, I can see how I could have stayed miserable and lonely, constantly blaming others for my situation. But I saw that other people needed me, and so I broke away from tendencies to wallow in my feelings of injury."

Joel came to the conclusion that suffering is something people do of their own choosing, even though they won't usually admit it, and that it is easier to blame someone else for what has happened, to try to make others feel as if they owe you something for what's been done to you.

Personal Involvement

Direct involvement in shaping society and in working for or with others usually enhances our own actualization. As we learn more about ourselves and others, the desire for individual responsibility and interaction with other people and in the affairs of the community in general increases; as we make more choices, life inevitably becomes more complex but also more interesting. We should be willing to work at problems, to take risks, and to try new ways of achieving results. Optimism fosters good personal relationships because it encourages others to initiate action, to express confidence, and to demonstrate more competent behavior.

Personal growth is reinforced by commitment to others and by the satisfaction that comes from being "involved." Focusing on issues outside yourself, without losing sight of your own perspectives, invariably elicits a positive response from others. Such an approach elicits a positive response because others enjoy being given attention, being made to feel that there is something worthy about them that makes people interested in them. Ideally, what you want for yourself should coincide with what is beneficial for others as well.

Interpersonal effectiveness increases when you relate with different groups and when you are comfortable with a variety of roles. Interacting with peers of the opposite sex, with children, with adults, and with the aged helps to develop a wide perspective. Well-liked persons are those who make others of any group feel accepted and involved (Keislar, 1961). Those who feel inferior tend to withdraw further or to compensate through aggressive behavior, which only increases alienation. Sometimes the family or the larger society does not provide an atmosphere in which authentic relationships can develop, but peers can sometimes meet the emotional needs that parents might have failed to answer; a negative experience with the parent of the opposite sex can be counterbalanced by a positive one with a peer of the opposite sex. The important point here is to understand that we can discover alternate sources for personal growth and need not yield to anger, despair, or recrimination.

Rogers (1961) suggests that, once we recognize the weaknesses and strengths of other people and ourselves, we should tolerate the weaknesses and pay greater attention to the strengths. It is likely that nonacceptance of a person's negative traits will cause the person to suppress or distort these aspects in order to find temporary relief; therefore, we should appreciate everyone for what he or she is—part of a common humanity.

Another way to achieve actualization is to pattern your behavior after the behavior of a person who has achieved actualization. This process, sometimes referred to as *modeling,* involves adopting behavior patterns that seem more efficient or more effective than your own. Such behavior changes usually occur only after extensive interactions between you and the person whom you admire and respect. Modeling does not, however, imply that you are merely acting out a role that does not belong to you; rather, it involves incorporating new patterns of behavior without changing your basic identity.

A recurring problem is how to become more outgoing, confident, and comfortable with the opposite sex. Martinson and Zerface (1970) used two procedures to investigate this problem. One group of dateless male students was offered ordinary counseling to overcome their fear of dating; another group was provided a social program including coeds who were interested in improving their social skills. The social program was found to be much more effective; that is, direct personal contact and social interaction proved to be more helpful than merely talking about the dating problem.

Incident

A female college student had been going with a man for some time. Due to his indecision and interest in other females, he decided to break up with her.

She had become more emotionally involved with him than he had been with her, and it was easier for him to make the separation. As a result, she lost interest in others and began to question her worth as a person. This is her story as she tells it.

Once I was really rejected by a guy. It really hurt. I began by dealing only with the present, with what I wanted out of life now. I didn't worry about what I was going to do in the future. Just moving on from day to day, trying to figure out what's happening, made me realize that things take care of themselves. I learned how to talk to people—everybody, friend or stranger. I tried to see them as they really were, as they came across to me, not through rose glasses. I opened up to them only when I got positive vibes, and if they were really messed up, I played it cool—relating, but with caution. I said to myself that, if I don't like myself, how can I ever expect anybody to like me?

I met a nice guy who kept a neutral attitude toward me. He had a badly bruised ego from some girl he was married to for a short time. He seemed lonely and really in need of loving, but at the same time he was afraid of getting too involved. I really empathized with him, though, because I think I know exactly what his ex did to him and what he was going through, so I tried to get through his defenses long enough to show him that all females are not beasts. He became a good friend, and he really appreciated my interest in him. This made me feel I was worth something. He saw me as a person—honest, trustful, likable—and I felt real good about myself afterward.

Self-Disclosure

Self-disclosure means opening up to others. Unfortunately, many people do not reveal much about themselves; they fear that if others know what they think and how they feel, they will reject them or view them with contempt. Certain people and societies even encourage misrepresentation of the actual self to uphold the myth that the person who "keeps things to himself" is "strong" and "mature." However, self-disclosure is a necessary step in establishing close relationships. Past generations enjoyed the benefits of the extended family (uncles, aunts, cousins, grandparents); that is, someone was always there to be a sympathetic listener or an interested advisor. There is no doubt that experiences with many intimate relationships early in life tend to increase the ease with which self-disclosure develops. Today's nuclear family (parents and siblings only) offers fewer opportunities for such interaction. Parents often work outside the home, children have programmed activities, and teens have part-time jobs. There seems to be less and less time for family talk, and thus many young people feel that no one really knows them. When people have little idea of what others think of them, they begin to wonder who they really are.

Jourard (1971) asked members of his family and certain colleagues what they knew of him and was surprised to discover that the person they described did not resemble the person he thought he was. He wondered what cues he had given them, what he had withheld from them, or what there was about himself that he had deliberately or unconsciously distorted in order to project this false portrait of himself.

Figure 2-2. Fulfillment can result from being open with friends who fully accept us for what we are. Photo by Shirley Kontos.

Jourard devised a questionnaire of personal information: He asked persons who "knew" each other to complete the form and then noted the items in which there was agreement. From these data, he speculated that clients who were less open about themselves (resistant) were apt to have more incapacitating problems. This assumption prompted him to test further whether or not self-disclosure is related to good adjustment.

Jourard's data revealed a positive relationship between self-esteem and self-acceptance and the tendency to reveal oneself to others, especially to one's mother; that is, the child whose mother inspires trust in him learns more easily to accept himself and to trust others later. Conversely, the more distant from its mother a child is, the less self-disclosing it is apt to be.

The main thesis demonstrated by Jourard is that presenting oneself to others genuinely and openly is a valid criterion of the effectively functioning personality.

A recent review of the research on the role of disclosing oneself to others as an indicator of good adjustment (Cozby, 1973) indicates that, for the most part, moderate disclosure of ourselves enhances interpersonal interaction, but too much or too little disclosure makes others view us as less well adjusted, thus blocking our social effectiveness with them. Consider, for example, if you met someone for the first time and you tried to become acquainted with that person in a short time by revealing your sexual fantasies and other such thoughts. That person would probably become scared and withdraw instead of getting closer to you. Sometimes even suspicion can develop. On the other hand, not saying anything at all and appearing sulky or disinterested, you may give out messages of being hostile, preoccupied, worrisome, and not liking others who are around you. They may perceive you this way and, in turn, withdraw from you. Ideally, we need to disclose ourselves gradually in a sort of mutual enterprise in which both parties each give enough time to the other for the closeness to build as more information flows between the persons involved. Also, the kind of person to whom we disclose ourselves makes a great deal of difference in how we disclose ourselves and in how much we disclose. For example, people sometimes feel comfortable confiding in a total stranger—a co-traveler, for example—but are afraid to speak openly to their spouse or parents.

Incident

From the time I entered high school until recently, no one has really known me as I am. I'm now a sophomore and as far back as I can remember I've been a loner and a "hermit." I guess I gave the impression that I was "cool" and confident, but inside I felt small and insecure.

One Sunday evening I had supper with a casual friend. After supper, we sat around and listened to music. She seemed to be in a good mood, and I kept on staring at her and at the ceiling—back and forth as if I had something to tell her. I gave her enough messages that something was on my mind, so she asked me if I was okay. I told her I wasn't happy, and right then and there I realized that this was the best time I would ever find to let myself go. I figured the worst that could happen would be for her to get up and leave. I told her what was bothering me, and she listened and gave me some pointers. In fact, she seemed happy that I had asked her for advice. She assured me I wasn't that bad and that she had gone through some of the same experiences before—feeling as if she didn't have friends or anybody to talk to. After that she sat next to me and told me about herself. We had a lot of the same thoughts and problems! It was a good feeling to share such "secrets." And when I talked to other people later, I realized I wasn't too different from anybody else.

Humanistic Identification

Feeling at home in the world, experiencing the feelings of others, and sharing universal goals are often part of humanistic identification (O'Connell, 1965). Humanistic identification generally refers to our assimilation, sharing, and partaking of those behavior patterns and attributes of other people and institutions that are valid, meaningful, logical, and beneficial for all persons. Through identification with the lives of others—for example, parents "living" through their children—it is possible to discover a new and deeper part of ourselves. Indeed, philosophers and people of wisdom seem to attain serenity and inner peace by "incorporating" themselves into the universe as a whole; that is, they do not consider themselves separate entities. To such people, "I" and "thou" are merely artificial separations between people. Everyone is one energy; individual egos are dissolved. With this feeling of oneness, people can empathize deeply with what is happening around them and come to accept things as they are, nonjudgmentally. Also, with this feeling of oneness, there is little opposition between individuals, and thus there is less energy given over to needless distress or conflict.

Incident

Barney got his degree in architecture, but he didn't want to work for a "rip-off" firm—one that builds shoddy houses in order to make big profits—and he didn't want to work for a boss whose basic philosophies might be inharmonious to his. He realized that he was happiest when he was working directly for people who needed him. He wanted to do something that made him feel good about himself, not that just brought in money. So he joined a group of missionaries and went to Africa where he designed and helped to build a school and a small housing complex. He worked from dawn to dusk, constantly wondering where the energy came from. There was no money involved, as materials were provided and food and shelter were shared. But the spirit of the village, the people helping, kept the project moving.

"For the first time in my life I met people who understood me as I am," said Barney, "and that was the greatest feeling I've ever experienced."

After the buildings were finished, Barney was sitting out in the country alone, watching the sun set behind a long chain of mountains, when he began to think about the millions of people in the world who exploit each other to make money and about how much energy is devoted to competition and technological advancement rather than to the production of food and the pursuit of understanding and love. He realized that he had helped to fulfill the dream, that he by himself *could* help change things—at least in a small way—with his own abilities, and that his words and thoughts were finally in harmony with his actions. "I see parts of me in everyone else," he thought, "and I sense that the feelings of others are inside me, as the inner world of my personality contains everything that's out there."

Interpersonal Competence

By doing the best we can (maximum performance) with what we have (endowment) we can reach maturity and achieve fulfillment (self-actualization). A practical way to facilitate self-actualization is to develop interpersonal competence (Fitts, 1970). Interpersonal competence refers to the ability to relate effectively with others, to deal efficiently with social situations, and to be capable to produce results with actions and behavior.

Combs and Snygg (1959) propose two ways of studying the competent personality: (1) observe how an adequate person actually functions and (2) explore how an adequate person perceives himself and the world around him. In observing how a person functions, competence may be judged by how effective people are in "getting things done," how stable they appear, how rationally and appropriately they behave with other people, and how self-confident they appear about themselves and their goals. Regarding the second and more subjective method of studying personality, competent persons seem to have a high regard for themselves—that is, think of themselves in positive ways; they are capable of accepting and living with all their experiences—positive and negative—and of making the best use of them; and they find it easy to identify with many other persons, even with the universe as a whole. We should stress here that genuinely competent persons are not bothered by their inadequacies. If, for example, they cannot swim or spell well, they do not seem upset by this weakness. It is as if they do not allow specific, acknowledged inadequacies to contaminate the rest of their personality. They do not accept their situation passively, however; they try to improve their situation, as they feel encouraged to try out new ideas and seek new experiences to bring about a desired result.

How do we go about enhancing interpersonal competence? First, we must be able to disclose ourselves through verbal and nonverbal (gestures, facial expressions) communication that is clearly understood by others. Since communication is learned, it can be changed, if necessary, and improved in the areas in which it is deficient. In short, we can learn how to disclose ourselves to others and, also, how to be more receptive to their messages.

Second, communication without emotion is usually ineffective and unrewarding. While communicating facts alone may not be very interesting, we can add depth to our conversation through our tone of voice, facial expression, gestures, eye contact, pauses, and the like; we can make dry, colorless material into appealing information. Expressing our feelings puts pleasure and vitality into our relationships, gives them greater meaning and significance, and draws us closer to the people with whom we're relating.

This idea leads us to a third point of interpersonal competence: accurate, honest, well-meaning verbal feedback has a strengthening effect on social competence and self-esteem. When others serve as a mirror, reflecting how we appear to them, we can modify the undesirable aspects of our behavior. For example, reviewing film clips of a football game has an important effect on the player who made a wrong pass or missed an important tackle. Seeing his performance as others saw it should help him to improve. Similarly, personality patterns that we refuse to acknowledge or of which we are ashamed may be perceived rather dramatically through the honest reactions of others. Such insight usually fosters a willingness to change and helps to sustain us during the sometimes tedious and demanding process of modifying unwanted personality patterns. We are more apt to change, and we are more apt to change others, not so much from criticism or "suggestions" but from support, warmth, care, respect, acceptance, and being liked by those who want to help us change.

A fourth aspect of interpersonal competence concerns control over emotions. While you may harbor a negative feeling toward someone, a *feeling* you cannot control, you are able to control the *expression* of that feeling. You can modify the way you project this feeling; that is, you can reduce its intensity, convey it with humor, balance it with praise. In short, you can avoid offending the person but still "mirror" the trait you feel is negative so that the person may begin to change.

Finally, a fifth quality of competence has to do with fostering behavior of a desirable nature in others. People usually treat us as we treat them, but our approach toward them is under our control. To a surprising extent we can elicit a pleasant or an unpleasant response from others. Sometimes we become convinced that we can say or do nothing of consequence in building a meaningful relationship. Yet, how we respond to someone determines how that person will respond to us; he or she "reads" our feelings and intentions and responds accordingly. Warmth elicits warmth; interest begets interest.

I have observed many students in group encounter sessions who initially felt that no one really cared about them. Operating under this assumption, they trapped themselves; when no one came to them first, they believed their assumption of unworthiness had been proved. In an encounter situation, they quickly realized that each person is responsible for his or her own isolation and that their own behavior, of which they were not always fully aware, was producing rejection from others. When they began to respond to the needs of someone else in the group, to show genuine interest in another, they immediately felt less isolated themselves. By helping others, each person had also helped himself.

Through productive interpersonal relationships, through communication and feedback, we begin to change. We become aware of how others react to us, and we adjust our reactions accordingly. We develop a capability to withstand stress and to develop our hidden potential.

Personal competence does not develop in a vacuum; it cannot grow without input from others in the social environment. On the other hand, we can become competent in spite of the poor quality of past experiences or our childhood upbringing.

Madison (1969) offers evidence to show that personality development in the college student is fostered by commitment to or engagement with challenging tasks whose mastery is within the student's range of abilities. Examples of such tasks might be to join clubs that have goals and interests that are similar to yours, to take up running and increase your distance each day, thereby convincing yourself of your increasing ability to do something on your own merit, or to enroll in a special class that teaches a skill like business correspondence or pottery. Typically, a student needs to improve social skills, discover his or her personal identity, grow in independence, and formulate goals. Achieving these ideals will help to put the student's life into perspective and prepare him or her for meaningful adulthood.

An empirical study to determine if academically superior college students attained optimum levels of psychological adjustment as compared with "average" students was conducted by McClain and Andrews (1972). Several variables emerged that relate to what we have been discussing about self-actualization. Persons who attained the most satisfactory level of academic adjustment were persons actively involved in numerous academic activities. They were able to work for long-term goals through the postponement of immediate pleasures and felt that scholarly pursuits had great value in their personal orientation. The superior students were more self-assertive, more intensely absorbed in their work, and able to use their intellectual capacities in a spontaneous, independent, and creative way. The academically superior students did not, however, actualize themselves in the area of human relationships and interpersonal involvement to the same extent as the average students. Superior students tended to disengage themselves from people for the sake of individual intellectual achievement, since much of scholarly work is rather solitary.

Incident

> If you wanted to find a person who felt inferior to others, I was that person. I felt everybody else had it made but me. I didn't expect anything from anybody, and when I played the role of the underdog it was because I felt like the underdog. What really affected me the most was when I joined the Hot Line as a volunteer who offers advice or help to distressed and lonely people who call in. The psychologist in charge made us first practice with hypothetical situations. This training made me feel confident for the first time in my whole life. I no longer felt like a shmuck; I thought I might really be able to help somebody. The first person who called just wanted to talk to somebody who would listen and accept him and understand. I felt I was listening to myself on the other end of the line! I really understood what he wanted and how he felt, and I poured out support for him. Then, he thanked me for the help I had given. I was really affected, but I almost had to laugh. Here I was, such a lonely person myself, making another lonely person feel so much better! So now I know that there's loneliness in others too, and I no longer go around feeling so sorry for myself.

All of us have an inner impulse to fulfill ourselves, an urge for optimal personal development. We also have inner promptings that guide us toward self-actualization, provided we are not unduly hampered or frustrated by severely negative environmental influences or unfortunate personal experiences. By yielding to this impelling force, we can discover a basic life theme by which we can live. In successful adjustment, these innate, propelling tendencies are positive and growth producing. Instead of repressing or canceling out what is negative, we can seek to foster what is positive in ourselves and others.

SUMMARY

In this chapter, we have reviewed the possibilities of achieving actualization through the development of social skills and through a commitment to others. We have described how it is possible through self-knowledge and empathy to transcend ourselves and to identify with universal goals. We have also tried to show how these possibilities exist within the realm of our own choice and initiative. The patterns of personal development described here are not merely for survival or to lessen pain and confusion; they can also broaden the dimensions of life.

Several avenues for achieving personal fulfillment were presented. Reaching out to others, caring for them, and thereby enlarging our own sense of personal worth and effectiveness is one way. Another way is to become self-directed—free from the support of others. A third way is participating in an encounter-group situation—that is, working through experiences with others rather than just reading or talking about them. Compensating for or ignoring an undesirable situation, working hard to correct our deficiencies, and overcoming obstacles of circumstance and habit are other possibilities for achieving fulfillment. Fulfillment involves knowing, accepting and taking risks, opening up to people, sharing feelings—both positive and negative—with others, and finding meaningful work. The recognition that others are like you, that your basic needs are similar to the needs of others, and that you have a responsibility for making the world a better place can open horizons of awareness that will give reason and direction to your life.

QUESTIONS TO THINK ABOUT

1. Recall a problem or difficult situation you had and how you eventually went about solving it. Did you use any of the methods presented in this chapter?
2. Can you think of other ways to fulfillment and actualization than the ones discussed in this chapter?
3. With which methods for actualizing yourself do you feel most comfortable? Do you believe these represent the most effective route for you?
4. Do you think that some of the methods for fulfillment presented here are inappropriate for some people because of their age, education, sex, or social class? Explain.
5. Can you recall someone you know who was dependent on others, who clung to a relationship and yet found it awkward and troublesome? How did the person depended upon feel?
6. Did you ever feel you wanted to get close to someone but then become fearful that you might become dependent on that person? If so, how did you eventually handle the situation?
7. Were you ever able to help others come out of their "shell" and relate with you more openly? How did you succeed in this? If you did not succeed, what do you think went wrong?

REFERENCES

Combs, A. W., & Snygg, D. *Individual behavior* (Rev. ed.). New York: Harper & Row, 1959.

Cozby, P. C. Self-disclosure: A literature review. *Psychological Bulletin,* 1973, *79* (2), 73-91.

Fitts, W. F. *Interpersonal competence: The wheel model.* Nashville, Tenn.: Counselor Recordings and Tests, 1970.

Fromm, E. *Man for himself.* New York: Holt, Rinehart & Winston, 1947.

Fromm, E. *The art of loving.* New York: Harper & Row, 1956.

Horney, K. *The neurotic personality of our time.* New York: Norton, 1937.

Jourard, S. M. Toward a psychology of transcendent behavior. In H. A. Otto (Ed.), *Explorations in human potentialities.* Springfield, Ill.: Thomas, 1966.

Jourard, S. M. *Self-disclosure: An experimental analysis of the transparent self.* New York: Wiley, 1971.

Keislar, E. R. Experimental development of "like" and "dislike" of others among adolescent girls. *Child Development,* 1961, *32* (1), 59-66.

Maddi, S. R. *Personality theories: A comparative analysis.* Homewood, Ill.: Dorsey, 1968.

Madison, P. *Personality and development in college.* Reading, Mass.: Addison-Wesley, 1969.

Martinson, D. W., & Zerface, J. P. Comparison of individual counseling and a social program for nondaters. *Journal of Counseling Psychology,* 1970, *17*(1), 36-40.

McClain, E. W., & Andrews, H. D. Self-actualization among extremely superior students. *Journal of College Personnel,* 1972, *13*(6), 505-510.

O'Connell, W. E. Humanistic identification: A new translation for Gemeinschaftsgefuhl. *Journal of Individual Psychology,* 1965, *21*(1), 44-47.

Rank, O. *Will therapy.* New York: Knopf, 1947. (a)

Rank, O. *Truth and reality.* New York: Knopf, 1947. (b)

Rogers, C. R. *On becoming a person.* Boston: Houghton Mifflin, 1961.

The Emerging Self

CHAPTER OUTLINE

I. Discovering personal identity
   A. Parental influences on development
      1. Love
      2. Ambivalence
      3. Sexual identity
      4. Rejection
      5. An unhappy childhood
   B. Family structure
      1. Family constellation
      2. Family climate
      3. The changing family
   C. Achieving independence
      1. Dependency
      2. Assertiveness
      3. Aggressiveness

II. Where do beliefs come from?
   A. Values
   B. Morality
   C. Attitudes
   D. Prejudice

III. Interpersonal behavior
   A. Group affiliation
   B. Roles

IV. Summary

In this chapter, we shall turn our attention to how we grow—how we become the persons we are. We will discuss what determines personality and the extent to which it is shaped by the family. We will discuss how emotional reactions persist from childhood and continue to affect us as adults, often without our full awareness. We will consider ways of achieving independence from our parents and shaping our own goals in life, for only through self-direction can we move toward actualization and fulfillment. Finally, we will compare conditions that foster favorable growth with those that often result in maladjustment.

DISCOVERING PERSONAL IDENTITY

Socialization involves a person's adopting patterns of behavior that incorporate the societal expectations and cultural requirements of his or her particular society. These elements of society may be moral and judgmental in nature (values, aspirations, modes of perception) or sociological (manner of dress, style of communication, forms of social behavior). Peers, political situations, and institutions such as school and church may also influence the socialization process of the individual. The development of *lifestyle* (a consistent way of reacting and coping) is influenced largely by the socialization processes occurring during the formative years of the individual (from infancy to about the age of 5).

The family and, of course, other groups to which we belong exert obvious as well as subtle influence on our lives. We can alter our beliefs and attitudes, but many of them become a very stable part of our personality and behavior. Have you ever noticed how certain mannerisms or speech patterns, as well as attitudes and values, are typical of a particular family? Or, for example, a person from another country may be dressed in American-made clothes, yet, there is something about his personality that suggests that his origin is different from ours.

The quality of socialization that we experience during childhood is a significant determiner of our adult behavior. However, even when early experiences of socialization are stifling or inadequate, we are not usually "damaged for life." For example, moderate restraints during early socialization—weaning, toilet training, and so on—are not necessarily frustrating and traumatic; for many children such socialization may even have positive effects (Thomas, A., Birch, H. G., Chess, S., &

51

Robbins, L. C., 1961). The child is apt to think of others' needs, to act more independently, to derive satisfaction from relating with peers, and to work and play more easily together with others.

Cooley (1964) describes how our notion of selfhood develops through the feedback that others give us. Thus, we often learn patterns of social responses that are dependent on the expectations of others. Such patterns can be seen in the ways that we speak, dress, eat, work, and play. We are "stamped" by cultural patterns so that our attitudes and actions can be compared to certain socially determined standards. However, we are not merely products of social-group influence. We have a great deal of choice regarding which groups we belong to and what roles we play within them. Thus, each of us remains unique, for the way we respond is never quite identical to the way others respond.

Parental Influences on Development

Two criteria are commonly used in evaluating childrearing methods and attitudes toward children: (1) do the attitudes convey acceptance and warmth as opposed to rejection and hostility and (2) do the methods involve restrictiveness and control as opposed to independence and permissiveness (White & Watt, 1973). There need not be so much concern with what the child is taught as with the psychological atmosphere and the parent/child interactions that are most likely to promote actualization for the child. What parents say and do directly affects the child. Parents' relations with each other, their tone of voice in speaking with each other and with the child, their mannerisms—all these give messages to the child. However, children may misinterpret their parents' behavior. That is, the child does not always perceive from the parent what the parent intends to say, what messages the parent wants to give. Parents always claim to have good intentions in mind, such as what seems to be in the children's best interest, but the ways in which they carry out these intentions often intensify the very problems they hoped to eliminate. The next sections will examine some of the behaviors that involve parental influences.

Love. The experience of love begins for infants when their parents shower them with affection simply because they exist; there is nothing the infant must do in order to receive this affection. Love is felt through parental closeness (proximity) and through the sensations of physical pleasures such as those experienced when parents hold, touch, and fondle the infant.

As babies grow physically and develop emotionally, they lose their sense of being the center of the universe. Gradually, they begin to develop an awareness of other persons and objects around them that may enhance their pleasure and gratify their needs. As they mature, they begin to find as great a pleasure in giving as in receiving. Parents and siblings are of the utmost significance in the child's development of this give-and-take attitude—that is, in his or her learning to love.

Mental, emotional, and sexual aspects are often involved in the meaning of love (Hirning & Hirning, 1956). Feelings of love may often be accompanied by thoughts or intellectual analyses of love—pleasurable fantasies, memories of the past, or ideas about the future. On the other hand, thoughts can stand in the way of expressing love; ego games, a very high or a very low opinion of oneself, the idea

Figure 3-1. The most important criterion for being a mother is being able to love. Photo by Shirley Kontos.

that one needs to appear "cool" to give a certain impression, and an attempt at mental control of a situation are all examples.

Actually, the feelings that go along with the experience of love are closely connected with the functioning of the autonomic (involuntary) nervous system. Emotions are related to physiological changes in our body through the nervous system. Hormones secreted inside the body are also associated with our emotions; thus, when we are tense or angry, the blood pressure rises, the heart beats faster, the muscles are strained, digestion decreases, breathing increases, pupils dilate, saliva lessens, and more sugar is secreted into the blood stream by the liver.

The sexual sensations of love are associated with certain areas of the body known as erogenous zones. These zones are located in the reproductive organs as well as in other parts of the body—the breasts, mouth, neck, thighs. Verbal expressions as well as physical gestures (facial glances, body language) can convey messages with sexual overtones and elicit a variety of sexual responses, which vary in intensity according to the prevailing mood of the persons involved and the nature of the situation. In general, when we speak of erotic love, we include sexual desire and attraction that contain elements of feeling and thinking, as well as of bodily sensation. When we say we love our friends, good music, food, a certain kind of scenery, our country, or God, we are emphasizing the intellectual aspects of love; love of a particular man or woman, however, is usually more strongly defined by the sexual-physical dimension of love. Love relationships do vary in degree, though, from person to person. Some people can experience a strictly intellectual type of love, some do not rely on physical intimacy as much as they do on intellectual intimacy, and some allow sex to play a more important role than verbal communication.

Our ability to love can be thwarted by the absence of loving models from which to learn. Children are normally spontaneous, uninhibited beings; they have fewer restraints in verbally expressing what they feel as well as in showing physical affection. As they grow, they learn from parents and teachers not to express themselves so openly but to hide their inner world—to appear "in control" of themselves. When such discipline is out of proportion, the thrust to reach out, to express oneself, to give of oneself—to love—becomes crippled or distorted. It is no surprise to discover that the parents of some delinquents (Glueck & Glueck, 1950) are distant and cold, showing little affection toward their children. As adults we may be loved because we love, but the child must first experience love from his parents before he can give love. It may well be that gang activities serve as a vehicle for venting resentment against others and that the relationships among the gang members may be an outlet for the delinquent's drive to love someone.

When a child learns to love, he or she also learns responsibility and, oddly enough, independence. Love is not a dependency relationship but a reciprocal bond. Loving others effectively and genuinely requires that we be independent persons, free to interact and become involved without fears of becoming trapped. Openness and honesty between parents and children and the communication of feelings without threats, intimidations, or demands is crucial to the development of love. Parents should not qualify their love: "I will love you *if* you become a doctor." The effects of such a qualification might cause the child to view love as a means of controlling others. Also, should the child fail to meet the conditions of love set up by the parent, he or she might feel doomed to rejection and to feelings of inadequacy for not being able to live up to what the parents expect. Instead of condemning a child for unacceptable behavior, parents should convey a steady sense of basic approval, in spite of their obvious disapproval of certain behavior. Emphasizing what the child does well instead of constantly discussing his or her faults strengthens the child's self-esteem. That is, praise is more effective in altering behavior than is criticism. Generally, a nonjudgmental attitude and a stimulating environment have a more positive impact on the child's growth than do strict preconceptions of what the child must do and become.

Ambivalence. Ambivalence refers to the opposing emotional attitudes that we may feel toward someone who is important to us—feelings that may even waver between love and hate. Such coexisting feelings are experienced by almost everyone; but we usually make a choice that will take us in the direction of one of the emotions. Sometimes, however, both emotions seem to exist with the same intensity, and they become locked in conflict. Conflicting attitudes toward oneself and toward others are typical expressions of this ambivalence in adult life. The crucial point here is that the "hate" portion is usually dominated by the "love" aspect. Indeed, this dominance is a sign of adult maturity. The balance can shift, however, and impair relationships with family members, and even with a mate, if ambivalence is not properly resolved at an early age.

Ambivalence begins in childhood. The infant is initially helpless; all its needs are gratified by another. The mother, as the nonconditional supplier of affection, food, warmth, and security, is associated with love. The infant's total dependence on someone else, however, cannot continue, and soon the child is expected to show signs of independence. Beginning with weaning, toilet training, eating, and later with impulse control, the child slowly learns socialized behavior. As the mother begins to make demands, she is no longer seen by the child as an "all loving" person who gives without question or qualification. The mother's subtle change of attitude creates resentment—even anger—in the child, which is not often verbalized openly. While the child continues to love the mother, he also "hates" her because she requires him to do things that he does not always want to do. Ambivalence, in short, stems from the dual role played by parents—mostly by the mother and sometimes by the father (with whomever the child is emotionally closer). They act as protectors but also as disciplinarians, and a dependence/independence conflict in the child results. As the child becomes an adult, however, he is expected to resolve these ambivalent feelings so that similar "hate" reactions do not interfere with adult transactions; he is expected to relate with others in the generally all-loving way his mother acted when he was an infant. Normally, with rewarding experiences, the positive side of ambivalence is strengthened and the negative one is weakened, as people respond more to our pleasant feelings than to our unpleasant ones.

Sexual Identity. Sexual identity begins to emerge when children see themselves as belonging to a particular sex to which certain socially prescribed behaviors are attributed. Each person's sexual identity is shaped by influences of the family and society as well as by biological traits.

Generally, both parents play an important part in the formation of sexual identity in children of either sex. However, a study by Heilbrun (1964) showed that well-adjusted males often had fathers who provided standards of desirable behavior, and girls with a healthy perspective of femininity often identified with their mothers, who were usually educated and who encouraged their daughters to become independent. While this evidence of mother/daughter, father/son training is obvious, the possibility of "people" models should be emphasized. We all have masculine and feminine qualities and traits as well as a basic human quality that transcends sexual roles. Therefore, an important focus in raising children might be to bring out more female qualities from males and more male qualities from females.

Figure 3-2. Sexual identity begins at home, generally with the parent of the same sex. Photo by Shirley Kontos.

Fathers are often more concerned about the sexual identity of their children; yet, a son's sexual identity is not fostered only by his father. Instead, peers, books, TV, and movies seem also to have a strong influence on male identity. Although the father's masculinity can serve to strengthen the son's, the son's personal identity seems to stem more directly from the care and the active interest the father showed (Lynn, 1974).

Sexual identity also reflects values learned from society. In western society, the female is traditionally emotional, tender, and passive, and the male is rational, strong, and aggressive. These stereotyped sexual roles (sexism) exist in all areas of our lives—in homes where parents want the son to play with toy cars and baseball bats and the daughter to play with dishes and dolls, at schools where male athletic directors do not allow females to compete in sports with males, and on TV and movie screens where the female is pictured as an "adornment" to the male figure who is the focus of attention and pride. The myth that the male is the breadwinner and the female the childraiser is, however, currently being challenged, since either sex can perform any of these functions. Such roles are strictly arbitrary and are set up by society, and there is a current trend with some people either to switch roles or to share the duties of each role. For instance, the husband may do the laundry, sewing, cooking, and cleaning, and the wife may perform activities outside the house. In essence, each treats the other as a person rather than as a member of a certain sex.

Sexual identity is also shaped by biological factors—that is, by hormones and other inborn sexual characteristics. For example, males are inherently more aggressive than females (Lynn, 1974). Certain alterations of mood appear to have a strong biological basis and sometimes to have a hereditary foundation. For example, hormones have a great deal to do with muscular strength and with emotional reactions.

To some extent, of course, everyone has both masculine and feminine qualities, with a natural balance between the two as an ideal. Often, however, when a person tries to assume aspects of the opposite sexual role, he or she may experience difficulties. Imagine, for example, the societal pressures that might befall a male student who decides to knit a sweater on the train or a female who goes out for the football team.

However, this particular moment in time is an exciting and challenging period of openness and change regarding sexual identity. There are new opportunities for both men and women to explore broader, more varied sexual roles. But there are also new responsibilities and even dangers. As the roles and expectations of parents change, the father's traditional authority may gradually decline, and the mother may become the initiator and leader. However, there is a danger that some women may merely imitate aspects of male behavior rather than define a fuller womanhood.

Rejection. Psychologists have long associated inadequate personal development with unsatisfactory conditions during childhood. Certain interactions between parents and children often impede the child's growth and maturation. One such interaction is rejection—parents' open expression of disapproval, which often nurtures resentment and anxiety in the child. Stable emotional development and self-realization are nourished by empathetic, nondefensive, supportive, and affectionate parents. However, children who are rejected or who erroneously perceive they are being rejected may lash out at the world in an attempt to retaliate or may behave submissively in order to earn acceptance and affection (Roberts, 1968).

Symonds (1939) compared rejected and accepted children who had been carefully matched on other variables and found that the rejected children were inclined to be rebellious, unstable, and hyperactive, while accepted children were stable, cooperative, and friendly.

Another study (Heilbrun, Orr, & Harrell, 1966) found that male college students who described their parents as controlling and rejecting had more difficulty performing conceptual tasks under conditions of appraisal and censure than did subjects who rated their parents as less controlling and rejecting. It seems, then, that persons who have been controlled and rejected as children are more sensitive as adults to evaluation.

Parental rejection can be expressed in two surprisingly different forms: overprotection and dominance. At first, overprotection may seem to be the opposite of rejection. However, the overprotective parent is often saying to the child: "I must do for you what you are incapable of doing for yourself. I am strong and capable, and you are weak and worthless." The parent, unknowingly perhaps, assumes that the child is inferior and inadequate, that the child is unable to learn from his or her own experience. Such a child is denied the opportunity to experiment, to learn for himself, to grow into independence. The child often comes to expect there will always be someone who will help him, and, thus, as an adult, he may tyrannize others by making excessive demands on them.

Levy (1943) studied the effects of overprotection with children whose mothers spent too much time with them (authoritarian control) and prevented them from becoming independent. In some cases, the children were obedient, courteous, and shy, and their social adjustment was marginal. In other cases, the children were arrogant and uncooperative in school, had difficulty forming friendships, and, at home, were unmanageable, rude, insolent, and aggressive. In follow-up studies, however, Levy found that most of these overprotected children went on to become reasonably well-adjusted, despite the dominance or over-indulgence of their mothers. The fact that most of the children had recovered, despite their being dominated or indulged by their mothers, indicates that at least they were assured of acceptance and love from their mothers—a condition that did not hamper their growth and actualization later in life. On the other hand, children who were deprived of maternal love and acceptance (conditions opposite to those in Levy's study) showed delayed or poor personality development (Goldfarb, 1945). Although deprivation appears to be more damaging to a child than overprotection, it is important to remember that overprotection does increase the likelihood of later maladjustment.

A recent report (Jacobs, Spilken, Norman, Anderson, & Rosenheim, 1972) found that college students with problems of emotional maladjustment rated their mothers as demanding and overprotective. These ratings differed significantly from those made by students who were free of emotional problems. Jacobs and his colleagues speculated that perhaps parents who expect their children to behave well, who make excessive demands on them, are themselves unable to serve as behavior models for their children. Perhaps they apply a double standard: "Do what I say, not what I do."

The second form of parental rejection is seen in overbearing dominance—that is, in "possessing" the child. Again, the child is forced to remain dependent and helpless. Both overprotection and dominance block the child's actualization by initially rejecting the child as a valuable human being. Controlling a child with threats or making excessive demands that, if unmet, will be followed by rejection often leads to the child's feeling guilty, hostile, frustrated, anxious, or depressed.

Discipline versus permissiveness remains a controversial topic for many parents. Although physical punishment may be temporarily effective, it tends to provoke aggression, resentment, and hostility in children (Hollenberg & Sperry, 1951; Sears, Maccoby, & Levin, 1957). Coercive methods are often ineffective because children either return the aggression or react too passively, submitting to their parents' physical size and strength (Nikelly, 1964). Neither method of discipline helps to foster desirable behavior patterns. Permissiveness without firmness and parental example, however, can also lead to behavior problems. A study by White and Lippitt (1960) illustrates this point. An experimentally induced authoritarian environment created discomfort and dependency in children, but when the subjects were subjected to a less repressive atmosphere they became more aggressive, hostile, and apathetic. Only when permissiveness is coupled with firmness and a positive parental example can it become effective.

Children should be accepted as they are and not manipulated or molded into the object of parental ideals. The authoritarian parent arbitrarily controls and forcefully manipulates the child into "right" conduct. A parent should be *authoritative* rather than authoritarian; that is, he or she must make clear to the child what is expected and must also share the reasons for these expectations. Such a parent must be oriented toward solving problems but supportive of the child's independent solutions. Discipline should be a two-way communication between parent and child (Baumrind, 1968). Children tolerate, even welcome, such discipline, especially when they know they are loved.

An unhappy childhood. If your current life situation is satisfying, you need not analyze your childhood to define what was "wrong" with it. There is always the possibility that, in attempting to justify a current behavior problem, you may search for experiences in your childhood that were not there or exaggerate or misinterpret incidents instead of dealing directly with the present problem.

For the sake of discussion, however, let us assume that your early years were genuinely unhappy ones. You can now use these same experiences as a spur to change, as the motivation to seek fulfillment. The college environment, in fact, provides many new opportunities to respond openly to reliable and responsive persons. But you must move outward to others instead of expecting them to "rescue" you. It is very possible to discover in peer experiences what you may have missed from your parents. In addition, there are counselors and other professionals to guide you (see Chapter 10). Finally, your entire educational experience can help you to discover your potential for change by encouraging insight, courage, and the willingness to act.

Family Structure

The family is structured, ideally, to hold its members together and to help them function effectively. Understanding the emotional attachments, sex and age roles, and rivalries and jealousies of family life can help you to understand how your own personality has been formed, how you may change, and how you may gain strength and happiness by living in harmony with parents, siblings, and relatives.

Family constellation. The positions held in the family by virtue of age and sex differences are referred to as the family constellation. Birth order (first, second, middle, last, or only child) is an important aspect of the family constellation and often governs many of the interactions between family members (Shulman, 1962). The way family members "see" themselves within the total family structure tends to make them behave in certain ways. The first born, for instance, may want to boss the youngest, or parents may expect more from the first child and tend to pamper the youngest. A daughter will probably be treated differently by her father than by her mother, and still differently by her brother.

The youngest child, like the only child, quickly learns that he or she has prerogatives as well as burdens. The youngest child can be pampered and overprotected, or it can be expected to follow too quickly in the footsteps of the older children.

Sibling rivalry refers to the competitive attitude that often exists among children in the same family. One child may see another as getting more attention or having a more desired position within the family. The first-born reigns as king in the family until the second child arrives to dethrone him, and this situation often sets sibling rivalry into motion. The older child may now feel displaced; he or she may attempt to compensate by being overly compliant or surprisingly aggressive or by acting resentful or sharply withdrawn. The importance of sibling rivalry, however, lies in its potential influence on our behavior as adults.

In a similar fashion, birth order within the family may affect later behavior. Research has shown that first-born children tend to be more conservative and conforming as adults. They also are inclined to be intellectually superior and to have a strong need to achieve (Schachter, 1959; Sampson, 1965).

Favoritism may also result from the family constellation. Favored children may never learn to defend their rights outside of the family because everything was given to them at home. On the other hand, unfavored children may always be battling for what they consider to be their rights and may never feel that they have received their just share. Parental expectations can also become a conflict area that drags on through adulthood. Some people never feel successful or satisfied, in spite of work well done and the commendations of others, because they persist in attempting to please the parents of their childhood who were never quite satisfied with their performance.

Certain patterns of reacting to stress are formed early in life and are based on the way the child operates within his family constellation. Various alliances and positions of power or weakness emerge, and no child fails to be influenced by the interactions peculiar to his family. The power and status we once held within the family are often reliable predictors of our adult behavior.

Family climate. The psychological climate in which a family operates is based initially on the beliefs and opinions of the parents and the methods and intensity with which such attitudes filter down to the individual children. Children observe their parents closely and soon pick up their traits, some of which are often used against the parents (for example, efficient methods of quarreling). In their later years, especially during their teens, children may be responsible for remarkable changes in family atmosphere, often developing distinctly different philosophies and sometimes changing parental opinion. These changes occur because the child comes in contact with peers of various sorts and is influenced by their opinions and beliefs. At the same time, the child begins to form his or her own individual identity and to stand apart from the parents; consequently, the whole family structure is reshuffled as the parents are forced to make some adjustments toward their maturing children.

Consider for a moment the family in which everything is measured in terms of money. The parents may talk about their possessions, their vacations, their homes, and their rich associates. Children raised in such a family may also be highly materialistic—engrossed in cars, clothes, and belongings. Yet it is not unlikely that a materialistic family atmosphere may also produce a son or daughter who rejects values based on wealth and is drawn instead by ideals of service or knowledge.

An authoritarian family climate can also be clearly identified. In such a family we find little humor or relaxation. Family members constantly fight with one another, and children soon learn to be loud and domineering to overcome the chaos that is prevalent when too many people attempt to exercise power. Yet, the painfully shy and withdrawn child may also be the product of such a family. Other family atmospheres may involve an emphasis on intellectual or creative matters, a pervading critical, hostile, and distrustful mood, or a tendency toward sincere, open communication.

The changing family. In times of rapid social change, of doubt concerning traditional values, of personal alienation and lack of outward direction and purpose, what type of family structure is most conducive to personal autonomy and fulfillment? Conger (1971) concludes that, in general, democratic and permissive parents who encourage autonomous (independent), responsible behavior and who give explanations for the behavior they expect from their children are most effective. Again, parental goals are best achieved when parents themselves set an example of democratic living. In the past, parents have held considerable power over their children; almost everyone shared the same values, and consensus lends itself to authoritarian structures. When society is stable, it is relatively easy for parents to pass down to their children their ideas of desirable behavior, but when rapid and vast changes are taking place, peers may become the reference group for a child or adolescent while parents are ignored (Mead, 1970).

Ideally, desirable development requires that both parents and children be equal participants in family mechanics and in the decisions that affect the child. Furthermore, there should be an open discussion of the issues, which is neither judgmental nor moralistic but which provides alternatives and options. The ultimate authority rests with the consequences of the decisions reached and not with the self-righteousness or powerfulness of parent or child.

Schaefer (1959) cites two general dimensions for parental behavior: love and acceptance as opposed to hostility and rejection and autonomy and permissiveness as opposed to control and restrictiveness. Although the effects of parental rejection or restrictiveness may at first be relatively inconspicuous, the child may eventually have difficulty in coping with situations outside his or her own family. Hostile and rejecting parents, for example, often foster hostility and rejection in their adolescents, while overcontrolling and restrictive parents may produce inhibited and shy children. The level of self-esteem in either case is low (Becker, 1964). Caution must be used, however, when interpreting the effect of parental attitudes on children; there may be specific trends, but there is great variation among individuals. Children in the same family may react in surprisingly opposite ways.

A warm and supporting relationship between parents generally helps to enhance a child's personal identity (Westley & Epstein, 1969). Inconsistent parents who ostensibly want their children to "grow up" but also want to maintain parental control create a situation that only confuses the child. In this circumstance, some children model their behavior after peers, using them as a reference group to balance parental inconsistency. It must be stressed that neither the constant presence of another person for security and decision-making nor the complete disengagement from others is an effective way to function; rather a delicate balance must be achieved, a position referred to as interdependence.

The family plays an important role in predisposing an individual to unique expressions of emotion. Affectionate, accepting, nonpunishing parents who emphasize responsibility and achievement usually raise children who have high self-esteem, show strong social feeling, and are generally well adjusted (Mussen, Rutherford, Harris, & Keasey, 1970). A recent study by Dewing and Taft (1973) indicates that parents of creative children used equalitarian childrearing methods (that is, treating children as equals), exhibited nonpossessive warmth toward their children, offered a stimulating environment for them, and encouraged self-reliance and activities outside the home. These findings emphasize the consistency of previous investigations; the quality of parent-child interactions generally is of crucial importance in fulfillment and actualization (Walters & Stinnett, 1971).

Achieving Independence

Some people never reach a significant degree of independence or self-sufficiency, while others become too independent, leading isolated lives or attempting to dominate the lives of others. There is a middle ground, however, that assures a reasonable personal independence and yet guarantees a life of significant interconnectedness with others. Independence is not synonymous with loneliness, neither does it connote freedom without responsibility for our actions. Although we tend to think of independence in personal, even selfish, terms ("I want my independence"), it is a condition that can only be achieved by moving freely within a framework of social responsibility.

Dependency. Dependent behavior involves relying on others for support, guidance, and protection—leaning on people to make decisions. During adolescence and early adulthood, we often waiver between feelings and actions of dependence and independence, especially in relation to our parents and other authority figures. We want to be free from their discipline, but we're not sure we want to be free from their protection. Financial and emotional independence is achieved only gradually, as we make decisions, assume responsibility, and acquire competence through new social and vocational skills. Although it is often very difficult for young adults to find positive, fulfilling ways of showing independence, the very desire for independence is itself a sign of approaching maturity (Nikelly, 1971).

Parents sometimes block an adolescent's progress toward autonomy because of their own strong need to preserve their position of power. They may attempt to maintain control by fostering feelings of guilt in the adolescent, thus making the road toward independence more difficult. We are all familiar with the father who seems to constantly remind his children how hard he has to work to send them to school for "the education I never had" or the mother who never ceases to remind her children how she cooks, scrubs, and irons so that "you can look nice and have a nice place to bring your friends."

The threat and uneasiness of separation from parents, or from any pleasant situation on which we have become emotionally dependent, is referred to as *separation anxiety* and can be experienced at any age. In less culturally advanced societies, there is often an abrupt shift from boyhood to manhood. There may be pain and difficulties involved in such a change, but at least the boy clearly knows when he has become a man. This knowledge can be helpful in spelling out his responsibilities and expectations when he becomes an adult. In our society, the period of adolescence is more prolonged; the shift into adulthood includes the early and late teens. During this period the adolescent reaches physical maturity but only gradually acquires emotional and financial independence from his or her parents. Attending college serves to lengthen the period of adolescence; students are neither children nor adults. They are usually not ready to commit themselves to marriage and a family or to contribute independently to society, and they are usually not completely financially independent.

In today's society, marriage is often postponed because members of both sexes seem to grant higher priority to developing themselves and achieving personal fulfillment. A satisfying career and independence seem to be stressed now more than ever before; being able to live with oneself seems to be more important than achieving happiness in a relationship that may involve dependence. This is not to say that sharing and intimacy are avoided; on the contrary, the emphasis of more young people today seems to be on personal development through interaction with others.

No one is independent of his or her environment or of the people in that environment. Indeed, adjustment depends largely on the quality and depth of our interpersonal relationships. Independence is not aloofness from society; it is freedom to move freely within it, to go in whatever direction we desire without being rebellious and entirely nonconforming. The basis for dependency is often found in the desire to achieve security by remaining subordinate to others. Such an unhealthy way of behaving is for some persons often rewarded or reinforced (strengthened) by the reactions of others (Horner, 1972). The dependent person may be rewarded because others do his work or assume responsibilities that are rightfully his, but dependency can also become a liability in securing a mate, advancing in work, or, most important of all, finding fulfillment within oneself.

Incident

I used to call my mom every other day and tell her what I had eaten, what I had done with whom, and what outfits I had worn. She would always give me advice and tell me the things I wanted to hear. On my 19th birthday, I called to ask her what I should wear to this party I was going to, and, for the first time, she refused to tell me. She said "You're old enough now to make your own decisions; don't ask me anymore." All of a sudden I felt really afraid. I felt lonely—as if nobody wanted me and as if I had no one to turn to who would listen. When I hung up, I just burst into tears.

This situation, although an extreme case, illustrates how dependency can provide temporary comfort to people but prevents their growth toward independence and actualization.

Most people do not enjoy the constant demands of a dependent person, but dependent individuals often exert remarkable control over the lives of those they see as stronger and more capable than themselves. Dependent people expect service, attention, and help, leaving the supporting person drained and used. Thus, the dependent person is able to dominate others through his ostensible weakness. In the following situation, we learn how one person overcame dependency.

Incident

Ever since grade school I felt sorry for myself when people didn't show me attention. In high school I dated anyone just to be with someone, but I felt that nobody really cared for me. Then I realized that I was being nice to people just to force them to like me. When I began going steady with this girl I liked a lot she told me some things about myself that I hadn't realized. She told me that I sometimes pretended that I was unable to keep my room clean, keep track of my account book, and hand in my homework on time as a means of getting her to remind me of what I had to do and in order to place her under my control; I couldn't earn attention and care from her any other way. She also pointed out that she felt that I was "buying" her off, because I would buy her gifts and take her to plays and then expect affection in return. So I began to change. I said "no" to her when she wanted to help me with things that I could do for myself, and I spoke my own mind when discussing touchy subjects with her rather than attempting to please her. I noticed that those who had not known me before treated me differently. It seems that, when you show you're free from needing other people to control and dominate, they respect you more. I found that out. When you act like you're strong, people treat you as strong, and you begin to feel like you're strong.

Assertiveness. A relatively new study (Alberti & Emmons, 1970) on assertive behavior (acting with confident conviction about the rightness of your course) helps us to distinguish it from aggressive behavior. Assertive people feel good about themselves; they do not hurt others or deny them their rights. Aggressive people, on the other hand, get what they want at the expense of others and tend to depreciate them.

Consider the following example: the soup you have ordered in a restaurant arrives cold. You can eat the soup as it is, without complaint; this is a passive response. You can, instead, call the waiter and ask him politely to take the soup back to the kitchen and have it heated; this is assertive behavior. Finally, you can raise your voice, tell the waiter that he is stupid and lazy, and demand that he serve you hot soup immediately; these are aggressive actions. Obviously, assertive behavior is more effective than aggressive behavior, and the goal is achieved without denigrating someone else. Passive behavior, in this example, hurts no one, but a life of cold soup is not a very cheerful prospect.

Passive and aggressive persons can learn assertive behavior by practicing assertive techniques in mock situations. They might, for instance, reenact the restaurant scene, choosing the words that will get them what they want without offending another person. The same sort of behavior can be extended to social relationships, school situations, and business transactions. Sometimes, of course, it is unwise to be assertive even though you are in the right—for example, when the other person is tired, in a hurry, upset, or harassed. Under such conditions, assertion might well be interpreted by others as aggression.

Incident

Every evening after supper, uninvited visitors showed up in our dorm room, and my roommate entertained them. It was beginning to get on my nerves because I couldn't study at all. I didn't have enough gumption to tell them to leave, but I knew that something had to be done. One evening when my roommate was out of town the crowd came in as usual. I told them what I had practiced so many times in front of an empty chair. I said politely "I have to study for an exam tomorrow, and I need the time right now. Let's get together when it is more convenient for all of us." It didn't take them long to leave, and they weren't really angry either. I think they just needed to see my point of view.

Aggressiveness. Aggression is an attack, either physical or verbal, that is intended to hurt someone. It can be expressed through hostility, attention-seeking behavior, rebelliousness, strong competition, or quarreling. Some psychologists feel that aggressive behavior stems from frustrating situations (the blocking of our needs to reach a goal). Other psychologists suggest that being deprived of personal freedom or of the necessities for life can lead to aggressive behavior. Prison riots or political revolutions are examples of such aggression. A less popular explanation for aggression is that it is natural; that is, it is pent-up energy that will be released when the proper cues from the environment are present. According to this explanation, aggression can be harmful, or it can be socially acceptable and even valuable. Sports, hunting, and even work might be interpreted as aggressive acts. A final theory is that, like many other patterns of behavior, a great deal of aggression is culturally acquired; that is, it is learned through imitation or modeling (Bandura, 1969).

Aggression can be provoked in children through physical punishment, inconsistent discipline, or excessive restrictions. Parents who withdraw their affection from their children as a means of discipline may also provoke aggressive behavior. On the other hand, the explanation of the possible consequences of undesirable behavior, the suggestion of alternative behavior, and the demonstration of suitable behavior by example seem to be effective ways of preventing aggressive behavior and still achieving the changed behavior that punishment and restriction were supposed to bring about (Bandura & Walters, 1963).

Another group of psychologists who believe that the expression of aggression is a learned pattern maintains that it can therefore be regulated (1) by failing to reward it, (2) by avoiding examples in which aggressive activity solves problems, and (3) by providing socially acceptable outlets for aggression. These psychologists maintain that, while we cannot wipe out frustration and aggression entirely, we can rechannel behavior into patterns in which the aggressive quality is not harmful. Perhaps an analogy with the conversion of nuclear energy into peaceful projects rather than warlike pursuits is helpful. Whether aggression is an instinct (unlearned) or learned behavior is not the real issue here. What must be stressed is that aggression can be shaped into something constructive, useful, and fulfilling. In short, aggressive behavior can become assertive behavior—not only more acceptable, but considerably more productive.

Can you suggest how the young man in the following example might begin to shape his aggressive behavior into more constructive and fulfilling actions?

Incident

I guess I felt that I couldn't let people get close to me; without fully realizing it, I kept them at a distance by the way I acted. I bullied them, made them angry, and found fault with them. It was no surprise that nobody wanted me around, and I ended up a loner.

I joined an encounter group but told everybody there how I felt about the whole stupid encounter process, and they asked me to leave. They thought I was being provocative, but deep down I was just scared. I think I am scared with everything that has people in it. I just attack and let them have it before they can attack me. It seems like I always have to be on top of things, or otherwise I am nobody. I always have to be fighting, looking for action, provoking somebody to react to me. When people are angry at me, I can handle it by being angry at them; but if someone is nice to me, it makes me scared and uncomfortable. I want to hurt them, to get them fighting with me; this is the only way I can reach people.

WHERE DO BELIEFS COME FROM?

The way we think and feel about things affects our behavior patterns. Behind our actions is a mental component formed from experiences—both pleasant and unpleasant—and beliefs. In this section, we will discuss how beliefs and experiences can help us to achieve actualization or can block our progress. The first three aspects of beliefs—values, morals, and attitudes—are usually positive and growth promoting, and the last aspect—prejudice—is a negative mental factor.

Values

Our values determine what we consider to be worthwhile, important, and desirable. They are always present, sometimes consciously, sometimes not, to guide our actions, to judge the action of others, and to subtly influence the people around us. Family, peers, and other social groups to which we belong all affect the formation of our values. Each individual sets up his or her own priorities—that is, a ranking of values. For example, a person may value sports more than socializing and, therefore, will cancel a date in order to attend a football game. One student may value friendship above material possessions, and another may value social status more than academic success. Some people value money as an end in itself and do not even care for the possessions that money can buy. Some may value hard work and honesty, while others scoff at what they consider to be naive or old-fashioned ethical values and stress the value of "knowing the right people" or being clever in social manipulations.

Not only do values differ among individuals and groups, but a clash of values can often occur within ourselves. Should we, for instance, buy an expensive car for its luxury and status or a small, economical and ecological vehicle that would provide the same transportation? Do we value a good figure and good health more than the pleasures of eating and drinking? In our capitalistic society, where free enterprise is encouraged and the advertising media are geared to the consumer, there is often a tendency toward self-indulgence, which may blatantly contradict basic health standards. Being influenced by the advertising of cigarettes and alcohol for the pleasure they give us when we already know the undesirable consequences is a typical example.

Whether we realize it or not, our values operate every time we make a choice. In fact, Spranger (1928) categorized people according to six broad value systems, granting, of course, considerable overlap in these divisions. People who place a high value on material things are the economic type. The religious type, on the other hand, finds value in philosophy and tries to comprehend the mystery of the world. The theoretical type values rationality and the pursuit of truth. The esthetic type values music, art, poetry, and creative and original pursuits, like sculpture and painting. The political type values power, competition, and influence. Finally, the social type values other people and friendship. Most of us belong to more than one category, but in general, we tend to react as one type more consistently than as the others.

The values that make us happy and that can be most easily applied by us are the ones we tend to retain. If, for example, friends, hard work, or religion add an important dimension to our lives, we are not likely to abandon the values that influenced such a structure of priorities. Actualized persons, however, do not merely mimic the values of their society or those learned from family or peers. Instead, they carefully choose values for themselves that add to their own growth and to the growth of others. Ideally, the values they choose are not inconsistent with reality or destructive. When values conflict, actualized persons are able, through their own experience, to make the most rational choice.

The notion of conformity is closely related to value structure. Riesman, Glazer, and Denney (1961) coined the term *inner-directed* for people who are self-directed, who have a strong and socially accepted sense of values and a solid conscience, and who behave more or less rigidly in agreement with the expectations of the social group to which they belong.

Other-directed people, however, are more adaptable and flexible; they change their attitudes and behavior according to the group they are with. They are sensitive to many values and standards and react to them quickly, with a pliable and yielding attitude. According to Riesman, Glazer, and Denney, the other-directed person has become increasingly conspicuous over the past 25 years, in such a rapidly changing society. However, the individual (whether considered inner-directed or other-directed) who trusts his or her own judgment and is guided by his or her own feelings will, in the long run, attain a superior overall adjustment to life and find genuine fulfillment.

Morality

Morality refers to standards of right or wrong, which are strongly determined by societal pressures. Sometimes moral behavior is difficult to define, because standards of right or wrong can vary from person to person and from group to group within the larger society. Abortion, for example, may be considered wrong, even sinful, by one person, a rational solution by a second person, and a positive good by still another. Our beliefs and actions, however, are not always consistent with each other. Consider, for example, the young man who does not believe in killing. When he is drafted into the Army, however, he must act under a philosophy of killing. Moral behavior may also vary with social class. One study (McKee & Leader, 1955) found that the lower the class, the weaker moral behavior is apt to be. Such a general statement might be questioned, however, since it may well be that people of a lower social class show aggression more openly and directly and are therefore more likely to be apprehended by the police. Middle- and upper-class people may conceal their immoral behavior by being discreet and "polished" in their unethical conduct. Purse snatching, for example, is a more obvious immoral act than is cheating on one's income tax.

Our moral values and conscience begin to develop in childhood. Parents love their children but at the same time expect proper behavior from them. Although children may be confused by this interplay of love and strictness, they usually grow up with relatively stable ideas about what is right or wrong, and they can appraise their behavior accordingly.

For the most part children learn from example and from reasonable explanation. Their moral ideas are adopted from adults whom they respect and who serve as models for them. Teaching morality is least effective by intimidation, threats, or punishment. Although punishment can bring "instant" results, it can also foster hostility and dependency (Zipf, 1960). Indeed, punishment can do permanent damage; a continually punished child may become timid, insecure, and overly sensitive, or, in retaliation, hostile and threatening.

A recent study (Yarrow, Campbell, & Burton, 1968) indicates that a strong conscience and a positive self-concept in the child form more readily if the mothers, for the most part, use reason, approval, and praise rather than physical punishment. When mothers are warm, affectionate, and accepting, their children are more likely to think of themselves in positive ways, to recognize what is right and wrong, and to do that which is ethically proper. Children whose mothers are distant and emotionally contained do not easily acquire these attributes. Acceptance and warmth accelerate the absorption of parental values.

In the final analysis, decisions are made on the basis of consequences to self and others, as well as on the basis of morality, although moral reasoning may change with age and experience. Kohlberg (1968) distinguished three stages in moral reasoning. The first stage is the preconventional stage (occurring in early childhood) in which the reasoning of right and wrong is totally self-centered. You do something good or right because of the return you expect. The second stage is the conventional stage (formed in later childhood), which is based on social expectations and community standards. You know what is right because it is what everybody else is doing. The third stage is the post-conventional stage (formed in late adolescence), which is founded on humanistic ideas concerning the welfare of all humanity and on the "sacredness" of life. You do what is right because of a higher value or feeling, not necessarily religious, outside yourself.

A strong conscience may indicate maturity and responsibility, but an overly conscientious person often becomes anxious over relatively trivial situations. The rigid perfectionist who makes large demands on herself feels guilty if her aspirations do not materialize. Guilt feelings out of proportion to the act are severely incapacitating, just as is the lack of appropriate guilt. A function of guilt is to regulate society and to help it operate harmoniously; guilt should not render individuals incapable of decision and action.

Attitudes

The development of our attitudes is greatly influenced by our physical, intellectual, and emotional growth. *Attitude* refers to a positive or negative emotional reaction toward an idea or thing; thus, we often speak of favorable attitudes or poor attitudes, even hostile attitudes. Because of their emotional strength, it is rather difficult to change attitudes. Often, environmental conditions—the physical setting or the interpersonal situation—must be changed before attitudes may change. When we assign value to objects or events, we are acknowledging their worth and usefulness to us. Thus, attitudes and values work together as a strong force in developing the drives and motivations that pull us through life.

Katz (1960) asserts that a person's attitudes are reinforced through the effects they may have. First, we are more inclined to hold a positive attitude toward someone who loves us or who makes us feel good because our self-concept and self-esteem are enhanced. By saying nice things to each other, lovers develop a positive attitude toward each other, but overly critical teachers may put their students on guard and foster a hostile attitude. Second, when faced with novel situations, we try to respond in a way that will allow us to cope. We classify the aspects of the new situation according to attitudes we have accumulated from previous experience. Thus, when we enter a foreign city for the first time, we tend to avoid dubious establishments in order to avert the possibility of getting cheated or being embarrassed. Third, certain attitudes express value either about things we believe in or about the type of person we wish to be. A person who aspires to become a writer may identify with and appreciate others who are interested in creative activities but may show little sympathy for military life and its objectives simply because it contradicts what he considers to be the essence of human expression.

Community attitudes can stifle our psychological and emotional development (Kennedy & Kerber, 1973). Consider for a moment the Protestant ethic, in which a person's worth depends upon his or her earning capacity and his or her standing in the community. The obvious emphasis on competitiveness and acquisitiveness continues in American society, although perhaps not with the intensity of a few decades ago. The results of such a dominating influence can often make us value power and material things over personal needs for affection, self-esteem, acceptance, and respect.

Another example of repressive community attitudes can be found in employment practices that sometimes discriminate against those without certain skills. For example, some jobs require practice experience from the applicant; however, the applicant needs a job in the first place in order to gain experience. In-service training programs have been devised in some communities in order to overcome this problem.

Thus, some segments of our population are denied an opportunity to share in the mainstream of our society and to reap its political and industrial benefits. As a result, they may become antisocial or aggressive and are often punished for such behavior rather than rehabilitated or re-educated. Individual responsibility and motivation are important, but the effect of social forces on the individual is highly significant.

The self-actualization process is not governed solely by the groups to which one belongs or by one's inherited characteristics. Rather, self-actualization is a product of forces found in childhood within the family and later in peer groups, at school, at church, in professional groups, and in the society at large. As children gradually mature physically, they gain increased mastery over their environment by developing skills (verbal, mental, physical) and independence from their parents. We are conditioned by society, but we also have the capacity to indicate the direction our lives will take, to create goals for ourselves, and to initiate and complete actions that will realize the blueprint we have outlined for ourselves.

Prejudice

Prejudice is a negative or positive reaction toward a person or group made on the basis of limited or false information. We can, therefore, be prejudiced for, as well as against, someone. Allport (1954) lists several reasons for the prevalence of prejudice: (1) it has historical roots in our society; that is, there have always been objects or people who were considered inferior or different; (2) economic inequality, competition, and exploitation breed hatred and envy; (3) prejudice is easily learned from parents, teachers, and peers; and (4) persons or groups who feel frustrated, discriminated against, and insecure tend to blame other people or groups for their situation (scapegoating).

Many of us have opinions that are fairly rigid and generalized but that do not interfere with our daily functioning; however, when we hold biased, unreasonable, and preconceived opinions of others, we are being prejudiced. Prejudice usually reveals our own insecurities rather than any actual and real differences among groups. The prejudiced person attempts to acquire a certain superficial leverage over someone whom he actually perceives as threatening.

Since prejudice is a learned response (consider children of different nationalities who play together without noticing differences in skin color or accent), it can be unlearned. After extended exposure to the group or individual in question, we can acquire more accurate perceptions. Thus, interaction with different types of people in school, in employment, and in social situations tends to reduce stereotyped thinking. The fact that nearly every ethnic group and religion has been the victim of prejudice in the past demonstrates that such negative beliefs do not stem from the real nature of these groups but from opinions and emotional attitudes about them.

Ethnocentrism—the belief of one ethnic group that it is superior to any other

Figure 3-3. Children are usually unaware of prejudice and get along well with one another. Photo by Arthur Nikelly.

such group—tends to polarize and prevent people from actualizing themselves.

One difficulty in eliminating ethnocentrism lies in the fact that prejudicial behavior tends to perpetuate situations that foster further prejudice. We may, for example, begin by denying women equal pay to that of men and then go on to describe them as hostile or aggressive for demanding equal salaries. Another facet of prejudice that tends to make these behavior patterns self-perpetuating is the isolation of people (either by choice or by societal pressures) because of color, religion, or ethnic origin. Isolation prevents new understanding and allows misinformation and misconceptions to multiply. People who are isolated or discriminated against usually feel out of place or inferior and may react in anger or respond in even more prejudicial ways. When, for example, a crowd of protesters perceive the police as hostile and the police perceive the crowds as hostile, a vicious cycle is formed, and the feelings and reactions of one group feed on those of the other. Later on, each group may be surprised to hear how its actions had been interpreted by the other; free speech had been perceived as mob violence, and law and order had become the denial of human rights.

Are there effective ways to deal with and prevent discrimination and prejudice? Educated persons tend to view others as equals and to grant them respect as individuals. It is therefore possible that our educational system works, to some extent, in eliminating prejudice. There is always the danger, however, that educated people may only have learned to conceal or mask their prejudicial behavior and to demonstrate it in more subtle ways.

Legislation has helped to ensure that individuals will be allowed to make the best use of their talents and skills, but much remains to be done. Minority groups are becoming more defensive of their rights and are seeking legal means to ensure equality. In the long run, acceptance of the plight and struggle of the minorities as a justified endeavor, in view of the oppressive society in which they live, may eventually lead not only to mere tolerance of one another but to a greater cooperation, closeness, and sharing on an equal basis.

Confusion and conflict thrive amidst stereotyped attitudes and interfere with fulfillment. Only when we become aware of our prejudices can we work to unlearn them and to discover more fulfilling personal relationships.

INTERPERSONAL BEHAVIOR

Group Affiliation

Belonging to groups is important for our personal development, for our fulfillment, and for our ability to cope. Interacting with others helps us achieve our goals, for isolation usually fosters ineffectual actions and unrealistic expectations. In business situations, at school, in the family, and in social situations, we receive the benefits of social interaction as we share common goals and values and work together for mutual benefits.

Affiliation refers to a basic desire to be with other people—people who may strengthen our personal identity through their support. We like to be with people who like us and who have pleasant personalities, who are similar to us in terms of beliefs or interests, whose values are close to ours, and whose activities and opinions are similar. We are often attracted to persons who make up for what we lack in ourselves; for example, a mothering-type person always seems to find a person who likes to be mothered. And we are drawn to persons who are competent, able, intelligent, and masterful (Stotland & Hillmer, 1962).

There is a need in us to feel that others know us. We want to feel rooted with others, to share in a larger setting of people. Most people want "strings attached" and seek others to feel close to and to depend on. If they go to a strange country or town, they usually have a tendency to look for someone they know; they may even try phoning "a friend of a friend." We may experience similar feelings when attending a party where we know few people or find ourselves ignored. More often than not we may develop a headache, become fatigued, feel nervous or depressed, want to leave the situation, or talk to the few people we know rather than meet new people. Young children in classrooms, college students away from home for the first time, and older persons who have retired often experience a feeling of not belonging and a sense of inadequacy or inability to cope. Feelings of isolation, then, can block or delay fulfillment or cause us to feel anxious (Schachter, 1959).

Another way to look at affiliation or belonging to a group is to consider the extent to which we are involved in its goals. Groups can be primary (for instance, the family), in which relationships are close and permanent, or secondary (for instance, a class), in which members share common goals but maintain more casual relationships. We belong to some groups in name only, while to others we have a deep commitment and sense of responsibility. Interestingly, the same group may produce quite different responses from different people. Some women affiliate themselves with a sorority on a casual basis, while others make close and lasting connections. Some people pay church dues and participate in only a most perfunctory sense, while others find the central meaning of their lives in church membership.

Group membership can enhance personal identity and self-esteem because of the support, approval, and recognition that group members often give one another. A group can also provide structure, suggest roles, strengthen competencies, and enrich interpersonal relationships. Group membership, however, can also be harmful if the group engages in antisocial activities or exploits a member's social weaknesses, physical handicaps, or poor family background. Groups can also require overconformity and thus destroy personal initiative and freedom. When individuals are dominated by a group, they merely assume an expected role and allow themselves to be controlled by those around them. Instead of building identity, such a group destroys confidence in the individual's ability to act independently.

When we identify with a particular group and use its standards to evaluate our own behavior, we develop in a certain social direction. Influential groups such as these are known as "reference groups" and help us to form attitudes, adopt values, and shape our lifestyle. Reference groups are particularly important for adolescents, who are in the process of breaking away from their parents to make their own lives.

We are all dependent on others for various reasons and in different degrees. Some groups we choose—professional organizations, political parties, sororities, fraternities, athletic associations—while we have little choice about our membership in others—ethnic or racial groups, groups based on social class, religious groups, peer groups, or groups based on sex identification. Sometimes we take the groups to which we belong for granted, realizing only when we move to a new locale (such as going away to college) how important our membership was. On such occasions we may suffer temporary setbacks, experiencing feelings of insecurity, loneliness, and indecision. Only when we identify with new groups do we again feel the strength that comes from shared beliefs and goals, similarity of interests, and mutual interdependence.

The major social changes of the last decade—such as the decline of the stable neighborhood, the rapid growth of suburbia, the increase of "singles only" living complexes, and the weakening of the stability of the family—have greatly influenced the creation and organization of groups. One strong group—the youth culture—has emerged quickly, often being unfairly stereotyped by the mass media.

Many adults view this group as a threat. Those who are dissatisfied with their own lives and the state of the world may welcome change, but those who are socially comfortable tend to see change as a threat that forces them to become defensive and to react in hostility against such groups as the youth culture.

Our world seems to offer fewer opportunities for people to come together, as compared with several decades ago, but many kinds of affiliation remain available for any persons who are willing to extend the effort to build bridges between themselves and others.

Roles

Roles prescribe how we are expected to behave and to interact with others. Such societal institutions as school, family, peers, religion, newspapers, and television train us to assume many different roles in order to function in a complex environment. Thus, teacher, student, maid, banker, child, and mother all have certain roles to assume in society—patterns of behavior that are consistent with the expectations of others. Of course a banker may also be a father, a husband, and a lover, just as the student may play the roles of son, scholar, athlete, and playboy.

Roles do not necessarily place limits on us, although sometimes they seem to. We do not necessarily lose our natural way of relating even within the framework of role expectation. As a matter of fact, our roles can help us to attain deep and serious relationships and to rise beyond social clichés. Roles are not necessarily rigidly imposed on us unless we conform to them blindly; rather, roles are helpers or facilitators, enabling us to move effectively within society without losing our real identity in the process.

Although sexual roles have seemed in the past to be rigid and predetermined, they have recently become less rigid, and considerable overlap of these roles is now generally tolerated. Most of us readily recognize the stereotyped female and male roles. A man who cries or a female football player seems inconsistent and unlikely, even though these activities are primarily socially determined rather than biologically determined. When people have a mature sense of their identity, they do not feel uncomfortable when performing duties associated with an opposite sex role. The husband who changes diapers and the wife who works as an architect are becoming more and more common.

Merely mimicking a role, assuming a part like an actor on the stage, can lead to frustration and can prevent development and fulfillment. The role must be a part of yourself; it must allow you to express yourself rather than force you to mask your true identity. We cannot pretend to love someone or to find satisfaction in work that does not suit us; conflicts will eventually arise. Sometimes we become "stuck" in a role and are afraid to "bust out" and adopt a role that is more compatible with what we really are. But we must dare to find the role that allows us to fulfill ourselves. Roles must represent our true selves instead of merely pleasing others and satisfying their expectations, or we become slaves to them and allow them to stifle our lives.

Sometimes we overplay roles and discover that we are shunned by others who recognize how insincere and "phony" our behavior is. It is generally believed that insecure persons tend to assume false or unnatural roles in order to place themselves in a more favorable light and to win acceptance from others. Consider, for example, the bright and relatively independent woman who plays the role of the "dumb" and dependent girl because she hopes that such behavior will attract a male's attention, or the male student who tries to appear independent, strong, and outgoing as a cover-up for his felt weaknesses in certain masculine areas. Such role-playing can be temporarily rewarding, but it is a behavior pattern that may backfire when others can see through the mask of an artificial role. In the long run, we may lose the admiration of others when they discover that we are basically different from the impression we have created through role-playing. While there may be risk in breaking certain roles we have come to rely on, the results can be gratifying because there is no longer any need for defensive, rigid behavior. By clinging to stereotyped roles, we elude others and function in an artificial world in which we have eliminated meaningful and lasting interpersonal relationships.

From time to time students make concerted efforts to identify with a particular group on campus that appeals to their needs or that they value for various personal reasons. However, the lifestyle of such a group may not always be consistent with the student's view of himself. He may conform to gain attention, recognition, acceptance, or status, but when the novelty wears off he wants to return to his earlier behavior. Joining a social fraternity may be an example of this kind of effort for the studious but essentially solitary young man. Joining a women's lib group may be an example for the young woman who is temporarily involved with the excitement of radical movements but basically holds a much more conservative and traditional value system. Either student may later wonder what "possessed" them to join that organization.

Roles are taught to us by our parents and conditioned within the larger society, but they are determined by our biological makeup as well. While most of us behave in basically consistent ways, we also play varying roles depending on the situation and the persons with whom we are interacting. We reflect that part of ourselves that corresponds to or is consistent with a certain aspect of the social milieu, but the basic core of our personality remains more or less fixed.

A conflict of roles may result when a person belongs to groups with different expectations. The female student who often assumes a passive, helpless role to place her dates into her service may encounter conflict when she joins a group that expects each of its members to be independent, outgoing, and assertive. A major problem is how to mesh personal needs with the requirements of a particular group. For many students, loyalty to different groups is difficult to achieve because of the conflicting requirements of each group. In some groups the "good life" means leisure, travel, and contemplative pursuits; in others it is the accumulation of wealth, social prestige, and power over others; in still others it is represented by a life of social service and humanitarian endeavor, regardless of material benefit. It is little wonder that students find it difficult to adapt to the expectations of such opposing groups.

Carroll (1964) explains the notion of "role lag"—the inability to shed earlier roles and to adopt more mature ones that are consistent and appropriate to a given age and situation. The pretty girl who was the teacher's pet in grade school and gained attention by being sweet and charming may have difficulty in college if she continues to use the same role; although it was effective at an earlier age, it is no longer appropriate, and it sets her apart from her peers. Roles change from age to age, from one situation to another, and the individual is expected to "keep up" with them—that is, to adapt without losing our individuality in the process. Sometimes we cling to old roles because new ones cause us anxiety; the retreat into a fantasy life where old roles can be maintained is often the route chosen by severely anxious persons.

Roles are also identified with various occupational groups—physicians, hostesses, athletes, college professors—but even within these limits, we can function as unique human beings and need not allow a superficial mask to hide our true selves. Every person undertakes activities consistent with his chosen role in life; and there is a general agreement between a person's behavior at work and the expectations of the larger society. Similarly, there must be consistency between how we view ourselves and the occupational role we exhibit if we are to find fulfillment in our work. Only when we can express our real nature in our work can we be said to be "occupationally suited."

How do we find our true role and belonging place? A unique way to understand our roles is through a group process called *transactional analysis,* in which our roles reveal themselves as we interact in a group (Harris, 1967). During this process, the therapist or facilitator observes each member's effective and ineffective ways of interacting with others, an interaction referred to as the "life script." The group leader then assists each member to alter undesirable behavior and to adopt more effective behavior. There are three ways of interacting—as a parent, adult, or child—and each role is acceptable as long as it is effective in a given situation and for the persons involved. For a wife to respond to her husband like a child is considered ineffective, just as is a fatherly reaction on the part of a husband toward his wife. Roles should match, and this is what the group leader tries to help accomplish. A further example of this method is presented in Chapter 10.

Group membership is vital for actualizing ourselves because we grow as we give and take within a group. Some of us have been fortunate to have been born into a group in which we discover a satisfying role as we make contributions to the group and are rewarded for them. Others of us have been asked to join groups or "have found our way" into groups that are rewarding. Another alternative remains, however. We can take an active interest in others—reach out to them rather than wait for their overtures to us. To learn to be ourselves we have to mix with others; for it is only in interaction that we discover the many facets of our identity. The following situation describes a person who found a new image of himself through group membership.

Incident

I was unhappy in high school and had no real friends. My parents never cared who I went around with; they had troubles of their own. So I ran around with crummy people like myself. None of us really belonged anywhere. Inside I felt rotten, and I didn't have the foggiest idea of what I wanted out of life. I had nightmares of falling down a high cliff or being lost in a forest and not being able to find my way out. It had gotten to the point where I was afraid to go to sleep and afraid to face the day. Here in college I am surprised at being dumped with other people who are so different from the ones I knew. People on my floor talked to me right from the start, and I felt more like everybody else. Nobody acted like there was something wrong with me, and I got to talking more. On week ends we went on bike trips, on Fridays we went drinking, and during the week we just talked. For the first time I found normal, exciting people, if you want to call them that, with lots of good ideas in their heads and many things to do. At first I sort of fed off of them, but now I think I add something of my own to the group. I think if you put yourself with the right people, with people who have their heads together, you can get to be a happier person.

SUMMARY

In discussing the emergence of the self, we have seen that personality is the product of innate potential as well as of social experience and that the quality of childrearing practices has a significant impact on later adjustment. We have noted how parental attitudes may determine how a child's personality develops and functions, and we have stressed the motivating force of early childhood experiences. The number and arrangement of family members also affect the behavior of every child. However, there are social factors outside the family that also shape our personality. As we gradually break away from parental control, our self-awareness grows, and we continue to struggle with the problems of independence as adults. Working through our original dependency upon our parents and forming emotional attachments to others help us to identify with society at large and to become concerned citizens as well as fulfilled individuals.

In reviewing the stages of emotional development, we have noted that children are at first fully dependent upon their parents. Their own helplessness dictates dependency. Later, they are expected to assume some independence, but they may resent this responsibility and interpret their parents' expectations as hostile and unloving. A child may interpret the fact that his parents no longer do everything for him as rejection. Most of us readily outgrow such feelings, since the taste of independence is pleasurable, but we have also seen the "clinging vine" who remains dependent on others for support as well as the overconfident person who is willing to manipulate others. Neither is engaged in a mutually beneficial relationship.

There is a link between the quality of the relationship between parents and their children and the child's capacity to give and to take love. Parental control and pampering have generally negative effects, but, in spite of such early experiences, we can build a satisfying and meaningful adult life. Ideally, we must untie the bonds of dependency that make us cling to our families and carry with us notions of what is right or wrong. We join a larger family when we become a part of society, establishing a new kind of harmony and interdependence. Belonging to the family of human beings ideally means working toward the common good while, at the same time, realizing our individual capacities to the fullest.

QUESTIONS TO THINK ABOUT

1. In what type of family were you brought up? Did it determine personality traits you may currently have?
2. Did you ever feel overly dependent or overly aggressive in situations in which, upon reflection, you would now behave differently and perhaps more effectively?

3. Did you ever experience a clash of values within yourself? How did you go about resolving it? How do you handle value clashes between yourself and others?
4. Do you catch yourself playing roles in order to impress someone? Under what circumstances? If you did not play that role, what results would you predict?
5. If you could change something in your personality, what would it be? Is there something about yourself that you like and would like to see reflected in the behavior of others?
6. Do you belong to a group with which you feel comfortable? Were there times when you had difficulty accepting the goals and purposes of this group? How did you resolve that conflict?
7. Can you place yourself in one category of values that best describes you, or can you rank three or four categories of values in order to create your own value profile?
8. Can you describe your own family climate? Does your family climate differ markedly from the family climate found in the homes of your friends?
9. Take a look at your own family. Who is the most passive member and who is the most aggressive? Who is closest to whom? Where are the alliances, and what are some of the sources of conflict? How do you fit into your family constellation?

REFERENCES

Alberti, R. E., & Emmons, M. L. *Your perfect right*. San Luis Obispo, Calif.: Impact, 1970

Allport, G. W. *The nature of prejudice*. Reading, Mass.: Addison-Wesley, 1954.

Bandura, A. *Principles of behavior modification*. New York: Holt, Rinehart & Winston, 1969.

Bandura, A., & Walters, R. H. *Social learning and personality development*. New York: Holt, Rinehart & Winston, 1963.

Baumrind, D. Authoritarian *vs.* authoritative control. *Adolescence,* 1968, *3*(2), 255-272.

Becker, W. C. Consequences of different kinds of parental discipline. In M. L. Hoffman & L. W. Hoffman (Eds.), *Review of child development* (Vol. 1). New York: Russell Sage Foundation, 1964.

Berkowitz, L. (Ed.). *Roots of aggression: A re-examination of the frustration-aggression hypothesis*. New York: Atherton, 1969.

Carroll, H. A. *Mental hygiene* (4th ed.). Englewood Cliffs, N. J.: Prentice-Hall, 1964.

Conger, J. J. A world they never knew: The family and social change. *Daedalus,* 1971, *100*(4), 1105-1138.

Cooley, C. H. *Human nature and the social order*. New York: Schocken Books, 1964.

Dewing, K., & Taft, R. Some characteristics of the parents of creative twelve-year olds. *Journal of Personality,* 1973, *41*(1), 71-85.

Douvan, E. A., & Adelson, J. *The adolescent experience*. New York: Wiley, 1966.

Dreikurs, R. Raising children in a democracy. *Humanist,* 1961, *21*(1), 15-24.

Forer, L. K. *Birth order and life roles*. Springfield, Ill.: Thomas, 1969.

Glueck, S., & Glueck, E. *Unraveling juvenile delinquency*. Cambridge, Mass.: Harvard University Press, 1950.

Goldfarb, W. Effects of psychological deprivation in infancy and subsequent stimulation. *American Journal of Psychiatry,* 1945, *102*(2), 18-33.

Greenwald, J. *Be the person you were meant to be.* New York: Simon & Schuster, 1973.

Harris, T. A. *I'm O.K.—You're O.K. A practical guide to transactional analysis.* New York: Harper & Row, 1967.

Heilbrun, A. B., Jr. Parental model attributes, nurturant reinforcement, and consistency of behavior in adolescents. *Child Development,* 1964, *35*(1), 151-167.

Heilbrun, A. B., Jr., Orr, H. K., & Harrell, S. N. Patterns of parental childrearing and subsequent vulnerability to cognitive disturbance. *Journal of Consulting Psychology,* 1966, *30*(1), 51-59.

Hershey, G. L., & Lugo, J. O. *Living psychology.* New York: Macmillan, 1970.

Hirning, J. L., & Hirning, A. L. *Marriage adjustment.* New York: American Book Company, 1956.

Hollenberg, E., & Sperry, M. Some antecedents of aggression and effects of frustration on doll play. *Personality,* 1951, *1*(1), 32-43.

Horner, M. S. Toward an understanding of achievement-related conflicts in women. *The Journal of Social Issues,* 1972, *28*(2), 157-175.

Jacobs, Spilken, Norman, Anderson, & Rosenheim. Perceptions of faulty parent-child relationships and illness behavior. *Journal of Consulting and Clinical Psychology,* 1972, *39*(1), 49-55.

Katz, D. The functional approach to the study of attitudes. *Public Opinion Quarterly,* 1960, *24*(2), 163-204.

Kennedy, D. B., & Kerber, A. *Resocialization: An American experiment.* New York: Behavioral Publications, 1973.

Klein, M. M., Plutchik, R., & Conte, H. R. Parental dominance-passivity and behavior problems of children. *Journal of Consulting and Clinical Psychology,* 1973, *40*(3), 416-419.

Kohlberg, L. The concept of moral maturity. Paper presented at the meeting of the National Institute for Child Health and Human Development Conference on the Development of Values, Washington, D. C., 1968.

Levy, D. M. *Maternal overprotection.* New York: Columbia University Press, 1943.

Lynn, D. B. *The father: His role in child development.* Monterey, Calif.: Brooks/Cole, 1974.

McKee, J. P., & Leader, F. B. The relationship of socioeconomic status and aggression to the competitive behavior of preschool children. *Child Development,* 1955, *26*(2), 135-142.

Mead, M. *Male and female.* New York: Morrow, 1949.

Mead, M. *Culture and commitment: A study of the generation gap.* New York: Doubleday, 1970.

Medinnus, G. R. Adolescents' self-acceptance and perceptions of their parents. *Journal of Consulting Psychology,* 1965, *29*(2), 150-154.

Mussen, P. H., Conger, J. J., & Cagan, J. *Child development and personality.* New York: Harper & Row, 1969.

Mussen, P. H., Rutherford, E., Harris, S., & Keasey, C. B. Honesty and altruism among preadolescents. *Developmental Psychology,* 1970, *3*(2), 169-194.

Nikelly, A. G. The psychological problems of democratization. *American Journal of Psychotherapy,* 1964, *14*(1), 52-56.

Nikelly, A. G. The dependent adolescent. *Adolescence,* 1971, *6*(22), 139-144.

Reuter, M. W., & Biller, H. B. Perceived paternal nurturance-availability and personality adjustment among college males. *Journal of Consulting and Clinical Psychology,* 1973, *40*(3), 339-342.

Riesman, D., Glazer, N., & Denney, R. *The lonely crowd* (New ed.). New Haven, Conn.: Yale University Press, 1961.

Roberts, G. L. *Personal growth and adjustment.* Boston: Holbrook Press, 1968.

Sampson, E. E. The study of ordinal position: Antecedents and outcomes. In B. Maher (Ed.), *Progress in experimental personality research* (Vol. 2). New York: Academic Press, 1965.

Schachter, S. *The psychology of affiliation.* Stanford, Calif.: Stanford University Press, 1959.

Schaefer, E. S. A circumplex model of maternal behavior. *Journal of Abnormal and Social Psychology,* 1959, *59*(2), 226-235.

Sears, R. R., Maccoby, E. E., & Levin, H. *Patterns of child rearing.* New York: Harper & Row, 1957.

Shulman, B. H. The family constellation in personality diagnosis. *Journal of Individual Psychology,* 1962, *47*(1), 35-47.

Spranger, E. *Types of men.* New York: Steckert, 1928.

Stotland, E. & Hillmer, M. L., Jr. Identification, authoritarian defensiveness, and self-esteem. *Journal of Social and Abnormal Psychology,* 1962, *64*(5), 334-342.

Symonds, P. M. *The psychology of parent-child relationships.* New York: Appleton-Century, 1939.

Thomas, A., Birch, H. G., Chess, S., & Robbins, L. C. Individuality in responses of children to similar environmental situations. *American Journal of Psychiatry,* 1961, *117*(9), 798-803.

Walters, J., & Stinnett, N. Parent-child relationships: A decade review of research. *Journal of Marriage and the Family,* 1971, *33*(1), 70-111.

Westley, W. A., & Epstein, N. B. *Silent majority.* San Francisco: Jossey-Bass, 1969.

White, R. K., & Lippitt, R. *Autocracy and democracy.* New York: Harper, 1960.

White, R. W., & Watt, N. F. *The abnormal personality* (4th ed.). New York: Ronald Press, 1973.

Yankelovich, D. *Generations apart.* New York: Columbia Broadcasting System, 1969.

Yarrow, M. R., Campbell, J. D., & Burton, R. V. *Child rearing: An inquiry into research and methods.* San Francisco: Jossey-Bass, 1968.

Zipf, S. G. Resistance and conformity under reward and punishment. *Journal of Abnormal and Social Psychology,* 1960, *61*(1), 102-109.

Chapter 4

Moving toward Self-Awareness and Identity

CHAPTER OUTLINE

I. Motivation
    A. Needs and drives: The forces behind motivation
    B. Growth motivation and deficiency motivation
    C. How motivation works

II. Emotions
    A. Emotions: What are they?
    B. Emotions: How do they develop?
    C. Dealing with positive and negative emotions

III. Cognition
    A. How does cognition develop?
    B. How can we improve our thinking skills?

IV. Social development
    A. When does it begin?
    B. How can we improve our social effectiveness?

V. Identity
    A. Ego identity
    B. Negative identity
    C. Identity formation: The major problem of adolescence and youth

VI. Self-esteem
    A. What is self-esteem?
    B. How may self-esteem be improved?
        1. Socialization
        2. New interests
        3. Career development
        4. Self-knowledge
        5. Listening
        6. Self-evaluation
        7. Mistaken beliefs

VII. Summary

In this chapter we will attempt to understand what motivates us to behave as we do. We will analyze emotional and rational processes affecting behavior as well as the role of socialization, and we will consider ways to eliminate or lessen deficiencies in these areas. Adapting to a rapidly changing world requires a remarkable combination of stability and flexibility, but knowing who we are and how we got that way can help us to understand our actions and to plan new alternatives.

MOTIVATION

Motivation is a force that propels us to act; it is usually inspired by an inner need to behave in a certain manner or by the importance of an external goal.

Motives change as we meet with new experiences. An inspiring teacher, a moving play, a deep friendship, or persuasion from those we respect and admire can play a significant role in changing our motives. Wanting to become a lawyer after observing a court session or finding ways to attain financial security after marriage are examples of how motivation and, as a result, behavior change.

We do not always fully understand our motives. In fact, it is believed by many psychologists that we are conscious of only a small portion of our personality or behavior, and that a large portion of it, which is unpleasant or threatening to us, is automatically put out of our awareness. There can be several reasons for a motive or none at all. We may get married for a long list of reasons but may walk barefoot in the rain simply because we enjoy it. Motives can be stimulated by the mass media as well as by more direct experiences. A beer commercial may motivate us to call for a pizza, and a rainy Saturday may motivate us to go home for the weekend rather than stay on campus for the football game.

Motives can change, especially when we are dissatisfied with things as they are. However, we must first recognize the motives involved in a behavior in order to understand the behavior and its effects on others and in order to experiment with new and different possibilities.

Needs and Drives: The Forces behind Motivation

An infant's survival depends initially on the environment. At first, biological needs and, later, social needs produce a state of tension that propels the infant to activity. This activity is aimed at reducing discomfort and pain; comfort and pleasure are the goals toward which drives are directed. These drives that have become linked with goals are called motives, and they grow and multiply as the child develops. Thus, an adult operates with an entire complex of motives.

It is sometimes difficult to separate motives that are inborn from those that are learned, but most psychologists today give more emphasis to those that have been learned (Hall & Lindzey, 1957). When motivation is prompted by physiological factors (hunger, sleep, survival, comfort, thirst), the force behind the motive may be considered a drive, but when motivation is directed toward achievement, wealth, education, recognition, and the like, it may be classified as a response to an acquired or social need. Although *drives, needs,* and *motives* are terms used interchangeably by psychologists, *drives* usually denote what we are born with, whereas *needs* and *motives* denote what we have learned from our parents, from society, and from the culture in which we were raised.

A psychological drive can sometimes be stronger than a physiological drive. Consider, for instance, the student who is studying for an important exam; his appetite may diminish, and he may even skip meals without noticing his hunger. Physical drives can also be modified by learning and experience; we are able to get along with less sleep or less food if our motivation to do so is strong. Most researchers would also grant that strong psychological needs, such as the need for security, for belonging, and for fulfillment, do exist. However, the basic physical drives tend to be stronger than psychological ones because they are associated with survival—that is, with maintaining the body.

As past emotional experiences mesh with a current situation, they arouse and support a goal-directed intention; in other words, the person is motivated. To be more specific, motivational behavior begins with the biological or physiological forces that energize us to action. These forces can stem from physical drives or from learned habits and childhood experiences. When we experience a situation that has the potential to activate these tendencies, we are generally prompted to act as we did in similar situations in the past, especially if these past experiences had positive value for us. Also, long-range intentions often alter or vitalize human motivation. Motivation, then, is a combination of drives and needs that may be governed by projected goals within a particular setting for action. For example, we may be very hungry (the physical need) at the drive-in (the setting or situation), but we order a cup of coffee instead of a milk shake because we are on a diet (thus showing the effects of a long-range goal on motivation).

Growth Motivation and Deficiency Motivation

When our basic drives are satisfied, we tend to reach out toward new experiences. Maslow (1955) refers to this impulse as *growth motivation*—that is, motivation based on a desire to extend ourselves because of the joy and satisfaction

Figure 4-1. We are motivated when someone we respect really cares about what we do. Photo by Shirley Kontos.

new experience might give us. However, when we act to make up for something that is absent from our lives, because of some shortage or deficit, our behavior, according to Maslow, is governed by *deficiency motivation*. For example, one student may attend college because she thinks she must do so in order to acquire social position and professional esteem (deficiency motivation), while another may enroll because of the interest she has in learning (growth motivation).

How Motivation Works

The following situation illustrates how motivation functions in a realistic setting.

Incident

As a child, Tom planted seeds and watched with fascination as his plants grew. His parents were enthusiastic and communicated their positive feelings about his interest in nature. In high school he made charts depicting the growth of plants and gave mini-lectures on the subject. As he read more, he realized that atmospheric and soil conditions affect the growth of plants, which in turn affects human lives. In college he broadened his knowledge by studying biology, chemistry, and psychology. As a sophomore he decided to specialize in ecology, a field that linked the past, present, and future together for him. His ego-enhancing past experiences directed him to select similar experiences that continued to enhance his self-esteem. Finally, the significance of his future goals further strengthened his direction and efforts. Thus, he acted on the basis of a series of consistent motives, each growing from a previous one and all brought together under a single future goal.

Success, however, is not the entire answer to the question of how human motivation works. Longstreth (1968) points out that curiosity, stimulus deprivation, and even boredom can be motivating agents under certain conditions. Outside obstacles that produce competing alternatives and, thus, create frustration or conflict can also motivate us to act. Such motivation is especially apparent if we are emotional about a given situation, since emotion produces energy that can be used to reduce the degree of frustration or conflict. Longstreth devised an experiment with a marble game to prove his point. He deliberately frustrated one group of children and discovered that the greater the induced frustration, the harder the subjects tried to perform effectively. In short, frustration can promote motivation to try harder.

Physiological drives are few compared to drives that are socially acquired. Socially-acquired drives obviously reflect the culture in which a person lives. Neither the need to control and dominate others, the need to obtain material possessions and to enjoy ownership, nor the need to have many friends and to cultivate strong bonds with them can be explained on the basis of biological needs. Social approval, in fact, is one of the strongest learned motivations and may spur individuals on to high achievement even if they must forgo many pleasures in the process. For example, a writer or scientist may sacrifice immediate satisfactions (cars, sports, clothes) in order to strive for goals that may establish his or her reputation and win reverence. History records similar strivings for social recognition. During the invasion of ancient Greece, the Persian generals, dressed in glittering clothes and surrounded by opulence, asked the Greeks what rewards were given to winners in the Olympic games. They were amazed that the prize was a wreath made from wild olive branches. The Persians could not understand why anyone would undergo such arduous preparation for such a simple reward! They didn't realize that it was the honor and prestige of winning that motivated the Greek youth of that time rather than the symbolic wreath.

Social approval and the desire for achievement are strengthened when they reduce anxiety, punishment, and rejection (social disapproval). In other words, positive consequences activate us to seek out situations and to behave in ways that will be awarded with approval, while situations and actions that meet with disapproval are avoided. For example, the student who wants to ask a girl for a date may not do so because he anticipates the humiliation of rejection; he finds the frustration of not dating her more tolerable than her possible refusal.

Conditions that prompt us to action affect our manner of thinking and learning. We tend to tune in to what is relevant at a particular moment and block out what is not immediately associated with our actions. This selectivity of motivation helps us to adapt to complex situations, to achieve competence within a specific situation, and to fulfill our goals with greater expediency. During an exam, for example, we may concentrate so intently that we obliterate irrelevant problems and issues from our consciousness. Or when we are with someone we care for, we may put all our emotional energy and power of attention on that one person; it is, for the moment, as if the rest of the world did not exist.

EMOTIONS

Emotions: What Are They?

Emotions are the underlying feelings associated with our actions and thoughts. Both psychological and physiological components are included in the generalized feeling of emotion. How and what we think and previous pleasant and unpleasant experiences can be part of the psychological side of our emotions; but emotions also have physiological components such as heartbeat, blood pressure, muscle tension, breathing, perspiration.

Social class may also account for differences in emotional expression. Lower class youth, for example, tend to act out conflicts and express anger; middle class youth, on the other hand, are more apt to respond introspectively, to express confusion over values, and to be verbally expressive (Douvan & Adelson, 1966). Naturally, emotions that stem from cultural patterns are easier to change than those based on biological factors, but it is difficult to distinguish between the emotional traits we were born with and those learned from social transactions.

Emotional responses generally reflect the quality of an individual's personal adjustment. Of course, we all have emotions that we feel to be authentic and genuine from within ourselves and that we are encouraged to express honestly. Emotions may become inappropriate when we try to express what others expect from us in a particular situation—when we fake an emotion in order to have some effect on others—or when we overreact to a situation. Crying in a teacher's office over a low grade in order to elicit sympathy and perhaps a better grade or laughing when someone gets hurt in a sports event are examples of inappropriate emotions.

Inappropriate emotions may be overt symptoms of an underlying problem, while emotions consistent with a particular situation usually imply personal well-being. The freedom to honestly express emotions, including being able to express negative emotions without guilt, reflects the behavior of an emotionally well-adjusted person. Self-acceptance and tolerance of others often play a significant role in emotional maturity, whereas, under- or overexpression of emotion and false or concealed emotion indicate an individual who has not yet grown to full emotional development. Fear of failure in the face of simple aspirations, wanting to express affection but not knowing how, and concealing feelings to appear more sophisticated or to avoid being rejected are examples of failure to actuate the emotional aspect of existence. Just as acceptance of ourselves and openness to new experiences enhance personal fulfillment, so does the acceptance of our emotions, even those that are negative. Mild negative emotions, in fact, often help to afford relief.

The intensity of emotional expression often determines whether or not such expression is considered appropriate. Feeling "low" for a long period of time because you failed an exam or becoming genuinely angry at the outcome of an athletic event are examples of overextended emotional expression. Some people seem to have difficulty spontaneously expressing emotion. Such people try to avoid emotional situations completely, or they may overreact, thus making themselves appear foolish or even irrational, or pretend to experience the emotional reaction that they feel others expect. Such false responses inhibit emotional development, which is personally satisfying as well as socially significant. Emotional behavior, like any form of behavior, can be misused or misinterpreted by others; however, emotional behavior, like other behavior, can be changed.

Emotions: How Do They Develop?

While emotions are to some extent innate, the manner in which they are expressed appears to be modified by early parental training as well as by social learning. Erikson (1950) amplified and modified Freud's developmental theory and described eight stages of emotional growth. All of us experience both the positive and the negative aspects of these eight stages; however, through the strength found in the positive aspects, we are able to go on to each new stage.

The first level involves our basic tendency to trust others for support. Such feelings go back to our earliest experiences with our parents, particularly our mothers, who fed and cared for us as infants. If a child does not feel that he can depend on his parents for nurture and support, however, he may develop feelings of mistrust that can lead to maladjustment later in life.

The second level of emotional development occurs in the second year of life. The child is expected to learn bowel control and personal autonomy, and he or she begins to feel more independent. Failure to develop in this direction may result in loss of parental affection, loss of self-esteem, and the growth of feelings of inadequacy and self-doubt. Between the ages of 3 and 5 (level three), children begin to imitate adult roles and to develop a strong sense of self-worth. Their failure to take the initiative, to think and act without being urged, however, may result in withdrawal or in feelings of guilt, jealousy, and doubt, which can later hamper their competence as adults.

The early school years cover the fourth stage of emotional development. Children begin to use their energies freely and independently. They work on their own, turning only occasionally to adults for support and guidance. As they are encouraged to grow, they learn to become effective with the skills they have at their disposal. If a feeling of industry and personal responsibility does not develop, a child may begin to feel inferior; for example, failure in school often produces severe problems in emotional development.

Highly relevant to the high school and college student is the fifth stage, lasting from puberty (approximately age 12) through adolescence and sometimes into early adulthood. Adolescents struggle to discover their true selves, to define a personal ideology, to prove their sexual attractiveness, and to determine a life direction. Failure to achieve these goals may result in value confusion, sexual disorientation, apathy, and the inability to accept authority or to find meaningful work. These are difficult as well as challenging years, for young people in high school and college must identify with many of the roles and goals of mature men and women.

In the sixth stage of emotional development, the adult should ideally have a full commitment to work, a satisfying social relationship with others, and a fulfilling sexual intimacy with one partner. However, individuals who fail to develop emotionally during the first five stages may become overly casual or even promiscuous in their relations with others or, on the other hand, may withdraw into antisocial or introspective behavior.

The seventh stage, middle adulthood, is characterized by family involvement and the production of offspring. This stage often demonstrates the ability of individuals to give of themselves to advance the welfare of others. Emotionally thwarted individuals, however, may find that this stage is characterized by inactivity and feelings of ineffectiveness. They may behave in selfish, unproductive ways. Lacking competence and resources, they may find that they are in a period of stagnation or immobility.

The eighth and last stage in emotional development involves an acceptance of the life cycle. The emotionally mature person recognizes that life is coming to completion and looks back on his or her past life with appreciation. There is no fear of death. In old age, as productivity declines, emotionally mature persons often try to make some sense of their existence—that is, put things into meaningful order. If the meaning of life or the reason for existence is not clear, older persons may begin to dislike themselves and feel as if their lives have been wasted.

Dealing with Positive and Negative Emotions

Most of us live by striking a balance between emotion and reason, for intelligence is a factor that may demonstrate itself in emotional, intuitive perceptions as well as in more logically ordered mental processes. Giving vent to our feelings and expressing our emotions is just as important as being able to think logically and act with reason and judgment. Depending on the stimulation and encouragement we receive from our early environment, emotions become strengthened in certain ways and stifled in others. We can observe, for example, that animated discussion occurs in certain families, while other families seem more reserved, even taciturn. In emotion-laden situations, some people react more intensely than others, but both positive emotions—such as joy, tenderness, humor—and negative emotions—such as anger, jealousy, fear—serve us best when they are *appropriate* for and in *proportion* to the particular situation. Becoming excessively depressed when someone offends you or laughing when someone is hurt are examples of disproportionate or inappropriate emotional responses.

People who feel comfortable about themselves will not become distressed if they occasionally withhold negative emotions or cannot find an opportunity to express their positive feelings. The important thing is that they have a choice whether or not to express themselves. They will work to strengthen their positive emotions and thereby increase their personal growth and their ability to present themselves effectively. Possible ways to strengthen positive emotions include writing down your thoughts and feelings or talking honestly with someone with whom you have a lot in common. Probably the best way to cope with unpleasant emotions is to examine their source. By acknowledging our negative emotions, we

Figure 4-2. Some persons cannot let their feelings come out freely for fear that they may appear foolish. Photo by Shirley Kontos.

may begin to understand their precipitating causes and then may attempt to avoid situations that may provoke us, or we may begin to substitute more positive emotional experiences, such as developing our creativity, getting involved in various activities, and building relationships with new people. Such action may lessen hostile feelings or reduce them to a level that does not interfere with productivity.

Our society seems to frown on strong expression of emotion. People intellectually acknowledge the restrictions placed on them by society; thus, they are afraid to shed the roles expected of them or imposed upon them. Because our emotional reactions are often contained or kept inside ourselves, we tend to behave rather automatically, allowing situations to trigger standard emotional responses. Our emotional repertoire is generally defined by what we anticipate in life and by what we have already experienced in the past. For example, a childhood memory of death may influence a person's present-day reaction to death, or the anticipation associated with holidays may occur during every holiday regardless of the particular circumstances. Finally, body chemistry, and even changes in the weather can influence our emotional reactions. For example, some persons become sluggish when the thyroid gland becomes deficient or apathetic when the weather becomes hot and humid.

COGNITION

How Does Cognition Develop?

Jean Piaget, a Swiss psychologist (Flavell, 1963), was a pioneer in the area of cognitive, or intellectual, processes (the way we learn, remember, perceive, and reason). He distinguished four significant stages in cognitive growth that, he felt, must be mastered in consecutive order. The sensorimotor phase, a period that occupies the first 18 months of life, comes first. Language has not yet been learned, and responses to people and objects are relatively simple. Children apply learned responses to different new objects. They generalize their responses from one situation or object to another. This process is referred to as *assimilation*. An opposite process, the altering of responses to handle novel situations, is called *accommodation*. The pre-operational phase, which lasts until the child is about 7 years of age, follows. Words and symbols begin to stand for people and objects, although the child is still bound to visual reality. The following five years constitute the third phase—the phase of concrete operations—in which the child handles qualitative relationships, deals with the properties of things around him, and thinks in terms of an object's potential instead of in terms of what it actually appears to be at the time. The fourth phase is called the formal-operation phase and occurs in children age 12 and over. The child is now capable of logical analysis and deductive reasoning; he or she may examine several possibilities and test alternative hypotheses before finally making a choice on the basis of empirical evidence. In short, children at this stage can operate on a formal, abstract, conceptual basis. Cognitive development, however, does not exist in isolation from emotional growth, and, therefore, we should keep in mind the brief survey of Erikson's theory presented in the previous section of this chapter.

How Can We Improve Our Thinking Skills?

Many psychologists believe that our feelings are often governed by our thinking. Certainly, the way we feel about ourselves affects how we think. If we have a low opinion of ourselves, our ability to cope suffers (Combs & Snygg, 1959). Along the same line, when we give others positive feedback, praise them for their contributions, and accept them as persons, they are strongly motivated to perform well and will likely show increased competence in solving problems (Hershey & Lugo, 1970).

Sometimes our actions indicate one intention, while our thoughts suggest another. For example, a student who appears to work hard in his courses may make obvious mistakes on his exams, almost as if he wanted to fail. His cognitive skills may be impaired by an emotional conflict, and his behavior may represent something like hostility toward his parents—a way of getting back at them without actually confronting them—or a way of punishing himself for something as unrelated to specific course work as breaking up with his girlfriend.

Solutions are not always as "neat" as we want them to be, but there are ways to become more effective in the cognitive areas. It is often helpful to define the problem by looking at it from different points of view; consider how others (real or characterized) have solved similar problems in the past, or ask the opinion of someone who is not intensely involved with your problem and who can thus give you an objective viewpoint. Avoid trying to solve problems when you are upset, nervous, tired, or in a hurry, and, if you cannot find a solution, postpone your decision for a time. Allow your mind to move to other things and return to the problem refreshed.

SOCIAL DEVELOPMENT

When Does It Begin?

Human development depends on biological maturation as well as on learning experiences; in other words, there is an interplay between physiological readiness and the opportunity to learn. Researchers like to describe human development in precise stages, each growing out from the full development of the previous stage; but these stages do not develop smoothly and uniformly in every person. Development should be viewed as a continuous and even somewhat erratic process; however, studying development in stages enables us to consider what tends to happen during a specific span of development in terms of social, intellectual, and emotional growth.

Robert Sears (Maier, 1965), a developmental psychologist, refers to three stages in social development. The first is the stage of total dependency on the immediate environment for the satisfaction of basic drives (hunger, protection, warmth, thirst, love). During the first few months of their lives, infants are the passive recipients of emotional supplies. Their needs build up tension, but as such needs are gratified the tension is reduced. Sears terms this stage the "rudimentary" period.

Infants soon become somewhat aggressive, making demands and showing greater activity and responsiveness toward their environment. They demonstrate a kind of inborn aggression when their needs are not met. From the age of 6 months to about 6 years, children occupy a stage of "secondary motivation." Basic drives no longer play the dominant role as new drives are socially acquired through interaction with others. A child, for instance, may play not to release pent-up energy but to satisfy his curiosity, to interact with his peers, or to gain a sense of mastery through play. Sears believes that this secondary period of both positive and negative social conditioning is crucial in the development of sexual identity and in the formation of a consistent view of the world. It is during this period that the basic personality structure that will last throughout the lifespan is formed.

The third stage in social development according to Sears involves "secondary systems," such as peer groups at school or in the neighborhood. Such groups may exert greater influence on an individual as models for action than do his parents. The importance of the immediate family gradually weakens, and societal institutions assume greater force.

As infants we are at first only aware of ourselves; later we begin to differentiate other "selves" and objects in the environment. In the process of development, we increasingly recognize the needs of others. As infants, we "take"; as adults, we often "give" more than we take. From love of self we shift to love of others—the highest and most desirable form of mature adjustment. Love for others grows out of trust, and trust in others emanates from a trust in oneself, which is usually fostered by parents who exercise control while providing freedom. Children cannot be pushed into autonomy; they must want to become independent. When provided with the proper family atmosphere, the child can become independent enough to meet his own needs without undue dependence upon others and may even assist others to achieve their own independence.

How Can We Improve Our Social Effectiveness?

A good way to encourage socialization is to become an active participant in a group. Your behavior may change as you accommodate yourself to group expectations and plans. By supporting the group's goals and intentions, by cooperating with its members, by sharing yourself with the group, you make yourself known to the group and become accepted by its members.

Acceptance by the group, however, must be preceded by self-acceptance. In short, you have to like yourself before you can expect others to like you. You must be willing to step toward others rather than expecting them to come to you.

Emotional and intellectual competencies obviously facilitate social adequacy. When reviewing our interpersonal relationships, we are usually aware of how others appear to us but may not be fully cognizant of how we appear to them. Perhaps the best way to achieve valid social interchange is to treat others as equals. Coleman and Hammen (1974) cite attitudes and actions that might prevent us from fully relating to others: (1) depending on others for support, (2) showing greater concern for self than for others, (3) resorting to competition and antagonistic behavior, (4) overconforming to the desires of others in order to secure their acceptance, (5) manipulating others for personal advantage, (6) being excessively assertive, (7) acting without self-esteem, or (8) withdrawing from others to avoid possible hurt or rejection.

Although examining the mechanics of a situation is an effective technique—for example, what went into a conflict, what were the obvious mistakes, what were the alternate responses—simply knowing what inhibits or destroys social adequacy will not bring about change. Only by living through corrective experiences, where new, alternate behaviors are shaped by respectful criticism and reinforcement, can we develop social skills.

IDENTITY

Agreement between how we view ourselves and how others in society view us results in a strong sense of personal identity. This sense of identity can vary at different ages and in different situations—within the family, at college, on the job—but it is often associated with the sense of competence and self-esteem.

Society has a large impact on personal identity. The ancient Greeks, for instance, stressed personal excellence in the form of physical feats, while, in the Medieval period, emphasis was given to saving one's soul and securing a place in heaven. During the post-depression years in America, values were oriented toward achieving financial security and economic independence, and thus Americans tended to discover their identity through economic success. Many young people today seek their identity in meaningful relationships, in intellectual rapport, and in the honest, unpretentious communication of feelings (Maddock, 1973) rather than through the acquisition of wealth, prestige, and power. It is not at all surprising to note the informal attire and manners on college campuses that go beyond social and class barriers. The emphasis seems to be on the humaneness of the person, not on what he or she purports to represent. Most young people today attempt to define their own lives, to discover unique and personal identities rather than to assume an identity imposed on them from the outside.

Adolescents may become concerned if their identity, at least as it is projected to others, does not meet social expectations. Such identity crises are not uncommon among college students. Because roles in college may differ radically from what they had been in high school or at home, college students may have difficulty discovering ways to respond that do not seem artificial or superficial. They may find themselves unable to choose a role to follow, because there are few standards by which to test themselves in new situations.

Contemporary society often fails to recognize individuality, and students, like employees and housewives, find themselves stereotyped into a mold that may prevent them from being themselves. In many colleges, you become a number—an identification number, a class number, a seat number, a course number, a telephone number, a floor number, a room number. This example, although extreme, shows just how mechanical and impersonal society can become in the name of efficiency and order. People often reminisce about "the good old days" when everybody was identified by friends and neighbors. People were more permanent, closer, and more supportive. There was always someone to turn to in difficulty. Today we are too often thrown together, whether on a college campus or in a large city; change and anonymity characterize our lives. The impersonal, industrialized society, the weakening of religious and parental influences, the dissolution of family and neighborhood ties all make the formation of identity a more difficult process than it used to be.

Ego Identity

There is another more specific kind of identity—ego identity—described by Erikson (1950). As children become increasingly skilled in verbal communication and in physical coordination and as sexual maturity begins to develop, they become increasingly concerned with how they appear to others. Erikson refers to this crystallization of personality as the formation of "ego identity" by which young people's innate and acquired abilities are integrated with the social roles at their disposal; in other words, the way they value or view themselves begins to coalesce with the way others value and view them. In addition, they sense a continuity between their past, what they are now, and how they will be in the future. Should this coalescence not concur, says Erikson, "role diffusion" takes place. Anxiety, aggressiveness, indecisiveness, depression, fear, and withdrawal are symptoms that may accompany or foster a confused identity. Even apparently well-adjusted persons may have difficulty defining themselves or maintaining consistency in their personality, beliefs, and goals. However, when the environment is relatively supportive, structured, and stable, identity develops relatively normally as we reach out toward a meaningful and fulfilling life.

Negative Identity

Normally we do not choose to emulate qualities that conflict with our basic lifestyle. Instead, identity is usually built on what we sense as our own; we avoid assuming the characteristics of others with whom we feel a certain conflict or disagreement. Negative identity, however, can occur; that is, we may adopt certain qualities that are directly opposite to those held by the significant persons in our lives, the persons after whom we would normally pattern our identity. For example, the banker/father who lives in a plush suburb, dresses impeccably, and mingles with the country-club set may have a long-haired son who wears discarded clothes, lives in a rooming house in a working-class neighborhood, and works at odd jobs only enough to sustain himself. The son seems to have defined his identity in direct contrast to the identity of his father (Erikson, 1962).

Identity Formation: The Major Problem of Adolescence and Youth

The uncertain world in which we live today may produce a "shock" reaction in adolescents who cannot adapt from the relative security of their infancy and childhood to the uneasiness and dismay they sense about the future (Toffler, 1970). These adolescents do not sense a stable present and cannot easily visualize a definite future. Greater social opportunities, freedom, and mobility have decreased the desire of youth to commit itself to a particular goal. The lack of continuity between the past and the future may cause the adolescent to stall his commitments in order to regroup his forces and to mobilize a new arrangement of attitudes and ideas to cope with the painful and frustrating problems of the future. Anger, guilt, apathy, or the single-minded pursuit of pleasure may be accompanying symptoms that reflect a more serious underlying disturbance. However, there seems to be a greater world consciousness developing among adolescents today—a concern with what will happen to all of us. Instead of formulating selfish goals that lead to material gain, many young people have adopted a world perspective. As a result, adolescent turmoil is often caused by large-scale moral issues such as war, sexism, and political and economic exploitation. The behavior of the young may be strictly ethical, although it may represent a violation of legal standards—for example, draft evasion, sit-ins, or the refusal to pay taxes to a government whose ideas you don't agree with. Today's youth sense that they have the freedom to act, to change, and to grow, but these very opportunities may also encourage indecision and withdrawal. Individual action often seems meaningless in the face of such enormous problems.

It may be helpful in discussing identity formation to consider three growth patterns of normal male adolescents moving into adulthood as described by Offer and Offer (1972), who studied middle-class, suburban high school boys and their families over an eight-year period. One fourth of the students showed continuous growth within this period; this minority had come from excellent environments and demonstrated an ability to cope with stress, to integrate societal norms, to tolerate or respect their parents, to establish a realistic orientation toward life, and to maintain self-esteem and self-control. They coped with unpleasant situations by isolating themselves from them or by denying that conditions were that bad. Thirty-five percent of the students studied showed a "mixed" growth. Their environment was not entirely free from various problems, and they often could not cope effectively with undue stress. There was usually a conflict with parents over values, and under stress these students were prone to anger and depression or to a projection of their difficulties onto others. Meaningful relationships with the opposite sex began later in life. Despite these negative factors, this group was able to show an overall adjustment about equal to that of the first group. One fifth of the subjects in the study, however, showed "tumultuous" growth. Their families experienced marital and emotional problems and were unsure of their values. The subjects lacked confidence and trust and were more prone to oversensitivity, introspection, anxiety, and depression than the other two groups. The remaining subjects in the investigation did not fit any of the three groups. The authors concluded from this study that emotional upheaval in adolescents is not always a sign of maladjustment, especially if young people show that they can cope with emerging stress.

The following incident may help illustrate several of the aspects of identity we have been talking about.

Incident

Even though I have a "good life," I often feel that every day is wasted. Everyone else I know has plans. Other people want a big house, a good job, money, but that's not what I want. Yet, somehow I feel as though these are what I *must* have. I seem to know only what I don't want rather than what I do want. I feel as if I am in a nonexistent state of existence. If I had an option to leave school right now, I wouldn't even know where to go. I feel younger now, in a funny way, than I did back in high school. I can't seem to make up my mind about anything.

Sometimes I nearly panic. Everything I see in the world seems so absurd and contradictory, and so many of the courses I'm taking don't seem to say anything to me. I wonder what's wrong with me. Am I really struggling to be free, or am I just immature and refusing to accept what my dad calls "responsibility"?

SELF-ESTEEM

Self-esteem—the value we place on our own worth as a person—influences our behavior in important ways. Our actions, even more than our words, are consistent with how we feel about ourselves. When, for one reason or another, we bypass or ignore those experiences that could affect us positively or distort and magnify those experiences that are unpleasant, our self-esteem suffers, and we may fail to utilize our capacities. Indeed, self-esteem may be the determining factor in inhibiting or releasing individual potential.

Many of our problems arise not so much because of environmental or personal inadequacies but because of our distorted perceptions of ourselves and our consequent unrealistic beliefs. As a result, we suffer more than we need to and often become disillusioned, unhappy, or depressed. Because of the importance of self-esteem as a condition of personal fulfillment and self-actualization, an overview of its nature and effects will be presented, and some of the conditions that may either accelerate or stifle its development will be identified.

What Is Self-Esteem?

Self-esteem is a subjective feeling about one's self that is often based on superficial criteria that vary from person to person; consequently, self-esteem is basically self-determined. The achievement of material, intellectual, artistic, or even athletic goals as well as social acceptance and consistency in behavior may contribute to the development of self-esteem (Ziller, Hagey, Smith, & Long, 1969).

Since we tend to measure self-esteem through achievements or through the admiration, love, and respect of persons important to us, we inevitably define it in rather arbitrary terms, often relying on values we learned in childhood to assess what is "good" or "bad." Should this subjective assessment be incongruent with the assessment of others, we may discover that we have overvalued or undervalued ourselves, that we hold an exalted or a minimal opinion of ourselves. Certain psychological difficulties, particularly with interpersonal relationships, can be traced to such faulty or eccentric perceptions of self-worth.

Self-esteem begins at a very early age and is strongly affected by how the child feels about his parents and other significant persons and how they, in turn, regard him; that is, the child depends heavily on the judgment of others because he is not yet old enough to be critical or analytical. It would be well to remember that it is not so much what parents say as it is their actual behavior that the young child perceives. Self-esteem is apt to be high in a person whose parents show warmth, encouragement, affection, and consistency, respect the child's feelings, and help the child to become independent. Research evidence, however, shows that having the

Figure 4-3. Children can be encouraged to take an active interest in the world around them. Photo by Shirley Kontos.

"right kind" of parents does not necessarily guarantee well-being later in life. Frank (1965) found no definite connection between the quality of an individual's early home environment and the patterns of parental interaction he experienced and his later adjustment to life. Frank concludes that parents of "normal" and "maladjusted" persons did not differ significantly in personality traits and that, therefore, parental personality is not a potent causative effect in the shaping of the personalities of offspring.

Brissett (1972) sees two distinct processes involved in the acquisition of self-esteem—self-evaluation and the realization of self-worth. Self-evaluation refers to how we feel we measure up to the ideals and standards expected by society, and self-worth refers to the sense of competence we experience when we are in control over what we are doing. Self-evaluation is defined by the values and attitudes of society, whereas self-worth comes from the person himself and is influenced by the person's own perceptions. That is, individuals' actions are congruent with their opinion of themselves, not necessarily with the expectations of others, although, of course, the two points of reference often merge. When people "play the game" according to society's rules, they may stand a greater risk of failing than when they pursue success in terms of a personal definition. Ideally, personal and societal ideals should be more or less consistent, if the society in which one lives gives priority to values that promote individual growth.

Unfortunately, many persons today wish to heighten their self-evaluation without recognizing that what is missing is a strong feeling of self-worth—a sense of direction that originates from within and is not dependent on external circumstances. Brissett maintains that our society programs us to think in terms of self-evaluation at the expense of self-worth. People are almost forced to compare themselves to others and to emulate them instead of growing within the bounds of what is possible for them. It is no wonder that many people who have achieved society's expectations of success continue to feel empty and lonely inside. Just as actors, they have followed a prescribed plot and portrayed the roles that the audience expected to see. Their energy was expended in reaching goals that had social significance (such as wealth, prestige, status), although these goals may have had little personal meaning to them. We can see, then, that self-actualization cannot be attained without genuine feelings of self-worth.

On the other hand, activities that offer personal satisfaction and encourage emotional involvement, even if segments of society tacitly disapprove of them, are apt to enhance self-worth because they are an extension of the self. In pursuing such goals, what we do flows from us; instead of merely shaping ourselves to fit a mold that society has created, we supply the generative force.

How May Self-Esteem Be Improved?

Research indicates that what counts most in the development of self-esteem is what you do rather than what you hope for. You may set up a fictional goal, an illusion, and work toward it as if it were real. However, failure and self-condemnation will necessarily follow if you have set up the wrong goal for yourself (Coopersmith, 1967).

A healthy attitude toward self and others stems from the capacity to deal with the present, to experience the here and now. A "good" feeling is created when an individual communicates what he feels to someone he trusts and respects. A feeling of contentment develops as he relates to what is seen and felt instead of to abstractions. A sense of self-respect takes form as he realizes that he is capable of making decisions and being responsible for them, that he can define existence within reasonable limits and enjoy it.

Bandura (1969) notes that persons who make lenient demands on themselves are more apt to give positive rewards to themselves and thereby reinforce their self-esteem than persons who impose stringent demands on themselves. It is only reasonable to assume that optimal conditions for enhancing positive self-esteem require that we begin by attaining that which is easily within our reach. In this way, we build confidence slowly and improve our chances to do better later. If we strive too high, we end up subjecting ourselves to failure and often labeling ourselves "mediocre."

Let us now discuss several ways to build self-esteem. These ways include learning new skills and experiencing new situations with work, exploring new, varied, and exciting interests, learning social know-how, and learning to relate with people effectively. However, these ways require also that we become more aware of ourselves and understand our strong and weak points, that we become able to listen with care and reflection, that we avoid mistaken and misleading ideas about ourselves and others, and that we refrain from being too critical with what we do and with our mistakes.

Socialization. Self-esteem is to some extent determined by how competent others think us to be. The type of evaluation one receives—positive or negative, approving or disapproving—influences competence, though a person with low self-esteem is less likely to improve than one who regards himself with greater self-esteem (Ludwig & Maehr, 1967).

Social participation of one's own choosing is often associated with positive feelings and happiness (Phillips, 1967). It is interesting to note that college students who participated in social and athletic organizations sought psychiatric help in significantly lower numbers than did students who were not involved with group activities (Segal, Weiss, & Sokol, 1965). Social belongingness and interpersonal interaction tend to foster good adjustment, especially if we seek such involvement of our own volition.

The way we think of ourselves affects our choice of friends, dating partners, and mates. Goodman (1964) found that people who value themselves highly are attracted to partners of similar caliber. Such persons usually have no need to compensate for personal deficiencies or to boost their egos by attaching themselves to someone better than themselves. Those who hold a poor opinion of themselves were drawn to partners with opposite traits; for instance, when a person is more comfortable yielding to the wishes of others, he or she usually seeks a partner who appears secure and "stronger." In other words, persons who accept themselves for what they are tend to choose someone like themselves as a partner; on the other hand, persons low in self-esteem tend to choose partners who are unlike themselves—that is, who have complementary characteristics.

When individuals are familiar with social reality—that is, what others expect of them and how society generally works—and know themselves well, they are able to alter their actions constructively instead of reacting defensively in order to avoid blame or to rationalize failures. Accentuating personal assets and minimizing liabilities will enormously strengthen self-esteem. As people come to like themselves, they gain self-respect; as they become of value to others and are needed by them, self-esteem increases.

Honestly expressing our feelings also facilitates viable relationships with others. The more we attempt to conceal negative feelings about ourselves, the more we are apt to employ strategies that alienate others who do not understand the real reasons for the actions they observe. On the other hand, expressing to others that we feel inadequate in a certain area or angry about something often helps them to interpret our actions and to respond appropriately. Individuals who consistently undersell or blame themselves inevitably feel depressed. Persons who have low self-esteem often behave in ways that invite others to reject them or to treat them as failures.

New interests. Adopting a variety of interests without pushing to excel in all of them can offer us an opportunity to gain confidence. The more we experience and the more we respond to the various facets of life, the greater the likelihood that we will not feel alienated, bored, or lonely. In our society, self-worth is unfortunately often measured by achievement, but connectedness with other people in the course of achieving can make us comfortable about what and who we are. Experiencing new and varied situations without concern for success can make us extremely liberated. However, achievement is a powerful force in the self-esteem of people who want to achieve, providing their goals are based on a realistic appraisal of their particular abilities. Avoiding goals that cannot be achieved is neither a "cop out" nor a sign of moral weakness; rather, it is a sign of awareness, courage, and reason.

Improving ourselves physically can also help to foster feelings of self-esteem. Physical activity often helps people to feel psychologically more at home with themselves. This feeling probably occurs because the body seems more efficient and because the release of energy involved with physical activity usually brings about a calming effect after the activity ceases. Improving the outer self, of course, is only a beginning, but it is an area over which individuals have control and in which they may find immediate reward. For example, a study by Koocher (1971) clearly demonstrated that becoming efficient in a new physical skill actually does enhance self-esteem. Using before and after measurements, he found that subjects who learned to swim thought more highly of themselves and came closer to the image of the person they wanted to be than did those who did not learn to swim.

Idleness and aloneness normally do not improve self-esteem. Often students cut themselves off, doing nothing, because they have no ideas of what to do. Fear of making mistakes or committing themselves to the wrong decisions prevents them from enjoying life; mature persons take risks and change their objectives flexibly as they move through life. Through trial and error we discover what we can master, and we begin to live in the present instead of merely collecting injustices from the past. Of course, predicting the consequences of a choice by balancing the advantages and disadvantages of the outcome helps an individual to feel more comfortable in making a given choice. Decisions are never perfect and there are always unknown factors. The idea is not to eliminate problems but to lessen them through insight and perspective.

The following incident dramatizes the first two suggestions in developing self-esteem—becoming comfortable with people and developing new interests.

Incident

All through high school I was a wallflower. The few friends I had were really messed up; it seemed that everybody who had problems was attracted to me. Everyone wanted to tell me their problems, but I had more problems than anyone. At that time I started swimming lessons. I kept practicing, and when I got into college I went to the pool almost every day. Being in the water seems to relax me emotionally as well as physically. I feel great after swimming. I worked up to a half mile a day, and I am still doing it now. I go to the pool frequently, and the guys there know me by now. We talk about our strokes, form, and things like that. In fact, I have dated three of them already this semester. I think many guys feel insecure around girls but try not to show it. I'm getting to feel a lot different about myself. I don't feel as if I'm trying to impress anyone; I'm just trying to be me. One thing I learned is to go where the kind of people are that you want to meet and to just be yourself. I discovered this by accident, but I wish somebody would have given me a helpful hint years ago. I really believe now that there's always somebody who is going to like you for what you are, if you only give yourself a chance.

Career development. Some people seem to know what career they want to pursue from childhood, while others find career choice a painful decision, often prolonged until they have gained considerable experience. Postponing this important decision is often wise, for merely following someone else's advice or choosing what seems readily available may later cause us considerable regret. Learning to do something well, especially when this decision is of a person's own choosing, is a tremendously important force in the development of self-esteem.

If you have not yet decided on a vocation, talk about the advantages and disadvantages of various careers with persons who are already involved in these fields or obtain occupational information from books—biographies and novels as well as the informational pamphlets usually available in the placement and counseling services in high schools and colleges. It might be helpful to work on a part-time basis in a field in which you may want to specialize. Because many occupations in our society are based on highly technical skills, we need to give considerable thought to deciding on and preparing ourselves for a career that fits our abilities as well as our aspirations (Tyler, 1961).

Career competency is of obvious economic importance to everyone, but its contribution to our emotional well-being is often overlooked.

It is unfortunate that many people make an unwise career choice and become bored with their work. Poor preparation and hasty decisions, however, are as responsible as mediocre talents for unhappy career choices. On the other hand, we must avoid making unrealistic choices based on parental pressure or the supposed glamour and prestige of a particular job. An honest assessment of your abilities is crucial.

It is impossible to be absolutely sure that you have made the right career decision, but you can reduce the risk of making a wrong decision by taking into account the reasons for your choice, the advantages and disadvantages of the profession, the satisfaction you expect from work, and an objective assessment of your personal qualities as well as your mental abilities or special talents. You may want to explore the opportunity for growth within a field and to avoid "dead end" jobs with little possibility for promotion and expansion. Satisfaction in your work, a sense of independence, opportunity for self-expression, and the chance to work with others, which builds a feeling of companionship and togetherness—all these are factors that contribute to achieving fulfillment through work.

Sometimes a student may feel torn between more than one talent or interest. Often these may be combined into one career. Consider, for example, the science writer who may have had interests in both literature and science and is able to express them both in one profession.

The *Occupational Outlook Handbook* describes over 800 trades and occupations, their earnings, their future outlook, and the training required. It also notes sources for more specific information. Examining such a volume may suggest new possibilities for you, as well as help you to make a realistic decision in terms of economics.

Career or vocational counselors often rely on various tests to determine special skills, abilities, and interests. They may also use instruments to assess how much you have learned up to now, what level you are likely to attain, and whether your weaknesses, if any, can be corrected. They also have special tests for predicting your suitability for specific careers: teaching, law, medicine, engineering. Personal traits such as your ability to work with others, how you handle failure, whether you are patient or flexible, or whether you are talkative, overly precise, or a follower or a leader—all may be taken into consideration by counselors in helping you select a career. The approach of the vocational or career counselor may vary, but in general he or she tries to give you as many facts about your area of career choice as possible. These facts, which are normally obtained through tests and interviews, include your feelings and attitudes about yourself—your aspirations, your capabilities, and your weaknesses—as well as information about specific programs of training and employment opportunities in general (Crites, 1974).

Personality problems often prevent us from making the best career choice. Fear of commitment, overdependence, the need to compensate for personal deficiencies, the desire to please parents, a refusal to give up the glamorous or the ideal, and constant comparisons of ourselves with others—any of these may interfere with choosing appropriate employment. While satisfying work can make us feel good and like ourselves better because we feel useful and esteemed by others, an unsatisfactory job can make us disgruntled and inclined to transfer our dissatisfaction to others.

Work is not merely "making a living"; it can push us into achieving our potential, or it can stifle and diminish our lives. Job satisfaction can never be evaluated in terms of money alone; there is always a "psychological income." All in all, the satisfaction we find in our jobs strengthens our self-image, our self-esteem, and our attitude toward ourselves. Compare how happy you can feel in a course you like and do well in with how bored you become in a required course for which you have no interest. Would you want to perpetuate the latter situation for 25 years?

Boring or unpleasant jobs are often only temporary or just a stepping stone toward more interesting employment. However, it is becoming increasingly common for people to change their professions, even relatively late in life and even when considerable new training is required. If our work makes us unhappy, we cannot actualize ourselves; thus, daring to begin a second career may be a valid option for many. Some of us, however, may not be in a position to risk the economic hazards of "recycling" our professional lives. In such cases, an avocation or hobby can make our lives more complete and fulfilling. The father of four who is unhappy with his life as a carpenter may not, for instance, be able to afford the time and money to retrain himself for a career as a teacher, but he may be able to work with young people in Scouts, church groups, or rehabilitation centers.

Approaching career choice with an open mind, with an attitude of flexibility, and with the willingness to invest some years in exploration and experimentation will help ensure that your work will enhance your self-esteem and help you to find fulfillment. Consider the following example.

Incident

I had a lot of trouble deciding what I wanted to do with my life. In college, I switched from chemistry to a business curriculum and then to physics. I ended up with an engineering degree, and the nightmares started. The factory where I worked was on defense money, which was cut, and I got laid off. I started a store with a partner selling blue jeans in a college town. We failed miserably, but I realized that I liked being with people more than with blueprints. So I took a teaching job at a small technical college. There were hassles with other teachers who had been there longer and were somewhat better trained than I. The stress was great; I even got high blood pressure. Then, as part of my teaching load, I was offered an opportunity to advise students with course planning. Quite a few of these kids had personal problems, and we got to talking. Several of them came back to tell me that I had really helped them a lot. I realized that I wanted to do something that kept me involved and that made me feel I was doing something worthwhile without getting caught up in a competitive rat race. I got a master's degree in counseling—three years of part-time work—but with my engineering background I got to be a top-notch counselor at a good engineering school. Knowing a lot about engineering and understanding the career needs of students gave me a perfect background for this job. I enjoy what I'm doing and that's the best feeling any person could ever have.

Self-knowledge. A key factor in developing self-esteem is to act like the person you want to be, provided that you do not pattern yourself after a person totally unrelated to your real self. Although this idea is easier said than done, at least you can observe others—what they do, how they feel, what they say—and then experiment with some of these actions. You can then begin to see what suits you most and what you really want from yourself. You begin to like yourself more when you behave according to the standards you actually want to follow.

Discussing attitudes and ideas with a variety of friends who may agree or disagree provides an opportunity for you to evaluate what is beneficial and what is unacceptable in your personality. This kind of feedback helps you to develop and maintain a realistic perspective about yourself. If, on the other hand, you select friends who say only nice things, you deprive yourself of constructive criticism that can encourage you to better behavior and more realistic attitudes about yourself and the world. When we dare to deal with what may be unpleasant about ourselves or others rather than merely seek situations that are comfortable or without stress, we often discover that our self-regard has risen considerably. We feel "right" about having hazarded ourselves.

Many young people today feel it is wrong to desire achievement, perhaps because they wish to avoid the harmful effects of ruthless competition. Yet, the desire to achieve is not synonymous with competitiveness. It is, in fact, an index of good adjustment. Of course, realistic assessments are necessary if frustration and anxiety are to be avoided. Lewin (1944) and his collaborators point out that realistic persons are more comfortable with what they "expect" than with what they "wish" to receive. Furthermore, repeated failure tends to increase tension and disrupt emotions, while success has the opposite effect. Repeated failure tends to reinforce frustration and induce inefficiency in our work, which is self-defeating and leads to further failure. Knowing our capacities and then setting our goals accordingly will usually help us achieve greater personal effectivenss, a fuller realization of our abilities, and a more satisfying sense of personal worth and self-esteem.

The acquisition of knowledge, in spite of the hostility many young people feel toward the "college scene," does enhance self-esteem, especially when you become an "expert" in a particular area. Bailey (1971) found that high-achieving college students have more realistic self-perceptions and a smaller discrepancy between how they rated their college ability and how their academic ability had actually been rated than underachievers of *equal* college ability. Acquiring a college education strengthens feelings of self-worth because so many people have been conditioned to associate feelings of personal competence, social effectiveness, and power with formal education (Stinnett & Stone, 1964). Some students today, rightfully rebelling against rigid grading systems and structured course requirements, also deny themselves the opportunity to excel academically and thus increase their chances to find success and security later in life. They may, in fact, tend to put too much emphasis on "achievement" in interpersonal relationships rather than truly exploring their personal limits, particularly in academic or intellectual matters. Unlike the previous generation, they are often willing to hazard much by offering themselves to others in genuine and honest relationships, but, also unlike their predecessors, they are not always willing to dare to find fulfillment through achievement in a more academic discipline.

There is no question that when we anticipate the results of our actions we feel in control of the situation—capable and competent. Tangible results help to tell us how effective we are. The student with a C grade often says "She (the instructor) gave me a C," but the student with an A usually says "I made an A." In truth, we are eager to express what we accomplish on our own, and we are anxious to find excuses when we fail.

In the following example, we see that by taking risks and showing initiative we can get to know our limits, obtain tangible results, and foster a better and sounder self-esteem.

Incident

I was sick and tired of sitting in my room waiting for someone to call and feeling sorry for myself. It finally dawned on me that it all had to start from me. So I mustered up enough courage to buy two tickets for a play and to ask one of the girls in my class to go with me. She refused by giving me some odd excuse; so I asked another girl, and she accepted. During the intermission, a couple of guys began to chat with us about the play and asked us to join them after. We had a good time, and I felt really good to be with some people for a change. One of the guys has become a good friend. I think it pays off to be a little daring and outgoing if you decide beforehand that you're not going to be worried by negative results. If you don't care what will happen, I think you can be more effective and less uptight in relating to people; it worked for me.

Listening. To become active listeners we must try to sense the feeling behind the words of the speaker, as well as the more obvious message. We should then respond to these feelings as well as to the words. When we attempt to put feelings out into the open, we promote warmth, trust, and understanding. Active listening encourages the talker to open up. It facilitates communication, and it helps the other person find solutions to his problems (Gordon, 1970). By reflecting the talker's feelings you nudge him into understanding them better and thereby being more in a position to do something about them. The talker acts more constructively when he feels appreciated and accepted for his feelings. Remember, however, that the problem he may present belongs to him, not to you; try not to scold, judge, or ridicule or to make his problem your own problem; by doing so, you deny him his rights as a uniquely responding individual.

Perhaps the following dialogues will clarify for you how important it is to hear the speaker's feelings as well as his words. Note in the second conversation how easily passivity can conceal a sharp edge of hostility.

Incident

(Active listening)

John: Linda turned me down when I asked her to go to a concert with me this Sunday.

Joe: You seem a little angry.

John: I don't know if I should ask her again.

Joe: You sound disappointed over Linda's whole attitude toward you.

John: I think she's got a good head on her shoulders.

Joe: Yeah. And you kinda like her that way, too.

John: I guess so. I don't like people who get too dependent on me. I get turned off.

Joe: Maybe it's a good idea to accept her for what she is.

John: I guess you're right.

(Passive listening)

John: Linda turned me down when I asked her to go to a concert with me this Sunday.

Joe: I think you should just dump her and find someone else.

John: But I like being with her.

Joe: She's stuck-up. Why bother with her? Ask someone else. Don't be a coward.

John: It's not that easy to be a friend with someone right away.

Joe: You'd better wise up.

Self-evaluation. We cannot entirely avoid evaluating ourselves and rating others, whether it is done verbally or nonverbally, consciously or unconsciously. But healthy self-esteem cannot be maintained in the face of constant comparisons with others. The mania for self-rating stems partly from a competitive society that pits one person against another and in which competition may even become an end in itself. Since judgments of what is "bad" or "good" vary from person to person and change from time to time, such inferences are apt to be harmful because they are subjective and can readily be drawn out of proportion. Preconceived standards often get in the way of genuine understanding. Another potentially harmful effect of self-rating is that when we rely on arbitrary criteria, "guilt" and "depression" often result when we fall short of these artificial standards.

When individuals feel self-confident because they have done something "right," they are making a value judgment about their actions and to some extent including themselves in this judgment; indeed, that is why their self-esteem is elevated. When they interpret an act as "bad," however—judging things against the way they "should" be—they also tend to equate the action with themselves, and their self-esteem consequently suffers. For example, if they are getting good (but not excellent) grades and they feel badly about themselves, it may be that they are indulging themselves with unrealistic expectations and punishing themselves with unfair comparisons. If they are constantly making unfavorable comparisons, they may find that their ability to function becomes seriously impaired. The depressed person often measures himself against a "should" system and, failing to meet expectations, labels himself in a distorted fashion as "bad." Unable to tolerate himself as he perceives himself, he becomes anxious and alienated from others. As his depreciation spirals, he draws upon it as proof for his low self-esteem and as justification for future failure. Breaking this circular and often unconscious reasoning requires that he learn to accept himself as basically *good* and to view only occasional actions as "bad," especially those that are harmful to himself as well as to others.

Often our interpretations of situations in which our self-esteem suffered were quite inaccurate or unreasonable. It often helps to discuss these experiences with others who may have undergone similar experiences. Their views may be quite different from ours, and their comments may help to restore a more objective perspective.

Habitual self-raters sometimes choose models who are something less than ideal and thus judge themselves by standards that are not generally compatible with their larger value systems. Consider the studious young man who does not think he is "successful" with girls and insists on comparing his dating profile with that of a good-looking "jock" with whom he has little in common. Self-raters, then, generally tend to be unrealistic about their abilities, either over- or underestimating them, and often seek a status that is not compatible with their real talents. They become frustrated in the process and often end up telling themselves that they are not good enough simply because they have accepted unrealistic or overly idealized goals. (Hurlock, 1974).

It is through activity, through achievement, through experimenting, and through involvement in different situations that we learn to change our self-concept and elevate our self-esteem. The opinions of others are helpful, but the elevation of self-esteem is largely a self-help project. Consider the way the young man in the following instance learned to accept himself without incessant comparison to outside standards.

Incident

As a child, I was taught to feel shame when I expressed my anger. It was "naughty" or "bad" to get mad. But I continued to have feelings of anger. In college, I became really concerned with the anger I was feeling. I became angry about losing a ping pong game or having somebody switch the channel on the

TV set in the dorm lounge. Then I took a psychology course, and I learned that anger is part of life and part of everyone, although one person can have more of it than another. So I said to myself "That's just the way I am," and from then on I didn't pay so much attention to my angry feelings. After all, I don't go around hitting people in a blind rage or throwing vases or pictures; I think some feelings of anger are natural. When you try to push such feelings away they keep on coming back; but when you just leave them alone and accept them they don't bother you that much.

Mistaken beliefs. Adler (1964) maintained that it is not so much that people and situations precipitate emotional conflict as it is the manner in which events are interpreted that creates dissension. When conclusions are based on false or erroneous assumptions, the behavior that follows is apt to be ineffective and disruptive. Adler stressed that thought is necessarily subjective and can be biased and highly personalized. Many of the difficulties we experience, therefore, do not actually stem from potentially threatening situations but are created by our *interpretation* of the situation.

The Greek philosopher Epictetus believed that we become anxious, depressed, or emotionally upset not so much by certain events or by the reactions of others toward us as by what we ourselves think about these events (Hadas, 1963). Using the teachings of Epictetus, Ellis (1962) developed Rational-Emotive Therapy, which focuses on our responsibility in creating our own problems. Ellis maintains that our values, beliefs, and attitudes create our psychological symptoms. Irrational, mistaken beliefs prompt us to react in ineffective ways to various situations and create anxiety, anger, depression, and loneliness, all of which work against our self-esteem.

Consider for a moment a person who has been insulted or mistreated in a restaurant. If he believes that everyone ought to love and respect him at all times (an irrational belief), he will feel anger or depression. If, on the other hand, he can admit the existence of mitigating factors—misunderstanding, conflicting interests, ancillary problems (rational beliefs)—he may merely react with mild annoyance. Thus, Ellis has been able to help people cultivate rational beliefs that prevent them from reacting in maladaptive, exaggerated ways. By disputing the irrational beliefs of his clients and pointing out more realistic ones that do not result in unacceptable behavior, Ellis is able to help his clients enhance their feelings of self-acceptance and thus lead more fulfilling and effective lives.

A common and unreasonable expectation among students is that nearly everyone ought to like them. Failure to elicit this response from others, they feel, is a sign that they have somehow failed. Such an unreasonable idea places one in a state of endless frustration. Students are often astute observers of the actions of others, but, at the same time, they often draw the wrong conclusions as to what these actions mean. If a student has a poor opinion of himself, he is apt to think that others share this opinion and he may interpret even the most insignificant cues as evidence that he is not accepted or appreciated. It is possible to help such a student to build a more reasonable perspective and to interpret the actions of others with greater tolerance toward himself.

People sometimes believe that changing the environment will produce a magic solution to their problems. For example, one student felt that if his father were a millionaire and his mother were a famous actress, he would not necessarily have any sort of psychological problems; he would be a happy person. A related irrational attitude attributes happiness and well-being to external factors. Such a student may relinquish responsibility for his own well-being, but, when he discovers that he cannot control all the factors in his environment, his feelings of helplessness and depression return. This fatalistic attitude soon becomes a self-fulfilling prophecy. Such a student can often point out alternate courses of actions to other persons, but he does not consider changing his own point of view. The person who seeks to change another shows his own desire to be in control rather than a genuine wish to improve someone else's well-being.

Another false assumption common to many people is that a normal and well-adjusted person always feels happy. Feelings of frustration and anger, they feel, indicate that "something is wrong." A more rational conclusion recognizes that every person has positive and negative feelings and that it is unjustified to associate negative feelings with emotional problems. Such students often associate unpleasant moods with personal weakness or lack of self-control. A related assumption is that, if you don't love everyone, you should feel "guilty." These attitudes are based on fictional goals that are almost impossible to reach.

People often avoid self-disclosure because they fear that others will reject them if they know how they really feel. Isolation offers such students a kind of protection, and they may find that escape mechanisms become more pleasurable than human encounters. Many students seek an atmosphere of safety and acceptance in various social groups. They maintain the unjustified belief that they must be liked by everyone, often without taking into account that they themselves do not like some of the persons they meet. Finally, they may project their own feelings of inadequacy onto others by attributing to them unacceptable traits that are actually their own.

Individuals, then, do suffer unnecessarily because of their faulty beliefs. Anxiety, depression, guilt, rebellion, frustration, or apathy may result from behavior based on erroneous convictions. When a student is unable to meet his unrealistic standards, he becomes the loser in a battle against himself and concludes that he is a victim or a failure in life. In the same way, making unrealistic demands on others leads to discontent and alienation; individuals tend to run away from those who cling to them or dominate them. Unrealistic assessments—whether they are deprecatory or excessively laudatory or whether they are self- or other-directed—inevitably lead to inappropriate and ineffectual responses, to interpersonal conflict, and to damaged self-esteem. Let us conclude by reviewing a case that illustrates how one young woman worked her way through the tyranny of her unjustified beliefs to discover a more satisfying set of standards.

Incident

I used to get upset when I felt that someone didn't like me or when I earned a low grade. I would panic when somebody I knew ignored me for no reason; somehow I felt that I was doing something wrong, that it was my fault. Actually, I wasn't doing anything wrong. I guess it all started when I was a kid and everybody paid attention to me. I liked it that way. When I got older, I began to notice that some people didn't give me the attention I was used to getting. This bothered me quite a bit, but now I'm beginning to get used to it. In fact, it would be ridiculous for the whole world to fall over me, as if I were someone very special. It's one thing to say that you can't expect everybody to love you and another to really learn to feel and accept the idea. It took me a long time. It's the same with grades, or, I should say, it was. I got all A's in high school, and here at college when I got my first B I thought I was going to flunk out. I thought that a good student doesn't make mistakes or settle for just average work. With grades, like with people, I felt I was a failure when I didn't live up to my expectations. Now I realize that my standards were too high to begin with. In fact, I know now that it's not a good idea to set such unreasonable goals.

SUMMARY

Motivation stems from the urgency to satisfy certain basic needs, but a large portion of it grows out of learned needs and out of an innate urge to reach a level of effectiveness that will activate our full capacities. Understanding our motives requires an objective view of the social environment as well as knowledge of physiological and psychological determinants.

Emotions play an important role in achieving full actualization, as do our cognitive abilities. Emotional development, like cognitive growth, begins in the family and extends outward to include the social environment. Thwarting our emotions and restricting our mental capacities affect our social development and limit self-actualization.

Identity develops through continuous adapting and growing as we interact with the environment. Physiological, psychological, and social factors act as motivating agents in goal-directed behavior. Some needs are innate while others are socially acquired, but the most basic motivating factor is the push toward self-fulfillment or self-actualization.

According to the old proverb, there is no point in running if you don't know where you are going. Yet much of life is an individual experiment, and we must often learn through trial and error. We must help ourselves as well as extend a hand to others. We must love and work; we must become independent and responsible; we must cope with problems, reach goals, and feel at home with ourselves and others.

We cannot think of self-identity without thinking of self-esteem, for both notions grow together within an individual. A young person's self-esteem is influenced by the appraisals of others, by the way in which he interprets and reacts to their evaluations, and by the degree of success or the status he attains. Self-esteem is also contingent upon the quality of the environment with which he interacts, but a person of high self-esteem can often affect the environment in positive directions while a person of low self-esteem seems to have less control over his environment. Meeting socially accepted standards of conduct, achieving proficiency in skills—particularly those that are career related—and exerting reasonable control over the environment are actions that contribute to self-esteem.

Experiencing the tangible results of our own accomplishments and enjoying a sense of social belonging and cultural identity help us to perceive what we are and what we can be. Acquiring expertise in a specific area also strengthens our self-esteem, as does positive appraisal from others. In short, success promotes self-esteem, but repeated failure creates anxiety, which causes us to fail again—a vicious circle that commits us to doing what lowers our self-image.

Sound self-esteem is part of social effectiveness and an indication of good adjustment, a stable personality, and a reasonable degree of self-actualization.

QUESTIONS TO THINK ABOUT

1. Did you ever go through a period in your life when you did not know where you were going or who you were? What happened? What advice would you give to a person who is going through a similar experience? Do you feel that negative identity is a particularly potent force in the identity formation of your contemporaries?
2. In what ways do you have difficulty expressing what you feel to someone?
3. Have any of the ways mentioned in this chapter for achieving self-esteem worked for you? Explain.
4. Do any of the pitfalls of self-rating apply to you? If so, how do you think you might resolve these tensions?
5. Have you ever felt unmotivated to do something, even when there were good reasons for doing it? As you look back and review the situation, can you explain why you felt the way you did?
6. Do you know anyone you would characterize as an active listener? If so, can you share some examples of how this person responds to emotional messages as well as verbal ones?
7. Choose a partner and spontaneously act out examples of passive and active listening. Perhaps another class member can suggest an initial remark on which to base your dialogue.
8. Have you ever encountered a situation in which you experienced new people and felt very comfortable being with them? What was the outcome of this experience?

REFERENCES

Adler, A. *Social interest: A challenge to mankind* (1933). New York: Capricorn, 1964.

Bailey, R. C. Self-concept differences in low and high achieving students. *Journal of Clinical Psychology,* 1971, *27*(2), 188-191.

Bandura, A. *Principles of behavior modification.* New York: Holt, Rinehart & Winston, 1969.

Brissett, D. Toward a clarification of self-esteem. *Psychiatry,* 1972, *35*(3), 255-262.

Coleman, J., & Hammen, C. *Contemporary psychology and effective behavior.* Glenview, Ill.: Scott, Foresman, 1974.

Combs, A. W., & Snygg, D. *Individual behavior.* New York: Harper, 1959.

Coopersmith, S. *The antecedents of self-esteem.* San Francisco: W.H. Freeman, 1967.

Crites, J. O. Career counseling: A review of major approaches. *The Counseling Psychologist,* 1974, *4*(3), 3-23.

Douvan, E., & Adelson, J. *The adolescent experience.* New York: Wiley, 1966.

Ellis, A. *Reason and emotion in psychotherapy.* New York: Lyle Stuart, 1962.

Erikson, E. H. *Childhood and society.* New York: Norton, 1950.

Erikson, E. H. *Young man Luther.* New York: Norton, 1962.

Flavell, J. H. *The developmental psychology of Jean Piaget.* Princeton, N.J.: Van Nostrand, 1963.

Frank, G. H. The role of the family in the development of psychopathology. *Psychological Bulletin,* 1965, *64*(3), 191-205.

Goodman, M. Expressed self-acceptance and interpersonal needs. *Journal of Counseling Psychology,* 1964, *11*(2), 129-135.

Gordon, T. *Parent effectiveness training.* New York: Wyden, 1970.

Hadas, M. (Ed.). *Essential works of stoicism.* New York: Bantam Books, 1963.

Hall, C. S., & Lindzey, G. *Theories of personality.* New York: Wiley, 1957.

Hershey, G. L., & Lugo, J. O. *Living psychology.* New York: Macmillan, 1970.

Hurlock, E. B. *Personality development.* New York: McGraw-Hill, 1974.

Koocher, G. P. Swimming, competence, and personality change. *Journal of Personality and Social Psychology,* 1971, *18*(3), 275-278.

Lewin, K., Dembo, T., Festinger, L., & Sears, P. S. Level of aspiration. In J. McV. Hunt (Ed.), *Personality and behavior disorders.* New York: Ronald, 1944.

Longstreth, L. E. *Psychological development of the child.* New York: Ronald, 1968.

Ludwig, D. J., & Maehr, M. L. Changes in self-concept and stated behavioral preferences. *Child Development,* 1967, *38*(2), 453-467.

Maddock, J. W. Sex in adolescence: Its meaning and its future. *Adolescence,* 1973, *8*(31), 325-342.

Maier, H. W. *Three theories of child development.* New York: Harper & Row, 1965.

Maslow, A. H. Deficiency motivation and growth motivation. In M. R. Jones (Ed.), *Nebraska Symposium on Motivation.* Lincoln, Neb.: University of Nebraska Press, 1955, *3,* 1-30.

Offer, D., & Offer, J. Normal adolescence in perspective. Paper presented at the 6th Annual Symposium of the Texas Research Institute of Mental Sciences, November, 1972.

Phillips, D. L. Social participation and happiness. *American Journal of Sociology,* 1967, *72*(5), 479-488.

Segal, B. A., Weiss, R. J., & Sokol, R. Emotional adjustment, social organization, and psychiatric treatment rates. *American Sociological Review,* 1965, *30*(4), 548-556.

Stinnett, E. R., & Stone, L. A. The meaning of a college education as revealed by the Semantic Differential. *Journal of Counseling Psychology,* 1964, *11*(2), 168-172.

Toffler, A., *Future shock.* New York: Random House, 1970.

Tyler, L. E. *The work of the counselor.* New York: Appleton-Century-Crofts, 1961.

U.S. Department of Labor, *Occupational outlook handbook 1974-1975 edition.* Washington, D.C. Bureau of Labor Statistics.

Ziller, R. C., Hagey, J., Smith, M.D.C., & Long, B. M. Self-esteem: A self-social construct. *Journal of Consulting and Clinical Psychology,* 1969, *33*(1), 84-95.

Chapter 5

Working toward Adjustment

CHAPTER OUTLINE

I. How we adjust
   A. Through purposefulness
   B. Through understanding our psychological states
      1. Anxiety
      2. Depression
      3. Psychophysiological problems
      4. Situational problems
   C. Most of us are well adjusted

II. How we protect ourselves
   A. Defenses of acting
      1. Compensation
      2. Substitution
      3. Identification
      4. Sublimation
      5. Restitution
      6. Malingering
   B. Defenses of feeling
      1. Repression
      2. Suppression
      3. Reaction formation
      4. Displacement
      5. Projection
      6. Regression
   C. Defenses of thinking
      1. Daydreaming
      2. Intellectualization
      3. Rationalization
      4. Devaluation
      5. Denial

III. Understanding maladjustment
   A. Stress
   B. Ineffective ways of coping
      1. Neurosis
      2. Psychosis
      3. Personality disorders
      4. Suicide

IV. Summary

What happens when things go bad for us, when we feel pressured by the people or situations around us? We may react in alarm, mustering up energy and defenses to put up a fight that will resolve or lessen the impact of the pressure. What are these defenses? How do they operate? What happens if they fail us? These are the major questions to be considered in this chapter. Hopefully, by understanding these processes better, you will be able to act with greater ease and tolerance when you experience harassment. By assessing your "battle strength" during a time of rest, you may be able to use your "forces" more strategically during actual distress.

HOW WE ADJUST

Life is an interplay between ourselves and the environment; we make changes in our surroundings, and our surroundings influence our behavior. Adjustment refers to an acceptance of growth and change within ourselves and a satisfactory relationship with others and with the environment. The acceptance of conditions that maintain stability and ensure social survival is a necessary condition for adjustment, but protest against a personally damaging social environment can also be a sign of good adjustment. Harmony, then, between what one believes and one's actual behavior within environmental realities is requisite for good adjustment.

Adjustment is based on a subjective feeling about ourselves rather than on how others see us. A student, for example, may have excellent grades, no financial worries, and many friends; yet, he or she may still feel depressed. On the other hand, the student who drops out of college to concentrate on playing the guitar may consider himself to be perfectly adjusted, but his parents may see his behavior as deviant and maladjusted.

Adjustment requires that we respond selectively to different situations, that we use trial-and-error approaches to problems, that we take risks occasionally and show good judgment, and that we make the best decisions on the basis of the facts that we may have. We must adopt flexible models of behavior if we are to accept change realistically and without frustration. Change is implicit in our development; yet, development also suggests a certain stability. We grow from a certain stage of

115

development while, at the same time, incorporating that stage into our current status.

Educational climate, which may involve such factors as whether the school is competitive, liberal, conservative, business-oriented, and so on, obviously affects student adjustment also. If a student has a sense of belonging in school and sees a clear purpose for education, his or her adjustment is usually good. Good adjustment may also involve a reaction to situations that do not promote human welfare and that suppress individual creativity. Indeed, consenting to conditions that may damage human well-being suggests maladjustment. Student protest and dissent, then, may be a sign of healthy emotional adjustment, for it often focuses on ideals such as humanitarian ethics, community feeling, and authentic human relationships. Student adjustment also requires the ability to create a rational dialogue between people of different viewpoints. Many university authorities and faculty have not always been responsive to this student need of talking as equals. Yet, in spite of this warfare between the generations, we must acknowledge that either the refusal to compromise or the unquestioning acceptance of authority indicates poor adjustment—in students as well as in other members of society.

How we react in college, or in any novel situation, depends on our past experiences. New situations often require that we correct and revise many of our former assumptions. In this sense, college provides an excellent opportunity for emotional growth and development of new coping skills. New experiences should be seen as a challenge for growth rather than as a frightening threat to our status quo.

Through Purposefulness

Psychological theory, as developed by Adler, Lewin, and Tolman, maintains that much of human behavior is goal-directed (Hall & Lindzey, 1957). Meaningful goals serve as incentives for action, especially when the objective to be attained will have positive effects. Activities tend to become boring or unpleasant if they are not reinforced by an end result that is beneficial and pleasurable. Without objectives, we may feel "lost"—a characteristic typical of persons who have a weak sense of personal identity. Such feelings may, however, be felt at times by persons who already have relatively clear objectives in life and a generally stable perspective. These feelings may occur because of temporary stumbling blocks, such as lack of money, unpleasant co-workers, conflict in the family, and so on. We might draw an analogy with the spectator at a play. Initially, the viewer may be confused and frustrated because certain parts of the play do not seem to fit; but, as the drama draws to a close, the minor parts fall into perspective and the author's objectives are fulfilled. Similarly, a student's experiences in college begin to make sense when viewed in the light of the final event—graduation and career preparation.

When a goal is altered, behavior also may change. For instance, if a person's goal to enter medical school becomes unattainable and, as a result, she feels anxious and insecure about it, she can deliberately change her goal to something she can attain, and hopefully the anxiety and insecurity will decrease. Hence, if certain behavior is unpleasant, it may be avoided if its goal is altered. A person, for example, who wants to avoid financial responsibilities (unpleasant experience) may postpone an immediate desire (marriage) for the sake of another aim (college degree). We see here that goal definition can strongly affect present attitudes and behavior.

Current behavior can never be totally explained on the basis of past experiences, for it is also shaped by how we view the future (Nikelly, 1962). In short, a combination of past events and future expectations meets in the present situation and propels an individual to undertake a particular course of action. For example, if you wish to design a model airplane, you must first have a mental image of it. You then rely on previously learned skills as you measure, trim, and fit the small parts together. All the detailed and miscellaneous tasks are not merely random tasks; they take on meaning in terms of the final construction. Similarly, life goals propel us to act as we do, constructing and fulfilling an image we have in mind, yet relying on knowledge and skills gained in the past. It is possible, however, to be pushed into action by the inner drive of an unfulfilled earlier experience or to overemphasize unfortunate and unpleasant past events and, therefore, to be disinclined to establish new goals—thus becoming past-bound instead of future-oriented.

It is encouraging to note that despite past failures we can alter goals and achieve future success. Not only can we learn from past mistakes, but we can change our goals so that they become more in tune with our abilities or with the circumstances at hand. When our expectations are too high, we invite failure—an easily predictable consequence when we do not make reasonable assessments of ourselves and the situations in which we find ourselves. While pessimism based on past failure can affect our thinking about the future, we can also make an effort to reconsider the future in an optimistic way. There is room for choice and freedom for action, especially if we do not erect rigid defenses, insist on perfectionism, or adopt pessimistic attitudes. Indeed, people who strongly hold that what they do is determined by the past may unconsciously view life in this manner because such rigid determinism permits them to avoid responsibility for their decisions.

Just as we may blame a failure-ridden past for our current problems or willingly accept the theory that the past controls our present life, we may also hold the "unconscious" responsible for our problems. Although much behavior is unconsciously motivated (that is, we are not immediately aware of the reason for our behavior), we should not conclude that everything we do is motivated by unconscious drives. Instead, we might begin by considering our problems to be conscious ones and by seeking effective solutions on that level. Practical and honest assessment is more likely to reveal new courses of action than is speculation about the past.

Through Understanding Our Psychological States

When we have problems, we often experience disturbing feelings, thoughts, or even bodily sensations that serve as indications that something is bothering us. Let us consider these psychological influences more fully.

Anxiety. Anxiety is often described as an uneasiness or tension about a danger or threat that we do not fully understand or recognize (Horney, 1937). When the threat is real—when its sources can be readily identified—we may assume that the anxiety is appropriate and probably manageable; however, when anxiety is out of proportion to a given situation or when it is evoked in a situation that is not threatening, we may be observing a reaction to internal threat. When a threat is external, the emotional response to it may well be fear; but anxiety is more anticipatory in quality and often occurs as a response to a danger that is essentially internal. According to Freudian theory, anxiety signifies that the mechanism of repression is not working well; that is, unwanted, unpleasant, and threatening impulses are reaching the surface and making the individual uncomfortable (Laughlin, 1967). Anxiety is, nevertheless, part of normal, everyday living; we cannot live without anxiety, but neither can we live with excessive anxiety.

Anxiety is often felt as agitation, restlessness, tension, uneasiness, and occasionally panic. "Butterflies" in the stomach, a "lump" in the throat, and shakiness in the hands are anxiety symptoms familiar to college students, especially during exams. Other physical symptoms may include perspiration, a rapid heartbeat, and dilation of the pupils. Mild anxiety may be viewed as beneficial because it keeps us alert and prepared to act (Roche Laboratories, 1968). Anxiety may even protect us from threat (Lief, 1967). In other words, when we experience fear or even anxiety we are given danger signals so that we may prepare ourselves to escape the situation. Severe anxiety, however, can interfere with our ability to function effectively, to think clearly, to focus effectively on our work, or to maintain an agreeable nature (Coleman, 1974). Motor coordination may also suffer, as we may fumble, stumble, make unnecessary mistakes, "freeze," become flustered, and so on. Severe anxiety may also cause insomnia, weight loss, loss of appetite, or vomiting. Drug therapy may be recommended by a physician or psychiatrist, but allowing the person to ventilate his feelings or removing him from the immediate stress situation are also effective means of reducing his anxiety (Kolb, 1973).

Slight anxiety may also be put to use, absorbed, and energized. Usually, our personality remains integrated and intact under mild anxiety, but we become more alert.

Anxiety can be generated by a variety of factors: resentment, rejection, failure, loss of self-esteem, competition, anger, feelings of inferiority or insecurity, parental pressure, inability to control unacceptable impulses, guilt, or failure to live up to certain standards (Coleman, 1964). Worrying about anxiety only intensifies the anxious state. The more we become annoyed with anxiety, the more it increases; we realize we are helpless to control it. Unfortunately, merely trying to forget about anxiety is rarely effective in reducing it.

Although anxiety may be characterized as a generalized state of tension, uneasiness, and fear, the causes of different anxieties differ radically. *Situational* anxiety refers to anxiety connected with a specific task—perhaps giving a speech in class or playing in a football game. *Social* anxiety stems from interpersonal or group situations in which unfamiliar people may make us nervous. *Neurotic* anxiety develops when there is a conflict within ourselves—for example, when we are unable to express our real feelings because they are considered socially unacceptable or because they would result in punishment. Consider for a moment the child who, through punishment, learned not to give easy vent to his anger. As an adult he may continue to carry the same feelings of anxiety and impending punishment whenever he becomes angry. Indeed, he may react irrationally in such situations (Guilford, 1959). Finally, *moral* anxiety is related to the urge to commit an act that violates one's conscience or ethical principles. Being tempted by the opportunity to cheat on an exam might create this type of anxiety. The anxiety you might feel over not reporting a theft you have witnessed is another example.

Since anxiety is a learned response to situations that threaten our security and self-esteem, cultural conditions are often a source of anxiety. In our society, for example, the failure to meet the expectations of one's social class can generate low self-esteem and feelings of failure that are often accompanied by anxiety. Similarly, the pressure for academic achievement produces considerable anxiety. Failure to live up to family expectations and, particularly, to achieve goals that have emotional meaning can also be a source of anxiety.

Anxiety can also be experienced with one person and transferred to another; that is, an unpleasant experience with one person may be generalized to other persons who were not connected with the original source of anxiety (Lief, 1967). A severely critical mother, for example, may turn her son against all females. Irrational verbal admonition or threats or emotional outbursts from parents can implant anxiety in a child who will continue as an adult to harbor fears over matters that are not considered threatening by others. A single incident in the past can establish a pattern of reaction in subsequent years. For example, having had a math teacher in high school who ridiculed your work can make you anxious and liable to perform poorly in a college math course. Such significant events with generalizing power are commonly known as *traumatic* incidents.

Anxiety can, in many instances, be lessened if we develop competencies for tasks or situations that threaten us. If you are unprepared for an exam or feel that your classmates have mastered the subject better than you have, you will very likely feel anxious. Thorough preparation and study will almost certainly reduce your anxiety.

Greater familiarity with an anxiety-provoking situation also tends to reduce anxiety. One of the purposes of freshman orientation is to familiarize students with a strange environment in order to lessen the anxiety often associated with the new college situations. Similarly, your hands may perspire or you may stutter and blush when you meet an unfamiliar person, but, with someone you know well, you may be able to talk freely and to touch physically without fear of rejection. There is no longer anxiety because there is no longer a threat or fear of the unknown.

It is also possible to reduce anxiety by verbalizing your anxieties to someone who is not threatening. Through repeated contact with such a person, you may begin to associate your anxious feelings and thoughts with more comfortable and pleasant feelings and thus may feel more relaxed when you experience anxiety-producing situations.

Physical activity of any sort is beneficial in making you feel more relaxed. Similarly, creative and pleasant work also reduces anxiety. The following is a good example of how physical activity helped to reduce anxiety for one person.

Incident

I wasn't doing very well academically, and because I was worrying about my grades all the time, I couldn't get down to studying. At night I lay awake for hours thinking about the things I had to do the next day. Sometimes I felt like screaming. I could hear my heart beating fast. I felt scared that something was going to happen. I knew it all had to do with school. I talked it over with an instructor in a course I was failing. He got me a tutor, and I got a B on the next quiz. That gave me confidence. Then I started to go to the gym to play basketball, and I found I could sleep better. I also played tennis and swam, and the relaxed feeling I got after the activity made me more able to enjoy both my work and the people around me.

When my grades picked up, I told my problems to my girlfriend. I was surprised to find out that she had gone through some of these same problems herself, that I wasn't the only one with these problems. I can see now that if you want to get the results, you have to realize that you have a problem in the first place. You've got to have the courage to let somebody know that you need help.

Depression. Depression involves a low-keyed mood, a lack of enthusiasm, a feeling of sadness, and a loss of interest in the environment. The depressed person often feels hopeless; that is, he has little to look forward to. More often than not, depression stems from low self-esteem, a poor self-image, emotional deprivation as a child, failure, or guilt.

Mendelson (1967) summarizes the causes of depression as follows: "To put it simply, self-esteem can be decreased and depression can be present because one feels lonely and unloved, unworthy, bad, guilty, unsuccessful, or inferior. And depression can be precipitated by the failure to obtain or by the loss of love or emotional supplies; by engaging in behavior or by experiencing feelings that cause one to feel guilty or unworthy; or by failure in the pursuit of goals, whether realistic or unrealistic" (p. 931). Mendelson also notes that lack of appetite, insomnia, fatigue, and loss of sexual desire may mask underlying depression in persons who are otherwise able to maintain a veneer of happiness, because depression decreases the instincts of pleasure, self-preservation, sociability, and hunger.

Boredom, social withdrawal, indifference, and lack of motivation for any clear-cut goal are characteristics also associated with depression. Such characteristics are typical of many adolescents, but if they are persistent and prolonged they may indicate a deeper problem of identity, guilt, hostility, or resentment. Depression is prevalent within our society. One in every eight persons, in fact, will experience a serious enough depression to require treatment (*Newsweek,* January, 1973). Frustration over social and political conditions, attempts to keep up with a rapidly changing society, and conflict over values are all factors that contribute to feelings of alienation and may be associated with depression.

Endogenous or primary depression originates from within, with no discernible precipitating stress. It is not clear whether psychological factors (such as guilt, inferiority feelings, or low self-esteem) or physiological factors (such as body chemicals and hormones) trigger endogenous depression. On the other hand, *exogenous* or secondary depression is caused by external stress factors, as when an individual reacts with depression to the loss of a loved one, to rejection, or to failure. Electroshock therapy or antidepressant drugs may be used to lessen depression, and the prognosis for alleviating depression is generally favorable. Indeed, many persons recover spontaneously, without any sort of treatment. Depression, however, is sometimes masked by a person's pleasant external appearance, while inner thoughts and feelings remain pessimistic (sometimes called "smiling

Figure 5-1. Depression consists of feelings of hopelessness, sadness, apathy, unworthiness, and helplessness; but fortunately it very often goes away with time. Photo by Shirley Kontos.

depression"). Suicide is often linked to prolonged and severe bouts of depression, and for that reason intervention may be crucial when "normal" recovery has not begun.

Feelings of mild depression are experienced by nearly everyone and are considered normal as long as they are not persistent and intensive. Such depression may involve a certain amount of sadness, melancholy, discouragement, and apathy.

Unexpressed resentfulness has also been cited as a cause for mild depression (Kolb, 1973). Mild depression is quite common among well-adjusted persons, as is mild anxiety. Certainly feeling "blue" or "in the dumps" when certain expectations do not materialize is a familiar experience. However, experiences such as these are only temporary; the person is not depressed in the real sense of the word. Mild depression can also be associated with a personal loss, whether real or imagined, whether emotional or material. Guilt for omitting or committing an act that violates one's ethical standards has also been cited as a psychological factor frequently associated with mild depression (Kolb, 1973). Actually, many of the situations that have the potential to elicit anxiety also have the power to create depression; indeed, some people may react to a situation with anxiety, while others may respond with depression.

Chronically depressed people, however, do present a serious problem. They frequently withdraw from social participation, limit their interests, and derive little enjoyment from life. Crying spells, awakening early in the morning without being able to fall asleep again, and loss of weight and appetite may also characterize their behavior (Ayd, 1961). Because of their self-depreciation, a preoccupation with suicide is also possible. Severely depressed persons, like extremely anxious individuals, may require medical attention, especially if they are potentially dangerous to themselves.

One difficulty in helping a depressed person is that his hopeless attitude toward himself and the future contains a built-in component of failure; he frustrates the efforts of those who want to help him because he considers himself unworthy of their attention. He may be quite unaware that he is manipulating others through his self-depreciation. It is easy to see that the moods of the depressed person serve ulterior purposes. They are not innate traits over which he has no control; rather, he uses them carefully. Many therapists adhere to the idea that feelings are motivated by conscious or unconscious goals and by the demands of the situation rather than being called "spontaneously" into play (Mahrer, 1970). If the behavior of a depressed person is reinforced, it becomes increasingly constant and more difficult to change.

There is no single method for coping with depression. However, there are certain relatively simple techniques that often serve to lessen such feelings. Some persons reduce depression by a change of scenery, by changing jobs, by finding a hobby, or by becoming involved in creative activities such as writing, music, or drawing. For others, physical activities may lighten the burden of depression.

The cause for depression is sometimes found in our immediate living situation. Often the loss of someone we love is a cause for depression. Rejection by someone we esteem or by a boyfriend or girlfriend is another likely cause. Substitute relationships may be difficult to find, but do help to make up for such losses. Failure in academics and the guilt that accompanies such failure also causes depression. Talking out such problems with someone you trust may help reduce your depression, because a good listener can help you to focus on the source of your depression rather than on your own feelings of inadequacy. A good listener may also be able to offer concrete suggestions and new alternatives. Often we feel depressed because we are avoiding what we know we ought to do. Facing up to obligations can have a remarkably heartening affect, as we note in the following situation.

Incident

On weekends and especially on Sundays I used to get real depressed. I didn't want to do anything. I would spend the weekend telling myself that I needed to catch up on my sleep. I was beginning to act like I wished I could fall asleep and never wake up again. During the week I had classes and was busy running around the campus and getting my work done. But those weekends were getting to me. I hadn't been socializing because I sort of expected the depression to come. I just couldn't go on like that. Finally, it dawned on me that when I was busy I didn't have these bouts of depression. Why not get busy on the weekends, I asked myself. So I went on a camping trip one Friday and got back late Saturday. I'd had a good time—no depression at all. On Sunday I went to a dinner with some friends. It was neat because we got to talking about photography, which I wanted to learn more about. Later that Sunday I got a little depressed, but the depression wasn't that bad because I realized that I had had a decent weekend. I still get depressed on Sundays late in the day, but it doesn't bother me like it used to. I think I solved the problem by doing things I like instead of hiding from everybody. Now I almost look forward to weekends as my chance to be with other people.

Psychophysiological problems. A psychophysiological reaction occurs when a physical symptom expresses an emotional conflict. The person experiencing the physical symptom may be quite unaware of its cause. Emotions can create physiological states, also known as psychosomatic problems, that are very real to the person experiencing them, but a medical examination may reveal no physical difficulties.

Actually we all experience mild psychophysiological reactions from time to time, especially in stressful situations. A pounding heart and inability to breathe deeply prior to an important examination, the choking sensation or "butterflies" in the stomach when encountering someone in authority whom we fear, the tightness in the neck or headache and nausea prior to making an important decision are examples of psychophysiological reactions. In each of these situations there is a threat, whether actual or only internally felt, that intensifies anxiety. The personality in distress "speaks" through physical symptoms.

The autonomic nervous system, which functions on its own, is involved in psychophysiological reactions, and their classification depends on the area in which the reaction occurs. These reactions may include respiratory (asthma, hyperventilation) and gastrointestinal (ulcers, hyperacidity) systems, the skin (itching, blemishes), and the musculoskeletal (headaches, muscle cramps), cardiovascular (migraine headaches, high blood pressure, rapid heartbeat), and genitourinary (dysmenorrhea, impotence) systems (American Psychiatric Association, 1968). Why some organs are affected instead of others is not fully understood, but some authorities speculate that anxieties tend to be expressed through the body's weaker organs or systems. It is also possible that personality factors and childhood experiences play a role in the selection of symptoms. Thus, therapy can only be offered after an intense study of a particular case, for there is no general rule that can be applied to all persons suffering from psychophysiological reactions.

A person is more likely to develop psychophysiological reactions when under pressure, even though the exact nature of the stress is not always known. Sometimes, of course, the source of stress is obvious—rejection, failure, loss of a friend. The student who develops stomach cramps prior to visiting his family at Thanksgiving may realize that he is anticipating the usual disagreements with his parents. In situations such as this, the distress in the organ(s) is the primary focus, and the anxiety is a secondary symptom. Anxiety and tension, then, through the innervations of the nervous system, flow into the body's organs and create symptoms similar to, even undistinguishable from, those of an actual physical ailment, and this is why a physical examination and laboratory tests fail to discover an organic problem. In such a case, the psychological factors involved must be discovered. Occasionally such symptoms disappear quickly and are not in any real sense psychosomatic; only when they are prolonged and annoying can they be classified as a genuine psychophysiological disorder.

Although a broad range of bodily dysfunctions (stomach and chest pains, diarrhea, indigestion, headaches) may be caused by emotional problems and fall into the general category of psychosomatic symptoms, it is generally held that the digestive system is more easily affected by stress than are the other organs.

Anxiety and depression are emotional states that may accompany psychosomatic symptoms; indeed, all the symptoms may stem from the same psychological problem. It is not uncommon for individuals to insist that their emotional problems have a physical origin, for such a stance allows them to avoid looking at themselves or admitting that there is "something mentally wrong." On the other hand, physical illness or poor health may cause emotional symptoms, such as the depression that may follow a bout of mononucleosis or the irritability that may result from a lack of certain vitamins.

Everyone has experienced mild psychosomatic symptoms that dissipate with time or when stress is no longer present; however, when the symptoms are severe and prolonged, medical intervention and psychotherapy might be necessary. Surprisingly enough, physical symptoms tend to lessen with psychotherapy sessions that explore the sources of anxiety as well as the means of coping with stress. Since the emotional state and the psychosomatic ailment are by definition linked together, only through the resolution of the former can the latter be remedied. One student describes this process very aptly.

Incident

I used to get these horrible headaches. My doctor said there was nothing wrong with me physically, but I still kept on having those headaches. Some of the girls in the dorm asked me what was bothering me; they said I looked real mad, like I was going to blow up at any minute. There was a lot of truth in what they said. I knew that I was angry at many things and that I kept my anger to myself. I was angry at the people at the library where I worked. It seemed like I was just a slave, running up and down, getting the books other people wanted, and I couldn't talk back to them even though I wanted to. Looking back I realized that I looked mad a lot of the time and probably turned people off. I talked to another girl, a senior, about this, and she said I should let out my feelings and that I should not let people step all over me. In the classroom I began to talk more and I was noticed in nicer ways. At work I got to be more firm; I looked the students directly in the eyes when I spoke to them, and I gave definite answers. Now my headaches are mostly gone. When I do get a headache, I ask myself what I'm angry at, and I try to let the anger out of my system without hurting anybody.

Situational problems. Reactions that subside as soon as a period of stress is over are defined as transient situational reactions. Transient reactions do not have appreciable or lasting effects on future behavior; indeed, were an individual to continue to react in this way after stress had diminished, we might well suspect a more encompassing problem.

Our reactions to temporary situations may depend on our age, the circumstances, and our experience. One child who is placed in a foster home may remain unhappy for a day or two, but another may find his situation unpleasant even after months. One 63-year-old may find retirement frustrating and boring, but another may adapt rather quickly to the new lifestyle. On occasion, however, therapeutic intervention may be required because an individual's reaction to temporary stress has not accommodated itself to general circumstances. In short, the stressful situation may have been transitory, but the response was not.

Relocating from home to college is another example of a transient stress situation. Many students temporarily miss the "good old days" of high school, when subjects were easier and friends more abundant. Now there are new pressures and demands, and students must learn new ways of coping. All of these factors can converge to create a stress situation. Students may react by cutting classes, sleeping late, arguing with roommates, or entertaining doubts about staying in college. But these reactions are usually only a temporary response to environmental stress. Most students soon adapt to the new situation.

Many other situations can cause transient stress: a toddler may seek attention through regressive behavior when a younger sibling is born; transferring from one school to another may cause temporary academic problems for an adolescent; or a young child may refuse to leave his mother's side for days after his father has left town to go to a company convention. Divorce, a school failure, a broken romance, unemployment—any of these may cause transient reactions of disgust, cynicism, apathy, or hostility. Duration is the criterion here; that is, a reaction that endures may well signal that the person is asking for help through behavior signals. You may be familiar with the following experience.

Incident

I went home after being away at college for a semester and visited my high school friends again. Some had already gotten married, so we didn't have much in common. Nothing that we talked about amounted to anything, but I had this feeling that I wanted to stay home and be with them again. I really missed some of the guys I had known for so long. We had done a lot of crazy things together. When I got back to college, I felt depressed. It seemed that things were unreal here, that I didn't belong in college anymore, and I wanted to go home again. I almost quit college—that's how deeply I felt. I knew there was nothing wrong with me; I lost my appetite, and I began to oversleep and to daydream. As a result, my grades dropped a little, but I managed to pick up before the end of the second semester. It's funny that this happened after I visited home, not when I came down here in the first place. I knew it all went back to that home visit, and I tried to have patience and give myself enough time to recover. The next visit home will probably be a lot easier.

Most of Us Are Well Adjusted

Students seeking assistance at counseling and health centers are usually reasonably adjusted persons who want to understand themselves better and who seek an encounter of an educational nature with a trained person who can serve as a guide for setting limits and defining boundaries. Certainly some students have serious psychological problems, but a large number are merely seeking information, searching for answers, and looking for feedback about themselves from a more or less objective source. Often they are anxious for clarification and reassurance about their behavior and social relationships. Nixon (1960) reports that 60% of the students who visited a psychiatrist at Vassar belonged to the category described above. Only 20% had relatively serious psychological problems. Communication with colleagues at other colleges led Nixon to conclude that comparable percentages were present in other areas of the country. Reifler and Liptzin (1969) report similarly that over 40% of those who seek psychological assistance have only temporary difficulties in personality functioning or are experiencing a negative reaction to a particular situation.

There is further evidence that adolescent upheaval is not as widespread as it has been suggested or that, when it does occur, it is generally of little consequence to the person in later life. Offer (1967) surveyed 103 "typical" adolescents over a period of three years and found all but 7% to be adequately adjusted. The emotional problems manifested by this small proportion did not reach psychotic proportions. In a mid-Manhattan project, however, much higher percentages were observed. One in every four persons studied there demonstrated an incapacitating emotional problem (Srole, Langner, Michael, Opler, & Rennie, 1962).

Walters (1970) investigated the incidence of emotional problems among students visiting the psychiatric unit of a large midwestern state university over a ten-year period and learned that nearly 36% had been classified as having a personality disorder. The majority of these were passive and withdrawn students, who had not fully actualized themselves. Close to 30% of the students had been classified under the label *neurosis;* of these, nearly half were mildly anxious, and another third expressed depression. Over 20% of the students who visited the psychiatric unit were classed as experiencing a transient, upsetting situation that had caused them to seek professional counsel. Only 6% of the total number of students were diagnosed as having physiological problems, and another 6% were classified as suffering from psychosis—a figure somewhat lower than that reported at other universities. Only about five in every one hundred students who visited the clinic, then, were actually found to be emotionally maladjusted. Walters also found that a significantly higher proportion of female students and Jewish students visited the psychiatric unit, a pattern that is confirmed by other studies. This higher incidence might be explained by speculating that these students tend to be more verbal regarding their feelings and problems and more favorably disposed toward the idea of therapy or counseling. Walters discovered further that a higher proportion of graduate students sought help than did undergraduates, perhaps because of increased pressures at that academic level.

The literature examining the causes and consequences of the emotional problems and/or maladjustment of college students is divided. Some view maladjustment as transient; indeed, in the long run the experience may even be beneficial, for the individual may be able to cope better with similar problems in the future. Others, however, consider the emotional difficulties of students as representing long-standing problems that may warrant long-term treatment. In this latter category, we often find medically oriented therapists who are apt to identify deep-seated conflicts, especially if these existed prior to the student's entry into college (Deutsch & Ellenberg, 1973). Psychologists and other nonmedically oriented professionals tend to view such problems as a normal stage of emotional development in which environmental factors play a large role (Nixon, 1960). Even among the therapists in the second category, however, recommendations for counseling or therapy are frequently made, for many problems may be alleviated more readily during the student years before personalities have crystallized into adult patterns. We can conclude, then, that most reported student problems are of a transient, situational nature. Most students are able to eliminate these problems with time, but some can be helped directly through counseling and therapy. Those few who are seriously emotionally disturbed in college do not seem to constitute a higher percentage than that found in society at large.

One authority on adjustment among college students notes that their problems have not increased or intensified during the last few decades (Farnsworth, 1970). The publicity given to student activism for social and academic reforms in recent years has focused considerable attention on their adjustment and may have distorted our perception of their emotional problems. There seems to be no characteristic peculiar to the college setting that causes any major maladjustment; neither does the stress of academic work appear to be a dominant cause. Instead, it seems that faulty but dormant development factors may be activated by the college experience. Farnsworth (1970) sums up the situation as follows: "Most of the serious psychiatric disorders found among college students have their origins in conditions in the home and in relations with other significant persons in the student's early life rather than in conditions encountered in the college. The latter are quite important but more often as precipitating agents than as fundamental causes of disabling conflict" (p. 473). As with any stress situation, it is not so much the nature of the pressure but its similarity to earlier, unresolved and buried conflicts that is the significant factor in determining whether or not stress will be keenly felt.

HOW WE PROTECT OURSELVES

Most of us exhibit mild tension or fear when we experience uncomfortable conditions, when our self-esteem is threatened, when we anticipate failure or rejection, and when we sense impulses unacceptable to our own or society's moral code. It is only natural, then, that we develop certain devices to protect ourselves from excessive anxiety or to help in its control. These responses are generally referred to as safeguard mechanisms or mechanisms of adjustment, because they assist us in maintaining control and self-esteem and help us to adjust to stress. Put another way, these mechanisms help us to maintain an equilibrium between our own needs and the demands of our environment.

Every living organism has the ability to survive—to protect itself from stress or to adapt to it. Certain animals, for example, develop thick layers of skin or special coloring to survive harsh weather conditions or to protect themselves from other animals. This principle may be extended to the mental and emotional life of humans, for the mind has the capacity to avoid, neutralize, or forget what has become unpleasant, disturbing, or intolerable. This ability not only helps to relieve tension and anxiety, but it also helps to reinforce feelings of security and self-esteem.

Some of these safeguards work automatically, while others are used in a more deliberate fashion. Often they shield us from the harsh realities of our inadequacies or the unpleasant aspects of our behavior. They often protect us from overconcern with ourselves, from the debilitating sense of a hostile or threatening environment, and from deep or overwhelming pessimism. On the other hand, if these mechanisms become intensified and rigid, they can also prevent us from functioning adequately in our environment. Discussing how these safeguard mechanisms function may help us to understand our own behavior more fully. And once we become aware of such mechanisms, we may be able to recognize them at work in the behavior of our friends, our parents, and our employers and thus learn to develop greater tolerance and understanding.

Although Freud's (1938) term *defense mechanism* refers to a generally unconscious process, most modern psychologists assume that the processes of these mechanisms operate along a broad continuum, from the fully unconscious to the nearly conscious. Like many other psychological terms, these mechanisms merely describe a human response, but it is safe to assume that, since defense mechanisms protect us against anxiety and maintain our self-esteem, these mechanisms must of necessity be deceptive, distorting events in order to make these events seem less threatening (Lazarus, 1963; White, 1964). Further, although these mechanisms are employed with varying degrees of awareness, an outside observer is usually better able to detect a mechanism at work and to identify its motivation than is the reacting individual himself.

Finally, defense mechanisms involve our *actions,* our *emotions,* and our *thoughts.* These three components do not exist in isolation, although one is usually more dominant in a given response (Hershey & Lugo, 1970). The next sections will discuss these three forms of defense mechanisms, offering for each an example typical of our everyday lives.

Defenses of Acting

Compensation

Incident

Mike had a clubfoot from polio that limited his social life. He was an excellent student and entered medical school without difficulty. He had always been interested in medicine and in helping people, but he noted that he was also attracted to the impressive image of a physician in a white coat who had the authority to order nurses around. Through his career choice, Mike seemed, to some extent, to be compensating for his inability to be with women on personal terms, but at the same time he was also fulfilling other interests and becoming useful to society.

When people attempt to develop a desirable trait in order to overcome an undesirable one, we say that they are compensating. It is admirable for students to attempt to make up for deficiencies by excelling in another area, as long as their choices are based on a realistic assessment of their own abilities and interests. If they make an unrealistic choice, however, they will not only be unable to compensate for the unacceptable trait, but they will also meet with additional failure and thus compound the original problem.

The physically well-developed student who has difficulty qualifying for a professional career because of an average academic record may compensate for his lack of academic achievement by excelling in athletic pursuits. He may win acceptance because of his excellence in sports. By the same token, the physically unattractive person may become proficient in a particular academic field, thereby winning admiration and respect. Some parents seek to compensate for their own failures by setting high standards for their children. For example, an uneducated, financially successful father may insist that his son acquire a college education, even though the son has little interest in college.

Compensation is one of the most reliable devices for adjustment, as long as the form of compensation used is socially desirable. Strong aggressiveness and unwarranted competitiveness are forms of compensation that may be considered unacceptable. Rather, people should try to overcome a personal weakness by achieving notable success in an area in which society may also benefit.

Compensation can occur in many areas of human behavior. There are, in fact, three recognized types of compensation: organic, social, and psychological. Organic compensation is found in bodily responses; the function of a damaged or defective organ, for example, may be taken over by adjacent organs. When a portion of the liver is damaged by disease, the healthy, undamaged portion compensates by producing new tissue. Organic compensation can also be seen in situations when an individual excels in an area that requires the use of a body part that was once weak. For example, persons have become skilled dancers or skaters after having had polio in their childhood. More vivid is the example of Demosthenes of ancient Greece who overcame his stuttering to become a famous orator. Social compensation may be demonstrated by students who dress in unnecessarily expensive or immaculate clothes or conspicuous hairstyles in an attempt to divert attention from their social inadequacies by drawing attention to their physical appearance. The "proper" clothes or a "perfect" appearance helps them to feel more comfortable in social situations. Finally, psychological compensation is illustrated by people who make up for personal inadequacies, such as poor physical appearance, stuttering, or social shyness, by developing admirable traits such as thriftiness, industriousness, or promptness. Such individuals may also choose careers in which they need not come in close contact with other people. Through this career choice, the individuals avoid exposing their social weaknesses, but they are rewarded through work that has social merit and public approval.

Substitution

Incident

Richard had been a very promising athlete in a small high school, but he had not done as well in the more highly competitive college scene. Because he had always been interested in sports and felt that his main talents were in this area, he had hoped to become a professional athlete. But he now realized that this goal was unrealistic. He decided to pursue a degree in physical education instead.

Richard was unable to reach his original goal; but, by choosing to study physical education, he remained committed to his interest in sports but under conditions in which his goals were compatible with his abilities. Richard's transposed goal, although less glamorous, was similar to his original one and allowed him to maintain his self-esteem and to employ his talents and interests.

Substitution is the mechanism by which people who are unable to reach their desired goals are able to relieve their frustration and anxiety by substituting a similar goal that can be attained. If people abandon seemingly unattainable goals, they may subsequently feel inadequate; if they persist in an unreasonable pursuit, they will probably experience the hurt of failure. Substitution is not an undesirable mechanism if the goal pursued is accessible and is comparable in value to the goal it replaces. However, the individual must feel comfortable with the "compromise" or alternate goal.

There are times, however, when a person should pursue his or her original goal—that is, when substitution is merely the means to avoid responsibility or hard work or when the person is unwilling to accept the consequences of the new choice. Guilt or fear, for example, may be at the root of the person's choosing compromise alternatives. Finally, making indiscriminate and repeated substitutions, such as "shopping around" for a career, may lead to feelings of inadequacy, especially if the person fails to achieve the substituted objectives. Not reaching any goals can make us feel left behind and insecure for not getting anywhere in life.

Identification

Incident

Joan, a pretty and popular girl, was elected queen of her high school. Everyone admired her and sought her friendship. As a result, she did not go out of her way to make new friends or to study seriously. Everything seemed to come to her without her having to make any real effort. She spent little time considering educational and vocational goals because she had already decided to major in the theatre arts. She imitated the gait, gestures, and mannerisms of actresses she admired, and she was even successful in adopting the voice of a favorite actress. She dated handsome men exclusively. The men were initially attracted by her physical appearance; however, they soon discovered that Joan lacked certain desirable intellectual and emotional qualities. Joan did not seem to realize that her identification with actresses and the resulting superficial and egotistical personality were restricting her personal and social growth.

Identification occurs when we develop strong emotional ties with another person, even going on to behave as if we were that other person. Students often imitate their instructors or other figures whom they admire and respect, adopting that person's gestures, phrases, and tone of voice. Aligning oneself with figures who have shown excellence and accomplishment can be a healthy way for young people to fulfill themselves and to give meaning to their actions. Such identification can provide an early sense of direction. When we begin to accomplish things on our own, the identification is transferred from the important "other person" to the task itself. Thus, the process of identification should not be interpreted as a sign of weakness or dependency but as an acceptable stimulus for personal growth.

Like most defense mechanisms, the process of identification is largely unconscious. When we admire someone and try to take on his or her characteristics and personal qualities, we are generally unaware of our actions. Identification in the form of "hero worship" may provide constructive values and guidelines that

Figure 5-2. Watching sports activities can help us vent our aggressions, as we can identify with the players. Photo by Shirley Kontos.

promote the development of personality. By identifying with "ideal" persons we give a positive direction to the growth of our personalities, provided that we do not lose our own identity in the process. We often identify with characters in novels and plays, and such empathic reactions can have a cathartic or growth-producing effect as we experience the fictional conflict and its ultimate resolution. Of course, we may identify with persons, groups, or ideals that are not socially approved (gangs, outlaws, radical ideals); such identification can be harmful rather than helpful. It is even possible to lose a sense of one's own identity. An extreme example of such identification (perhaps mixed with other mechanisms) is found in people who have lost all contact with reality and believe themselves to be another (often god-like) personality (Napoleon, Hitler, Manson) with a special mission to transform the world.

Sublimation

Incident

Nick was an active, outgoing, and socially rebellious boy in high school. He had been a leader of a gang that committed a variety of delinquent acts (such as thievery and vandalism). In college he began to realize that he could not function as a student if his rebelliousness continued. During his first year in college he took a course in criminology, which led to an interest in becoming a probation officer. By becoming a probation officer, Nick continued to deal with delinquents on an exciting level, but in an altogether different relationship. Although Nick was still considered aggressive, his socially unacceptable actions were now redirected into a responsible, socially useful channel.

Sublimation is the process of channeling conventionally unacceptable drives into activities that are socially approved and desirable. Sublimation is considered to be one of the healthiest of mental mechanisms. Sexual and aggressive urges, particularly, are transformed and directed by this means into channels of activity that promote the welfare of society and of the individual—as in the case of the boy who learned to fight in order to survive in his tough neighborhood who later became a successful boxer.

Since sublimated behavior is highly respected by our society, it often leads to a feeling of competence and fulfillment, as aggressive and sexual drives are discharged in ways that are accepted or even esteemed by others. Excessive sublimation rarely becomes a problem unless an individual uses this mechanism as a means of evading major problems.

Restitution

Incident

Don felt guilty for having made his girlfriend pregnant and for the fact that she got an abortion, which was against his moral principles. Although he talked the matter over with his religious adviser, he could not put his mind at ease. He tried to compensate for his act in many ways. He made a point of being home early every evening; he attended church regularly; he even enrolled in a religion course. His social conduct in college became exemplary; he became a model student. He participated in various student organizations and so favorably impressed his adviser with his impeccable moral conduct that he was appointed as a counselor for freshman students. Don made amends by becoming an ideal student through redemptive and purposeful activity.

Restitution is an attempt to relieve the guilt and anxiety caused by having acted against one's moral code. Restitution can be an unconscious act, without apparent repentance, but there is often a conscious element of regret that spurs one to make up for wrongdoings by actions from which others derive benefit. For example, the student who failed to return a book to the college library may make a donation to the library fund years later.

The mechanism of restitution has helped to form many great people throughout history. St. Augustine is a good example. During his youth he had been prodigal, but in later life he attempted restitution through his writings, which inspired and elevated the early Christian Church to new heights. King David, in the Old Testament, is another example. After violating the rules of society by sending a man to the front lines of battle so that he himself could marry the man's wife, he became severely depressed and began restitution by expressing his repentance and faith in his famous psalms. Similarly, many persons have attained sainthood in the church by denouncing their sins, by gaining new self-insights, and by performing outstanding deeds. The effect of active restitution can be powerful in social and humanitarian terms as well as in intensely personal ones.

Malingering

Incident

Dorothy was unprepared for her final exams. She had missed many classes during the semester and had often been able to manipulate people and get out of unpleasant tasks by feigning illness. As a child she had derived a great deal of attention whenever she complained of feeling sick. On the day of one exam, she woke up too late to go to class. She immediately went to the college infirmary, complaining of "illness." The physician found nothing wrong with her. She then attempted to have her exam rescheduled to a more convenient date. Dorothy felt embarrassed when the dean inquired why she had not reported to the infirmary when she had been "ill" earlier in the semester. Her trick of malingering had been exposed.

Malingering is the deliberate feigning of physical symptoms in order to avoid an unpleasant or threatening situation. Unlike many other adjustment mechanisms, we are well aware of what we are doing and what we expect to gain.

Malingerers do not experience physical pain; they are simply acting deceitfully in order to avoid undesirable situations. Malingering reflects a certain amount of immaturity and passivity and, in the long run, is an ineffectual way of coping. The fear of discovery, the threat of humiliation, and the presence of guilt create a heavy additional burden, which we may find even more painful than the situation we seek to escape.

Defenses of Feeling

Repression

Incident

     Ann seemed unable to prolong a friendship with any boy she met in college. As soon as she felt herself becoming emotionally involved, she spontaneously developed a hostile attitude and rejected the young man. She did not know why she got "cold feet" or why she experienced this negative attitude.

     Ann had never been close to her father. At an early age, when she had been dependent on him, he had not understood her needs and had ignored her feelings. As a result, Ann, while desiring to form a close relationship with a male, would suddenly break away, even if the young man had given no indication that he might reject her. Her repressed experiences of fear associated with rejection by her father continually prevented her from forming close emotional ties with men.

Repression is considered one of the most basic defense mechanisms. Through this process, unpleasant or dangerous past experiences, thoughts that arouse shame and guilt, feelings of failure, and the expression of hostile impulses and unacceptable drives are automatically kept away from the conscious mind so that we feel more comfortable with ourselves.

Repression may become a problem when numerous experiences must be concealed. It is possible to invest too much energy in maintaining repression; the energy might be used more constructively in dealing directly with a specific unpleasant situation. Too great a reliance on repression produces anxiety, thus causing us to feel uneasy without knowing why. It is possible for individuals to see themselves "without problems," but they are probably deceiving themselves through repression. Such persons may become alienated from their real personalities since so many of its aspects have been obliterated. In summary, then, repression is universal and helpful when it obliterates minor unpleasant incidents and allays the anxiety connected with them. Excessive repression, however, can cause intensified anxiety.

Suppression

Incident

     Sue's boyfriend was angry because he felt she did not pay enough attention to him in social situations. As he described to her the details of her behavior, she swallowed her pride and refused to argue back. Instead, she listened to him sympathetically and displayed no hostile emotions, although she actually felt as angry as he did. Sue avoided further conflict and embarrassment by withholding her real feelings toward her boyfriend who was making, she felt, unreasonable demands.

Through suppression, we hold back or "forget" feelings and thoughts that are not condoned by society or are threatening to us. This mechanism is similar to repression in that an unpleasant or unacceptable feeling or thought is pushed out of awareness. In suppression, however, we act deliberately; in repression, the act takes place without conscious effort.

Some individuals may deliberately avoid the expression of anger by refusing to speak, even by pressing their lips tightly closed. A person who feels abused by his or her date may become unusually silent and withdrawn during the evening. By relying on the mechanism of suppression, a person may avoid actual or potential danger; no one is hurt by unkind words or actions. If, however, the suppression of feelings is a deliberate attempt to "get even" or to express resentment, it may disrupt rather than promote human relationships.

Reaction formation

Incident

Andy had accepted a blind date. When the prospective girl was pointed out to him from a distance by his friends, he became angry because she did not meet with his expectations. However, if he had expressed these feelings, he would have been acting immaturely, and he would have embarrassed his friends and the girl. As he shook hands with the girl, he became cheerful and polite. Toward the end of the evening he complimented her and went out of his way to express his thanks for a pleasant evening. By being kind and cooperative, he had concealed his hostile, antisocial feelings toward his date and had redeemed the evening for everyone involved.

Reaction formation is demonstrated when we behave in a manner precisely opposite to what we really feel like saying or doing in order to avoid conflict or social condemnation. A student, for example, may show kindness toward and interest in another student for whom she really feels considerable dislike or even hostility. Another example is the student who is angry because he has failed an exam and yet approaches his instructor in a polite and charming manner. The reason for reaction formation is to rescue the person from saying what he or she really thinks, which may be a sign of foolishness and immaturity.

Reaction formation can be an asset. For example, using reaction formation in an effort to keep our "cool" instead of panicking when confronted with danger and threat can indeed help us to overcome the problem; other people, in fact, may accept and credit our positive approach. It is true, on the other hand, that reaction formation is a form of concealing and distorting, but it is a mechanism with merit because it enables us to cope with situations that would cause difficulty if we said what we actually thought or acted as we really felt. It usually represents the lesser of two evils, and it is a mechanism that seldom leads to further difficulty. Within this context, reaction formation is a desirable mechanism, but if we were to employ it indiscriminately we would ultimately project an image that was not representative of ourselves.

Displacement

Incident

Ann did not want to return to college because she was failing. She had been unable to convince her mother of the rightness of this course of action and had consequently developed strong negative feelings toward her mother. Ann returned to the campus with great reluctance. During her first class session, she disagreed on a minor point with her instructor, a woman about the same age as her mother. Ann's irritation in class was so apparent that the instructor asked her to stay and discuss her feelings. Ann intimated that the instructor had been stubborn, demanding, and inconsiderate of other people's feelings. Although Ann was not aware of it, she had simply transferred her feelings about her mother to her instructor.

Displacement is the transfer of unacceptable feelings or thoughts from the person or situation that aroused them to another person or situation. Often, if we were to behave as we really feel toward the source of our feelings and thoughts, we would experience undesirable consequences. A student who failed an exam, for example, may be angry at her professor; yet, she dare not express these feelings to the professor. Instead, she unloads her feelings on someone else—her roommate, perhaps—and the consequences are not severe. The student, through the mechanism of displacement, finds relief as she expresses her anger and pent-up feelings of hostility to someone who is unlikely to reject her or to bring about dangerous consequences.

Displacement can often be helpful if we unload negative feelings and frustrations on inanimate objects, but we may experience "backlash" if we displace our feelings on other people. For example, if a student uses her roommate as a scapegoat for difficulties with a boyfriend, she may risk losing a girlfriend as well. In the long run, it is preferable to work through difficulties with the person directly involved rather than to displace negative feelings to an "innocent bystander." Displacement, though, is often tolerated, and, in fact, society often approves of such tactics. We can, for example, "beat" someone we dislike by outdoing the person academically or in sports. By putting the unacceptable feelings to work in constructive ways or in neutral areas of actions, no one is injured and problems may be averted.

Projection

Incident

Mary was a fairly attractive girl but unreasonably shy and withdrawn. As a young girl she had not been allowed to participate in social groups because her strict parents feared that she "might get into trouble." She was not allowed to be herself at home and was often reprimanded when she expressed her own views. Her parents had wanted to plan her whole life. As a result, she harbored a poor image of herself, both socially and academically in college. She never felt that she belonged there. She withdrew from others because she felt they were "phony" and "empty," but she also feared that they might criticize her. Although she felt inadequate and inferior, she attributed these negative feelings to others rather than to herself. They were somehow to blame for her shyness and social failure. She avoided them because she thought they regarded her as inadequate and inferior—feelings that were really part of a self-evaluation that she was unable to accept.

Projection is the mechanism by which individuals perceive their own undesirable personal characteristics, thoughts, or attitudes as belonging to other persons or groups. They use projection as a protection against admitting the deficiencies in themselves. They can willingly attribute to one other or others what they may be unwilling to accept in themselves. For example, if a student has not won acceptance by a particular group in college, he may resent and dislike the group. However, rather than admitting these feelings as part of himself, he blames the group for showing hostility toward him. When his own feelings are seen as emanating from the group, he is relieved of them. Sometimes personal assets are also projected onto others, and an individual sees only good qualities in other people. Through this positive process, the individual unwittingly hopes that others will overlook or tolerate his shortcomings.

The mechanism of projection operates widely and in varying degrees, and often without our awareness. It is, in fact, difficult to avoid projecting because the way we feel and think about the world reflects our own needs and characteristics. In short, the way we perceive the objective world often reveals our inner, subjective world. For example, the unmotivated student who receives low grades and who describes his instructors as "dull and disorganized" may well be ascribing to them his own self-image.

Regression

Incident

Diane, a graduate student, had been crying all day in the dorm because her boyfriend had left her. She felt totally helpless and unable to control her feelings. When Diane went to see a counselor on the floor, she appeared in blue jeans, a sweatshirt, and gym shoes. She chewed gum noisily, wore her hair in a girlish ponytail, and giggled as she entered the counselor's office. When the counselor pointed out that Diane wasn't acting her age, she broke into tears.

When Diane found herself in a trying situation, she had reverted to a behavior pattern from the past because it was comfortable and reassuring. By acting like a little girl, Diane had retreated into a situation in which she could cope more easily.

Regression involves a reversion to a chronologically earlier phase of behavior that is characteristic of less mature functioning. In short, under stress, we often ward off anxiety by acting in a manner that is inconsistent with our age. By acting childishly, we create a situation in which less is expected of us. The student who feels uncomfortable and inadequate in social situations may "clown" around in order to conceal his tenseness. The student who has difficulty communicating with her parents or boyfriends may gain attention through "baby talk" or by crying over irrelevant matters. By reverting to less mature behavior, such people absolve themselves of the responsibility that the situation may demand.

Those who are prone to regress to childish behavior when faced with difficulties are usually those who have been dependent on parents or other strong figures. Basically, such persons lack confidence and feel that they cannot relate responsibly to the adult world. When they cannot achieve goals through conventional behavior, they act immaturely (pouting, giggling, crying, screaming, making childish demands, behaving stubbornly). By acting as a child, they hope to be taken care of by someone else; and very often this tactic proves successful, for their actions compel others to treat them as children and thus make few demands of them.

Defenses of Thinking

Daydreaming

Incident

Ted was a handsome teenager who had never had a date. He felt anxious in the presence of girls and had difficulty engaging in even casual conversation with them. He became panicky at the thought of telephoning a girl. Ted liked to take long walks alone on Saturday nights, imagining that he was with an attractive blonde who was very fond of him. His fantasy continued as he imagined another girl—a brunette this time—who was equally in love with him. The girls began to argue over who actually owned him. He enjoyed watching the argument, displaying a wide grin as if he were actually witnessing the event. People who happened to be strolling by noticed his grin and wondered what he was thinking about. Finally, Ted resolved the conflict by imagining that he escorted both girls, one on each arm.

Daydreaming (wish-fulfilling fantasy) constitutes a temporary mental retreat from seemingly dull and routine everyday activities. All of us daydream nearly every day, finding temporary relief from boredom and enjoying moments of relaxation during which we often regroup our energies in order to face duties with greater strength.

Daydreams may depict powerful or extraordinary feats or scenes of humiliation and suffering. Students often fantasize that they are great heroes or that they possess unusual physical beauty. Or, they may suffer in their daydreams in order to elicit revenge or pity, possibly from someone in real life who has rejected them. In other words, the content of daydreams is dependent upon the needs of the dreamers, their feelings toward others, and their unfulfilled aspirations. The content of daydreams changes with age. Children often daydream of possessing objects, while adolescents and young adults often have sexually oriented fantasies.

Daydreaming of excessive duration and intensity is undesirable in terms of adjustment. Prolonged withdrawal from the environment temporarily delays or ultimately prohibits the achievement of realistic goals. When students become conditioned to daydreaming, they may find it difficult or even impossible to shift their energies to the world around them. On the other hand, daydreaming can be a satisfying experience when it occurs in short intervals and at appropriate times. For example, students who daydream toward the end of the day, after they have prepared the next day's assignments, may find relaxation and comfort, even encouragement, in their fantasy world.

Intellectualization

Incident

Ray never had time for dates and denied having any sexual needs or thoughts, belittling anything of a sexual nature. He felt unable to cope with practical and concrete matters, but he was able to express himself verbally and to describe situations in a highly abstract way. He tried to avoid interpersonal difficulties by secluding himself and, therefore, had no real friends. Instead, he derived immense gratification from books. He controlled his feelings and emotions excessively in order to prevent the possibility of behaving in socially unacceptable ways. It seemed that he had quelled the threat of his own emotions by becoming abstract and theoretical.

Anything of an emotional nature can be threatening to certain individuals, and the safeguard of intellectualization, like many other protective devices, is quite appropriate if not carried to an extreme. Through the device of intellectualization, we are able to detach ourselves from situations that might require us to act more emotionally than we wish. Teachers, nurses, policemen, and so on are prone to intellectualize emotional situations and, as a result, are often perceived by others as detached and undemonstrative. Moderate intellectualization is a merit for most of us, since the control of emotions contributes to logical thinking and to effective action under duress. Excessive intellectualization, however, may result in role-playing or in other forms of self-delusion. The student who does not express how he or she really feels but hides behind abstract pursuits (such as music or art) may find the ordinary activities of life uninteresting and may begin to experience a general feeling of emptiness, weariness, and depression as a result of this imbalance.

Rationalization

Incident

Tom had called several girls for a date over the weekend and had been refused by each. In spite of his disappointment and his feelings of unpopularity and even physical unattractiveness, he returned to his residence hall and announced to his roommates that he had to stay in all weekend to prepare a paper to hand in on Monday and to study for a quiz Tuesday. Obviously, these were not the real reasons for his remaining in the dorm to study; however, these reasons were acceptable to him and to his friends. It was easier for him to make up reasonable excuses than to admit his feelings of rejection and humiliation.

Rationalization is a mechanism by which we create plausible reasons to justify acts or ideas that are actually based on altogether different reasons. By relying on this device, we may excuse failures or condone acts that would otherwise damage our self-esteem. Rationalization is a mechanism frequently used by students. The student who shows undesirable behavior (cheating, drinking, studying just enough to get by) may attempt to make such behavior appear reasonable and even justified by insisting that "everybody else does it" or that social experience is a more valuable part of life than formal education.

Devaluation

Incident

Although Judy was selected as one of the finalists in a beauty contest, she failed to win. She consequently declared that "beauty is only skin deep" and that "brains are what really count." She went on to note that it was superficial to seek out others merely on the basis of physical appearance and that beauty contests ought to be abolished because they emphasized false and misleading values. In fact, she continued, she was glad not to have won the contest because she respected herself too much to be known only as a pretty girl. People, she felt, should admire her for her personality and intellect rather than for her physical appearance. Finally, Judy expressed contempt for any girl who aspired to enter a beauty contest.

Devaluation is a form of rationalization through which we minimize the importance of an event or condition in order to render it less threatening or painful. The student who receives a low grade in a course can feel less anxious about it when he says to himself or to others that the course has no real purpose in his curriculum or that what is to be learned in the course will never be of use to him. Thus, we often prefer to "believe" that a goal was not worth attaining rather than to admit that we simply failed to reach it.

While devaluating our environment may sometimes enhance our self-importance, in the long run this mechanism may cause further anxiety. If we constantly depreciate others, we invariably alienate ourselves from them. Further, we may tend to generalize from one devalued incident to similar incidents. If, for instance, we have devalued one English teacher, we may similarly depreciate all instructors in that department, or, indeed, all teachers.

Denial

Incident

Marianne was scheduled for doctoral examinations but seemed relatively unconcerned about the ordeal of facing a panel of professors and answering difficult questions. She claimed that the instructors knew her and the quality of her work because she had taken courses with them in the past. She felt they had always liked her and that there was no reason to fear failure now. She added that her professors were basically understanding persons who were there to help rather than to hinder her progress toward an advanced degree. She felt no compelling need to study intensively or to worry about the approaching exams.

Denial is a special form of rationalization in which we refuse to accept a fact as fact when it represents a major threat. Relying on this device, we may, at least temporarily, avoid a real problem by refusing to accept it as a threatening or unpleasant actuality. The student who was rejected by his girlfriend or who received a bad grade may refuse to admit to himself for days that these events really happened. He deceives himself by pretending that nothing harmful actually occurred; and indeed, he continues to function as if nothing had actually happened. If he did admit that these events occurred, he would become anxious and unhappy.

The mechanism of denial undoubtedly enables us to find temporary protection from threatening situations and to experience less anxiety. In the course of time, the threat may diminish, or we may become able to cope with it more effectively; for example, if we can counter with alternate plans, the impact of facing failure is less traumatic. Excessive and prolonged denial, however, can prevent the discovery of realistic solutions. At best, this mechanism allows us to "turn off" those aspects of our environment that threaten us, and we tend to become more interested and involved in areas of our lives that enhance our well-being and self-esteem. At worst, denial merely allows us to postpone what must be eventually faced. In some instances, for example, a person may not strive to overcome the problem that originally caused him or her to use the mechanism of denial. When the problem is not resolved, the unavoidable confrontation with the problem sometime in the future may bring on more distress.

UNDERSTANDING MALADJUSTMENT

Psychologists prefer not to label maladjusted behavior as "abnormal" or "sick," for the ominous connotations of those terms do little to help the person readjust. Instead, the terms *poor adjustment, maladjustment,* or *faulty adaptation* are preferred. Therapists often refer simply to the person's inadequate or mistaken ways of coping or to their deficient motivation.

Psychologists maintain that since an individual has learned to become maladjusted, he is also capable of learning other patterns of response and of ultimately achieving actualization. Often maladjustment is a direct result of a poor environment. Children of the ghetto, for instance, may experience difficulty in adjusting to public schools with a middle-class orientation; faulty childrearing practices may foster misconceptions or unresolved resentments, which may later hamper a child's adjustment to other authority figures. Poorly adjusted parents may provide poor models for their children to follow, and certain patterns of maladjustment may thereby be passed on from parent to child. Hereditary factors have also been thought to play a role in maladjustment, although evidence is not conclusive. Perhaps the cycle of maladjustment is best summarized by Bosselman (1969): If innate predispositions (intelligence, physical traits, efficiency for adapting) meet obstacles (social constraints, parental rejection, environmental deprivation, peer intimidation) in early development, the individual may seek rigid, over-blown defense mechanisms (projection, denial, regression, reaction formation, repression) in order to protect the personality under stress. Later, such an individual may meet with additional stress, which will further strengthen these defenses and possibly cause a severe type of maladjustment—even neurosis or psychosis.

Stress

When the demands of life seem threatening, we experience stress. Stress can also stem from physiological causes—from fatigue, disease, or injury—but our primary concern here will be with psychological stress resulting from our individual interpretations of interpersonal events. Stress is caused by such manifestations as fear of rejection, low self-esteem, anticipation of failure, and frustrated need for achievement—all of which make psychological demands that can overflow into physiological stress (for example, feeling tense before an exam or becoming frightened when someone is hurt). Psychologists attempt to help people cope with stress by eliminating it, by preparing them to overcome it, or by changing their attitudes toward it.

Maladjustment may develop when we are unable to change, when we are inflexible and cannot reach a compromise between need and stress, or when we fail to persist in a course of action that is necessary for effective functioning and self-enhancement (White & Watt, 1973). A college student's pouting to gain attention

Figure 5-3. We feel anguish even more when we go through a crisis without being able to share it with someone. Photo by Shirley Kontos.

and sympathy is an example of his or her inability to change—that is, develop behaviors that are consistent with chronological age—for such behavior is typical of a pre-school level of emotional development. Secondly, a person has to learn to respond differently to new situations. Changing a goal or a course of action often becomes necessary to reduce stress, and flexibility is important in reaching such a compromise. In other words, we should change our course of action when we realize that we cannot maintain the energy to achieve a certain goal. Finally, when a student develops skills in one area and neglects those in another—for example, emphasizing intellectual activity (studying) at the expense of social relationships (dating)—he often experiences an uneven growth that can make him anxious later on when he must confront change. His failure to develop more general skills for effective functioning creates undue stress.

We have seen how the inability to shift from one type of behavior to another, as demanded by the environment, can create a stressful situation, but the inability to continue what we are doing when we are threatened by stress can also signify maladjustment. Consider, for example, the high achiever who "gives up" because continued success implies more responsibility than he can handle or because he fears that his academic success is alienating him from his peers. Another example (Horner, 1972) involves women who fear success because such assertiveness is traditionally contrary to society's expectations and to the female stereotype. Despite their talents, women may avoid competition, choosing to forfeit success rather than to assume a role that might generate anxiety and result in rejection, resentment, and confusion.

Ineffective Ways of Coping

Too many changes in our behavior as a result of stress and conflicts may interfere with our work, with our interpersonal relationships, and even with our ability to express ourselves. Demands and expectations of parents, peers, and society at large can also reduce our ability to cope. Our emotions may get out of hand, and we may distort or misinterpret what we see around us. Repetitive failures, severe competition, prolonged frustrations, and the inability to satisfy our needs (love, belonging, security, esteem) can cause us to respond in nonadaptive ways. Let us consider here some of the ineffectual responses of maladjustment.

Neurosis. The most common emotional pattern of maladjustment is neurosis. A neurosis is usually caused by a conflict within oneself or with some aspect of the environment. It is often accompanied by anxiety or depression, which the individual senses acutely but is unable to control or lessen (Coleman, 1964). The neurotic person does not experience disorganized thinking or gross distortion of his perception of reality, but his coping mechanisms usually become rigid and exaggerated in order to help him control the anxiety. If these coping devices are too weak, anxiety may "spill over," causing what is known as "free floating" anxiety. The individual may then experience such physical disturbances as headaches, stomach cramps, fatigue, crying spells, insomnia. Medication may be used to reduce these interfering physical symptoms so that the person, with the help of psychotherapy, can identify the locus of his anxieties and adopt better ways of coping. As he comes to understand the nature of his conflict, he can learn to respond to it in ways that do not produce anxiety. He may learn to avoid anxiety-producing situations or to adopt a different attitude toward them.

Occasionally, the psychological symptoms of neurosis are strengthened and maintained so that the person may win attention, hold control over others, run away from responsibilities, gain material rewards and special privileges, and, of course, make others feel sorry for him.

There are neuroses other than those producing anxiety and depression: phobic neurosis, obsessive-compulsive neurosis, conversion neurosis, and dissociative neurosis (American Psychiatric Association, 1968). *Phobic neurosis* refers to a fear of an object or situation (dogs, heights, darkness) that is out of proportion to the real threat. Such a fear is often recognized as irrational and inappropriate by the person affected, but he or she is unable to do anything to lessen the fear. Individuals experiencing an *obsessive-compulsive neurosis* are overly concerned with certain aspects of living (cleanliness, punctuality, politeness) and literally drive themselves to behave in certain ways. Such people become anxious if they do not perform these compulsive acts. They may, however, become even more anxious when they realize that they cannot get rid of these undesirable symptoms. In *conversion neurosis,* an individual develops severe physical symptoms that have no organic basis. These may become so severe that they prevent the individual from working effectively or relating to other persons. A *dissociative neurosis* involves the temporary loss of identity in the form of amnesia or fugue, usually in situations that are causing an individual anxiety. By obliterating himself, so to speak, he avoids facing the threatening situation. These four neuroses do not commonly occur; however, anxiety and depression as described earlier under general neurosis are frequently found.

Psychosis. Psychosis is the most severe and incapacitating type of maladjustment. Psychotics have lost contact with reality, are not fully competent to manage their personal affairs, exhibit inappropriate behavior and illogical reasoning, and tend not to be accountable for their behavior, although this last point is controversial (Szasz, 1961). Some therapists, for example, feel that psychotics are aware that their behavior is different from others' behavior and that being labeled "psychotic" absolves them from the responsibilities of life. They prefer to be taken care of by society, even though they are capable of working and of contributing to society when they work under structured and supervised conditions. If the psychotic person has deteriorated to the point of incoherent and bizarre behavior, he is potentially dangerous to himself and to others, and hospitalization may be required.

Psychotic persons usually do not have the emotional stamina and interest in the environment to aspire for achievement or to compete. They are usually too preoccupied with themselves to have much time for other things. Their moods are apt to change abruptly, and their behavior is often irrational.

In the lower socioeconomic sectors of society where the stress of living conditions is great, there seems to be a greater incidence of psychosis (Hollingshead & Redlich, 1958). These sectors of society tend to limit enriching experiences and espouse more rigid attitudes toward life, which make it difficult for their members to handle stress effectively. Psychotics generally cannot tolerate change, and their simple and rather negative views about life tend to make them fatalistic and self-depreciatory. The independence and resourcefulness required in the competitive college scene place additional pressure on the psychotic individual. In certain borderline cases psychotic persons have a keen insight into their personalities and maintain excellent contact with the world. For example, a small number of psychotic students are able to attain excellent grades (Kiersch & Nikelly, 1966).

Psychosis may have an organic (bodily) basis; that is, damage to the tissues of the nervous system or brain (concussion, tumor, lesion), toxic substances in the blood stream (alcohol, arsenic, barbiturates, infection), or deterioration of the brain cells or arteries due to old age may significantly alter an individual's psychological responses. In such instances, the psychosis may be acute (for example, in the case of a brain infection) or chronic (for example, the gradual deterioration of the brain in old age). Symptoms of acute psychosis include memory loss, disorientation of time and space, intellectual impairment, and poor judgment. Chronic symptoms may include erratic manners, eccentric behavior not previously displayed, changes in speech and gait, and alteration of mood. Medical intervention is usually indicated in the treatment of organic brain disorders (Rosen & Gregory, 1965). Organic psychosis may appear suddenly and disappear after a short time with no appreciable organic deterioration. Reactions to psychedelic drugs, alcoholic intoxication, or infection are examples of this kind of psychotic reaction; that is, the person returns to normal after the toxic substance has been eliminated from the body. For the most part, however, psychotic behavior is caused by environmental factors—one's early childhood experiences or a sudden and unpleasant unexpected event. This type of psychosis is called functional psychosis because the symptoms are not based on any known physiological change or damage.

There are several types of functional psychoses, but the most common is schizophrenia—a condition characterized by a loss of interest in the environment, by a lack of initiative, or by emotional withdrawal and little feeling about things. Nearly two-thirds of the patients in mental hospitals in the United States are schizophrenics, and the odds are that one in every 100 persons in the United States will develop schizophrenic symptoms (Lehmann, 1967). Schizophrenic characteristics include regression (often to an almost infant level), inappropriate or blunt emotions, strange or bizarre ideas, and fantasies that are not validated by consensual experiences. One drastic form of psychosis is the paranoid type of schizophrenia, during which an individual entertains delusions (false beliefs) that make him think of himself as strong and powerful (Coleman, 1964), hallucinates (sees and hears things that are not there), and often becomes violent and even threatening to others whom he feels are against him (American Psychiatric Association, 1968). Hospitalization and medical intervention are often necessary.

Current treatment for psychotic persons consists of a combination of several approaches including family therapy, social habilitation, vocational training, group psychotherapy, and drug therapy. Medication can be effective in preventing or reducing the recurrence of psychotic symptoms, but a cure involves long-term treatment. The student must be given support by those around him and enabled to utilize his talents to become a useful member of society.

Personality disorders. Individuals with personality disorders usually do not experience conflict or anxiety, as they do with neuroses; instead they seek to externalize their problems through outward actions. They do not generally develop psychological symptoms but often respond in immature ways that may upset others and run counter to the values and regulations upheld by society; they are often referred to as deviant, antisocial, or sociopathic. Thus, passive and strongly socially sensitive people, rigid and inhibited individuals, aggressive persons who get into trouble with their friends or with the law, alcoholics, drug abusers, delinquents, or sexually deviant persons all may exhibit personality disorders that tend to create conflict for them with others, with authority, with the law, and with society's moral code. Such people usually cannot handle frustration effectively and often become indecisive, rowdy, defiant, manipulative, dependent, or demanding. They are often quite able to rationalize their behavior, even though they give in to impulsive expression at the expense of others and with little consideration for the possible consequences.

There are several underlying factors associated with personality disorders, especially those of an antisocial nature. Some authorities maintain that a hereditary weakness is present—an innate inability to learn social values, to adapt, or to become properly socialized (White & Watt, 1973). Such an explanation may be comforting to therapists who often feel helpless to change antisocial personalities; however, not everyone holds such a pessimistic view. Some psychologists argue that neglectful and rejecting parents who use inconsistent and punitive discipline foster antisocial behavior in their children (McCord, McCord, & Zola, 1959). Aronfreed (1968) believes that those with personality disorders have not been exposed to proper learning experiences from their parents and have not had the opportunity to incorporate the moral values of society into their own personalities. Reasons for this may be that association with peers who displayed antisocial or deviant behaviors strongly affected their development or that such behavior "paid off" and was thus reinforced in them. In short, they never learned to behave as socially responsible persons. Although they may exhibit excellent verbal abilities, there is little underlying feeling to reinforce their verbalizations; in other words, there is no empathy, genuineness, or social consciousness—the hallmarks of the self-actualized person (Cleckley, 1964).

The exaggerated personality disorders are the ones of significant consequence. Let us consider several of these commonly observed personality disorders in more detail. Passive-aggressive persons may cope with pressure by withdrawal or inactivity; they may seek support from others on the one hand or show opposition and obstructionism toward them on the other. Such people often manipulate others by being overly passive, indecisive, or stubborn. Uncontrollable outbursts of anger in the face of stress mark the aggressive side of the personality, while the passive side is often exhibited by poor judgment, a frequent change in goals, or poor coping strategies. Hysterical persons are prone to emotional, vain, and dramatic bids for attention; such behavior may sometimes be seductive. Mood swings from euphoria and optimism to feelings of futility and hopelessness without apparent cause are typical of the cyclothymic personality.

A number of patterns of deviant sexual behavior may also fall within the general category of personality disorder. Exhibitionism, which involves exposing oneself (usually the genitals) to a member of the opposite sex, is one such example. Sadism and masochism (the giving and receiving of pain in association with sexual pleasure) and voyeurism (the compulsive need to view persons as they undress or have sexual relations) are other examples. Fetishism (the direction of sexual interest to objects or parts of the body, such as underwear, perfume, or legs, that have only symbolic value in representing a real person) and transvestism (the wearing of clothes typical of the opposite sex) constitute still other types of personality disorder. Fear of the opposite sex, feelings of sexual inadequacy, punishment and subsequent guilt for appropriate sexual interest as a child, unpleasant experiences during the period of psychosexual development, and, occasionally, biological factors are possible explanations of sexually deviant behavior (Eaton & Peterson, 1969). Psychotherapy is often helpful in these cases, especially when such problems are detected at an early age and when the person wants to change his or her behavior.

Suicide. Suicide, the second leading cause of death among college students, is of growing concern to parents and faculty alike. Although the suicide rate among college students seems slightly higher than that of the noncollege population (Farnsworth, 1966), the differences noted may be due in part to the more accurate reportings of suicides in college.

While some suicide attempts are made by psychotic individuals, most attempts are made by persons who are responding to a stressful or critical situation that they feel they can handle in no other way. Despondent persons who have no resources for help or who lack the personal stamina and flexibility to deal effectively with stress situations may seek a way out through suicide. Although some suicide attempts are made only to gain attention and to elicit sympathy, many are genuine distress signals that signify that the individual is experiencing a situation with which he or she cannot cope. Suicide attempts are sometimes an individual's way of retaliation; the individual may hope to "get even" with someone who has failed him, to make others feel guilty, to force them to succumb to his wishes, or to punish them for not having given in to his desires (Karon, 1964). In short, the suicidal threat or attempt is often a hostile message intended to stir up guilt feelings or responsibility in some other person.

Since guilt is often felt by persons with suicidal thoughts, suicide attempts may be viewed as efforts to avoid responsibility for past actions. When an individual admits his guilt by threatening suicide, he may win the sympathy of others and may make his transgression appear less serious. In short, his declaration of guilt may mean to him that he need suffer no further consequences.

Suicide attempts are usually precipitated by a specific situation of family or interpersonal conflict. A follow-up study of 45 adolescent suicide attempts revealed that these persons had often made previous attempts that had gone unnoticed or ignored (Barter, Swaback, & Todd, 1968). Although we cannot generalize from one study to all suicides, this finding contrasts with the popular notion that those who threaten suicide never really carry out their intentions. Those young people who required hospitalization often made subsequent suicide attempts after leaving the hospital, usually in conjunction with conflict at home. The rate of suicidal behavior was significantly higher among those adolescents who had sustained difficulties with parents, who had suffered the loss of a parent or of another close person, who had maintained a limited social life, or who were dependent on others for emotional support.

What brings more college students to suicide than their noncollege peers? A thorough study of suicides in college (Bruyn & Seiden, 1965) reveals that most of these young people had given previous warnings of their intentions and were experiencing emotional problems of various sorts. The precipitating factors in these suicides were poor interpersonal relationships, social withdrawal, personal rejection, feelings of alienation, excessive worry about academic work, and undue concern over physical symptoms. Other reasons for suicides among college students involve disappointment with love relationships, frustration with grades, feelings of low self-worth, alienation, loneliness, and lack of life goals. Fortunately, many potential suicides can be averted through proper psychological intervention.

SUMMARY

We no longer need to view ourselves as "ill" when we experience personal problems or find that we are not coping well with the problems of everyday life, since most of us have abandoned the idea that everyone must reflect an ideal pattern of normalcy. We have found that we are free to grow and to become what we are without constant comparisons to theoretical means or norms.

For our purposes, the best definition of normality involves the progressive course of psychological growth, in which an individual is without significant incapacitating symptoms and is generally moving toward satisfying intrapersonal (within oneself) and interpersonal relationships; in short, such a person feels at home with his self and with society. Such normality involves understanding goals and developing the ability to cope with stress.

We have discussed the function of goals—how we need to choose them and to discriminate among them, having in mind the consequences that might follow.

To cope with stress we may rely upon the natural protection within us called defense devices. Such mechanisms allow us to reduce anxiety and feelings of failure over small problems and to "let off steam in spurts," thereby preventing an intolerable build-up of tension. Bypassing the real problem is not necessarily ideal behavior, but it may prove to be a temporarily more desirable course of action than facing the "cold facts." As long as our efficiency and our social functioning are not impaired, we need not fear these mechanisms. Indeed, the ability to identify these devices of behavior in ourselves is a sign of being mentally sound.

While most personal problems and conflicts fall within a range that the average person can handle for himself, there are psychological symptoms that are severely incapacitating and require professional intervention. Unfortunately, many persons would rather tolerate a marginal, frustrating existence than seek counseling or therapy.

Many of the specific causes of maladjustment are not fully understood; in most instances a combination of heredity and social, family, and personal factors are responsible. Our attitudes toward those who are severely maladjusted are changing for the better through increased understanding of the factors associated with emotional problems. We no longer regard such persons as "sick," deliberately irresponsible, or innately incorrigible; instead, we tend to consider the severely maladjusted as persons who have not had the opportunity to learn appropriate coping behavior, who have not experienced positive rewards in their lives, and who have not found growth-producing environments wherein they can build fulfilling interpersonal relationships.

Psychosis is a major departure from the ordinary symptoms of emotional problems and represents an unreal and faulty perception of reality that renders personal adjustment extremely difficult if not impossible. Neurotic manifestations are expressed typically in the form of anxiety or depression and are relatively easier to manage, as the person is in basic contact with reality. Psychophysiological problems are physical complaints that reflect emotional conflicts; these disorders usually involve organs of the body that are innervated by the autonomic nervous system, which, in turn, is significantly affected by our emotions. Our behavior can also become maladjusted through damage to or the degeneration and poisoning of various brain or nerve cells; these are organic disorders, which may be acute or chronic. Personal peculiarities that are not generally disturbing unless they are highly out of proportion are referred to as personality disorders. Suicide attempts are often a plea for attention or a means of communicating anger and may reflect a genuine emotional problem.

The behavior of the vast majority of college students falls within the reasonably well-adjusted range. Most of those who seek professional help for their problems do so because they wish to become more competent in their social relationships, to alter aspects of themselves they do not like, and to learn to cope more effectively with various pressures both in and out of college.

QUESTIONS TO THINK ABOUT

1. Have you ever felt anxious about something or depressed over an unpleasant situation? How long did these feelings last, and what did you do about them?
2. Have you ever done things that brought on feelings of anxiety or depression? Looking back now, what might you have done to prevent these feelings from coming?
3. Which of the defense mechanisms described in this chapter do you rely on? How do they help you to feel better?
4. Which of the defense mechanisms do you feel would not restrict your efforts to actualize yourself? Which ones do you think might limit self-actualization?
5. Have you ever noticed others using defense mechanisms of which they were not aware? Were these people effective in maintaining adjustment? Were there possible dangers?
6. Can you think of any defense mechanisms that you learned from your parents? Can you recall an experience from childhood that you think caused you to begin using a mechanism that you continued to use because it lessened your feelings of inadequacy or increased your self-esteem? Explain the situation. Do you still rely on that mechanism?
7. Are there any defense mechanisms that you feel you have only recently adopted? If so, can you explain why there are such recent additions to your behavior repertoire?

REFERENCES

American Psychiatric Association. *Diagnostic and statistical manual of mental disorders* (2nd ed.). APA, Washington, D.C.: Author, 1968.
Aronfreed, J. *Conduct and conscience.* New York: Academic Press, 1968.

Ayd, F. J., Jr. *Recognizing the depressed patient.* New York: Grune & Stratton, 1961.

Baker, R. W. Incidence of psychological disturbance in college students. *The Journal of the American College Health Association,* 1965, *13*(4), 532-540.

Barter, J. T., Swaback, D. O., & Todd, D. Adolescent suicide attempts: A follow-up study of hospitalized patients. *Archives of General Psychiatry,* 1968, *19*(5), 523-527.

Bosselman, B. C. *Neurosis and psychosis* (3rd ed.). Springfield, Ill.: Thomas, 1969.

Bruyn, H. B., & Seiden, R. H. Student suicide: Fact or fancy? *The Journal of the American College Health Association,* 1965, *14*(2), 69-77.

Cleckley, H. M. *The mask of sanity* (4th ed.). St. Louis: Mosby, 1964.

Coleman, J. C. *Abnormal psychology and modern life.* (3rd ed.). Glenview, Ill.: Scott, Foresman, 1964.

Coleman, J. C. *Contemporary psychology and effective behavior.* Glenview, Ill.: Scott, Foresman, 1974.

Coping with depression. *Newsweek,* January 8, 1973, 51-54.

Deutsch, A., & Ellenberg, J. Transience vs. continuance of disturbances in college freshmen. *Archives of General Psychiatry,* 1973, *28*(3), 412-417.

Eaton, M. T., Jr., & Peterson, M. H. *Psychiatry* (2nd ed.). Flushing, N.Y.: Medical Examination Publishing Company, 1969.

Farnsworth, D. L. *Psychiatry, education, and the young adult.* Springfield, Ill.: Thomas, 1966.

Farnsworth, D. L. College mental health and social change. *Annals of Internal Medicine,* 1970, *73*(3), 467-473.

Freud, S. *A general introduction to psychoanalysis.* Garden City, N.Y.: Garden City Publishing Company, 1938.

Guilford, J. P. *Personality.* New York: McGraw-Hill, 1959.

Hall, C. S., & Lindzey, G. *Theories of personality.* New York: Wiley, 1957.

Hershey, G. L., & Lugo, J. O. *Living psychology.* New York: Macmillan, 1970.

Hollingshead, A. B., & Redlich, F. C. *Social class and mental illness: A community study.* New York: Wiley, 1958.

Horner, M. S. Toward an understanding of achievement-related conflicts in women. *The Journal of Social Issues,* 1972, *28*(2), 157-175.

Horney, K. *The neurotic personality of our time.* New York: Norton, 1937.

Karon, B. P. Suicidal tendency as the wish to hurt someone else. *Journal of Individual Psychology,* 1964, *20*(2), 206-212.

Kiersch, T. A., & Nikelly, A. G. The schizophrenic in college. *Archives of General Psychiatry,* 1966, *15*(1), 54-58.

Kolb, L. C. *Modern clinical psychiatry* (8th ed.). Philadelphia: Saunders, 1973.

Laughlin, H. P. *The neuroses.* Washington, D.C.: Butterworth, 1967.

Lazarus, R. S. *Personality and adjustment.* Englewood Cliffs, N.J.: Prentice-Hall, 1963.

Lehmann, H. E. Schizophrenia. I: Introduction and history. In A. M. Freedman & H. I. Kaplan (Eds.), *Comprehensive textbook of psychiatry.* Baltimore: Williams & Wilkins, 1967.

Lief, H. I. Anxiety reaction. In A. M. Freedman & H. I. Kaplan (Eds.), *Comprehensive textbook of psychiatry.* Baltimore: Williams & Wilkins, 1967.

Mahrer, A. R. Interpretation of patient behavior through goals, feelings, and context. *Journal of Individual Psychology,* 1970, *26*(2), 186-195.

McCord, W., McCord, J., & Zola, L. K. *Origins of crime.* New York: Columbia University Press, 1959.

Mendelson, M. Neurotic depressive reaction. In A. M. Freedman & H. I. Kaplan (Eds.), *Comprehensive textbook of psychiatry.* Baltimore: Williams & Wilkins, 1967.

Nikelly, A. G. Goal-directedness: A practical goal for psychotherapy. *Mental Hygiene,* 1962, *46*(4), 523-526.

Nixon, R. E. A challenge for the college mental health service. *Student Medicine,* 1960, *8*(4), 340-343.

Offer, D. Normal adolescents. *Archives of General Psychiatry,* 1967, *17*(3), 285-290.

Reifler, C. B., & Liptzin, M. B. Epidemiological studies of college mental health. *Archives of General Psychiatry,* 1969, *20*(5), 528-540.

Roche Laboratories. *Aspects of anxiety.* Philadelphia: Lippincott, 1968.

Rosen, E., & Gregory, I. *Abnormal psychology.* Philadelphia: Saunders, 1965.

Seiden, R. H. Campus tragedy: A study of student suicide. *Journal of Abnormal Psychology,* 1966, *71*(6), 389-399.

Srole, L., Langner, T., Michael, S., Opler, M., & Rennie, T. *Mental health in the metropolis.* New York: McGraw-Hill, 1962.

Szasz, T. S. *The myth of mental illness.* New York: Harper & Row, 1961.

Walters, O. S. Prevalence of diagnosed emotional disorders in university students. *The Journal of the American College Health Association,* 1970, *18*(3), 204-209.

White, R. W. *Lives in progress.* New York: Holt, 1964.

White, R. W., & Watt, N. F. *The abnormal personality* (4th ed.). New York: Ronald Press, 1973.

Chapter 6

Learning, Coping, and Communicating

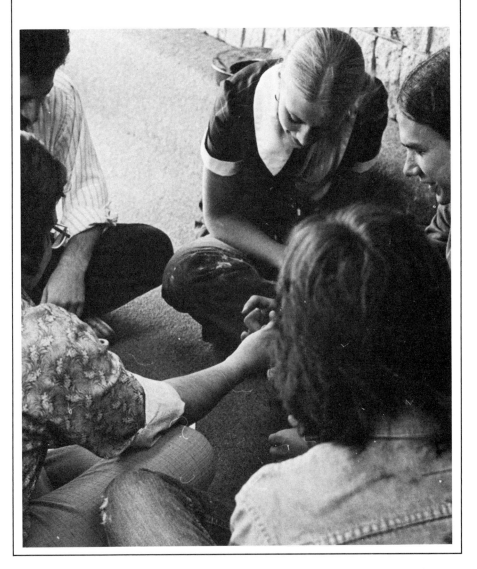

CHAPTER OUTLINE

I. How we learn

II. Better ways to solve problems
   A. Studying effectively
   B. Planning ahead
   C. Gaining from experiencing failure
   D. Avoiding fallacious thinking

III. Understanding coping behavior
   A. What is coping?
   B. Can competence for coping be developed?
   C. Ways of coping
      1. Neutralizing stress
         a. Concession
         b. Toleration
         c. Changing our attitudes
         d. Disengagement
         e. Restructuring
         f. Blocking
      2. Achieving psychological equilibrium

IV. Communication
   A. Levels of verbal communication
   B. Can verbal communication be improved?
   C. Nonverbal communication

V. Summary

The fast pace of change, the increased demands of American living, the new skills needed for us to keep up with ever-progressing ideas and experiences—all these require us to think fast, act quickly, relate well with others, and learn rapidly if we are to behave effectively. We find ourselves constantly pushing ahead and relying on self-direction, on our own skills and experiences, and on our own beliefs and goals rather than on traditional values or the "old way" of doing things. In spite of this orientation toward the self, however, we often find it difficult to experience personal growth and fulfillment within the sometimes fractured, always pressured, contemporary life mode. If we are to achieve actualization as well as enjoy satisfying interpersonal relations, we must facilitate and maintain our abilities to learn and to cope with stress and become competent in sending, receiving, and interpreting verbal information.

HOW WE LEARN

Learning involves gaining knowledge, skills, experience, and understanding that produce a lasting and observable change in behavior. What we think of ourselves, what kind of goals we have, and the quality of our past experiences all affect our learning processes.

Learning processes often involve the use of language and the ability to discriminate when and how to respond to another person. Indeed, effective functioning depends to a large extent on the quality of verbal communication. Words can convey abstract concepts and enable us to communicate rapidly and effectively. The use of words to express feelings is extremely important in achieving self-actualization. Being able to verbalize important experiences can give us relief from pent-up emotions and open new vistas of self-understanding.

There are two broad categories of learning: conditional and instrumental. Conditioning generally means that learning is fostered by something from outside the learner. In instrumental learning, however, the learner occupies a more active position.

The learner is normally *passive* in conditional learning even though his nervous system is learning from stimulus cues. He associates objects and labels, behavior and words and, as a result, is able to make new relationships and draw inferences and conclusions. A consciousness of selfhood emerges as he applies verbal ideas to his own behavior. A word by itself, in the absence of stimuli, can also arouse a response; that is, the word takes the place of the thing it represents. Assume, for example, that a young person associates the word *love* with acceptance, affection, and esteem. Later, the word love need only be mentioned for him to experience a pleasant sensation. The human mind makes a vast number of associations of this type; thus we may respond to word symbols in emotional ways without always fully understanding how these associations were initially formed. As the nervous system and brain mature, what were once relatively simple associations become a vast network of connecting symbols that are activated by many possible combinations of stimuli at a particular moment. Responses that produce satisfaction are reinforced, while pain-producing responses are avoided. Suppose that a young man meets a person with blonde hair for the first time and likes him almost immediately without really knowing him at all. A possible explanation involves his having generalized pleasant associations with blondes in the past to all blonde-haired persons. If, however, a blonde *girl* rejects him, he may begin to discriminate among blonde-haired persons according to sex. If he later meets a blonde girl who does not reject him, however, the association of rejection may disappear; the association with rejection becomes extinct. A relatively new technique that helps us unlearn undesirable conditioning is referred to as behavior-modification therapy and is discussed in Chapter 10.

In instrumental learning, we obtain results from what we do, from our actions. When we say or do something that brings pleasant results, our actions are reinforced; but when our actions produce harmful results, that behavior is abandoned. If, for example, you do not date because you are shy, you can acquire some social know-how, apply it, and perhaps obtain some good results; these social skills, then, become ingrained because they worked for you. The social skills were learned, as in conditioned learning, but the initiative came from your own actions. Instrumental learning, like conditioning, can take place automatically and without our full knowledge of its process. Four contingencies are necessary if instrumental learning is to be effective. We must be motivated to act, and the act must be followed by a reward. We must be able to produce the correct response, and, should we fail, we must be motivated to try until we succeed.

Social behavior is also governed by the fact that we tend to copy the behavior of those who are significant to us, a behavior pattern called *modeling*. Teachers often use this method to change undesirable behavior into more acceptable forms; they provide themselves as a "model" for effective behavior that the student can adopt as his own, or they discuss experiences of others in history, literature, or current events who have shown judgment, coping behavior, benevolent actions, rational thinking, or the ability to make positive decisions.

BETTER WAYS TO SOLVE PROBLEMS

Before you consider solving a problem, it might be helpful to gather all the facts related to it. The more you know about what can be done, the greater the number of alternatives you will have at your disposal and the easier it will be to discover a realistic and effective solution. Unbending attitudes and rigid approaches only limit your ability to choose a workable solution. Try to set aside stereotypes and biases about people or events or you may blind yourself to the very solution you are seeking. It is often helpful to consult others, for their objective viewpoints may suggest alternatives that you were totally unaware of.

Stress or preoccupation with personal matters hampers our ability to make decisions. Flaws in our reasoning, such as depending on generalizations, faulty logic, wrong conclusions, and circular reasoning, may also prevent us from arriving at reasonable solutions. Decisions made under emotional pressure are generally less successful than those made with deliberation and careful study of the consequences. However, the most important part of the decision-making process is to abide by the choice you have made.

Studying Effectively

Since the earliest times, there has been a philosophical tendency to separate the rational or intellectual aspect of humans from their emotional nature. Ideally, there is a balance and fusion between these two aspects, but frequently one develops out of proportion to the other. There is the stereotype of the intellectual—controlled, precise, articulate, detached—and the stereotype of the emotional person—impulsive, involved, erratic. Yet individuals cannot achieve their potential when they stifle one part of their nature. We have discussed how emotional competence can be strengthened; now let us consider how we may improve the quality of our intellectual responses, which deeply affect our self-esteem and overall fulfillment.

Since students' ability to learn is judged by the quality of their academic work, let us consider first the problem of how to study. Long hours of study without intermission or diversion are not as effective as distributed study periods interspersed with physical activities. When the material you study is relevant to your goals, your motivation to study will naturally be stronger. Assessment of your work—from teachers, peers, and yourself—helps you to understand your deficiencies and to capitalize on your strengths. Some tasks are more easily learned when there is a carry-over between tasks. For example, from math you can switch to physics with little difficulty (positive shift); one subject may assist in the learning of the other. However, a science major may have difficulty in determining the meaning of a poetic passage that she finds alien to her major interest (negative shift).

There are other factors that seem to govern effective learning: a clear idea of why you want to learn, an environment conducive to study, efficient study skills—note taking, summarizing, reviewing, and the use of study aids when necessary—and the use of tutors, tapes, outlines, and charts (Voeks, 1970).

Mental flexibility also facilitates intellectual growth because it encourages us to solve problems in innovative ways. As problems change, so must our skills. Indeed, this tenet is as important in coping with life's problems as it is in coping with academic situations. Flexible attitudes keep us functioning within realistic limits; at the same time such flexibility fosters new solutions and intellectual growth.

Incident

I always wondered why I was in college in the first place, because I had difficulty doing my work from the very beginning. There were many times

Figure 6-1. Living in the academic world is often very different from living in the real world. Photo by Shirley Kontos.

when I would usually want to flip through a magazine or watch the tube rather than do the work I was supposed to do. My grades were getting low, and I worried quite a bit. Then I talked it over with a couple of my friends who were doing above-average work, and they gave me some pointers. For one thing, they told me that I daydreamed too much, thinking about what I could do and what I should do. (I would always see myself at the beach in Fort Lauderdale.) They made me realize that I wasn't happy, and therefore I couldn't study my best. It's not that I'm not bright or not college material; it's because my mind grazes at other, more pleasurable, pastures to make up for what I lack here.

Well, these friends sort of moved me into action, and the first thing that happened was that I started studying with some new female friends I had made. At least I could talk with a girl while I worked. As my elaborate daydreams lessened, I began to do better academically. I was praised for my enthusiasm and dedication, and this really helped, especially when the praise came from these female friends. Once I felt that others were taking notice of me, I began to feel more motivated to study. I wanted to be here, to belong to this place, because I had something going for me here. Man, I tell you, life is much brighter when someone tells you you're a good guy.

Planning Ahead

Even though we sometimes seem to have little control over our thoughts and feelings, we can control our actions. We are generally free to choose a particular action, depending on its immediate consequences for us and its influence on our future. For example, quitting school for easy money may restrict a person to a lifetime of uninteresting employment, and chronic criticism and complaint may sentence a person to a lonely life or superficial relationships. The list can go on and on. We have the power to avoid an action because of undesirable consequences or to perform an action because we want certain consequences. If you think some people are "just lucky" or that "things always turn out" for them, perhaps you should observe their behavior more closely. Almost inevitably their present (and past) actions are the determinants of their future situation.

Incident

My grandparents used to tell me that the wise man begins cooking his dinner before he gets hungry. Well, I didn't pay any attention to that saying until I got to college. There I discovered that you can't let things go for too long without experiencing trouble. I had the attitude that things will perk up by themselves and that everything will work itself out. Well, I learned one thing fast; success doesn't come on its own. I nearly flunked out my first semester, but I did learn that you've got to do something to make success happen. My roommate said it even better; you have to give something if you want to get something. I know this doesn't always work, but there's a lot of truth in it. I began to think out what I wanted from life, from college, from people, and then I set out to earn these things. When I got myself in order, things began to happen in the order that I expected and wanted. It's not that my goals and values became materialistic or exploitive, it's just that I began to see how the future is seeded by the present.

Gaining from Experiencing Failure

Some of us find it difficult to follow advice or example and must learn through experience—even at the price of repeated failure or pain. We can become aware of the likely consequences of certain actions by listening to what others tell us or by experiencing the situation ourselves; however, learning through actual experience (called *processing* by O'Connell and O'Connell, 1974) often has a more lasting effect on us. Reading and discussing are useless experiences unless they eventually result in direct action that solves a problem. The following situation illustrates this point.

Incident

My younger sister dropped out of high school and married against my parents' wishes. They tried to tell her what it would be like to be married to an irresponsible, happy-go-lucky guy like Joe, but nothing they said really got to her. She went ahead and got married anyway. Joe was only a year older than my sister and didn't want to sentence himself to an 8 to 5 job. He had dropped out of high school too and couldn't find a decent job anyway. A year later my sister got a divorce. She came home and clerked in the grocery store while she finished earning her high school credits. We all loved her at home, and we still do. She went on to college, and now she is getting her Master's Degree in Special Education. She has learned her lesson, I guess, and she is dating a sensible, caring, and dependable guy whom she plans to marry eventually.

Avoiding Fallacious Thinking

From time to time we are unknowingly subjected to various types of erroneous information and persuasion. In a free society such as ours, a number of groups deliberately attempt to influence us to think and behave in a certain way. This distortion process generally involves *propaganda*, which relies heavily on emotional appeal. Propaganda is used for both positive and negative purposes in the mass media (newspapers, advertising, TV, radio, books, magazines) as well as in political speeches, religious pronouncements, and rumor. Of course, all of us influence one another in ways in which we cannot always be fully aware. But there are more obvious pitfalls in the area of communication that we can avoid when we recognize them as false and do not allow them to influence us.

A comon propaganda technique is to attack the integrity and credibility of an individual rather than to criticize his or her actual thinking or deeds. Words like "radical," "Marxist," "subversive," "atheist," or "anti-American" are emotionally persuasive to persons who already have negative opinions about these adjectives. Another technique is to gather negative material with little or no regard for its validity and to ignore completely the other side of the story in order to prove a point. We can "prove" that a college education is not worth the money and time involved by gathering only statistics that show how wasteful it is to attend college; the contradictory facts can be deliberately omitted. A third way to influence people emotionally is to use socially acceptable descriptions or catch-all phrases in which little relevant information is offered. A candidate for political office may be a "real American," or Pepsi may make you feel "really free." However, neither of these descriptions really presents concise or significant information. Another technique for deceiving others is for a person to be represented as simple, honest, and just like everyone else in order to win over those who value such personal attributes. For instance, in Nazi Germany, Hitler often posed with children in order to foster a paternalistic image of himself, hoping to convince others to think well of him. Another technique is to associate a particular goal (usually undesirable) with an idea or symbol that people already believe in. For example, the war in Vietnam was for "honorable peace" and the preservation of democracy—ideals that many did not dare to question. Finally, persuading people to support an idea, product, or method of behavior on the premise that "so and so is doing it" (that is, asking people to jump on the bandwagon) can be used effectively to get across a desired message.

UNDERSTANDING COPING BEHAVIOR

While the mechanisms of defense considered in Chapter 5 operate automatically to lessen anxiety and to protect our self-esteem, we can also learn to cope by relying on our judgment, by utilizing past learning and experiences, and by examining our intentions. We can make a deliberate effort to investigate what is wrong and then act on the basis of a realistic assessment of the problem, of our abilities and resources, and of the logical consequences of our actions.

It is well to keep in mind that people making decisions today generally rely less on tradition and authority than they do on their own inner capacity and on the insight gained from previous experiences. Such a process is liberating, but it also places increased demands on the individual; he or she no longer expects to merely follow a code prescribed by society. Coping with these new demands can result in frustration (the inability to reach a goal) or in conflict (the inability to decide between two choices). However, contemporary society does provide general patterns of response, such as respecting the rights of others and focusing on behavior that will promote growth in others and benefit society, that allow for personal development while meeting certain societal expectations. Indeed, the degree to which self-actualization is achieved by individuals is contingent upon the extent to which they see themselves as part of the society. Problems arise when individual needs conflict with the values and experiences shared by others within the larger society. In other words, we need methods that we as individuals can use to circumvent or to solve some of these larger difficulties; we need to know when to "run away" and when to "stand and fight." Let us examine some of these methods in the following pages.

What Is Coping?

Coping refers to how we react to danger or threat (stress). The way we appraise threat (*primary appraisal*) depends on our needs, our convictions, and our knowledge of the possibilities for action. Our evaluation of the effectiveness of a particular coping pattern is termed *secondary appraisal* (Lazarus, 1966). Effective coping requires a realistic understanding of present needs, an awareness of alternatives, and the ability to discriminate between the available alternatives in order to initiate the most effective courses of action.

Lazarus (1966) observes that coping behavior is learned rather than instinctive, and that, under conditions of heightened stress, coping behavior may become more ineffective. "More adaptive and reality-oriented forms of coping are most likely when the threat is comparatively mild; under severe threat, pathological extremes become more prominent" (p. 162). Essentially, then, mild stress is dealt with through rational, constructive patterns of coping; but when we face severe stress, we may panic, regress, and become disorganized or even delusional. Feeling "low" for a month or two because your girlfriend left you and asking yourself why it happened is understandable, but developing a chronic sensitivity to what people say about you may become a serious nonadaptive pattern of behavior.

Coping with frustration is a frequent occurrence in everyday living. A feeling of tension is created when a psychological need is blocked or when it competes with other needs. Murray and his colleagues (1938) describe several important needs, or motives, that can involve us in conflict. The need to excel in activities that have social significance, the need for friendship (affiliation), the need, for some, to be influential and controlling are all motives that can create tension and fears. However, we must rely on our coping ability; we must choose from among alternative behaviors, basing our decision on a behavior's effect on ourselves as well as its consequences on others.

We may cope with stress through the manipulation of threatening conditions or persons so that they become potentially less dangerous. Lazarus (1969) notes that preparation against the possibility of threat helps to lower the anxiety associated with it, just as we build shelters against destructive weather or innoculate ourselves against disease. For example, one of my students adopted an interesting coping behavior to meet the stress of possible rejection when he asked for a date. He always made alternate plans in case the date did not come through so that he could switch to a second course of action immediately. This other course of action diverted him from brooding over rejection.

There are instances in which people may not perceive alternatives to stressful situations; they may become apathetic, inactive, and immobile. Severely depressed persons tend to behave in this manner, as they sense their inability to cope and their helplessness. Even in acute situations, however, coping ability is not usually as weak or the situation potentially as dangerous as the participant sees it.

Stress situations seem to be handled more effectively with a detached, analytical attitude. Lazarus, Opton, Nomikos, and Rankin (1965) showed a stress-inducing film (fingers being cut with a ripsaw) to a group of viewers; another group of viewers was told that the film had been performed by actors; a third group was asked to concentrate on the plot, on the interaction of characters, and on the outcome of the story, without concentrating on the personal injury. The emotional response in the last group, as measured by skin conductance and heart rate, was the lowest; the response of the middle group was intermediate; and the first group demonstrated the highest emotional-stress response. Thus, it seems that the less emotionally involved we are, the greater our ability to cope. Consider the surgeon and nurse who constantly deal with patients in critical situations; by remaining emotionally aloof, they are less likely to impair their judgment. But, the situation may be quite reversed if one is asked to intervene in a serious accident that involved a loved one.

Any situation that offers alternatives can cause stress and increase anxiety. When both alternatives are undesirable an avoidance-avoidance conflict is present—for example, having to choose between attending a boring lecture or staying home to cut the grass. When the choices are pleasant, an approach-approach conflict is in evidence—for example, choosing between an attractive date or a ride in a Jaguar. An approach-avoidance conflict refers to a pleasant/unpleasant combination—for example, desiring a college degree but being required to take courses that are uninteresting or irrelevant. Because most situations offer several options, making decisions becomes a laborious and perplexing process that can cause anxiety and discomfort.

When we seek to complete a task or solve a problem, we are confronted with several courses of action. First, we can make a direct assault, meeting the situation with constructive or destructive behavior. (In the latter instance increased anxiety and frustration will usually result.) We may attempt to manipulate the environment in order to accommodate our goals, or we may make an effort to change ourselves. Of course, effective action depends on an intelligent assessment of the facts in a given situation. Often we do not have enough facts to make the best decision, and so the most effective solution at that certain time may be to curtail efforts or to make only a partial decision. Second, we can withdraw from a painful situation or from one that we cannot handle well. That is, we may avoid confrontation or become oblivious to surroundings that are intolerable. We may deliberately limit our activities to those that produce pleasurable experiences; we may put off undesirable tasks, or we may isolate ourselves from situations that arouse our feelings of insecurity. Third, we can compromise, should the first two possibilities fail us. For example, we may want to go hiking on a certain day, but it is raining. So, rather than giving up the hike altogether or going despite the rain, we may postpone the hike until the next day.

Coping responses are not always socially acceptable forms of adjustment. Consider, for instance, a student who is failing in college. He may attempt to improve his study habits or reduce his academic load. He may change his curriculum, enroll in a different college, or leave college altogether. But another level of adjustment to poor scholarship can be for him to blame his teachers for "incompetence," to question the value of a college education, or to condemn his high school for having failed to prepare him for college. He may also develop debilitating physical symptoms such as intense headaches, insomnia, diarrhea, or persistent fatigue. An even less socially acceptable response is an attempt to stave off the reality of academic failure with drugs, sexual promiscuity, or antisocial "gang" behavior. Finally, a student may evolve totally irrational explanations for failure; for example, thinking that he must withdraw from classes because the food in the cafeteria is poisoned. A student need not progress through all these stages in order to reach the last one, for each level can be experienced independently of the others. In fact, most of us have responded at many of these levels without consequences of any significance. The last two responses, of course, involve us in behavior that will not be tolerated by society. It is important to add that when behavior at any of these levels is reinforced, it tends to persist.

In summary, by assessing a problem and evaluating alternatives, it is possible to reduce anxiety. We can cope with stress by altering the situation or by denying what is happening in order to make conditions more tolerable. At the same time we must continue to function as competently as possible in order to achieve or approximate our original goals or to formulate new ones. Stress is an ordinary part of life, and learning to cope with its milder forms not only increases resistance to future stress but also builds self-esteem and enhances our ability to act effectively in new situations of stress.

Can Competence for Coping Be Developed?

Bruner (1965) notes that personal competence depends not so much on intellect as on the ability to reach out and to magnify cues in the environment; through such "amplification," individuals can learn to respond more effectively to the environment and to exert some kind of control over it. It is not the environment, however, that exerts a constricting influence and makes an individual feel trapped and stifled; it is the individual's interpretation of and reactions to the environment. The ability to recognize the factors in the environment that limit our growth and those aspects of our personality that prevent us from experiencing and integrating diverse ideas is crucial in developing effective coping behavior. The mark of educated people is not their fixed ideas about themselves and life but the flexibility and tolerance they show toward alternatives and the respect they hold for objectivity and valid evidence. Essentially, learning to cope is adapting through self-change to a changing environment, and the end result of this process is a sense of competence and fulfillment.

When we feel inadequate in a situation, regardless of whether or not we are, we become anxious and frightened. Students may be anxious before an exam because they are not fully prepared, because they fear competition, or because they are concerned over the probability that they will be nervous during the test and consequently fail.

Although we are apt to feel anxious under stress, especially when the task is a measure of our strength or a validation of our self-image, it is possible to avoid becoming overly emotional. We can at least minimize the emotional effects by examining antecedent circumstances and uncovering the real reasons for our fear. Also, it is better to accept the fact that you are nervous than to tell yourself you "should not" feel tense; accepting the condition lessens its effects while trying to deny it only aggravates the symptoms.

Combs and Snygg (1959) have also suggested that we need to feel adequate in order to cope with life's demands. In fact, a major goal of psychotherapy is to help a person *feel* more competent as a human being in order to *become* more competent. These authors point out that a sense of adequacy depends on a person's view of himself as well as on the views of others toward him. As feelings of adequacy are developed through respect from others, the opportunity to share progressively in decisions and actions, and increased exposure to situations that invoke assertive responses, the individual becomes stronger and more able to meet the demands of the situation directly and consciously without distortion and without mechanisms for self-protection. Such a response is situation-oriented, flexible, and realistic. In short, one can become a problem solver—even in times of stress—if responses are based on fact and on conscious effort. And, realistic self-appraisal is probably the most important "fact" we must obtain.

In a demanding situation, we can mobilize our processes of discrimination and our past experience. While we are obviously affected by personal needs for esteem, security, success, and the like, we can nevertheless appraise the situation realistically and choose the best possible response. We need to see things as they are and not as we wish them to be. Emotion is present in almost all behavior—especially in behavior that responds to stress—but emotion cannot be allowed to cloud the responder's objectivity in appraising himself in terms of skills and values as well as in assessing the demands of a particular situation. A moderate amount of feeling helps to motivate us, but strong emotions can weaken our ability to reason.

Smith (1968) elaborated on the characteristics of personal competence and concluded that competence is reflected in a basic optimism about our ability to master the environment—an optimism that is a result of a positive self-evaluation and realistic goals. Such an attitude encourages us to set goals slightly above previous ones but within a realistic range, for overcoming reasonable challenges serves to stimulate the growth of even stronger feelings of personal competence.

Smith (1968) goes on to suggest that the fulfillment of basic needs and particularly the development of language skills increases feelings of competence. Through words we heighten our awareness of our surroundings; with speech we are able to experience other people more fully. With more words at our disposal, we are able to learn faster; we become increasingly able to manipulate the environment, and thus we enhance our feelings of competence. (Have you noticed how people become readily frustrated in a foreign country when they know only a few words of the native language?)

Adkins (1974) maintains that, although formal education can help us to actualize ourselves, it operates in rather remote and indirect ways. He proposes that we initiate a "fifth curriculum" from kindergarten through college, which he calls the "Life-Coping Skills Curriculum." Such a curriculum would focus on how we can go about solving the problems of normal personal development, on how we can deal with crises, and on how to cope with growing up, with marital problems, with interpersonal relationships, and the like. Most philosophers and historians agree that life is becoming increasingly complex and confusing, and it is not unreasonable to assume that we need to acquire more knowledge and improved skills if we are to cope successfully with the problems of living.

Ways of Coping

We are not born with all the coping skills that we will need, but the fact that we must learn these complex responses is often overlooked by our parents as well as by our educational institutions. So little is taught us that we often approach the entire problem of achieving fulfillment, securing love, and managing to cope with distorted or unrealistic notions, misinformation, and incredible naiveté.

O'Connell (1973) lists some realistic considerations that can be integrated with our own experiences to help develop effective coping behavior. You can recognize that what is real for you—that is, how you actually feel about yourself—may not be equally real for others, for each person bases his or her actions and feelings on private reasons. The suburban banker and the ghetto dweller have different economic views; the teacher does not view an examination in the same way as the student who failed it. You alone are responsible for limiting or expanding your feelings toward others; you alone will have to decide whether you want to belong or not to belong; you alone must decide what to think about yourself. Avoid being trapped in inferior/superior roles or locked into power struggles, for growth cannot occur in such relationships. Equality and cooperation are more effective behaviors than domination or submission. If the former cannot be achieved, however, state your feelings, propose better solutions, and, if all else fails, withdraw from the situation.

You need not be a victim of your environment, for you can select, reject, interpret, and "arrange" it according to what you want. To some extent, you can change a situation to fit your needs. You can also look for similarities between yourself and others and build on these. Emphasizing differences only blocks the fulfillment process and creates distances. You may concentrate on the consequences

Figure 6-2. The demands of living have many faces, and we have to cope with each of them differently. Photo by Shirley Kontos.

of what you are doing. Try to anticipate what effect your actions will have on others. Use possible consequences as a guideline for what to do and what to avoid at a particular time. Maintain your sense of humor so that you may live more harmoniously with your conflicts, with yourself, and with others. Humor acknowledges the absurd and accepts the contradictory; it respects the way we are as people—our differences, shortcomings, appearances, and personal characteristics.

In addition to O'Connell's useful possibilities, there are three important areas to examine in our discussion of effective coping behavior—how to neutralize stress, how to achieve emotional release, and how to maintain hope. We will consider each of these and their relationship to coping behavior. Our theoretical discussion will be clarified in each instance by the narration of a specific incident.

Neutralizing stress. Stress, in the form of frustration and conflict, can originate from within us or be forced on us by the environment. We are in control when a state of equilibrium exists between our inner capabilities and the exterior demands. Ambiguity toward a situation or lack of familiarity with it, however, raises the level of stress and anxiety and makes the task of coping more difficult. When stress is overwhelming and our skills and personal adequacy cannot meet its demands, we are likely to act to protect ourselves; instead of confronting the situation, we tend to turn inward and examine ourselves. Further, when a desired goal produces conflict, stress intensifies as we approach the goal.

As an example of such coping behavior, consider one nation threatened by another. When diplomacy and political maneuvering fail, the threatened country begins to arm itself, thereby drawing energy away from useful and fulfilling goals. Much must be sacrificed for protection and safety needs. Indeed, the normal life of the nation is curtailed and even crippled in order to maintain preparedness against possible threat; security becomes more important than growth. A similar situation exists when a person cannot cope with an exterior threat and turns inward to protect himself. Initially such a response may be harmless, but if it is prolonged it will weaken and paralyze the person and prevent him from coping directly with the danger.

There are many ways to defuse conflicts between ourselves and others, and our choice often depends on the nature, length, and intensity of the conflict as well as on the personality, age, education, sex, and social status of the people involved. Although we may not always choose the most desired method of coping, in general our response will fall into one of the following categories.

• *Concession.* Making concessions is a deliberate way to cope with stress; when each person involved is willing to yield on certain demands, an accommodation can be reached. By giving up an immediate claim, we often gain in the long run, and the harmony that we may attain may be well worth the price of capitulating to someone and easing the strain of conflict. Although a middle position is never entirely satisfying, it may represent the best choice. Instead of expecting others to change, often we must make the initial move ourselves. The ability to compromise is not the measure of a weak personality; rather it may indicate resourcefulness, flexibility, and insight. Particularly in interpersonal relationships, conceding enhances closeness and harmony, and many possible conflicts can be avoided. The following instance demonstrates this process.

Incident

I lived with my grandparents for a while and found that many of their ideas turned me off. Both of them were still living in the past, and every time I tried to explain how I and the younger kids felt, they would put up an argument. I never seemed to get my chance to talk. I didn't want to hurt their feelings because of their age and because I knew that, in spite of everything, they loved us kids, so I went along with them, sort of giving in to their schedules, meals, and daily habits rather than risk their love and friendship. Giving them their own way about little things helped me get along better with them. I never really felt trapped in the situation because I was always aware of what I was doing. My actions were deliberate and, therefore, weren't irritating to me.

• *Toleration.* It is surprising to observe how many conflicts may be avoided simply by letting them exist, by refusing to allow them to interfere with our lives. "Going with the flow" is often an effective way to overcome conflict. Fighting a situation may only aggravate tension in the person and produce more anxiety than the conflict is really worth. Some Eastern religions advocate a passive stance toward adverse living conditions—that is, accepting things as they are and as natural in one's life. Drought and famine are accepted as part of the cycle of time in some Asian countries whereas we, in the United States, become worried when such conditions occur in our country. Consider, for example, a college curriculum with certain required courses. The faculty has devised a program that hopefully meets specific career goals, but the students enrolled may feel that their needs are quite different. The process of education may proceed quite normally though as long as disagreements remain at an acceptable level, and neither the faculty nor the students are unduly burdened by the conflict. We can live with differences of opinion as long as they are not out of proportion to the situation. Here is how one person exhibited toleration.

Incident

Several years after we got married, I realized that my husband and I had certain basic personality differences. He was more introverted, more intellectual, and I was more expressive, more outgoing. I like people, and I like to talk and share my feelings.

I went through a period of examining our relationship, and I came to the conclusion that I'm willing to accept these differences between us. We have so many other things working for us that I don't feel lost or out of place in our marriage. And, although I wish he'd respond to things at my emotional level, I'm learning to understand his reactions too. In fact, his quiet responses sort of balance my emotional "highs." We're a good couple.

• *Changing our attitudes.* When a situation cannot be changed or when the persons involved are not willing to alter their ways and views, attempting to change the situation and its participants may only intensify the conflict. It is easier to accept such situations if we remind ourselves that they are only temporary or if we concentrate on shifting our attitudes to adapt to the situation. An irritable roommate who has trouble with final exams is a good example of this type of conflict. Since life will be "back to normal" after exams, an attempt to alter the situation is not necessary. Being courteous and avoiding direct confrontation may be enough to ease the temporary strain. In essence, your attitude toward your roommate has changed, and the conflict no longer exists. Similarly, you cannot change your parents, but you can change your stance toward them and thus minimize conflict.

Incident

When I got out of high school I had some ideas about myself that I now realize were false. I thought I could breeze through college, pick the teachers I wanted, attend the classes I liked, and graduate without trouble. It didn't take me long to realize how wrong I was. I almost gave up college because I felt that I was being pushed into courses that had no relation to what I wanted to do. But I stayed on to finish even though the college was calling the shots, not me. I just said to myself that what I wanted most was the degree, and I would do whatever it took to get it. After all, everybody else was in the same boat.

Once I changed my view, I felt a lot better. I didn't complain, and actually I just didn't think about it much anymore. I realized that you can't change the system, but you can change your opinion about the system and thus free yourself from being hassled.

• *Disengagement.* We can disengage ourselves from conflict by diverting our attention to something else. From time to time situations arise that seem to invite conflict; we seem to be expected to fight or to give in. Neither alternative represents a solution: if we win by fighting, we can expect revenge from the other's defeat; if we give in, we deprive ourselves of our basic equality with others. When locked into this kind of situation we can best maintain our integrity by refusing to become involved in the conflict, no matter how tempting it may be. By choosing to disengage ourselves, we are not "copping out;" rather we are promoting a state of harmony within ourselves and with others—not as winners or losers, but as equals.

Incident

My roommate sometimes makes demands on me that are totally unjustified; he really gets on my nerves. Then I have this impulse to get into a fight or argument with him, but I don't do that. I just pick up my stuff and go to the library and study there. By the time I get back, my roommate has fizzled out, and I can talk with him. I learned this from my mother when I was just a kid. Sometimes I threw tantrums to get her attention, but she would just go to the bathroom and sit there reading magazines. By the time she got out, I was calmed down. I find that freeing myself from a situation that is potentially explosive is a good way not to get hurt. When some guy argues with me over something, I just walk away. I ignore his invitation to tangle with him over something I don't give a darn about. I simply refuse to become someone's enemy without good cause.

• *Restructuring.* Our relationships with people are in continuous flux, and our ways of coping must change accordingly (Arkoff, 1968). As circumstances, needs, and values from the past are outgrown, new ones appear. Past solutions are not necessarily appropriate in the present or feasible for the future. For instance, wives of the past were mainly homemakers and childraisers, and husbands worked outside the home to earn money. Young couples today, however, have to restructure their behavior in tune with the way society has evolved—that is, with an emphasis on equal responsibility for the homekeeping and money earning for each spouse.

Theories of child discipline, for example, have changed from authoritarian to democratic, and each theory requires different resources, although the fundamental problem may often seem quite similar.

In the past, obedience was synonymous with good behavior, an understandable notion in societies dominated by kings or other absolute rulers and in societies in which fathers ruled their homes in uncontested authority. Using force to control a child today, however, may encourage authority-challenging behavior. Today's democratic attitude assumes that parents and child are equal. The relationship between parents and child has been restructured into an equalitarian transaction in which the child suffers the logical consequences of his unacceptable behavior (Dreikurs & Grey, 1968). Indeed, natural consequences are a more logical system than reward and punishment, for consequences reflect the inevitable outcome of the child's misbehavior. The child learns to accept responsibility for his own actions rather than merely to accept the punishment doled out to him by a superior, self-righteous parent. Thus, we must restructure our attitude toward our children in agreement with a philosophy of equality, and they must learn that the consequences of their actions are the criteria that determine whether or not they will persist in certain behavior. The following incident shows how restructuring works.

Incident

My parents came from Europe, and I was brought up strictly. The strictness worked in our family because I wasn't exposed to any other form of discipline. I was made to feel that there were people above me and people beneath me, and I had to obey those who were superior to me and to "browbeat" those inferior to me. You can imagine that this game didn't last long. By the time I got to high school, I could see that we should all be treated as equals, even though we are not all the same in height, talent, strength, or interests. For a while, I secretly hated my parents for treating me as they had, but I soon realized that the past didn't matter because I was now old enough to lead my own life. I think the best way to cope is to learn from your own trials and errors rather than to take orders from others who "know better," even though they really may know better.

• *Blocking.* We can of course become deadlocked with someone over an issue, and failing to resolve it, we remain "at war" with the opponent. Neither person is willing to change his attitude or to accept the conflict and try to live with it. Such a stance is not the same as merely postponing a solution temporarily, for we continue to have difficulty relating with the person, always expecting the issue to erupt. Blocking is the least effective way to overcome conflicts, for when communication fails, frustration increases.

Blocking most often occurs between children and parents or between siblings, but peers can also harbor a seething anger while exhibiting outward cordiality, especially in social situations. Occasionally, even lovers will hesitate to mention a disagreement between them, hoping to avoid negative feelings that might interfere with their blissful existence.

Incident

My boyfriend always counted on me to help him with his term papers because I am much better in English. He got a bad grade on one paper, and he was worried about having to repeat the course. He came complaining to me. He wanted me to get into the act, which was his act really, and go with him to his instructor and explain his difficulties. I quickly realized that I was being made part of his problem, and he made me think I owed him my support. I told him pointedly that he was entirely responsible for his work, that he would have to choose how he made the improvements, and that he would have to do the work and accept the outcome. Although I love him, I don't want him to think that he can always count on me to help with the difficulties he may have. I didn't want to make his problem my problem. He never accepted my views on this situation, and we just didn't talk about it anymore. But the battle was still there, covered up. Neither of us gave in, but the problem seemed a deadweight to us both.

Achieving psychological equilibrium. We often contend with minor stresses and pressures by demonstrating patterns of psychological behavior that lessen the impact of these stresses.

One common way of lessening the impact of experiences that bother us is to discuss them with someone we can trust. The other person may share his or her reactions to similar situations, and we can gain new insights into how to cope.

Incident

I always go to my roommate and tell her how I feel when I get a bad letter from home or have troubles with my boyfriend. She always listens. Even though she does not tell me what to do, she sometimes talks of her own similar experiences. And the fact that there is someone there I can talk to helps a lot. Also, she never seems to get upset when I tell her these things, and that by itself makes me feel real good and more in control of myself.

Sleeping is another emotional response to stress. When we dare not face a problem because of our fears and insecurities, we may seek to avoid the entire situation by sleeping. Sleep is not necessarily a "copout," for a temporary withdrawal from a problem may allow us to face it later with greater equanimity.

Incident

I am usually a calm person; little things don't bother me. But the other day I got a bad grade and got very upset. It was not what I had expected. It was a Friday evening, but I didn't want to do anything and I hated to spoil anybody else's Friday. I felt very tired, so I went to bed early. I curled up and slept for 12 hours straight. When I got up, it was nice outside and I had almost forgotten the bad grade. I did a lot of studying that week-end, and on the next quiz, I got a much better grade.

Flight into activity is another emotional way of relieving tension, and many persons experience this type of release in physical exercise or work. When people remain in one position for much of the day, there is a tendency for them to become even more anxious or depressed when they are frustrated or under pressure. An outlet through physical work or recreation is often amazingly beneficial. One person explains it in the following way.

Incident

On the phone the other night, Jane told me she was going to be busy for the next month. When I hung up, I felt very tense and angry. I just couldn't take "no" as an answer from her. I felt that I had to do something. I paced up and down my room, but that didn't work so I went to the gym and played basketball for two straight hours. When I got home, I took a shower and I didn't feel so bad about myself. I felt that I had purified myself of the bad feelings by working hard.

Another release of tensions that helps us to cope with stress is crying. Often, we may feel like crying but refrain from doing so because we fear that others may assume that we are weak. Some people tend to cry only when they are alone; yet, crying in front of someone else can be helpful in helping us to get over an unpleasant situation. Instead of allowing the tension to build up within us, we can express it through crying, something we all learned as infants. Often we feel relieved after tears, especially if crying is followed by support from someone who cares for us and understands.

Crying can be a manipulative gesture—"turning on the tears" to win the sympathy and concern of others—but it can also be a genuine expression of sorrow and hurt. One student related the following recollection of crying.

Incident

I always considered myself to be a stable person, but after I had mono for several weeks and missed a lot of classes, I got upset when talking to a teacher in her office. I was depressed about the work I had missed. In fact, I felt so weak— physically and mentally—I thought I just could not make up the work. I burst into tears in her office, almost without realizing that I had. She was very sympathetic and listened carefully to my feelings about her course. She had always liked me, and I had been a good student. She knew my crying was genuine because of my illness. She recognized that I was not crying for sympathy, and she knew that I wanted to do the work for the class. She told me not to worry, that she was on my side.

Laughing in the face of an uncomfortable situation is also a way of dissipating tension. Everyone recognizes the fact that we tend to smile when we meet people for the first time even though we are a bit anxious or insecure. Similarly, some people scoff at a situation that is potentially harmful as a way of coping with that situation. Laughter can hide hurt feelings or mask self-doubt. It can serve as a cover-up and as a release of emotions without making us appear foolish. Consider the following instance.

Incident

My relatives are very serious people and often get excited and angry at one another or shout when they discuss politics or financial matters at our house. When they visit us the atmosphere gets very tense; however, I spontaneously start mentioning humorous things that happened to me during the day, and everybody starts smiling. The atmosphere gets to be more relaxed.

Through thinking and self-examination, we can analyze a situation that has hurt us—taking it apart and trying to find out why it has given us pain. Although reflection is not always an effective way of coping because we do not normally take an active stance when reflecting, it can nevertheless help us to gain new insight into our own actions as well as into the particulars of a given situation. Reflection can become the basis for changed behavior. This process is described in the following example.

Incident

My boyfriend wanted to break up with me, and I got terribly upset. I left my room and went to the park and sat on a bench all by myself. I looked at the squirrels and at the birds. I felt melancholic and lonely. I began to think about what had happened between us and how we had gotten together in the first place. I tried to make sense out of it all. The way I saw it was that there were so many differences between us that he was not for me and I was not for him. I concluded that things would not have worked out anyway, even if we did stay together. Of course, I was still hurt, and I thought that maybe in all fairness I was entitled to be hurt. After all, we had gone together for one whole year.

When I am by myself and can think things out without interference from other people, my mind gets clearer. I can focus on what I need to think about and come up with good results. I stayed in the park half the afternoon, but when I got back to my room I felt that I had begun to resolve my problem. I wasn't happy, but I no longer felt so insecure and depressed.

Hope, defined as anticipatory fulfillment, can help to circumvent stressful, unpleasant experiences and to avoid despair (Korner, 1970). Anticipatory behavior is related to coping behavior in that current stress is eased through the expectation that future events will provide solutions; looking forward to relief in the future lessens tension in a crisis situation.

Certain criteria must be met before hope can be effective as a coping device. (1) Hope must have a realistic basis; the future alleviation of current stress must be feasible. (2) Hope is not synonymous with wishful thinking or childish demands. (3) Hope is not based on promises or gimmicks that falsify and deceive. Rather, hope involves reasoning and logic; it consists of an emotional commitment based on belief and confidence, and it is founded on a reasonable assessment of probabilities. Hope can prevent panic, disorganization, and apathy—all poor coping devices. Indeed, one of the main tasks of the therapist is to build hope in otherwise hopeless clients who would give in too easily without using their abilities and resources properly.

Incident

I think many of the problems we experience come from the fact that we feel inferior and incompetent inside ourselves. When we try to relate with people, we get defensive because we're wrapped up thinking about what others are thinking about us. It's a self-centered, vicious circle. We appear unfriendly and disinterested, and people think we don't care about them. So they walk away from us feeling rejected, and we in turn feel rejected because they walked away from us! If we try harder and look earnestly for somebody to care about or love us, people get turned off because we look too eager. That only makes us doubt ourselves more. We exaggerate our shortcomings; we get lonely and scared; sometimes we even panic or lash out at the world. The situation snowballs, and we can lose hope. We get to feeling like displaced persons.

But I've found that if you have hope, if you think in terms of a time in the future when things will not be so bad, the down feelings will pass more quickly. You've just got to see that future and work toward it. If it's a sensible expectation, it can happen for you. You make it happen.

In my case it's college and my career. I want to work with kids. People tell me I'm good at it. Now I'm plugging through college, and, when I have doubts, I just think of the future and a good, worthwhile job. What I'm hoping for makes my life now easier to put up with.

COMMUNICATION

Human beings are separated from the animal kingdom in several ways. One of these ways is that we communicate primarily through words that have complex, representational meanings. When we are skilled at communicating our ideas and competent in the use of words, we interact better with others, we get things done, and on the whole we are more able to fulfill ourselves. In this section we shall consider three main topics—verbal communication and its various levels, how verbal communication may be improved, and, finally, the nature of nonverbal communication.

Levels of Verbal Communication

Bernard and Huckins (1975) describe five levels of communication. They begin with the least desirable level of communication, the fifth level, characterizing it as manipulative, deceptive, and exploitive. Conversing at this level is not "straight." The words cover up real feelings in order to set up a beneficial or manipulative situation. Misunderstandings may occur, and motives are often obscured. What a person says at this level is usually not what he or she means. While this kind of communication does not usually take into account the other person's feelings, it may have merit, especially with people we do not know well. If our intentions are merely to create a friendly dialogue, there is little harm in such transactions, especially at the beginning of a conversation that might lead to a more genuine relationship. At a party, feigning interest in a guest's trip to Asia is an example of an innocuous use of this level of verbal communication.

Giving factual data with little emotion, without distortion of the facts, and without hidden meanings is the fourth level of communication described by these authors. The approach is usually mechanical and impersonal; lecturing, presenting news, and reporting on research are typical examples.

The third level of communication involves interpersonal communication and expression of feelings about society and others; others are now viewed as real people

Figure 6-3. Society can give us conflicting cues or messages that are impossible for us to live by. Photo by Shirley Kontos.

rather than as objects. This level involves an exchange of emotions and a concern for things that have personal meaning and significance. Our views on life are checked against those of others, and social harmony and feelings of closeness result from this mutual exchange of ideas. We talk freely about what we feel, think, and see, and we respond with consideration to the reactions of others.

The second level of communication involves feelings, attitudes, and thoughts inside ourselves. At this level, we are concerned with the meaning of existence and with a definition of who and what we are. When these thoughts are shared, we often experience greater self-acceptance; however, it is often difficult to put these thoughts into words. Introspection, meditation, and self-disclosure fall into this category. Levels two and three actually complement and reinforce each other and lead to greater social perceptiveness and self-understanding.

The first level of communication involves a spontaneous, emotional, ecstatic experience within the individual that is difficult to express in words. Such an experience tends to take place in persons who are creative, unboundaried, and at peace with themselves and the world. The experience is often a revelation in some form of the pure love that is a basis of humankind and of the unifying power of this love.

It is important to note that the middle three levels of communication can work together to promote personal effectiveness, accuracy of perception of one another, high self-esteem, and better self-understanding. Interaction in situations that stimulate personal exchange help us to move rapidly from level four to level two. We acquire insight and confidence so that we need not rely on level five, which is superficial and maintains social distance between the communicants.

It is only fair to observe here that relating verbally can have drawbacks. Too much talking often inhibits action; the talkers may become so wrapped up in the talk that they put off acting. Verbal relationships are not always on an equal footing; one person may do all or most of the talking (thus creating a situation of control rather than intellectual intimacy), or one person may be a lot more adept at talking (thus creating a situation of frustration and feelings of inadequacy for the other person). Consider, for example, a student on a date who monopolizes the conversation so that his partner is kept at a distance. He is thus protected from the emotional closeness that he fears by directing the conversation toward topics that he can handle and away from those that may pose a threat to his self-esteem. Often such a person is quite unaware of his verbal manipulations but may readily recognize this defense when it is identified for him.

Communicating with others is a major factor in developing feelings of self-worth, effectiveness, and fulfillment. With trusted friends, we can often check or verify our perceptions and interpretations, thus creating a situation in which, through others, we see our real selves without fear of humiliation and rejection. Once we have this objective insight into our personalities, we can modify those aspects of ourselves that interfere with our effectiveness.

Can Verbal Communication Be Improved?

Bernard and Huckins (1975) suggest five methods to promote effective communication. First of all, relating communication to the present—what's going on at that moment—instead of to the past or the future assists the listener in "tuning in" to what the words mean. It is easier for the listener to understand and respond directly to something that everyone is experiencing simultaneously. Second, it is helpful to exhibit personal feelings and emotional reactions while you are communicating. There can be, for example, a dramatic release of feelings in a person who breaks down and cries while talking with close friends. A third way to improve communication is to rely on a personal, subjective viewpoint in your verbal communication rather than to present the feelings and thoughts of others. Presenting thoughts and ideas from your own frame of reference instead of in the third person (which leaves you out of the problem) is a helpful technique. Fourth, being an active listener, giving verbal and facial clues, establishing eye contact, and following your intuition all serve to promote communication. Finally, speaking in specifics instead of in generalities is helpful. Talk, for example, about your joys, fears, decisions, problems, instead of discussing impersonal, philosophical abstractions. Intellectual platitudes have little bearing on direct communication and tend to keep the communicants emotionally apart.

Effective verbal communication also depends on how skillful we are in handling constructive feedback. Fitts (1970) offers several standards by which feedback can be judged. First, is the criticism generated by the motive to be of help to the receiver or to harm or humiliate him? Second, is the criticism requested rather than volunteered? People receive feedback best when they need it. Third, does it focus on what the other person is saying or doing rather than on the person herself—for example, "Your information lacks proof" rather than "You are a prejudiced person"? Fourth, does it relate to specifics rather than to generalizations—for example, "Your tone of voice frightens me" rather than "I hate you"? Fifth, does it point to the present rather than to the past? Sixth, does it describe what the other person is doing or saying rather than being judgmental and moralistic? Seventh, is it I- rather than you-oriented? That is, are you telling the other person how you feel, how that person affects you, rather than telling him what you think about him—for example, "I feel uncomfortable here" rather than "You are a nervous person"? Eighth, can it be tested and verified for agreement? Ninth, is it aimed toward something the receiver can change (you cannot lower the height of a tall girl)? Tenth, is it confirmed by others? If only one person thinks you are stingy, you may not have a problem.

Inability to put your feelings and thoughts into words is an obstacle to self-fulfillment. Watzlawick, Beavin, and Jackson (1967) suggest that improvement occurs if we talk about how we are communicating with each other, if we stop and reflect on the tone and depth of our verbal content, and if we try to determine whether we "got" across what we wanted to say.

These authors also suggest having a third party observe two persons in a dialogue and then offer feedback as to what actually occurred. Such a process can take place, for example, between a married couple that is having problems communicating and an observer who acts as a catalyst to facilitate communication. Often the observer can help the couple discover the basis of their problem; the observer can be more "objective" because he or she is not part of their problem.

Nonverbal Communication

Nonverbal communication (gestures, facial expressions, posture, tone of voice, physical closeness) like verbal communication is inevitably entwined in the process of socialization and strongly influences our interpersonal competence. Certain aspects of nonverbal communication (tone of voice and physical contact) precede verbal communication and have a strong effect upon the growing child. Even as adults, however, we are sensitive to nonverbal cues, although we may be quite unaware of that level of expression.

The messages we give through posture, gesture, and facial expression are popularly known as *body language* (Fast, 1971). It is generally held that over half of our communication involves nonverbal expressions (Birdwhistell, 1970). Very often we give messages by the way we stare, by how we sit or move our hands, or by the tone of our voice. As a result, if the listener fails to decode our body messages correctly, misunderstanding will result. Consider the following example.

Joe: How've you been, Mary? I haven't seen you for a long time.
Mary: Okay . . . I guess. (Mary pauses and stares out the window with a sullen expression.)
Joe: You're not saying much; are you mad at me?
Mary: I'm not mad at you. I just had a fight with my parents, and things are up in the air right now. I'm thinking what to do about it.

We can see how the message received in this example was based on a faulty interpretation of cues. Joe concluded that he had somehow been the cause of Mary's distant behavior. The messages he picked up were not the ones she intended to give, but they were the ones he "heard."

Close friends or partners in relationships often communicate by eye contact, by tone of voice, or by how they touch each other. A wife, for instance, may know her husband's mood by the way he greets her at the door. Some persons are very sensitive to the feelings of others even when talking to them over the telephone, and they are more often right than wrong when they sense that the speaker is tired, anxious, depressed, or happy. Most of us have encountered persons who give much away through gait, manner of speech, facial expressions, hand gestures. However, be aware that cues can often be misread, even in those we know well. For example, people with seductive eyes may be giving out sexual vibrations without being fully aware of what they are doing, just as certain prolonged glances may be perceived as containing a "special" message.

Touching is a sensitive area in our culture because physical contact has been inhibited for so long by traditional morals. In certain other cultures, however, touching is more customary and is used to express casual friendship as well as closeness. A bearhug in Russia is an entirely appropriate greeting but in England it may be viewed quite differently. When a person in France kisses a friend hello, his or her behavior is completely acceptable, but the same gesture in America may have a different connotation and may result in a misunderstanding. The point here is that body language may be decoded differently, not only because of cultural differences but also because of personal styles. It is important to recognize that others respond to our body language, accurately as well as with misunderstanding, and that their response to us is always to some extent governed by this "silent" but powerful form of communication (Scheflen, 1973).

SUMMARY

In this age of constant change and continuous demands, our ability to cope may be severely tested. While we rely on built-in mechanisms of defense, we must also deliberately seek alternate ways to circumvent or resolve the difficulties we encounter. In this chapter we have seen how personal competence and the learning of specific skills can help us cope more effectively with stress.

Understanding how we learn can help us to solve problems more readily and perhaps even prevent the impact of stress. We can learn to study effectively and thus make college a less stressful situation; we can learn to program our behavior to obtain desired results in the future; and we can just go ahead and fail, as painlessly as possible, and then start all over again, having learned from experience.

We have also discussed how to neutralize stress situations by adopting certain attitudes or by exhibiting certain behaviors, such as concession, toleration, and disengagement. We can also cope by releasing pent-up feelings through laughter or tears, through talking out a problem with a trusted friend, or through engaging in a flurry of activity that provides temporary relief.

Finally, we have discussed the importance of verbal communication, not only in our interpersonal relationships, but also in our search for fulfillment. We have pointed out the various levels on which verbal communication occurs, and we have stressed the importance of nonverbal forms of communication. We have tried to emphasize that the listener is as important as the speaker and that only through effective feedback can communication be sustained.

Specifically, we have shown how, by strengthening our skills of learning, coping, and communicating, we can overcome stress with greater ease. Recognizing the nature of stress and understanding our own strengths and weaknesses help us to choose ways of coping that are effective and help us to avoid anxiety or depression. Improving our ability to communicate verbally, for example, is known to help us in coping with interpersonal conflicts; yet, it is a technique that can be learned and practiced without much basic change in our personality. When conflicts are difficult to change, we can manipulate our own attitudes and reactions. When we alter our habitual ways of reacting to the conflict, we may succeed in bypassing it or in viewing it in such a way as to avoid involvement and hurt. If we devote too much energy to merely protecting ourselves from stress, we waste energy that might be spent more constructively. Finally, maintaining hope and a stoic attitude are highly effective coping devices. If self-actualization is the end goal of our existence, then coping is a means toward this end.

QUESTIONS TO THINK ABOUT

1. Can you recall a difficult situation in which you had to make a choice among several alternatives? How did you cope with that situation? How did you reach your final decision?
2. After considering the several possibilities for coping with stressful situations, can you identify any on which you tend to rely? Did you learn a new way of coping that you did not know before?
3. Do you have difficulty in verbal communication? Why do you suppose you have this difficulty? How might you improve in this area?
4. Have you ever tried to cope and failed? Looking back, what were the reasons for your failure?
5. Can you recall experiences with nonverbal communication? How did you respond? Do you think your interpretation of the nonverbal message was accurate?
6. Did you ever go through a period in your life when you did not know how to cope with a rejection, plan your time effectively, express anger, express emotional intimacy, or give and take orders? If so, can you recall how you coped with that situation? Was your coping behavior satisfactory? Would you respond to the same problem in the same way today? If your response would be different, why do you think you have changed?

REFERENCES

Adkins, W. R. Life coping skills: A fifth curriculum. *Teachers College Record,* 1974, *75*(4), 507-526.
Arkoff, A. *Adjustment and mental health.* New York: McGraw-Hill, 1968.

Bernard, H. W., & Huckins, W. C. *Dynamics of personal adjustment* (2nd ed.). Boston: Holbrook Press, 1975.

Birdwhistell, R. L. *Kinesics and context*. Philadelphia: University of Pennsylvania Press, 1970.

Bruner, J. S. The growth of the mind. *American Psychologist*, 1965, *20*(12), 1007-1017.

Combs, A. W., & Snygg, D. *Individual behavior* (Rev. ed.). New York: Harper & Row, 1959.

Dreikurs, R., & Grey, L. *Logical consequences: A handbook of discipline*. New York: Meredith, 1968.

Fast, J. *Body language*. New York: Pocket Books, 1971.

Fitts, W. F. *Interpersonal competence: The wheel model*. Nashville, Tenn.: Counselor Recordings and Tests, 1970.

Korner, I. N. Hope as a method of coping. *Journal of Counseling and Clinical Psychology*, 1970, *34*(2), 134-139.

Lazarus, R. S. *Psychological stress and the coping process*. New York: McGraw-Hill, 1966.

Lazarus, R. S. *Patterns of adjustment and human effectiveness*. New York: McGraw-Hill, 1969.

Lazarus, R. S., Opton, E. M., Nomikos, M. S., & Rankin, N. O. The principle of short-curcuiting of threat: Further evidence. *Journal of Personality*, 1965, *33*(4), 622-635.

Murray, H. A. *Explorations in personality*. New York: Oxford University Press, 1938.

O'Connell, W. E. Social interest in an operant world: The interaction between operant and existential-humanistic thinking. *Voices*, 1973, *9*(3), 42-49.

O'Connell, V., & O'Connell, A. *Choice and change*. Englewood Cliffs, N.J.: Prentice-Hall, 1974.

Robinson, F. P. *Effective study* (Rev. ed.). New York: Harper, 1961.

Scheflen, A. E. *Communicational structure: Analysis of a psychotherapy transaction*. Bloomington: Indiana University Press, 1973.

Smith, B. M. Competence and socialization. In J. A. Clausen (Ed.), *Socialization and society*. Boston: Little, Brown, 1968.

Voeks, V. *On becoming an educated person: An orientation to college* (3rd ed.). Philadelphia: Saunders, 1970.

Watzlawick, P. J., Beavin, J. H., & Jackson, D. D. *The pragmatics of human communication*. New York: Norton, 1967.

Chapter 7

Adjustment to and Growth in College

CHAPTER OUTLINE

I. Must we experience problems in college?
   A. Insufficient motivation and indefinite goals
   B. Learning to avoid problems

II. A closer look at adolescent adjustment
   A. Problems are normal
   B. Problems are temporary
   C. The importance of peer relationships

III. Living arrangements for personal growth
   A. Choosing where to live
   B. Coeducational housing

IV. How college students change
   A. Student-faculty relationships
   B. Alienation
      1. Causes of alienation
      2. Overcoming alienation
   C. Understanding loneliness
   D. Loneliness versus aloneness
   E. Causes of loneliness
   F. Reactions and responses to loneliness
   G. Mind-altering substances
      1. Drug abuse
      2. Alcohol abuse

V. Summary

Technological advances and the rapid pace of change in our society make higher education increasingly imperative. In addition, the period of adolescence has been extended in our culture beyond that of many other cultures, including our own of only a generation ago. Since so many of us will spend so much time in college, it is only natural that we want to know how to find fulfillment during those years, how to relate meaningfully with our fellow students as well as with our instructors, and how to cope with the problem of growing up in college. This chapter, then, will examine this period of rapid and intensive change, discussing different ways to adjust, and ways to overcome loneliness and alienation, and ways to achieve maximum personal growth through experience.

MUST WE EXPERIENCE PROBLEMS IN COLLEGE?

College education can make us more aware of ourselves and of the world around us as well as foster critical thinking and mature judgment. The college setting not only provides us with new opportunities to expand knowledge but also encourages us to develop new and meaningful personal relationships. Indeed, attending college may help broaden our perspectives toward people in general, as we are exposed to more persons, more knowledge, and more experiences, and introduce us to the basic issues of adult living. Some of these issues might be relating effectively with others, deciding upon a meaningful and fulfilling career, knowing ourselves as best we can, establishing a satisfying marital relationship, and finding a place and purpose for ourselves in society. College education encourages the development of the total person—not just the intellectual person. On the whole, college attendance promotes emotional development and intellectual fulfillment and increases independence, awareness, sensitivity, and self-expression (Newcomb & Feldman, 1969).

It is easy to seriously question many aspects of the educational scene today. Should academic institutions, for example, emphasize such societal issues as peace, equality, and justice, or should they concentrate on professional training? Do colleges truly educate, or do they only give graduates a "union card" to professions that guarantee a high income? Some students feel that real learning is unrelated to lectures and reading assignments and is only achieved by experiencing life itself—that is, increasing self-awareness and expanding our knowledge of the world through contact with and involvement in it. These are not easy issues to resolve, and teachers and educational administrators as well as students must enter the dialogue if creative and valid solutions are to be found—solutions that are relevant and palatable to the young and yet acceptable and beneficial to the total society.

Insufficient Motivation and Indefinite Goals

Motivation to attend college varies from student to student, depending on how each regards his or her capabilities and expectations. Many students seriously seek a good education and can be said to be intrinsically motivated; others, however, attend college because of external pressure and are, therefore, said to be extrinsically motivated. There is evidence that student motivation to go to college and to do well academically may be strongly determined by having parents with a high educational level, being in a high social class, and/or performing well in high school (Trent & Medsker, 1967). Of course, many potentially capable students never go to college, and students who were mediocre in high school often do well in college, because predictive indicators do not neatly encompass factors like newly won insight or persistence.

Overall adjustment has a lot to do with success in college; lack of confidence, personal inefficiency, parental conflicts, social interests, poor study habits, personal problems (loneliness, anxiety, depression)—any of these may cause a student to fail in college. The greater the discrepancy between how students rate themselves and what they value as socially desirable, the greater the likelihood that they will experience adjustment problems (Heilbrun, 1963). Academic difficulty may stem from a personality problem; sibling rivalry at home, for example, may determine a young person's choice of a prestigious profession for which he or she has no aptitude. Similarly, poor peer relationships, lack of personal autonomy, or unresolved parental conflicts can affect students' academic performance, even though they are good "college material."

Having no goals at all or harboring goals that are incompatible with one's abilities are also associated with underachievement in some college students (Taylor, 1964). Health, financial, and interpersonal problems, along with poor study habits and insufficient preparation in high school, are all potential factors that can affect academic achievement negatively.

Underachievers often have not actualized themselves in other areas of their lives besides the academic one. Earlier and more basic needs such as self-regard, peer acceptance, and belonging must sometimes be met before the academic underachiever can actualize himself in the college setting. When underachievers were placed in a discussion group in which problems of motivation, conformity, success, communication, and study habits were aired in a democratic atmosphere, their academic performance improved and their level of self-actualization increased (Leib & Snyder, 1967).

Learning to Avoid Problems

How, then, can you achieve the most from your college years? Interacting with others lets you know where you stand. It is reassuring to know that others experience many of the same doubts that you do, and it is also helpful to observe how others go about resolving indecision and determining a course of action. We all react to input from others, and stubbornly attempting to figure everything out on our own can create avoidable problems. Occasionally, those who feel lost in college find that exploring the situation with students who seem to know where they are going is extremely helpful. Even reading biographies of those who found a purpose for themselves in life can be helpful for some of us. Organizing your life around a plan, hierarchy, or order within which you can tackle one problem at a time can lessen unnecessary worries. If you place your goals without regard for your priorities or interests, you may often be faced with deciding which goal is the most important. It is also important to acknowledge your weaknesses and take advantage of your strengths—putting the strengths to work, allowing them to expand, and permitting them to play the dominant role in your life.

A CLOSER LOOK AT ADOLESCENT ADJUSTMENT

The adolescent and early adult period of life is perhaps more trying than any other period. There are often contradictions occurring in the way the adolescent is treated by society and at home—that is, in the roles he is expected to assume. For example, at work he may be respected as a serious, mature person, but at home he may be ordered about like a child. Such contradictory treatment often occurs precisely as young people are struggling to define themselves and obviously complicates this task (Rogers, 1972).

As a result of these conflicting pressures, young people may identify with the superficial values of their peers rather than accept the more difficult developmental tasks of achieving gradual independence, of establishing satisfying social relationships, or of becoming a contributing member of society. Further, parents are often as confused about adolescence as adolescents themselves and may openly express their anxiety and guilt feelings. Young people, in turn, respond with caution or even cynicism to parental expressions of inadequacy, and the conflict may well broaden. It is difficult for adults to steer a course between "giving in" and "dictating" to teenagers. Adults tend to prescribe oversimplified rules for adolescent conduct, while at the same time using young people as the scapegoats to vent their own conflicts. On the other hand, young people often indulge themselves in pointing out the foibles and follies of adults and mocking their "righteous" authority. Perhaps one obvious corrective lies in not treating youth as an inferior, troublesome breed or adults as all-knowing and infallible. Parents need not be so insistent upon the respect of their children that they forget to grant the rights of youth to err and to learn through experience.

Problems Are Normal

It is generally held by psychologists that the problems of adolescence—apathy, criticalness, rebelliousness, moodiness, superficiality, defiance, impulsiveness, cynicism, irresponsibility—constitute a more or less normal and transient manifestation of emotional development. In fact, many clinicians go on to suggest that the absence of these disturbances suggests the presence of an underlying personality problem that may surface later in another form, especially under the duress of adulthood (Lindemann, 1964).

One of the most familiar adolescent experiences is the identity crisis so aptly described by Erikson (1950). During this experience, adolescents try to establish a logical connection between their childish and less mature behavior and the new roles that society expects of them as adults. It is a process of reevaluating earlier patterns of behavior, of gaining greater self-awareness, and of making a link that allows them to view the past, the present, and the future with a consistent perspective. Erikson (1956) maintains that the crisis in identity gradually resolves itself through trial-and-error behavior and through experimentation with different roles; gradually the adolescent comes to value and view himself in ways that are compatible with how society recognizes and accepts him. Commitment to a profession and to a philosophy of life with which the individual is comfortable usually resolves the crisis in identity. At the other extreme, however, a person may remain indecisive, functioning on only a day-to-day basis without perceptible goal-directedness. It is important to remember that although these problems are considered normal in the adolescent, they are apt to indicate deeper conflicts when they occur in the adult. A severe identity crisis, according to Erikson, can occasionally be pathological if it is prolonged into adulthood and if it is marked by negativism, isolation, self-destructiveness, and extreme pessimism.

It is interesting to note that adolescent turmoil was not found among adolescents in the Israeli kibbutzim (Zellermayer & Marcus, 1972). Positive development was noted and attributed to early and continuous socialization of the young people with peers, to their participation in the structure and goals of the group, and to the fact that the children were raised by adults other than the biological parents. In short, the nonexploitive and highly ethical structure of the community emphasized psychological siblingship and the acceptance of each individual as a person in his or her own right. Further, such a structure limited the duration of the adolescent period and appeared to be more effective in averting the problems of adolescence than an extended, unstructured adolescence. As a result, interpersonal relationships, social responsibilities, and trust were enhanced within the kibbutzim, and alienation was significantly curtailed.

The labeling of personality as "healthy" or "abnormal" can lead to connotations of a scientific nature that may obscure the real nature of psychological problems. Instead, normality should be viewed as an ideal state of functioning that no one ever reaches; this means that everyone is maladjusted to some degree. Another viewpoint of "normality" involves statistical averaging; that is, if a large number of people in a given population suffer from the same affliction, its prevalence may denote a normal phenomenon. However, the affliction (for example, alcoholism) may still be incapacitating to the individual and detrimental to the larger society. Weiner (1970), reviewing research based on the general population of adolescents, concludes that, except for a small percentage of extreme cases of psychological disturbance, adolescents can be considered normal persons who do not differ significantly in degree of maladjustment from the adult population.

Problems Are Temporary

Only a century ago, adolescents assumed a reasonably well-defined role by the time they reached their late teens; they had already found a direction in life and had identified themselves with a life task that was to become their career. Now life is more complex; greater freedom and choice necessitate more decisions. With the prolongation of the adolescent period because of college and post-college training, students run a greater risk of experiencing a crisis in identity. Nixon (1966) fully agreed with Erikson in this respect, adding that confusion over attitudes toward authority, siblings, career, and sex reduces the student's ability to cope with many of life's issues during this period of development.

The effects of family situation on adolescent adjustment have been studied extensively. Adolescents in stable and harmonious families, for example, exhibit a better ability to communicate and greater trust, autonomy, and confidence than do young people in less exemplary families (Peck, 1958; Murphey, Silber, Coelho, Hamburg, & Greenberg, 1963; Marcus, Offer, Blatt, & Gratch, 1966). While such observations appear logical, it is not fully understood exactly why some adolescents lead normal lives even though their parents are overtly maladjusted. Frank (1965), after extensively reviewing the literature, concludes that it is not just the family that generates adolescents' problems. Other, more complex, social factors, such as peer and authority pressures and subjective experiences, often prompt adolescents to form erroneous, biased conclusions about themselves and their parents.

It also happens that persons who are maladjusted tend to view their parents as maladjusted. Nikelly (1967) asked a group of college students to describe their mothers. A group receiving therapy viewed their mothers as more pampering, more overprotective, less concerned for their personal welfare, and less tolerant than did a control group. Vogel and Lauterbach (1963) compared the family patterns of pre-college subjects experiencing difficulties with those of normal adolescents and found that the former viewed their mothers as more controlling than did the normal subjects. Just as we cannot know fully whether disturbed parents necessarily cause disturbance in their offspring, so must we avoid the assumption that strong identification with parents is necessarily an index of good adjustment (Sopchak, 1952). For example, with the growing emancipation of the female and the consequent changes in her role, a weak identification of a young woman with her mother may not necessarily reflect a personality disturbance. Finally, with relatively few exceptions, many problems of adolescent adjustment are transient and likely to fade as a student progresses academically and becomes emotionally closer to his or her peers.

The Importance of Peer Relationships

There is no doubt that meaningful peer relationships help to sustain personal identity and enhance actualization (Douvan & Adelson, 1966). As the family moves toward decentralization and as urbanization and technology intensify feelings of alienation, there is little question that feeling close to someone of your own age or status influences adjustment in positive ways. By the time you enter college, you have probably experienced with your own parents the typical conflict between the generations over values, goals, and lifestyles. College offers an opportunity to "replace" parents with other knowledgeable and mature adults. If we had no one except our parents after whom to model our behavior, we might become limited and even rigid. The greater the variety of people we are exposed to, the more we can enrich our own perception of what and how we want to be. It is always possible that, despite their best intentions, your parents did not provide positive or useful models for you to follow. Acknowledging this possibility may make it easier for you to explore the many new possibilities for models that college offers.

College life is a new experience—personal, social, and academic—and it is natural for students to turn first to their roommates, or friends, or dating partners for solutions to new problems. The quality, duration, and intensity of a relationship is a far more important measure of good adjustment than is the quantity of superficial, "visible" friends. However, we often hesitate to make social overtures because we fear rejection. At times we interpret the actions of others as signaling rejection when actually we have erroneously interpreted facial expressions, gestures, or mannerisms.

Every stage of human development is confronted with stress conditions that the individual must resolve, and it is not surprising that many such problems arise as the natural outcome of the transition from childhood to adulthood. Often these problems are intensified by the college scene. Many students, for example, feel that they must excel in college, but they have not been prepared emotionally to meet the demands of academic stress. Such students may find it easier to isolate themselves socially for the sake of academic success. There is, of course, a tendency for adolescents to experiment with different lifestyles, as expressed in their changing attire, interests, manners, and general behavior. Certainly some of these attempts are genuine efforts to find a meaningful self-identity, but, in some instances, students are merely seeking attention or aspiring for acceptance by a particular group.

Knowing what we want is one thing, but putting it into practice is another. It may well be that the closely knit family and country way of life of the past created conditions in which one did not have to try so deliberately to become close to someone else, to make friends; family and neighbors cared, virtually by definition, and the style of living was friendly from necessity. Nowadays we must often define what kind of people we want as friends and then go out and find them. Our expectations can be unrealistically high, making frustration and disappointment inevitable. Nevertheless, to the extent that we can change as we grow, we are capable of establishing meaningful relationships and fulfilling ourselves.

Incident

Deep down I want to get close to someone, someone I can tell exactly how I feel, someone who won't put me down or laugh at me. It seems, though, like you can't trust anybody; people are out to get you any way they can. Every time I meet someone I like, I always have this feeling that I have to watch what I say and be one step ahead so I won't make mistakes. I want to be honest about myself, but I'm afraid I won't be liked if someone gets to know me the way I am. I want to be emotionally and intellectually intimate with someone, but it's not so easy to find someone who is willing to be your friend in the same way. Some people get scared off right away when you try to become close with them; I guess they got their hang-ups from their parents. I never saw my parents show affection openly to each other, and their friends are very stuffy, self-righteous, self-protecting people who are afraid to show their feelings. I love and respect my parents, but that isn't the way I want my life to be.

LIVING ARRANGEMENTS FOR PERSONAL GROWTH

The assignment of compatible roommates has become increasingly difficult in college residential facilities. Personal habits, social philosophies, and sleeping and studying patterns affect a student's psychological well-being as well as his or her academic achievement. Some university administrators have suggested that roommate compatability might be ensured through the use of modern computers. Students would be matched on the basis of personal habits elicited through computer questionnaires, and hopefully the quality of dormitory life would be enhanced. Students, on the other hand, have tended to seek alternate living situations: co-ops and communes, rooming houses, trailers, apartments, and even rather free-floating, temporary quarters. Just how important is a student's living situation, and how does it affect his or her education and self-actualization?

Choosing Where to Live

Social changes, especially the surge toward greater personal freedom, have altered the traditional dormitory living style on college campuses. Many students feel that, if society considers them mature enough at 18 to vote and to serve in the army, they should also be allowed to live the kind of life they prefer, as long as no one is harmed. Colleges, on the other hand, feel obligated to "provide for" students, and students often resent this paternalistic attitude. Further, some administrators prefer that students live in campus housing in order to maintain financial stability within the existing university structure. Somewhere between these two positions lies a realistic solution—a campus living style in which students can function academically while they continue to grow as persons.

Students today feel fairly capable of handling themselves without direct college supervision, particularly with respect to housing. Their exodus to independent living accommodations, although indicating an understandable resistance against the lack of privacy in supervised dorms and against the starkly functional surroundings of dorm rooms (that often leave a student's emotional and aesthetic needs unfulfilled), does breed difficulty when such arrangements foster situations that encourage premature emotional involvement or constant distractions from academic pursuits.

College officials' concern about making the mechanics of dormitory life more responsive to students, accounting for individual needs and tastes, and rendering such living more economical may eventually encourage more students to return to dormitory housing.

Coeducational Housing

In response to the exodus from college dorms, as students seek to escape regimentation and control, some universities have sought to compromise by housing both male and female students within a single dorm, in segregated areas or floors. By bringing all students together in the sharing of dining, recreational, and study facilities, residential morale would hopefully be improved and realistic interaction between the sexes would be encouraged. Students would be apt to treat one another on an equal basis, with openness and informality. Because of these experiences, mate selection may later be based on more mature and realistic attitudes rather than on impressions created in formal academic settings or artificial social "occasions." Mixed dorms, however, have also developed problems; visitation regulations are often violated or virtually nonexistent, and the common dorm problems of privacy are also present.

Acting on hints from previous surveys, Schroeder and LeMay (1973) tested students before and after they had lived in a coed dormitory. They found that spontaneity, naturalness, self-identity, acceptance of self and others, and the ability to get close to others had increased significantly, especially when compared with the ratings of sexually segregated students. Early experiments seem to indicate that coeducational living promotes interpersonal competence, increases mature awareness between the sexes, and calls for greater sensitivity to the needs of others.

Recent evidence also suggests that coeducational living makes males and females feel less self-conscious in each other's presence and less bothered with traditional sexual roles (Reid, 1974). Casual nonsexual relationships developed more easily, but casual sex was no more prevalent than in any other type of dorm. Students felt free to do what they wanted to do and were less concerned with whether or not they were considered sexually desirable. Coresidential living seems to afford more opportunities for real relationships and for emotional growth by members of both sexes.

HOW COLLEGE STUDENTS CHANGE

Leeper and Madison (1959) have coined a term, *reintegration,* that facilitates our understanding of student actions and reactions in college. Reintegration refers to the fact that we tend to behave in a new situation in ways that are similar to how we behaved in comparable past situations. For example, the emotional relationships you formed with parents and significant peers prior to entering college often persist; persons who remind you of your parents trigger your emotions and cognitive processes (thoughts, memory, perception) and cause you to respond in a familiar fashion. Often students encounter difficulties because college and pre-college expectations are quite different. The old patterns simply do not "work." Thus, the students must develop new competencies and "grow" in order to properly adjust.

Consider the situation of this college freshman.

Incident

Pat intended to major in Art Education. In high school he had been an excellent student in the physical sciences, and his mother had urged him to enter a medical specialty. But Pat "dabbled" with writing poetry and, despite his mother's objection, decided to enter an artistic field, even though he was not as fully talented in this area as he was in science. He felt that artists were more "independent" than persons in other professions. His poor academic performance in college, however, necessitated constant tutoring, and most of his teachers felt he should be in another field.

Pat's father was described as an "easy going" person who remained aloof when a decision was to be made in the home. Pat wanted encouragement from his father, but he never received any strong support from him. As a result, he relied heavily on the opinions of teachers and peers regarding decisions, and often these opinions confused rather than helped him. Pat preferred dating passive, dependent girls who did not "hassle" him and who tended to agree that he should become an art major. But such passive girls made his dates a drudgery; he referred to them as "drags."

Since Pat was not doing well either academically or socially, he sought counseling. He discovered that he preferred passive girls because he associated aggression with his mother. He also began to understand that he was trying to major in art because it stood in opposition to what his mother wanted. He did not want to be dominated and "feminized," and so he was seeking to define himself in opposition to his mother. He had sought out "strong" figures (primarily teachers) to take the place of his weak father. In grade school and high school, these reactions had posed no significant difficulty, but the college environment was too broad a field for his former patterns, and approaching adulthood meant that Pat could no longer play games with himself. As he came to understand why he was behaving as he was, he was able to concentrate on learning alternate responses based on new insight into his earlier experiences, particularly his relationship with his mother.

Madison (1969) collected accounts of students' personal experiences, from which he documented student change during the college years. The student culture—as manifested in extracurricular activities, student subgroups, personal friendships, personal contact with faculty, inspiring content of specific courses, and direct confrontation with success or failure that required innovative, coping strategy—was found to have a significant impact on personality. Old misconceptions about self-expectations were corrected in the light of college reality, and a new organization took place that enabled students to achieve a sense of control over their present life and the future. As students were exposed to unfamiliar styles and attitudes, they adopted new perspectives on life.

Student-Faculty Relationships

Considerable attention has been given to the study of peer and parent-child relationships, but few significant studies have been made regarding interactions between faculty and students. This situation is somewhat surprising since students spend considerable time with faculty, and it might reasonably be assumed that student behavior is influenced by faculty models in many ways. One study (Jacob, 1957) shows that the personal influence of the instructor has a greater impact on student attitudes, values, and beliefs than does the curriculum content or method of instruction.

Ideally an instructor's task is not only to impart knowledge but to create an atmosphere in which students want to learn. Education should be a cooperative venture shared by both faculty and students. While many instructors meet these criteria, others contend that students should "adjust" to the classroom or to the temperament of the faculty. The student who is able to accept the fact that the course is more important than the personality of the instructor is likely to be able to cope with the situation, but the student who allows the situation to degenerate into a power contest with the instructor by being tardy, uncooperative, disinterested, cynical, or critical more often than not becomes the loser. Of course, when a large proportion of students in a class agree that an instructor is unfair or incompetent, it is to their benefit to seek redress through administrative channels.

Although some instructors do abuse their authority over students, students may often harbor negative attitudes toward all faculty members because of what adults in general symbolize. The majority of students, however, accept the negative traits, as well as the positive traits, of their instructors and tolerate whatever discomfort is involved. An instructor's personality may hinder the educational process, but rarely can it stifle the process unless students give up their responsibilities.

Good relationships with teachers can help sustain the enthusiasm necessary for learning as well as influence the student's personality development in positive ways. Often teachers affect students more than peers or parents. Students usually want to be respected by those who teach them, and many students become disillusioned when these expectations are not met. The difficulty is compounded when students react abrasively to negative traits in their instructors. Often students magnify these traits out of proportion to their real importance, overlooking the fact that teachers are not immune from emotional problems or personal conflict. Sometimes students find it difficult to separate the instructor's personal views from the objective data that he or she covers in the course. The more impatient or disagreeable students become in this situation, the greater the likelihood that they will elicit a similar unpleasant reaction from the instructor. Students often fail to realize how much they contribute to instructional conflicts and overlook the fact that they as well as instructors have a responsibility in maintaining productivity within the classroom.

Although many books have been written about how instructors are to deal with the problems of students, there is very little information on how students are to cope with the faculty. Unfortunately, some faculty members underestimate students, failing to realize that many students today are extremely sophisticated and knowledgeable. Other teachers view involvement with students as "unprofessional"; indeed, such teachers may be afraid to become too close to their students. At the other extreme are instructors who become overly involved. A student may have no one to turn to in times of distress, and an instructor, often against his or her better judgment, may act in a way that only intensifies the problem. Despite the probability of severe repercussions, sexual attraction can become a factor in student-instructor relationships. A student may at first be intellectually attracted to

Figure 7-1. A pleasant and inspiring teacher can be more important than elaborate classrooms and textbooks. Photo by Shirley Kontos.

a teacher of the opposite sex, but soon may become emotionally involved. Young people in the process of becoming independent may respond to the attention of an older, more established faculty member, or the teacher may succumb to the admiration and naiveté of a younger person. Faculty members can unwittingly (or deliberately) promote this kind of relationship, especially if they have family problems of their own. Mature judgment is expected from faculty members, but the student is often equally responsible for infractions of behavior that can lead to difficulty for both.

Alienation

Halleck (1966) defines alienation as an estrangement from society's values, from the important persons in one's life, and from one's own feelings; it is often reflected in the lack of a clear identity. Through his work with adolescents and young adults in college, he identifies seven types of behavior that characterize alienation.

1. Poor self-concept: the student has only a vague idea of who he is, what he wants, and where he is going.
2. Inability to communicate: he usually distrusts adults, which makes it difficult for them to reach out toward him in meaningful ways.
3. Severe and sudden bouts of depression: the student is aware of stress that he cannot handle, which causes depression; his depression may be accompanied by suicidal thoughts. Even when his depression is lifted he continues to feel bored, apathetic, and unhappy.
4. Present-bound: he is unable to look forward optimistically, to commit himself to goals and meaningful aspirations. He drifts from one situation to another without sustained action.
5. Sexual activity: a full sex life may be typical of many alienated students, but, for the most part, their actions are unfulfilling and meaningless. There is usually no love or commitment to the partner, and sexual expression is often mechanical, joyless, and compulsive. Many may experience impotence.
6. Wasteful, ineffective behavior: many young people cannot study effectively or complete an academic assignment; they may work slowly, daydream, or sleep excessively.
7. Drugs: the use of drugs has almost become the trademark of the alienated person.

Causes of alienation. Feelings of alienation often have their origins in family, school, and peer relationships. The family, marriage, and other societal institutions are undergoing rapid changes and becoming increasingly complex; as a result, standards of behavior are less stable and well-defined. In the meantime, social injustices—such as race and sex discrimination, war, poverty, and double standards of ethical behavior—help to create an atmosphere of pessimism and an attitude of helplessness. Some students feel that the proper priorities of our country are denied and that the quality of life will continue to deteriorate unless unjustified wars, capitalistic imperialism, and personal arrogance are denied (Mullaney, 1970).

Brown (1968) discusses five social values that contribute to alienation. (1) The pressure to compete and succeed, whether for wealth or grades, drives away those who cannot accept this way of life and makes them withdraw from active participation in the society. (2) Urbanization decentralizes and depersonalizes life; close personal relationships weaken. (3) People are expected to adjust so that the complex social machine can function smoothly; such adjustment inevitably curtails individualism. (4) Equality is often expressed only in words. Those who control have difficulty accepting others as equals, while those who are controlled, although designated as equals, are confused about what equality really means. (5) Doing and achieving are often given a higher priority than care and compassion. Business and contractual obligations may take precedence over rewarding human experiences, and youth who may seldom have experienced human closeness and intimacy are afraid to show these emotions when the opportunity arises.

When society becomes too complex, too threatening, too demanding, we find adaptation difficult and may choose alienation as an alternative. We may develop defenses so that we can be more flexible in the face of stress, or we may "numb" or desensitize ourselves thereby reducing the possibility of injury to ourselves. But such isolation robs us of the opportunity for fulfillment; the processes of alienation remove us from the mainstream of activity and from experiences that are humanizing and meaningful.

Not only can we feel alienated from our surroundings and from other people, but we can also experience self-alienation, or estrangement from our true selves. We may often try to imitate an ideal image and, in the process, become further alienated from our essential selves. We may sometimes use self-alienation as a defense against anxiety-provoking situations, although deep inside us we yearn for emotional involvement (Weiss, 1961). We may use self-alienation to justify detachment and to avoid feelings of anxiety, rejection, and fear or the responsibility of commitment. Many philosophers have said that the less we want, the freer we become, but for many young people the lack of emotional involvement is only a protective measure against potential failure. While such a measure may allay anxiety temporarily, it hinders optimal emotional growth in the long run.

Self-alienation is often instigated by overly demanding parents; strong parents, primarily due to their own needs, have forced dependent relationships upon their children. As a result, most of the child's energy is expended on defensive measures against the parents who have made the demands, at the expense of independence, spontaneity, and empathy.

Overcoming alienation. To know intellectually why we need not be alienated from ourselves is not sufficient; rather, we must experience what it is like to accept and like ourselves. We must acknowledge that our own self is our best, most intimate friend. Only when we come to accept ourselves can we begin to love others. Self-acceptance makes one less guarded and defensive, and such openness often leads to more effective adjustment (Weiss, 1961). Helping individuals to recognize that, in a sense, the "enemy" comes from within and that the dynamic energy to exorcise the "enemy" lies within us all is a major goal of therapy. Often the therapist may point out the lively, moving, colorful content of the person's dreams in order to prove that there is a vital, energetic inner side to the person that has been repressed in daily life.

It is not easy for an alienated person to risk investing in others, but, if such an "opening up" occurs in an atmosphere of acceptance and openness and is followed by a positive response, success can be achieved. Often the self-alienated person fears involvement because he fears he may lose control over a situation. What happens in many instances of therapy, however, is that the therapist shows his or her own humaneness and feelings first and then indirectly "seduces" the client to do the same without the client's being fully aware of the process. Through another person or other people, then, the self-alienated person comes to terms with himself and develops an identity that he can call his own (Weiss, 1961).

Obviously there are no set rules for dealing with feelings of alienation, but there are courses of action and points of view that may help to alleviate intense alienation.

You might experiment with as many courses of action as are possible (including temporarily dropping out from a situation to help lessen your feelings of alienation), even if you are unable to visualize a clear-cut goal toward which to work. Only through action can you discover your potentialities. Realize, of course, that you are not completely punched, folded, and mutilated by society, parents, friends, religion, and school but that you make yourself. You are the ultimate authority on your own behavior. Anything can influence you, but only if you allow

Figure 7-2. Loneliness is estrangement from life and the world, but aloneness can be a personally rewarding experience. Photo by Shirley Kontos.

it to. Lose yourself in something you enjoy, even if it is "only a hobby." Find something that gives you distinction, an identity of your own. And finally, you might let your genuine feelings of love flow freely, for love works both ways, and to have someone loving you is one of the most identity-supporting situations of all.

Understanding Loneliness

Loneliness refers to the feeling that nobody knows you or cares about you, an increasingly widespread experience of our time. Political, religious, and social estrangement—that is, people feeling apart from the political process, removed from organized religion, and unable to affect other people or groups directly—as well as increased social mobility, contribute to this situation (Keyes, 1973); and young people, because of childhood disappointments, conflicting peer relationships, and personal frustrations, are often particularly vulnerable. They are not experienced enough to cope with such conflicts, and unfortunate experiences often make a serious impression on them.

Loneliness is similar to alienation; however, its primary concern involves only the lack of social relationships rather than a distance and dislike for many aspects of life and society. Also, the alienated person may find friendship with others whose feelings and attitudes are similar and, although lonely people seldom find one another, they may not always feel alienated.

Loneliness versus Aloneness

Let us begin by drawing a distinction between loneliness and aloneness. People who are *alone* have chosen to be alone and do not feel impaired or unhappy in any way. After their temporary withdrawal from society, which may help them to gain strength and to function more competently upon their "return" to society, they quickly return to normal social relationships. Many cultures have maintained customs of retreat or vigil whereby persons spend time alone, fasting and reflecting, but emerge with a sense of renewal and enthusiasm, ready to resume their activities. Loneliness, however, encompasses a feeling of isolation and estrangement from others. Its definition is broad enough to include feelings of powerlessness to direct one's life, of estrangement from the controlling economic structure, of political disaffiliation, of impersonality in human interactions, and of a general unpredictability concerning the future (Lystand, 1972). In a sense, everyone is born alone, but most of us manage to transcend our loneliness through marriage, work, creativity, and love.

Despite the seeming universality of the experience of loneliness, there has been relatively little research on the subject. Except for novelists, songwriters, and poets, most people are reluctant to acknowledge feelings of loneliness, often trying to conceal their loneliness (Fromm-Reichmann, 1959). Close interpersonal relationships among lonely persons are virtually nonexistent; the personal contacts of the lonely are apt to be superficial or merely functional.

Causes of Loneliness

It is quite understandable that ill, aged, and confined persons should feel lonely (Burnside, 1971), but why should adolescents and young adults feel lonely and isolated? A recent national survey showed that over half the people in the United States have an increasing sense of alienation, powerlessness, disenchantment, and futility. In fact, the number has nearly doubled over the past seven years (Harris Survey, 1973). The respondents in the survey expressed dissatisfaction with things as they are; they felt that their personal opinions did not mean anything to anyone; they believed that those who governed the country were more interested in their own welfare than in the welfare of their constituents; they felt that the rich were unfairly favored.

Why do we become lonely when there are so many people around us? Individuals can become lonely by misinterpreting the actions of others. They may feel lonely and unable to reach out for people because they believe that no one really likes them or that they will not be accepted for what they really are. They may also be afraid of becoming too dependent on someone else and thereby increasing their chances of getting hurt. Loneliness can also stem from an uncertainty about the purpose of life.

There are several major types of loneliness present today. College students often feel isolated upon their arrival on campus, much as immigrants might feel "out of touch" in a strange and perhaps inhospitable land. In these instances, the differences in place, in companions, in customs, and even in language may cause confusion and insecurity—what we might call *cultural loneliness.* Another kind of loneliness is exhibited by the "loner," the person who adopts a lifestyle of isolation. Such people may complain that no one really knows them well, but at the same time, they rarely go to the trouble to know anyone else; they usually prefer to be alone most of the time, to remain unmarried, and to develop few, if any, close friends. This kind of loneliness is almost a personal characteristic and usually does not bother an individual in the same way as loneliness that is suddenly thrust upon him. A third type of loneliness is *imposed loneliness,* such as that imposed by military posts remote from normal social contacts, by prisons, or by physical conditions such as debilitating age. Although such loneliness may be temporary in nature, it can be extremely stressful. A fourth type of loneliness is *existential loneliness*—a feeling that the individual is totally responsible for himself and therefore alone. In this context, the struggling person may often attempt to find some order in nature and society into which he can fit (Keniston, 1960).

Another classification has been made by Moustakas (1961); he distinguishes between neurotic loneliness (when a person is estranged and alienated from his own feelings) and existential loneliness (loneliness as a natural experience of the human condition but for which the individual can compensate by being socially responsive and useful). In a more recent essay, Moustakas (1972) maintains that loneliness can serve as a positive force in life, just as aloneness can, because it brings us closer to our selves and promotes self-awareness. He goes on to make a critical and relevant point; if you cannot make it on your own, you are likely to have difficulty making it with someone else. Within this perspective, loneliness has its proper place in the range of human emotions, for through the pangs of loneliness we come to value human compassion and affection.

Most sensitive persons from time to time experience one or another type of loneliness. It is only when loneliness becomes persistent and exaggerated, dominating one's life, that it inhibits or threatens the actualizing process. Consider, for example, the loneliness of this college student.

Incident

Sometimes I don't know what I'm here for; life seems so empty. Everybody is cold and selfish, and nobody gives a damn how you feel. I'm caught in the rat race, running around and doing things, but I'm not getting anywhere. I always feel I am in the same place. I walk to classes feeling like a blob of protoplasm. I take notes and pass exams, but I still don't know what a college education is for. I'm not learning anything anyway. Nobody seems to care how I feel, and sometimes I wonder whether I'm becoming numb myself.

Alright, I say, I'll have my degree; I'll hang it on the wall. But what good is the degree when I haven't yet found the purpose of living? If you're not happy, nothing is worth anything to you, and, besides, material things just disgust me. Sometimes I wonder if I am here just to make a living, but if that's the only reason I'm here, then I see no point in struggling. I'll probably get a job, marry, have kids, get old, and die; so what's the use? There's just something missing.

It's hard to make friends, and, when someone shows even the faintest interest in me, I begin to wonder what he sees in me that he likes. I don't know why I even bother to get up in the morning. I can't seem to be myself; I'm so conditioned by society and the environment that everything I do seems to be just an echo of the social conditions around me—not me.

It seems that life passes by, and I'm an outsider, a stranger living in enemy territory. I feel like running away and going to sit under a tree somewhere in the country, alone. It seems like when I'm close to nature I can figure out things about life a little easier, without having to play the roles and games that society wants. The real me is a person who wants to love, to be together with someone nice and accepting who's easy to talk to and who doesn't need a show or a game in order to like me. But you know, doc, I'm scared to go out and do what I want to do because people are going to laugh at me and call me foolish. If you try to do something genuinely nice, people will think you're crazy or phony. But if you play the game you're alright. Do you think people can really be happy in a life when they have to pretend to be what they're not?

Reactions and Responses to Loneliness

The fabric of modern society does little to relieve individual loneliness. Social mobility, competition, the quest for power and independence, and weakened family ties limit the growth of deep personal relationships (Slater, 1970). New attitudes and casualness toward sexual expression have also contributed to this loneliness. Indeed, when the sexual aspect of a relationship becomes intensified, the relationship may lose some of its emotional and intellectual depth. People, however, often seek a sense of personal satisfaction and a deeper emotional experience through sexual intimacy or physical affection. In most instances, though, they not only do not find lasting contentment, but they may feel even lonelier afterwards. Ideally, sex is a consequence of a relationship that is already flourishing; sex by itself is a poor alternative for loneliness.

It is, however, entirely possible for a lonely person to understand his or her condition and to become motivated to relate to others (Moustakas, 1961). It goes without saying that loving and caring is an antidote to loneliness, but how can such ties be initiated? Being sensitive to the feelings of others and attentive to their needs is an effective means of eliciting interest from others. Such actions, when not mere politeness or feigned interest, may begin a potentially meaningful relationship. When you express concern over the happiness of someone else, he or she feels wanted and esteemed, attitudes that, in turn, alter how that person views you and can thus open avenues of communication that can lead to the expression of affection. Group therapy, in which closeness and understanding are possible with less threat to the lonely person, offers another realistic beginning. As the participants experience sharing and commonality within an accepting situation, they may begin to free themselves from their own constraints and become more responsive to others. Often a shift from an intellectual to an emotional level of response encourages spontaneity and growth as well as a new understanding of one's self and others (Buhler, 1969).

Often we can relieve loneliness by taking even a casual interest in others, by sharing accomplishments, and by fulfilling simple social obligations. Being less selective in one's choice of companions and contributing to the needs of others are also good techniques to alleviate loneliness. An old proverb says "You must first smile at the mirror if you want it to smile at you." Some students become frightened at the prospect of emotional closeness and possible rejection and prefer to maintain distance as a safeguard. Thus, to protect themselves, they may adopt an intellectual approach to life and attempt to avoid emotional commitments in spite of their desire for affection and intimacy, concentrate on their undesirable physical appearance or social inabilities, treat others as if they wanted to be rejected (blaming everyone and everything except themselves for their loneliness), or conceal their loneliness through excessive activity. It is not unusual for students to keep "busy" on weekends in order to avoid facing their loneliness. Cheerful preoccupation can of course be therapeutic, particularly if loneliness is only a temporary or short-term condition, but determined, almost compulsive "busyness" may signal that the individual is refusing to confront the realities of his lonely situation.

Mind-Altering Substances

A characteristic of our society, and of its young population in particular, that has aroused considerable discussion during the last decade is the drug problem, which includes alcoholism as well as other forms of drug abuse. In the following discussion, we will emphasize not so much the temporary changes in ourselves and in our perceptions that drugs bring about, but whether or not such substances can help us to achieve actualization and self-fulfillment.

Drug abuse. The illegal and abusive use of drugs during the last decade has been widely publicized; however, there is a fair amount of disagreement among researchers regarding the effects of drugs.

The mind-altering drugs are used primarily to alter sense perception and emotional responses and to escape temporarily from reality. Individual responses to these drugs vary according to the user's personality, his expectations, and the mental set and physical setting of the user when the drug is taken. Sadava (1972) reviewed the literature and found four stages of drug use among college students. The *experimentation* stage is the student's initial involvement. When the effects have been experienced, the student may go on to the *casual* or *chance* usage stage. When usage becomes more consistent and regular supplies are required, the student has entered the *occasional* or *"weekend"* stage of usage. Finally, when drugs have become integrated into the student's lifestyle on a daily basis, he is said to be in the *regular* usage stage.

Einstein (1970) offers an overview of these psychoactive drugs. *Stimulants* (benzedrine, dexedrine, cocaine) activate the central nervous system and relieve depression and fatigue. *Depressants* (seconal, phenobarbitol, amytal, opiates) relax the central nervous system, reduce anxiety, and lower the blood pressure. These drugs, of which the narcotic heroin is the most commonly abused, also foster a mild state of euphoria. Thus, the narcotics normally used in medicine to relieve physical pain may also be used to relieve emotional stress. Heroin may serve in addition as a defense against feelings of alienation or inadequacy. *Hallucinogens* (LSD, peyote, mescaline, psilocybin) induce perceptual changes and distort the senses, as they interfere with the electrical activity of the brain. LSD may stir up opposite emotions simultaneously in the user; large doses may bring on exhilaration and "insights" or generate depression and confusion. Frequent users may become panicky and suspicious of others, usually while they are under the influence of the drug. They may even experience "flashbacks" many months after their last dose. Surveys show that these flashbacks, difficult to prevent or predict, seem to be a major factor in deterring students from experimenting with hallucinogenic drugs. *Deliriants* (glue, gasoline, paint thinner) are volatile chemicals, which, when inhaled, produce mental confusion, irritability, drowsiness, slurred speech, and/or intoxication. Prolonged use may cause physical damage, such as inflammation of the vital internal organs.

Marijuana is probably the most commonly used drug among students (Tart, 1971). Because it can produce the effects of nearly all of the previously mentioned drugs, it belongs in a category by itself. Increasing the consumption of marijuana may change feelings of relaxation and euphoria into those of mild excitement. Perceptual distortions, panic, and other severe mood swings may also follow. The user may also lose social initiative and become passive and withdrawn. In our society, which values competition, aggression, and upward mobility, marijuana seems to be an effective way for people to say "no" to the system. The use of marijuana rationalizes their desire to drop out from society. Marijuana, like the hallucinogens, can trigger a bad trip in the emotionally unstable person (Snyder, 1971). However, most marijuana users look upon marijuana as a social catalyst and do not see themselves as addicts any more than their parents who engage in social drinking or use tranquilizers or aspirin see themselves as addicts (Ray, 1972).

A report by the National Commission on Marihuana and Drug Abuse (1972) reveals that about 24 million persons in the United States have tried marijuana and that approximately eight million are still using it. Most users are apt to be experimenters and fall within the adolescent and young adult age range. The same report cites that, insofar as is known, marijuana is not addictive, does not produce harmful physical effects, and does not normally lead to the use of harder drugs.

The negative reaction against marijuana stems, at least in part, from the generation gap; indeed, the question of marijuana has become a battleground between the generations. The introversion and passivity associated with smoking marijuana contrast sharply with the traditional values of our society—action, progress, achievement, and aggression. For oldsters, who value initiative, marijuana has become nearly synonymous with "laziness." And for many, the primary argument against marijuana is that it is illegal.

As with tobacco, coffee, and alcohol, however, it is possible that one may become psychologically, if not physiologically, dependent on marijuana (Fort, 1973). Thus, it is important to ask here whether marijuana and other drugs contribute to actualization and genuinely promote emotional development or whether they simply encourage "copping out" from stress situations in everyday reality. There seem to be two distinct views in answer to this question. One view holds that it is more desirable to confront stress for what it is—to deal with it without distorting it or blunting our senses to it—and that, during the important

Figure 7-3. Drug abuse reflects not only human unhappiness but also a problem with today's society. Photo by Shirley Kontos.

developmental years, adolescents will learn more through confronting and attempting to solve problems than by running away from them. The other view is that the pleasure, euphoria, and relaxation involved in marijuana consumption and the accentuation of the bodily senses offer a fuller experiencing of the world and a stronger awareness of oneself. However, since experiences vary according to the subjective expectations and personality of the user, questions about marijuana use cannot be resolved by ready generalization.

Some of the previously mentioned drugs are present in medications routinely prescribed by physicians for relieving tension, pain, or fatigue, which seems to make their use harmless enough, or even therapeutic; however, there is danger when these drugs are taken without prescription by a depressed or nervous individual. Surely a preferable course for distressed persons would be to find the reasons underlying their anxieties or lack of interest in life.

Prolonged use of drugs may develop unwanted side effects that can become a greater nuisance to the users than the problem they originally wanted to escape. As the body learns to tolerate a drug, the user may be inclined to increase the dosage or switch to a more potent drug. Eventually, psychiatric treatment, hospitalization, or medical treatment may be necessary because the user cannot function effectively physically or mentally.

Drug users may also discover that their social contacts have become limited to people with similar problems, and they may discover that they have jeopardized opportunities to broaden their social experience. Consuming drugs without medical justification is usually a rationalization that helps the user avoid confronting his real problems (Laskowitz, 1971). However, there is no evidence that any drug has a permanent effect in altering one's outlook on life positively (Conger, 1973). Drugs may prove especially harmful to the teenager or young adult who has not achieved a secure sense of identity. The intake of drugs at this stage is likely to hinder rather than to facilitate the development of his personality, since drugs do not allow him to learn to cope with problems in a realistic fashion. Although the user may initially benefit from drug intake by peer acceptance, new confidence, and a brighter outlook on life, these effects are only temporary and cannot be attributed to any beneficial chemical effects of drugs. Since the effects of drugs often depend on what the user expects them to be, the psychological release he experiences through drugs occurs only on a symptomatic level.

Several surveys related to drug use suggest that social pressures and need for approval are significantly present in drug users, while marijuana users demonstrated a lower need for social approval (Scherer, Ettinger, & Mudrick, 1972). Other studies (Hogan, Mankin, Conway, & Fox, 1970) reveal that marijuana users are not necessarily maladjusted persons but are often poised and confident, show a wide range of interests, are skilled in interpersonal relationships, and are higher in achievement motivation than nonusers. Heavy marijuana users, however, were found to be more dissatisfied and maladjusted when compared with light or moderate marijuana users (Hogan et al., 1970; Cross & Davis, 1972). The increase in marijuana use has also been associated significantly with an increase in creativity, adventuresomeness, and the search for novel experiences (Victor, Grossman, & Eisenman, 1973). We might add that Victor's survey also found that, as marijuana use increased, the extent of reported experience with other drugs also increased. These results, however, are general in nature and cannot be applied to individuals, as each person has different reactions to the different drugs.

Some attitudes toward the precipitating causes of drug use are based on mere speculation or on the study of isolated and relatively small groups of users; however, Sadava's in-depth study (1970) of drug use among college students disclosed nine possible causes: (1) alienation from society and the quest for a new meaning of life, (2) desire for excitement and stimulation, (3) rebellion and disenchantment, (4) unfulfilling interpersonal relationships, (5) lack of and need for self-identity, (6) escape from sexual drives, (7) relief from stress and anxiety, (8) curiosity and search for novel stimuli, and (9) search for pleasure and happiness.

Psycho-emotional, semi-philosophical reasons for drug use, however, are not the only explanations. Many adolescents who use drugs may be modeling their behavior on parents who are also drug users (Smart & Fejer, 1972). A survey of several thousand adolescents indicated that when parents, as reported by their children, used alcohol, tobacco, and/or psychoactive drugs (tranquilizers, antidepressants), adolescents tended to use psychoactive and hallucinogenic drugs. This link of drug usage between adolescents and parents seems to indicate a pattern of conditioning or modeling.

Research findings on the correlates for drug use have tended to be inconsistent because methods of investigation and definitions of drug users vary widely from study to study. However, there seems to be no single reason for drug usage; rather, several causative factors seem to operate at the same time. A recent review (Braucht, Brakarsh, Follingstad, & Berry, 1973) attempted to bring together results in which some agreement could be found. This report noted that suggestibility by peers, availability of drugs, use of various drugs by parents, and poor parenting (domineering, overprotective, or rejecting parents) are factors often associated with drug use among adolescents. Young drug users generally tended to be immature, selfish, and insecure and to come from the middle and upper social classes.

Some individuals condone and even encourage the use of drugs to relieve boredom and feelings of alienation. They are often attracted to consciousness-expanding drugs, hoping to find a shortcut to fulfillment because the promises implicit in our society have somehow never materialized. Through the use of chemical agents, they often hope to experience an inner reality, to discover facets of themselves that were hitherto unknown, and to compensate for the dissonance they sense between society's promises and the actualities of daily life. They assert that the controlled use of drugs is less dangerous than the chronic use of alcohol and tobacco, which, they maintain, have been proven harmful but have not been declared illegal because of government and business interests. On the other hand, others maintain that there is no justification for introducing additional "harmful" substances into the body and that a person should develop inner resources to overcome boredom and isolation.

Alcohol abuse. Although the use of marijuana and hallucinogens has aroused much controversy recently, alcohol remains the most abused drug in the United States, the drug that causes the heaviest financial and social burden to society (U.S. Public Health Service, Alcohol and Health, 1971).

Contrary to popular belief, alcohol is a depressant, not a stimulant. People relax under the influence of alcohol and pent-up feelings of hostility and aggression are often released. Initially, the intake of alcohol makes an individual feel uninhibited, even lively, but the gradual increase of alcohol intake produces lethargy and sleepiness. It is not surprising that shy and insecure persons are attracted to alcohol because it allows them to escape the difficulty of coping directly with life's pressures. Anxious or depressed persons also find temporary refuge in alcohol because it permits the temporary forgetting of problems. Alcohol consumption enables some people to elicit the attention, pity, or understanding that they need from others.

Prolonged and heavy use of alcohol can produce mental deterioration, depression, memory loss, physical incoordination, disturbance in the thinking processes, and sometimes a loss of contact with reality. In addition, the nervous system, muscles, heart, kidneys, blood vessels, liver, and stomach can all be adversely affected from the overuse of alcohol (Fort, 1973).

Social drinkers consume alcohol to induce feelings of conviviality and mild relaxation or sometimes to stimulate their appetite. Because alcohol has a sedative effect on tension and anxiety and because its use is associated with pleasant experiences (conversation, socialization, celebration), it may also be used in situations that are normally avoided due to fear (Conger, 1956). Consider, for example, shy and inhibited persons who under the influence of alcohol may "have the nerve" to ask for a date, to talk about themselves, to initiate conversation, or to become sexually aggressive. The pleasant effects of alcohol unfortunately become the reinforcers for increased consumption, for we seek to repeat those experiences that give us pleasure.

According to one study (Blum, 1969), college students who drank tended to be either more liberal and dissenting or stronger socializers than did nondrinking students. Intensive drinkers showed more religious, political, and athletic interests, were more pessimistic about life, and tended to be involved in family disagreements. This group was also more likely to have tried other drugs besides alcohol than was the light drinking group.

It is difficult to say whether alcoholism is an exclusively social or psychological maladjustment or a physical disease; it is possible that the two are related as cause and effect. There are an estimated 100 million social drinkers in our country, and perhaps around ten million of them are alcoholics. And there has recently been a significant increase of alcohol consumption among high school students (American Medical Association, 1973). A combination of individual or group therapy and medical treatment can help return the alcoholic to a productive and fulfilling life. However, to be treated effectively, the alcoholic has to want to stop drinking. One way to treat alcoholism is through aversion therapy—pairing alcohol intake with a drug that induces an unpleasant reaction, like vomiting. Another program of treatment is through an organization called Alcoholics Anonymous, in which former "addicts" are usually effective in helping an alcoholic because they can speak from experience. Experts are cautiously optimistic about the treatment of alcoholism, but they predict that around two-thirds of all alcoholics can recover from alcoholism if they receive early and proper treatment (American Medical Association, 1973).

SUMMARY

Motivation to attend college varies widely from person to person, but academic achievement and adjustment to a new style of living are experiences that can effectively promote growth and self-realization. The college years offer challenges that students may accept—growing through failure as well as success— or refuse—reducing their field of operation and the range of their capabilities.

Important changes occur within the student years. Young people are forming a personal identity, often independent of parent models; they are seeking a philosophy of living that will accommodate both personal and societal demands; they are establishing meaningful relationships with their peers and attempting to align sexual drives with personal values.

Adults have been both fascinated and perplexed with the adolescent period, and their reactions have ranged from a joyous, sometimes humorous, acceptance to scorn, and even deep pessimism. Parents and teachers alike find their involvement with adolescents a difficult and sensitive occupation, and they are often at a loss as to how to proceed.

With the increase of liberal views in society, college students have adopted new lifestyles and chosen more independent living accommodations, which, they feel, maximize self-expression and a natural way of living. However, the coeducational housing experiment has seemed to demonstrate that on-campus living arrangements can also provide opportunities for personal growth and greater self-fulfillment.

The college experience requires new ways of responding, new insights, positive attitudes, and flexibility. Students must accept much that is new without giving up what was valuable in their past. The student subculture has considerable impact on the personality of the student, as he seeks to discover a suitable and viable lifestyle that does not merely imitate that of others but that reflects his own identity.

It is considered appropriate for students to find new adult models from within the faculty of their college. It should be remembered, though, that college instructors themselves often have difficulty in relating with others. Even a learned person may have personality disturbances, and such a model of behavior can indeed be frustrating to a student.

Students often suffer acutely from feelings of alienation. Loneliness can be strengthening, but if it is prolonged, it can also hamper self-actualization. Forces of depersonalization in modern society increase feelings of loneliness, and learning to cope with isolation will depend on how much we have fulfilled ourselves in other areas of our lives. Increasing our social feeling, committing ourselves to meaningful goals, and doing the things that give us satisfaction are ways to dispel the plague of loneliness. We can transcend the state of loneliness through meaningful human relationships.

We have talked about alienation as estrangement from the values of the society, from meaningful goals, from being in touch with oneself, and from one's feelings. Loneliness, on the other hand, tends to refer more to social isolation—the feeling that nobody cares, that no one knows you.

Drug use is a characteristic of the student subculture that has aroused considerable controversy. Investigators are still trying to define exactly what the effects of various drugs on the human personality are. And while the effects of drugs and the permanence of the effects vary from person to person, there is no evidence that drugs will make a person happier or better adjusted in the long run. However, an increased reliance on drugs may well allow individuals to conceal or mitigate internal conflict without facing up to its real implications.

QUESTIONS TO THINK ABOUT

1. What is your reason for attending college? Is it predominantly your own, or does it belong to your parents? Have you been conditioned to feel that going to college is the "right thing to do"?
2. Have you experienced any significant problems since you came to college? How did you go about solving them, and how successful were your methods?
3. How are living conditions at your college? Do you find that they increase opportunities for personal growth, or do you feel isolated and restricted?
4. Have you noticed any changes in your personality since you began college? Have others seen any changes in your personality?
5. Have you experienced loneliness or alienation since you came to college? If so, how have you coped with these feelings? Did you rely on any of the ways described in this chapter? Did they work effectively?
6. Have you had any experience with drugs? If so, what were your reasons for

taking drugs, and what were the effects of drug consumption? Do others with the same experiences share your views?

REFERENCES

American Medical Association. Alcoholism: Is it a treatable disease? *Modern Medicine,* 1973, *14*(20), 33-36.

Blum, R. H. *Society and drugs (Vol. II): College and high school observations.* San Francisco: Jossey-Bass, 1969.

Braucht, G. N., Brakarsh, D., Follingstad, D., & Berry, K. L. Deviant drug use in adolescence: A review of psychological correlates. *Psychological Bulletin,* 1973, *79*(2), 92-106.

Brown, W. N. Alienated youth. *Mental Hygiene,* 1968, *52*(3), 330-336.

Buhler, C. Loneliness in maturity. *Journal of Humanistic Psychology,* 1969, *9*(2), 167-181.

Burnside, I. M. Loneliness in old age. *Mental Hygiene,* 1971, *55*(3), 391-397.

Conger, J. J. Reinforcement theory and the dynamics of alcoholism. *Quarterly Journal of Studies on Alcohol,* 1956, *17*(2), 296-305.

Conger, J. J. *Adolescence and youth.* New York: Harper & Row, 1973.

Cross, H. J., & Davis, G. L. College students' adjustment and frequency of marihuana use. *Journal of Counseling Psychology,* 1972, *19*(1), 65-67.

Douvan, E., & Adelson, J. *The adolescent experience.* New York: Wiley, 1966.

Einstein, S. *The use and misuse of drugs.* Belmont, Calif.: Wadsworth, 1970.

Erikson, E. H. *Childhood and society.* New York: Norton, 1950.

Erikson, E. H. The problem of ego identity. *Journal of the American Psychoanalytic Association,* 1956, *4*(1), 56-121.

Fort, J. *Alcohol: Our biggest drug problem.* New York: McGraw-Hill, 1973.

Frank, G. H. The role of the family in the development of psychopathology. *Psychological Bulletin,* 1965, *64*(3), 191-205.

Fromm-Reichmann, F. *Psychoanalysis and psychotherapy.* Chicago: University of Chicago Press, 1959.

Halleck, S. Therapy of the alienated college student. In J. Masserman (Ed.), *Handbook of psychiatric therapies.* New York: Grune & Stratton, 1966.

Harris. Survey as reported in Champaign-Urbana *Courier,* December 7, 1973.

Heilbrun, A. B. Social value: Social behavior inconsistency and early signs of psychopathology in adolescence. *Child Development,* 1963, *34*(1), 187-194.

Hogan, R., Mankin, D., Conway, J., & Fox, S. Personality correlates of undergraduate marihuana use. *Journal of Consulting and Clinical Psychology,* 1970, *35*(1), 58-63.

Jacob, P. E. *Changing values in college.* New York: Harper, 1957.

Keniston, K. *The uncommitted: Alienated youth in American society.* New York: Dell, 1960.

Keyes, R. *We, the lonely people.* New York: Harper & Row, 1973.

Laskowitz, D. Drug addiction. In A. G. Nikelly (Ed.), *Techniques for behavior change.* Springfield, Ill.: Thomas, 1971.

Leeper, R. W., & Madison, P. *Toward understanding human personalities.* New York: Appleton-Century-Crofts, 1959.

Leib, J. W., & Snyder, W. U. Effects of group discussion on underachievement and self-actualization. *Journal of Counseling Psychology*, 1967, *14*(3), 282-285.

Lindemann, E. Adolescent behavior as a community concern. *American Journal of Psychotherapy*, 1964, *18*(3), 405-417.

Lystand, M. H. Social alienation: A review of current literature. *The Sociological Quarterly*, 1972, *13*(1), 90-113.

Madison, P. *Personality and development in college.* Reading, Mass.: Addison-Wesley, 1969.

Marcus, D., Offer, D., Blatt, S., & Gratch, G. A clinical approach to the understanding of normal and pathologic adolescence. *Archives of General Psychiatry*, 1966, *15*(6), 569-576.

Moustakas, C. E. *Loneliness.* Englewood Cliffs, N.J.: Prentice-Hall, 1961.

Moustakas, C. E. *Loneliness and love.* Englewood Cliffs, N.J.: Prentice-Hall, 1972.

Mullaney, A. The university as a community of resistance. *Harvard University Review*, 1970, *40*(4), 628-639.

Murphey, E. B., Silber, E., Coelho, G. V., Hamburg, D. A., & Greenberg, I. Development of autonomy and parent-child interaction in late adolescence. *American Journal of Orthopsychiatry*, 1963, *33*(4), 643-652.

National Commission on Marihuana and Drug Abuse Report. Washington, D.C.: Superintendent of Documents, U.S. Government Printing Office, 1972.

Newcomb, T. M., & Feldman, K. A. *The impact of college on students.* San Francisco: Jossey-Bass, 1969.

Nikelly, A. G. Maternal indulgence and maladjustment in adolescents. *Journal of Clinical Psychology*, 1967, *23*(2), 148-150.

Nixon, R. H. Psychological maturity in adolescence. *Adolescence*, 1966, *1*(3), 211-223.

Peck, R. F. Family patterns correlated with adolescent personality structure. *Journal of Abnormal and Social Psychology*, 1958, *57*(3), 347-350.

Ray, O. S. *Drugs, society, and human behavior.* St. Louis: Mosby, 1972.

Reid, E. A. Effects of co-residential living on the attitudes, self-image, and role expectations of college women. *The American Journal of Psychiatry*, 1974, *131*(5), 551-554.

Rogers, D. *The psychology of adolescence.* New York: Appleton-Century-Crofts, 1972.

Sadava, S. W. College student drug use: A social-psychological study. Doctoral dissertation, University of Colorado. Boulder, Colorado: University Microfilms, 1970, No. 70-23749.

Sadava, S. W. Stages of college student drug use: A methodological contribution to cross-sectional study. *Journal of Consulting and Clinical Psychology*, 1972, *38*(2), 298.

Scherer, S. E., Ettinger, R. F., & Mudrick, N. J. Need for social approval and drug use. *Journal of Consulting and Clinical Psychology*, 1972, *38*(1), 118-121.

Schroeder, C. C., & LeMay, M. L. The impact of co-ed residence halls on self-actualization. *Journal of College Student Personnel*, 1973, *14*(2), 105-110.

Slater, P. *The pursuit of loneliness.* Boston: Beacon, 1970.

Smart, R. G., & Fejer, D. Drug use among adolescents and their parents: Closing the generation gap in mood modification. *Journal of Abnormal Psychology*, 1972, *79*(2), 153-160.

Snyder, S. H. *Uses of marihuana.* New York: Oxford University Press, 1971.

Sopchak, A. Parental "identification" and "tendency toward disorders" as measured by the Minnesota Multiphasic Personality Inventory. *Journal of Abnormal and Social Psychology,* 1952, *47*(2), 159-165.

Tart, C. T. *On being stoned: A psychological study of marihuana intoxication.* Palo Alto, Calif.: Science and Behavior Books, 1971.

Taylor, R. A. Personality traits and discrepant achievement: A review. *Journal of Counseling Psychology,* 1964, *11*(1), 76-82.

Trent, J. W., & Medsker, L. L. *Beyond high school.* Berkeley: University of California Press, 1967.

U.S. Public Health Service. *Alcohol and health.* Washington, D.C.: Superintendent of Documents, U.S. Government Printing Office, 1971.

Victor, H. R., Grossman, J. C., & Eisenman, R. Openness to experience and marihuana use in high school students. *Journal of Consulting and Clinical Psychology,* 1973, *41*(1), 78-85.

Vogel, W., & Lauterbach, C. G. Relationships between normal and disturbed sons' perceptions of their parents' behavior, and personality attributes of the parents and sons. *Journal of Clinical Psychology,* 1963, *19*(1), 52-56.

Weiner, I. B. *Psychological disturbance in adolescence.* New York: Wiley, 1970.

Weiss, F.A. Self-alienation: Dynamics and therapy. *The American Journal of Psychoanalysis,* 1961, *21*(2), 207-218.

Zellermayer, J., & Marcus, J. Kibbutz adolescence: Relevance to personality development. *Journal of Youth and Adolescence, 1972, 1*(2), 143-153.

Chapter 8

Sexual Fulfillment

CHAPTER OUTLINE

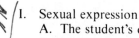

I. Sexual expression
   A. The student's dilemma
   B. Underlying motives
   C. Management of the sexual drive

II. Sexual ethics
   A. Defining a personal ethic
   B. The "new" morality

III. The dating scene
   A. Why do we socialize?
   B. What is love?
   C. Fear of intimacy

IV. Fulfillment through marriage
   A. Why do people marry?
   B. Alternatives to traditional marriage
      1. Group marriage
      2. Two-stage marriage
      3. Contract marriage
      4. Open marriage
      5. Communal living
      6. Part-time marriage
      7. Triads
   C. Living together without marriage
   D. Divorce

V. Other forms of sexual expression
   A. Masturbation
   B. Homosexuality

VI. Summary

We now plunge into perhaps the most perplexing and controversial area of human experience—sexual expression. Because of the many psychological and sociological factors associated with sexuality, and especially because our attitudes have undergone rather dramatic change during the last decade, sexuality is a much discussed topic in college, in the media, and in society at large. Some people welcome the present openness of sexual expression as a needed remedy to the Victorian attitudes of the past, while others regard sexual permissiveness as a harbinger of doom. Only the future will tell to what extent this most basic impulse has been altered.

This chapter will focus on changing attitudes toward sex, on emerging forms of sexual expression, and on the meaning of love and marriage. In addition, divorce, dating, masturbation, and homosexuality will be discussed.

SEXUAL EXPRESSION

Despite the widespread interest in the subject of human sexuality, there is much misinformation and contradiction. Many persons today, for example, remain sexually inhibited, while others place increasing importance on physical relationships. Thus, it is difficult to accommodate the diverse ideas about sexuality, both objective and subjective, within a single discussion. To begin, I should distinguish between *sex*, which refers to an inborn, biological aspect of ourselves, and *sexuality*, which encompasses a broad range of learned factors—values, attitudes, experiences, motives, and even knowledge. Sex is associated with reproduction, while sexuality is bound up with identity and role.

The Student's Dilemma

During the past decade, sexual values, patterns of socializing, and modes of sexual expression have changed rapidly, creating perplexing situations for many students. The development of the "pill," for example, has had an enormous impact on the quality of interpersonal relationships. Besides allowing more sexual freedom and openness, the pill has given the female a more equal status with the male. She can choose a partner or initiate a sexual relationship without the fear of pregnancy and thus commitment (Kaats & Davis, 1970). It is interesting to note that our attitudes in this area have changed so rapidly that texts on marriage and dating that researched dating patterns less than a decade ago are no longer applicable. It is not surprising, therefore, that students find it difficult to formulate an ethical code to guide their sexual behavior. No one presumes to tell them what their sexual conduct should be; they must decide for themselves, and they must live with the consequences of their decisions. Students have many options regarding their sexual behavior that range from extremely liberal views to repressive attitudes toward sex (Williamson, 1972), but often they do not fully understand the consequences of their behavior until after involvement in a sexual relationship. Only in retrospect can they evaluate what was harmful or beneficial. It has always been easier to talk about objective biological facts than to discuss ethical questions concerning sexual intimacy, and it is not surprising that students frequently reach the wrong conclusions regarding predictable consequences and possible alternatives. The problem is further compounded because sexual partners often do not communicate on the same level; sexual intimacy for one may carry an entirely different connotation than it does for another. Often enough, students may be motivated to seek sexual involvement not because of biological needs but because of social pressure from peers. Indeed, the sexual drive is intensified or diminished by psychological and social factors, and these factors complicate an individual's formulation of personal sexual ethics (SIECUS, 1970).

On one point, however, psychologists can speak with reasonable assurance: Sex for sex's sake alone is more apt to create problems than is sexual expression as a part of a total relationship. This is especially true for females, who traditionally have attributed a deeper meaning to sexual experience than males have. The female, then, has in the past been more apt to suffer psychologically from the consequences of casual sexual involvement than the male. As in any undertaking, individuals must be aware of their motives, although it is especially difficult to be objective about sexual motives. Maintaining individuality, mutual equality, and trust are important aspects of sexual motives that students would do well to consider before sexual involvement (O'Neill & O'Neill, 1972).

Sexually intimate couples who see each other as potentially permanent mates are often able to express a mutual feeling of care and understanding and to maintain a premarital sexual commitment. They are willing to accept the consequences of their behavior and establish a nonexploitive, mutually satisfying relationship. However, it is often difficult to separate neurotic motives—dependency or the need to control another—from a genuine and healthy relationship. Sometimes students who are involved in a dependent relationship prefer to rationalize their behavior in order to justify it, rather than extricate themselves from an unrewarding relationship. Experimenting with sex before marriage may, for some persons, limit sex to a physical level alone, produce mistrust and suspicion if sex is not fulfilling for both, create feelings of one's being used by the other, or encourage a disregard for marital fidelity later; but abstaining from sex out of fear, guilt, or inhibition can have equally undesirable consequences.

No one questions the enormous power of the sexual drive or the fact that other forces—social and spiritual—have given it shape and direction. Some of these forces have made the sexual drive a creative power—that is, a way of discovering the positive aspects of another person, and a new way of perceiving the world, since the feeling of affection for one person may extend to others as well. Other forces have inhibited the natural expression of the sexual drive. Students should, therefore, as part of their total education, examine the conflicting beliefs and attitudes and select those that are consistent with their goals. A humanistic ethic that places sexual expression in proper perspective and takes into account love as a primary ingredient (Sorensen, 1973), the well being of the individual, and the goals of humanity would seem best.

Underlying Motives

Sexual behavior reflects the entire personality of an individual. Just as some persons eat for psychological reasons without being hungry, others may indulge in sex without actual physical desire. The following psychological motives often directly influence sexual activity.

1. *To obtain acceptance.* Sex offers a kind of security and may be used to achieve acceptance, especially if the individual concerned feels unattractive. Sexual contact can be a way to express gratitude for favors or it can be initiated out of "duty" to the partner.
2. *To defend against loneliness.* Sexual contact can guarantee human communication for those whose lives seem otherwise barren. It provides temporary companionship and a sense of belonging. For lonely individuals, the sex act can be a transitory alleviation of feelings of isolation.
3. *To avoid emotional intimacy.* Some persons use sexual intimacy to avoid an emotional union; intimacy on a physical basis alone eliminates the threat of emotional involvement. Sex can provide excitement, release, and pleasure, without feelings of responsibility toward the partner.
4. *To overcome inferiority feelings.* Some people use sexual conquests to compensate for feelings of inadequacy. However, their anxiety in sexual relations may often produce impotence, premature ejaculation, or frigidity.
5. *To demonstrate power.* The sex act may be used by certain individuals to demonstrate power over their partners. One partner can dominate the other by withholding affection; the sexual act in this case becomes an expression of aggression. Sexual unresponsiveness, in turn, may suggest unconscious revenge. Sexual victories are sought to improve the individual's self-image (Shulman, 1967).
6. *To offer comfort.* Sexual expression may take the form of comfort given by one partner to the other who is hurt, humiliated, or depressed. Sexual contact brings consolation.
7. *To experience suffering.* Some individuals indulge in sex in order to make themselves suffer, using sex to satisfy their masochistic desires. For example, one partner may view the other as having "animal needs" to which he or she must submit.
8. *To cause trouble.* Sex may be used to rebel against authority. Flirting with everyone in sight, falling in love with a married person, or pursuing someone

just to alleviate boredom are some examples of this kind of behavior, which can often be attributed to deep-seated conflicts or dissatisfaction with how the individual feels about himself (Shulman, 1967).

9. *To show hostility or contempt.* Sex can serve as an outlet for aggression or hate or as a means of degrading the partner. In these cases, sex is divorced from tenderness and affection. For example, prostitutes may show boredom or ask their clients to hasten the act; in so doing, they degrade their clients as their clients are degrading them.

10. *To promote relaxation and pleasure.* Sex may be used to relieve tension and anxiety. Hidden strain and nervousness are momentarily alleviated, although the source of these feelings is not eliminated. Nocturnal emissions ("wet dreams") provide an unconscious release of anxiety in the absence of sexual intercourse. Another alternative that provides release of anxiety is masturbation.

11. *To procreate.* If the desire to procreate is the *only* reason for sexual intercourse, it may take away the pleasure from the act. Also, dissension may develop between partners if their reasons for sex are different. And when two people become unhappy over sex, they may also become unhappy over other aspects of their lives.

Healthy human sexuality involves erotic pleasure within a context of tenderness and affection. Jourard (1974) cites several factors that contribute to healthy sexual enjoyment. (1) Being satisfied with other aspects of our lives—work, friends, leisure—can help us enjoy sex more. The reverse is also true; that is, when we are sexually gratified, we generally relate better to our work, to other people, and to other activities. (2) Relative freedom from unpleasant childhood experiences with sexual expression generally promotes a wholesome attitude toward sex during the adult years. Being taught that sex is "dirty" or being punished for masturbation are examples of childhood experiences that can affect adult sexuality in the form of uneasiness, fear, shame, and even impotence or frigidity. (3) Accurate sexual instruction is a significant factor in sexual enjoyment because much of sexual behavior is learned. When parents are not honest with their children's natural curiosity about sex, negative attitudes and false beliefs can develop that can affect later sexual responsiveness. (4) Loving the partner, communicating freely, and caring for each other's needs can make the sexual act rich and beautiful.

Management of the Sexual Drive

People who understand themselves and recognize what they want from life are usually able to place sexual expression in its proper perspective; that is, they are neither tormented by nor captive to their sexual drive. Many students, however, cannot establish satisfying and fulfilling ways of sexual expression. Parental conflicts, feelings of guilt, immaturity, unfortunate sexual experiences during a crucial period of emotional development, undernourished self-esteem—any of these factors may prevent a couple from deriving joy and pleasure from sex. When the sexual act becomes empty and meaningless, the frustrated persons may "quit" altogether or may go on, even overdoing the sexual activities they dislike without knowing why.

SEXUAL ETHICS

There can be no single view on sexual ethics within a pluralistic society such as ours, but we can examine facts and discuss experiences in order to make decisions on sexual behavior that will bring us joy and fulfillment rather than guilt and grief. Discussing alternatives does not mean that we must condone particular kinds of sexual behavior, but we must try to understand the range of sexual activities if we are to put this important experience into meaningful perspective (Kirkendall & Whitehurst, 1971).

Defining a Personal Ethic

Despite the subjectiveness of sexual ethics, certain general principles seem to apply without moralistic overtones. A lack of trust between sexually involved partners may cause psychological harm; it is unethical for people to act against their own moral standards or to persuade other people to act against theirs; making false promises, manipulating others into betraying their principles, disrespecting the rights of another's weaknesses or needs constitute unethical behavior, and sexual involvement under any of these conditions may cause injury to at least one partner; before engaging in premarital sex, the individual should consider the possible consequences—including guilt and rejection—and be willing to accept them; although there is some sexual aspect in nearly all forms of love, sex by itself does not always contain love.

As we have suggested earlier, views on premarital sex and sex without love vary widely. Ellis (1958) states that persons may enjoy sex without love, especially if they do not experience guilt, which is most often produced by conditioning and social taboos. Klemer (1970) has challenged Ellis on this point and feels that sexual restraint has a positive effect on personality; young people should first have a framework of ethics on which to base their sexual behavior. Another view holds that premarital sex is acceptable when it is conducive to the welfare and happiness of those involved and when no one is exploited or hurt because of the relationship (Fletcher, 1967). Another point of view maintains that the consequences that follow the sexual relations must dictate whether sex should take place or should be avoided (Hamilton, 1970); whether sexual activity will improve a given interpersonal relationship is still another criterion (Kirkendall, 1960). Bowman (1965) feels that sexual exclusiveness is most important in physical intimacy and that affection is highly desirable when intercourse before marriage is contemplated.

Confusion in semantics often creates problems of communication. For instance, to "make love" means to engage in sexual intercourse; yet, copulation is possible without love. Physical attraction or sex technique cannot provide a foundation for a relationship or help it to grow. There are, of course, instances in which both partners agree from the beginning that the relationship will exist on a physical basis alone. While the physical dimension of sexual expression is necessary and pleasurable, it is also possible for two persons to transcend the physical experience and find in each other intangible qualities that attract and bind them together (Fromm, 1956).

There is no doubt, however, that sexual attitudes are being re-evaluated by young people and that a new approach toward sexual expression is emerging. This sexual ethic appears to focus on the quality of sexual expression, on the destruction of the antisexual ethic that stifled sexual fulfillment, and on the importance of affection, caring, and love between sexual partners (Otto, 1971). "The issue is not whether sex occurs before or after marriage, but rather what the significance of the relationship is in terms of appropriateness, maturity, choice, responsibility, intimacy, and similar factors" (Garfield, Marcus, & Garfield, 1971, p. 252).

The inhibitions of the Victorian ethic created an artificial situation in which young people frequently found themselves on the defensive; sexual expression was often constricted, clandestine, or unnatural. The male may have had to "con" the female into sex, and the female was afraid of being "tricked." It was difficult to behave honestly. Students today, however, are more apt to talk openly about sex and to avoid playing "games" with each other; they feel more equal with each other than their parents did when they dated. Students, in fact, are not so afraid to touch and kiss each other, to show affection without embarrassment, or to be uninhibited about their bodies. Such behavior is considered healthy and growth-producing. When sex is not expressed hypocritically, when it is not associated with guilt, secrecy, or mystery, it becomes more positive, constructive, and fulfilling (Farnsworth, 1970).

Evidence as well as more indirect information from students indicates that guilt feelings over premarital sexual intercourse are decreasing. Sorensen (1973) found that 80% of the males he questioned and 72% of the females answered affirmatively the statement "It's all right for young people to have sex before getting married if they are in love with each other." Students appear to be more open in discussing sexual matters, less inhibited physically, and more accepting of alternate attitudes toward sexual expression. The sexual behavior of a large number of students is consistent with their beliefs and values and cannot, therefore, result in subsequent guilt. It is the meaning that sex has for the two persons involved that young people emphasize rather than criteria of "good" or "bad" established on arbitrary, abstract, and dogmatic principles (Reiss, 1964).

It is important to recognize that the term "sexual revolution" may well be exaggerated. On the basis of his own recent findings and on reviews of previous investigations, Offer (1972) concludes that there has not been any dramatic change in sexual behavior and attitudes among adolescents during the last 30 years. It may well be that we sense a "revolution" now because we talk more openly about sex than we did a few decades ago. Although Simon, Berger, and Gagnon (1972) report an increase in premarital sexual intercourse among females, their analysis of the data does not consider this pattern a radical departure in sexual attitudes because the women did not engage in sex in a casual or uncommitted manner. The authors further contend that the belief in the "sexual revolution" may cause anxiety in those who have not yet experienced sex; indeed, if this speculation is correct, there may yet be a sexual revolution. Contrary to the belief that the majority of our youth is experiencing a decline in moral values, Fredrickson (1972) found that a sample of middle-class college students from the Midwest endorsed social responsibility, stable family values, and ethical responsibility toward society at large.

On the other hand, McCary (1975) recently reported a trend toward greater sexual activity and more liberal attitudes toward sex. Similarly, a recent survey at a four-year public college in northern California indicated that 72% of the females and 83% of the males in the survey engaged in premarital sexual intercourse (King &

Sobel, 1975). In addition, this survey suggested that there is a continued emphasis on stable, affectionate relationships as part of sexual expression in a social and emotional context and a lessening of the double standard. Such limited studies, of course, are only indications of what is happening; we cannot conclude that these findings apply to students in all other areas and colleges.

No one can deny that sexual intercourse is a very pleasurable outlet, whether within the boundaries of marriage or not, but since sexual expression involves another person, it is inconsiderate for one partner not to consider the well-being of the other (Kirkendall & Anderson, 1973). Regardless of political and social orientation, nearly all of the students I have come in contact with mention the intervening component of love as enhancing sexual pleasure. People free of bias and misinformation and devoid of significant personality problems should be able to decide for themselves what their actions should be in light of their personal convictions and philosophies.

The "New" Morality

Sexual ethics have changed in recent years as the pendulum has swung from the repressive sexual attitudes of earlier generations to a more liberated view of sexuality (Rubin, 1971). Older generations attempted to inhibit sexual expression and encouraged sublimation, denial, rationalization, and displacement in order to stave off the sexual drive. Thus, romantic, ethereal approaches to love relationships developed. In contrast, today's "new morality" involves an increased interest in the technical aspects of sexual activity (Katchadourian & Lunde, 1972). Too often, however, this interest in the sexual aspects of an individual is divorced from concern about the individual as a total person, and interpersonal openness, honesty, communication, and freedom with regard to the sexual drive may lose force when emotional and mental intimacy weakens. Indeed, some people may have become "sex machines" as an antidote to the Victorian philosophy. At its extreme, the new morality maintains that individuals satisfy their sexual urges in the same way that they gratify the hunger or thirst drive; that is, they can take and give physical love without commitment or responsibility.

Cultural changes, including increased equality and extended education for women, seem to be responsible for the apparent increase in the sex drive of women, rather than an awakening of a dormant biological instinct or increased hormone activity. The female sexual drive appears to follow a pattern set by cultural sanctions; the older ethics conditioned the woman to restrict her sexual and emotional needs; the new morality demands that these needs be fulfilled. When a society disapproves of female orgasm, it develops females who do not experience orgasm (Kornhausen & Kornhausen, 1965); thus, in previous years many females did not know that orgasm existed. Now they frequently ask for professional assistance if they do not experience orgasm (Greenson, 1967). As women become more interested in asserting their rights, their feelings of sexuality take on greater force. We see here a strong influence of culture on sexual expectation and behavior.

There is evidence, however, that women today experience fewer guilt feelings about sex and that a commitment to marriage is less important in regard to premarital sexual relationships than it was only ten years ago (Bell & Chaskes, 1970). Certainly the availability of contraceptive devices has had an impact on this attitude change, even though the possibility of venereal disease is still present. Occasionally during the course of psychotherapy, a female may state that from time to time she desires sexual relationships with a compatible male for the sake of sex alone, in much the same way as a young man might desire sex for physical release. It is not impossible that the biological sexual intensity in the female is becoming stronger and closer to that of the male and that suppression of sex through social learning has in the past made the female more passive and less sexually demanding. At present these ideas are only speculations, but further studies on the personality of women under fewer sexual restraints will shed more light on this emerging issue.

It does not appear, however, that the decline in sexual repression has brought an end to emotional problems, neuroses, or sexual aberrations. On the contrary, sexual freedom seems to be associated with as much emotional disturbance as sexual repression. Neither repression nor casualness seems to be a realistic guide in sexual conduct, and the current liberal attitudes toward sex afford students few guidelines for sexual morality. The ensuing confusion may make it difficult for students to find the kind of relationship that they actually desire. They often tend to look at sex rationally rather than to follow either impulse or rules blindly, but sex is a complicated matter, and the responses involved cannot be so easily categorized. Studying sex apart from other personality traits may have scientific value, but sexual expression in real life is affected by numerous nonsexual factors. There are often fallacies in seemingly reasonable arguments: premarital sexual activity is alright "as long as no one gets hurt," or premarital sex is not wrong when "love makes it right." In the first place, it is difficult to be sure that no one will get hurt; in the second place, students do not always know what they mean by "love," for the word is deceptive and may be used for secondary gains rather than as an expression of genuine affection.

It is difficult for some young people to acknowledge that genuine sexual revolution does not mean sexual licentiousness and exploitiveness but sexual equality—a sense of inclusiveness between the sexes and a sexual freedom that includes the freedom to love and to express tenderness and affection (Barclay, 1971). People who feel that playing "games" and assuming "roles" are necessary aspects of their sexual lives are not expressing themselves honestly but are caught up in a form of sexual tyranny.

Despite heated discussions in the mass media and sometimes within the family, there is little concrete evidence that sexual promiscuity (casual and indiscriminate sex) on the campus or in society at large is increasing. Some evidence, however, indicates a general increase in sexual experience before marriage, usually between emotionally involved partners who intend to marry (Packard, 1970). A two-month survey of high school students and their counselors and teachers in a large metropolitan area found that teenagers are becoming involved in sexual experiences more often and at an earlier age than their parents did (Chicago *Sun-Times,* 1973).

THE DATING SCENE

Dating practices have changed rapidly during the past few years as students have moved away from the formality typical of dating in the past. There is less pressure to date; casual, informal, and relaxed relationships among young people

Figure 8-1. Socialization patterns have changed from a rigid social etiquette to more natural and casual relationships between the sexes. Photo by Jody Ellyne.

are increasing. Students tend to avoid elaborate planning for dates and instead seek more spontaneous encounters based on the sharing of ideas. Many students feel that dating should not be a competitive "game" but a casual "getting together." The male is no longer expected to "call the shots," and expenses are often shared. Couples are more apt to get together on the basis of how they think or feel rather than on the basis of their social status or physical appearance; frequent dating, just to be dating, is no longer a mark of status. Students today do not feel a strong need to conform to group expectations, and their rejection of artificiality in social relationships thus carries over into dating practices.

Why Do We Socialize?

The primary objective of socializing is to increase our opportunities to relate to others on a social basis and thus broaden our experiences so that we may understand our own personalities better as well as the personalities of others (Douvan & Adelson, 1966). Students develop emotionally and intellectually as they relate with others and are thus aided in the growth of their personal identity. Such broadening of experience may also later enable the student to make a mature choice of a mate (Rogers, D., 1972). Dating also encourages etiquette, poise, the sharing of mutual interests, and participation in social and recreational functions. When socializing becomes a means for securing social "props" or boosting an individual's ego, however, it loses its real purpose and becomes superficial and "diluted," promoting relationships that will not sustain two people in any meaningful way. Sexual activity can make dating more interesting; however, sex cannot restore a relationship that lacks stability and depth and may even lead to misunderstandings that can destroy an initially favorable relationship.

What Is Love?

Since love can mean so many different things, we might consider first distinguishing among the most-often thought of kinds of love. Infatuation (romantic love) is most often based on unreasonable and foolish notions about another person; we tend to see in that person what we want to see and to ignore what we do not like. In this respect, romantic love can be "blind." It is often based on physical attraction rather than on an objective and realistic appraisal of the person. Romantic love is also characterized by possessiveness and exclusiveness ("You belong to me alone.") Such a romantic view of love is gradually being replaced with a more realistic attitude that emphasizes the enjoyment of the present, the similarities between the sexes rather than the differences, and a greater feeling for belonging to the "world community" (Kilpatrick, 1974). Mature love is built on knowing someone well and recognizing and receiving that person the way he or she is. It is also based on feeling deeply liked and accepted for what you are (Rubin, 1973). Trying to avoid hurt or rejection by not letting yourself be fully known prevents a loving relationship from developing.

Despite such distinctions, love will probably always mean different things to different people and even to the same person at different times in his or her life. I asked some of my students to jot down a definition of love based on their own experience. Here are some of the definitions they gave.

Love is an emotional reaction combined with a physical relationship.

Love is showing your deepest emotions for a person.

Love is making someone else happy, a feeling that gives you contentment that grows all the time and never seems to reach a peak.

Love is an attraction, both physical and emotional, based on viewing a person from a positive rather than an idealistic point of view.

Love is trusting someone and showing yourself as you really are and not being ashamed of what others think of you.

Love is caring for someone's feelings and happiness as much as you care for yourself.

Love is to feel comfortable with someone even with the full knowledge of his or her problems and faults.

Love is accepting someone as completely as you accept yourself.

Love is thinking about the needs and desires of another person before your own.

Love is honesty and trust and being happy with and enjoying another person.

Love is intimate sharing with another person.

Love is the security that grows with mutual affection and understanding.

Figure 8-2. Love is intimate sharing with another person. Photo by Shirley Kontos.

Herman and Snyder (1962) have put together the ideas of many others in an attempt to show the difference between mature and immature love. When love develops out of sexual attraction—that is, on a "first sight" basis—when it involves demands and possessiveness, when it is characterized by alternating feelings of attraction and doubt, it is apt to be an immature love. Desiring to change the partner "for his or her own good," envying the partner's personal achievements or possessions, and seeing in the partner only what you wish to see are also characteristics of immature, ineffectual love relationships. Having doubts about whether the relationship will last or prolonging it strictly for personal gain are also features of a faulty love interaction.

Mature love, on the other hand, is based on mutual trust and respect. It is a secure relationship because it is based on each partner's acceptance of the other as he or she is, not as he or she might be. The feelings of love are relatively stable and are not grounded in one partner's desire for power or control. Sexual expression is an important aspect of this relationship, but mental and intellectual intimacy are also involved. Mature love is built on the premise that the growth and advancement of one partner is shared and rejoiced in by the other and that any reasonable differences that may exist between them are an "added attraction" to the relationship because such differences make the relationship more challenging and enlightening for both (Herman & Snyder, 1962). Here is an example of what a mature love may involve.

Incident

Before we got married, my husband and I sat down one day and drew up some ideas on what our marriage should be like. We agreed that we would be lovers, friends, and partners, but most of all we wanted to accept each other realistically, as unique and special individuals. We hoped to share the things we both wanted to feel and do without losing sight of the fact that we are two separate persons with lives of our own. What we share should strengthen us and make us grow through the other's presence, not limit our individuality or inhibit self-fulfillment. We belong *with* each other, not *to* each other, and we should try to tune in to each other's needs while remaining true to ourselves. We vowed not to feed *on* each other but to grow *with* each other. We will try to give as much as we take from each other and respect the few differences that we have. With these attitudes in mind, we hope for more experiences in the future that will make each of us a more beautiful person because together we are more than either of us could have become alone.

Fear of Intimacy

Intimacy, ability to share, and openness are much desired qualities that pave the way to greater fulfillment. However, some people experience difficult emotional barriers against such qualities. Kangas and Solomon (1975) mention several obstacles to intimacy: Fear of dependency, when dependency is viewed as a sign of weakness, fear of losing ourselves in the identity of another person, fear that our feelings may make us look foolish and stupid, fear of getting hurt, put down, or rejected, fear of not obtaining love, fear of being possessed by someone else or trapped in a relationship, and fear of taking chances. All in all, it is the strong person who can risk being vulnerable, who can reach out to new experiences, and who dares to ask others to value him or her.

There are many kinds and degrees of intimacy. Intimacy begins in the womb, and after birth it may be expressed through cuddling, sucking, and caressing. Later, intimacy may be attempted with mother substitutes such as soft objects, toys, and pets. As we grow older, intimacy is demonstrated in social conduct (shaking hands, embracing); sometimes human objects of intimacy are replaced by inanimate objects, such as alcohol or cigarettes. The next stages of intimacy involve verbal exchanges, eye contact, and hand, mouth, body, and genital intimacy (Morris, 1971). Such direct physical intimacy can, however, be associated with fear and guilt and may cause people to look for other forms of intimacy, such as dancing, massage, or talking to a therapist. Some people, of course, can become intimate on an intellectual, philosophical, or spiritual level; that is, their minds are on the same wavelength, and they experience a certain mental rapport with each other. And some people may seek to become intimate with themselves through masturbating.

FULFILLMENT THROUGH MARRIAGE

The majority of individuals ultimately seek some form of personal intimacy with a member of the opposite sex by the time they reach adulthood, and the most common way to establish this intimacy is through marriage.

Why Do People Marry?

Attitudes and expectations about marriage have changed considerably in recent years. While some aspects of the old notion of marriage—security, love, children—still survive, other aspects are no longer so widely accepted. The changing role of the female as housekeeper and mother is, perhaps, the most obvious case in point, but other changes involve the decreasing importance of social pressure, legal regulations, and religious customs related to marriage. Indeed, sex itself is no longer considered by many as a chief motive for marrying. Instead, young people today tend to look upon marriage as an important opportunity to find self-esteem, acceptance, and a means toward self-actualization. Psychological reasons for marriage, then, seem to be more operant today than economic or social reasons. The idea of a "convenient" marriage—one based on the partner's health, social class, or economic stability or on a need for security—seems to be overridden by the idea of a happy and growth-producing companionship. While many still use traditional characteristics as a basis for choosing a partner—similarity of social and educational background, for example—others choose their partners primarily on the basis of the partner's respect for personal freedom. For them, marriage encourages greater personal intimacy while preserving their own unique lifestyles. They would rather not enter into marriage than enter one that curtails or eliminates their freedom (Otto, 1973).

It goes without saying that traditional sex roles are disappearing, and in many modern marriages we observe that both partners do exactly the same type of work in and out of the home (Reiss, 1971). Thus, for many young couples, marriage is a liberating situation in which one partner acts as a stimulus for the growth and inspiration of the other. Despite these changes in attitudes, however, there continue to be problems concerning role expectations, lack of communication, and undue attachment to parents. Personal problems that were not resolved before marriage often take on renewed force in marriage and prove genuinely detrimental to the new relationship.

Incident

We were married two years ago, and I am beginning to realize that my husband wants to have the same marriage his parents have. I get up and make him breakfast, and then I drive him to work. I work around the house all day, do the shopping, keep things nice. Supper is ready when he comes home. He says he brings in the money, and my job is to take care of him and the home. He

Figure 8-3. Regardless of what kind of marriage contract we choose, most of us understand marriage to be an intimate union of mutual tenderness. Photo by Shirley Kontos.

never does anything around the house unless I ask him. When we dated, he was a lot more considerate. He did things for me; I felt important. But we never discussed what my role would be after we married. I guess I expected the consideration he showed me before we were married and thought that he would be as open with me now as he was then. When I do something outside our routine, I feel I have to ask him because otherwise he gets this sulky look on his face. Some evenings we sit and watch TV and have nothing to say to each other. I wonder how I ever got into this situation; are other marriages like ours?

Incident

My wife is the best friend I ever had. When I was dating in college, girls just sort of came and went; there was nothing steady in my life. But I can really depend on my wife.

I work around the house and take care of our kid as well as any woman. We don't think who's going to do what work, we just think in terms of what's to be done. We don't do things for each other because we should but because we want to. We both treasure our personal freedom; we try not to tie each other down. We're not upset when we happen not to agree on something; we accept our differences because we have so many things in common. We have times when we want to be alone, but our time together is strong and beautiful. I know she's always there, and she feels the same way with me. We don't live only for each other, but there's care and affection and we both know it.

Most of us have given some thought to marriage and have certain expectations and even dreams about what marriage will bring. When undergraduate students in a large Midwestern state university were asked what they wanted and expected from marriage, they submitted some very enlightening replies.

I want to be able to retain my personality and have my wife retain hers also. I hope we can share the things we have in common and still learn from our differences. Rather than molding both lives to one pattern, I hope we can find happiness in new experiences and new challenges.

In my marriage I expect to stay at home and take care of my kids and my husband. I hope to be able to keep a nice house for when he returns from work. I'm sure I'll be comfortable being at home all day raising a family.

I expect two people to respect the fact that they are two individuals and that marriage must be a mutual give and take. One of the parties should never feel submerged by the other. Total honesty and airing of feelings is required. I expect honest disagreement, but nothing should shatter the foundations of a marriage based on respect and love.

I want my marriage to possess security, a sense of unending closeness, and open communication between us. I want a marriage that has the strength to endure all situations and the ability for growth. I want togetherness, but it must be based on true feelings.

I want my marriage to be permanent, without any doubts about our mutual love. I expect an everlasting bond of love and respect in my marriage, but I want to be treated like an equal with my husband. I am a career-oriented person; you won't find me sitting at home. I expect to keep myself and my spouse happy, but we'll have to work together to achieve that goal and to resolve our problems.

I hope for a lasting marriage—one in which both of us can find enjoyment and contentment in life together. I expect love and fidelity that goes far beyond the joy of the wedding ceremony. I expect to learn how to share myself completely with another person and to make personal sacrifices that I've never had to make before. I want to rise each morning knowing that I'm making someone else's life a little more pleasant.

Alternatives to Traditional Marriage

Most of us are familiar with the traditional marriage in which the husband becomes the major money earner and family provider while the wife manages domestic affairs, including the rearing of children. As traditional marriage has been judged confining, monotonous, and unfulfilling and as equality between the sexes has increased, new marriage styles have emerged (Rogers, C., 1972). While each of these has its advantages, shortcomings are also apparent, just as in traditional marriage.

Group marriage. A relatively new arrangement is group marriage, which involves three or more persons of both sexes (Ellis, 1971). Such a group seeks the companionship and intimacy associated with traditional marriage but also desires greater freedom and emotional openness, including somewhat flexible sexual involvements. As more persons interact in intimate ways, however, relationships can become extremely complicated. There can be too many "third wheels" in such situations as well as subtle rivalries and intricate power struggles.

Two-stage marriage. The anthropologist Margaret Mead (1971) speculated that two stages of marriage might offer a solution to the problems of failing marriages and increasing divorce. In the first stage, *individual marriage,* the couples would legitimately marry for companionship and love. There would be minimal financial obligations and an agreement not to have children. Should a couple choose to dissolve the arrangement, a divorce would be easy to obtain. If a couple decided to have a child, they would move on to *parental marriage.* By this time, they would have demonstrated their emotional compatibility and financial capability of raising children. In this phase, divorce would be difficult, and the children would be protected. To some extent, many couples who postpone beginning a family are, perhaps somewhat unconsciously, working out this two-stage arrangement within the boundaries of a traditional marriage.

Contract marriage. Another alternative to the assumed permanency of traditional marriage is a renewable contract. Instead of signing a contract to remain married to the same person throughout life, why not make the contract valid for only a stipulated period so that it may be renewed only if so desired by both partners? Such an agreement might encourage partners to remain more considerate of each other, especially as the date of expiration approaches. On the other hand, one partner might exercise the option to negate the contract, while the other was quite unprepared—particularly in terms of possible alternatives—for a termination of the marriage. Also, in such trial marriages, there may be a feeling of lack of permanency in the relationship; one or both partners may feel that the door is always open if something goes wrong.

Open marriage. The types of marriage I have described so far—with the possible exception of group marriage—are closed marriages, in the sense that *one* partner more or less fulfills the expectations and needs of the other—financial, emotional, intellectual, and sexual. Open marriage, however, stresses perfect equality and the freedom for each partner to find his or her own way to personal growth (O'Neill & O'Neill, 1972). Each partner is free, therefore, to have sexual relationships with others and to discuss these openly. Obviously not everyone could tolerate such circumstances—especially those who are dependent on their spouse, those who feel insecure about themselves, or those who feel that their spouse might abandon them—but there are couples who seem able to maximize their own love and trust through extramarital relationships.

Communal living. Students interested in relating intimately to a small group of people have been deeply attracted by communal lifestyles. Such living arrangements require sharing and ensure acceptance, yet often grant considerable freedom through economic cooperation and through the abolishment of arbitrary social rules (Roberts, 1971). Students who are interested in testing themselves but who also want protection in case of failure are often attracted to communal living. Rather than living with someone about whom they care deeply and risking possible failure in maintaining that relationship, they choose communal living, where there is considerable sharing and intimacy of feelings in an unassuming atmosphere of freedom and openness. It is possible to find nonpossessive love without any significant amount of guilt in such a living arrangement. Each member has the opportunity to experience the association of other persons without feeling "tied down" to any one person. However, problems involving privacy, jealousy, misunderstanding of expectations and obligations, and conflict of loyalties do arise.

Part-time marriage. In our mobile society, some married couples are forced to separate because their work involves long separations and frequent geographical relocation. Some couples, therefore, maintain the option to separate if relocation seems desirable for either partner. For some persons, such an arrangement is unthinkable, but for others, those who are more independent and who do not plan to have children, this arrangement ensures their freedom and mobility while providing many of the benefits of more traditional marriage (Whitehurst, 1975).

Triads. For three persons who like and understand one another and who can allow intimacy between the other two at times, living together as a trio can bring comfort and support, unique closeness, and convenience. The benefits can include better child care, less opportunity for loneliness, equal distribution of household chores, and financial advantages. For some, the amount of love and opportunities for sharing are increased with a third person (all the members of the triad may be of the same sex). Of course, there can be conflict, jealousies, and tension if all the members of the trio are not suited for this type of living or are unwilling to contribute equally to the family unit (Whitehurst, 1975).

Living Together without Marriage

Students in counseling sessions report a growing number of problems in relationships that involve living together without marriage, although such arrangements may initially prove to be convenient and pleasurable, as well as meaningful.

Responsibilities develop when two persons live as husband and wife without marriage, and one partner may be unwilling to assume his or her share of these responsibilities. Of course, the same can be said for married persons who are unwilling to fulfill marital obligations, but the risk appears to be higher among unmarried couples living together. Partners who live together do not always share the same motives; that is, what is casual commitment for one may be permanent commitment or emotional dependency for the other. One partner may wish to possess the other exclusively, while the other partner may require freedom to relate emotionally and/or sexually with others. This tension may strain the relationship so that jealousy and possessiveness become the dominant elements. If one partner leaves, the other may experience frustration and depression or feel exploited and abused. Subsequent relationships for the rejected partner may become guarded or viewed with suspicion.

There are social pushes (peer pressure, economic advantages) as well as personal motives that encourage students to live together without marriage. Many students seek an intimacy and sensual awareness that they feel has been denied them by an industrial and technocratic society. By living together they hope to learn to express their real feelings, to reveal themselves through emotional spontaneity and valid sexual expression, and to find self-realization and self-fulfillment. Nevertheless, these relationships are often of short duration because there is no contractual statement of permanence, because parental and legal disapproval of cohabitation may subtly affect those who are not quite sure of their moral philosophy, and because many students are only experimenting with personal encounters and have not yet formed a stable identity.

For some, living together may develop their confidence so that they can successfully marry in the future, but failure in living together can make some reluctant to enter into intimate relationships later. Thus, they may continue to seek protection through a series of short-term liaisons.

Separations after living together can be as painful as a legal divorce. The following situation reveals how one partner became a "casualty" and had to seek psychological assistance in order to find better ways of coping with her basic problem of dependency.

Incident

Ann is a shy and hesitant freshman from a sheltered home who dated only occasionally in high school to avoid "putting up with different guys all the time." At college, however, she met Ted, a senior, and she began to date him regularly. Occasionally she stayed with him overnight because it was too late to walk back to her dormitory; moreover, her roommates bored her. The following semester Ann moved into Ted's apartment for convenience and shared expenses with him. On weekends Ted wanted his freedom; he drank beer with his friends, watched ballgames on TV, read magazines, played basketball, and, in general, lived like a bachelor. As he became evasive and noncommittal in the relationship, Ann felt lonely and neglected. She concluded that he did not care for her any longer, and she began to feel sorry for herself. She lost interest in sex and felt used by Ted whenever he approached her. She realized that Ted wanted to have all the benefits of married life without being married. When Ann decided to move out, she felt "trapped" again. She had difficulty finding a vacant room in the dormitory in the middle of the semester; besides, she did not want her parents to find out. Her academic work deteriorated as she began to miss classes. She became increasingly depressed. She overslept constantly in order to escape her unpleasant situation. After consulting with a psychologist, Ann became aware of her dependency and how she had gone about resolving it, possibly as a reaction to her strict parents.

In spite of the risks involved, living together seems to be gaining acceptance among college students. In one study (Thorman, 1973), interviews with persons living together indicated that the vast majority did not take the matter casually but maintained affection and loyalty between themselves. Instead of taking each other for granted, as with the traditional marriage, they tried to make their "nonmarriage" a liberating experience for each other. In this survey, the couples felt content with each other and did not feel trapped or frustrated in any way. Each maintained their own friends and only rarely was there sexual adventure with other partners. Love, not sex, was the force that brought the couples together, according to this survey. The mutual sharing, the honesty and lack of pretense, and the quality of the relationship seemed more important than sex alone.

Another study (Macklin, 1974) found similar results. Cohabitating students did not differ from noncohabitants in academic performance, in their desire to marry eventually, or in family background. Very few had refrained from sexual relations for moral reasons, and most of them began to live together because an opportunity presented itself. Their partners were monogamous, and their emotional attachment was strong. Companionship, security, convenience, and enjoyment were important aspects of the arrangement. Sex was not given as the primary reason for living together; instead, students maintained that the decision had been based on the desire to get to know someone well and to share experiences with that person. As the relationship grew, so did the sexual intimacy. They found living together a fulfilling, growth fostering, and maturing experience.

Apparently both partners can benefit from living together, even when one partner decides to leave. Consequences, of course, depend on the expectations and attitudes of the persons involved, on their initial agreement concerning commitment, and on their personalities. Consider the following successful separation made by a young couple who had enjoyed living together without marriage.

Incident

After living with Judy for a year, Don considers taking a job in another city. Judy begins to evaluate their relationship and the possible consequences of separation. She concludes that living with someone and the experience of loving someone has given her confidence and the knowledge that she could make a go of marriage. Judy feels that she has enough strength to accept the separation gracefully, particularly because Don never makes her feel rejected or exploited. Both consider their living together as a "pleasant summer vacation that has to come to an end like all good things" and feel more mature as persons than a year ago. Judy's fleeting depression is accepted as a natural consequence of the relationship, showing also that her association with Don had substance and meaning. Each had acted as a catalyst for the other's growth. Judy has become aware of what to look for in a man who will some day become her husband. When Don leaves, she begins to date other men with apparent success and without depression.

Much of the information reported here is necessarily one-sided because it came from students who sought clinical help with problems associated with living together. Obviously, students do not need help and are happy living together without marriage.

What is important is the student's understanding of himself, his freedom to choose, and his acceptance of the consequences of his actions. In the final analysis, every person behaves according to the experiences that have affected the development of his unique personality, his individual interpretations of these experiences, and the particular nature and conditions of his encounters with the opposite sex. The effects of living together are, therefore, as variable as the personalities of the persons involved. However, it does seem fair to caution students that difficult consequences may result from living together outside of marriage.

Divorce

Divorce often has a deeply negative impact on spouses and children. If divorce cannot be prevented, efforts should be made to ensure that the spouses do not lose their self-respect or suffer overwhelmingly from feelings of guilt, inadequacy, failure, and loneliness.

Divorce occurs in every segment of our society, particularly among those who marry in their teens. One study (Berelson & Steiner, 1964) shows that divorce is more common among persons who did not know each other well before marriage, who had short engagements, and whose parents were divorced. Divorce also seemed to be more prevalent among persons who were less educated, who had different religious faiths, and who did not attend the church of their faith. Of course, personality factors such as emotional instability, alcoholism, undue attachment to parents, and homosexuality can also cause divorce.

Many view the dissolution of their marriage as a sign of personal failure, and thus it is to be expected that divorce leaves people at least temporarily depressed. Divorced people may fall out of circulation, so to speak, as they begin to lose social contact with their still-married friends, since feeling and acting like a single person may not be so easy for those who have come to depend on someone during marriage. Divorced people tend to re-evaluate themselves and their lives, and such personal soul-searching can bring about personal growth.

Children also experience stress in the process of their parents' separation, but the ultimate detrimental effects of divorce on children may be fewer than those experienced by children who continue to live with quarrelsome, unhappy parents. It is not unusual, however, for children to feel guilty or punished by the divorce of their parents.

Financial difficulty is often given as a reason for divorce. Infidelity is also a commonly cited cause for divorce, but marital unfaithfulness usually reflects other problems, most significantly, perhaps, the inability to communicate or to feel close to each other. Failure to satisfy a spouse sexually can be a problem, but that too may reflect something deeper—emotional distance or simply lack of love toward each other. Indeed, many couples are divorced psychologically long before they are legally divorced. When psychological needs go unmet, couples are separated, regardless of whether or not they continue to live together.

Marriage counseling can help, especially if a couple seriously wishes to save their marriage. A divorce is more likely to be averted when both partners make sincere efforts to save their marriage.

Krantzler (1973), a psychologist who is himself divorced, has studied the problems that divorced persons go through and has suggested that we view divorce not as an experience in failure but as a growth-producing situation. Look at divorce as a stage of living from which to learn and move on. Krantzler points out that the persons whom he counseled after divorce went through a period of self-examination that helped them to find themselves and to become even happier persons than they were before.

OTHER FORMS OF SEXUAL EXPRESSION

The liberal trend in sex in our society has fostered a more tolerant view of different forms of sexual expression, and we are becoming more accepting of alternate needs and of variant lifestyles. Different forms of sexual expression are not necessarily inadequate or inappropriate, but many people, in spite of the relative values and attitudes in our culture, find that what is different is for them "deviant" or "unhealthy." As we mature and experience new ideas, however, we often come to reevaluate what we believed in the past to be forbidden or perverted.

Masturbation

Despite lingering superstitions, it has never been established that masturbation causes harm to an individual (Committee on Human Sexuality, 1972). It may, in fact, be helpful in preparing a person for intercourse, for sexual technique is to a large extent a learned expression (Pomeroy, 1969). The damage inherent in masturbation is related to our attitudes about it and to the possibility that masturbation may compulsively replace meaningful heterosexual relationships. In general, however, masturbation can be considered a prelude to sexual intercourse, although the need for a release from sexual pressures in the absence of a heterosexual partner can serve as a strong motivating force in masturbation.

Homosexuality

Homosexuality refers to sexual desire toward a member of the same sex. Occasional homosexual dreams, admiration for the body of someone of the same sex, or a physical appearance more like someone of the opposite sex are not necessarily indicative of homosexuality. Latent homosexuality refers to heterosexually oriented persons who have repressed or "hidden" homosexual desires. Such feelings may come out under the stress of alcohol, prison, or the loss of a spouse (Kolb, 1973). Homosexual "panic" may be experienced by people whose sexual orientation is fully heterosexual but who may at times have irrational fears that they are indeed homosexual. Such individuals may experience occasional homosexual dreams or daydreams and may become unduly anxious in the company of known homosexuals or if they experience sudden, close contact with members of their own sex (Freedman, Kaplan, & Sadock, 1972).

Mothers of homosexual males have been found to be over-protective and seductive (Bieber, 1962). Such a mother often discourages her son from engaging in heterosexual behavior and encourages him to participate in feminine activities.

Often she shows a preference for her son over her husband (Bieber, 1962). Such a boy finds it easy to identify with his mother but often discovers that he is not accepted by his father. This rejection further discourages the development of masculine attitudes; the boy is likely to grow increasingly distant from his father and increasingly dependent on his mother. It is also entirely possible for an aggressive and dominant father to make a son feel threatened if he shows masculine behavior, such as becoming independent from his family or being aggressive in sports. Indeed, the child may assume that, through masculine behavior, he may lose his father's affection; he does not dare to compete with this powerful figure. Thus, the boy becomes noncompetitive—passive and nonmasculine—to eliminate the danger of parental rejection. It is also possible for a child's misinterpretations of his parents' behavior to account for his sexual orientation, regardless of the overt personality characteristics of his parents. There are in addition a variety of other psychological and social factors that can explain, in part, the genesis of homosexuality—guilt, hostility, dependency, low self-esteem, poor identity (Hoffman, 1968).

There is little substantive research regarding homosexual females, but speculation based on clinical experience suggests that a somewhat opposite situation prevails in their parental relationships; that is, closeness toward a seductive and possessive father is countered by distancing from the mother.

We are not, of course, justified in drawing conclusions from a limited number of studies about how homosexual behavior develops. Many other factors contribute to homosexual behavior, and not all homosexuals are exactly the same, either in their personality makeup or in their reasons for becoming homosexual. It should also be mentioned that negative social reinforcements in attempts to relate with the opposite sex and positive social reinforcements in relations with the same sex are also important in encouraging homosexual behavior.

If there is strong motivation for a homosexual to change in a heterosexual direction, therapy can be of benefit. There is no definitive evidence that homosexuality constitutes a biological and inherited trait; on the contrary, acquired social and psychological influences seem to have a more dominant effect in shaping sexual identity than inborn traits (Brecher, 1971). Often the development of heterosexuality is inhibited by a learned fear of the opposite sex.

Homosexuality is subject to much current debate (Lesse, 1973). Is it a "disease" or merely an alternative way of life? Homosexuals often experience intense prejudice as well as punitive laws because of their deviation from the sexual norm. Only when society's view of homosexuality as an "illness" is discarded will homosexuals be treated without hostility and discrimination. The "sickness" image imposed on them denies them the right to live as they wish. They often subconsciously incorporate society's intolerant attitudes and thus develop psychological symptoms for which they may need psychotherapy.

Most homosexuals do not wish to change their behavior, and those who do may do so primarily because of social pressure. Homosexuals want to be accepted as useful members of society on the basis of what they contribute and through their innate worth as human beings. Several organizations have been established to help them assert their rights as equals.

The American Psychiatric Association no longer classifies homosexuality as an illness or as pathological or deviant behavior. It has taken issue with discrimination against homosexuals in work, housing, education, and other areas

(*Psychiatric News,* 1974). For those homosexuals, however, who are disturbed about their sexual orientation and wish to change it or to learn to live more comfortably with it, the Association has defined a new category of behavior— *sexual orientation disturbance.* In other words, homosexual orientation is no longer considered a disease, a mental illness, or a physical abnormality, and treatment is recommended only when the homosexual experiences distress and considers his sexual orientation personally undesirable.

SUMMARY

Changing attitudes toward human sexual expression have generated confusion recently over the choice of a fulfilling sexual lifestyle. In the past, social institutions and family training dictated authoritatively the course for each individual, but the task has now become a test of personal responsibility based on needs and consequences. Slowly but surely, however, sexual expression seems to be taking a comfortable place within the total perspective of human existence. As we understand, experience, and appreciate sex and sexuality, we discover that it too fosters fulfillment and becomes an agent of our self-actualization.

The new social ethic asks for an increased tolerance of alternate lifestyles, decreased suppression and distortion of feeling, and greater opportunity for the satisfaction of human needs, including sexual needs. Although students cannot be taught or told which sexual lifestyle to choose, they may be better able to make a choice for themselves if they are well informed about the alternatives. Socializing can encourage growth through improved interpersonal awareness and a better understanding of oneself.

Although the sexual "revolution" may have been overdramatized, there is a discernible trend toward more open, honest sexual relations. Females have become increasingly career-oriented and independent and behave more forthrightly in sexual matters. Some males respond in more contemplative and passive ways. The change of sexual attitudes has produced new alternatives to satisfying the sexual drive: sex without affection, sex with commitment for marriage, and living together without marriage.

The institution of marriage is also experiencing gradual change—greater equality of the partners, increased sharing of experiences, and less sexual role discrimination. Alternate marriage styles have also emerged, which aim at developing more fulfilling and enriching experiences than traditional marriage offers. In spite of the increasing rate of divorce, most young people continue to enter the arrangement with anticipation and expectation.

New information fosters new understanding, and masturbation and homosexuality are no longer treated as ominous and morbid phenomena but as sexual alternatives. Masturbation is considered simulated practice for later sexual experience, and homosexuality is accepted as an alternate lifestyle.

QUESTIONS TO THINK ABOUT

1. Were you ever attracted to the "wrong" person? What was the outcome of the relationship?

2. What is your reaction to a couple's living together without marriage? If you have had experience with this arrangement—personally or through friends—discuss some of the problems and benefits encountered.
3. Do you believe that living together or any other alternative will replace traditional marriage? Explain.
4. How comfortable do you feel over the changing roles of males and females? Do you feel equal with members of the opposite sex? Does sexual equality have any disadvantages?
5. Have you ever discussed marriage goals with friends of the opposite sex? Was their attitude toward marriage similar to yours? What problems do you think you might experience in marriage?
6. How would you define love? Have you ever experienced the type of love that you describe?
7. Do your views on masturbation differ from those of your parents? How? Have you ever discussed this subject with them? If not, why?
8. What is the attitude within your community toward homosexuality?

REFERENCES

American Psychiatric Association. APA rules homosexuality not necessarily a disorder. *Psychiatric News*, 1974, 9(1), 1.
Barclay, A. M. Sex and personal development in the college years. In D. L. Grummon & A. M. Barclay (Eds.), *Sexuality: A search for perspective*. New York: Van Nostrand, Reinhold, 1971.
Bell, R. R., & Chaskes, J. B. Premarital sexual experience among coeds, 1958-1968. *Journal of Marriage and the Family*, 1970, 32(1), 81-84.
Berelson, B., & Steiner, G. A. *Human behavior: An inventory of scientific findings*. New York: Harcourt, Brace, Jovanovich, 1964.
Bieber, I. *Homosexuality: A psychoanalytic study*. New York: Basic Books, 1962.
Bowman, H. A. *Marriage for moderns* (5th ed.). New York: McGraw-Hill, 1965.
Brecher, E. M. *The sex researchers*. New York: New American Library, 1971.
Committee on Human Sexuality. *Human sexuality*. Chicago: American Medical Association, 1972.
Douvan, E., & Adelson, J. *The adolescent experience*. New York: Wiley, 1966.
Ellis, A. *Sex without guilt*. New York: Lyle Stewart, 1958.
Ellis, A. Group marriage: A possible alternative? In H. Otto (Ed.), *The family in search of a future*. New York: Appleton-Century-Crofts, 1971.
Farnsworth, D. L. Sexual morality and the dilemma of the colleges. *Medical Aspects of Human Sexuality*, 1970, 4(11), 64-94.
Fletcher, J. *Moral responsibility: Situation ethics at work*. Philadelphia: Westminster Press, 1967.
Fredrickson, L. C. Value structure of college students. *Journal of Youth and Adolescence*, 1972, 1(2), 155-163.
Freedman, A. M., Kaplan, H. I., & Sadock, B. J. *Modern synopsis of psychiatry*. Baltimore: Williams & Wilkins, 1972.
Fromm, E. *The art of loving*. New York: Harper & Row, 1956.
Garfield, S., Marcus, S., & Garfield, E. Premarital sex from an existential

perspective. In H.E. Otto (Ed.), *The new sexuality.* Palo Alto, Calif.: Science and Behavior Books, 1971.

Greenson, P. R. Masculinity and femininity in our time. In C. W. Wahl (Ed.), *Sexual problems, diagnosis, and treatment in medical practice.* New York: Free Press, 1967.

Hamilton, E. *Sex before marriage.* New York: Bantam, 1970.

Herman, R. L., & Snyder, E. C. *Marriage.* New York: Wiley, 1962.

Hoffman, M. *The gay world.* New York: Basic Books, 1968.

Jourard, S. M. *Healthy personality.* New York: Macmillan, 1974.

Kaats, G. R., & Davis, K. E. The dynamics of sexual behavior of college students. *Journal of Marriage and the Family,* 1970, *32*(3), 390-399.

Kangas, J. A., & Solomon, G. F. *The psychology of strength.* Englewood Cliffs, N.J.: Prentice-Hall, 1975.

Katchadourian, H. A., & Lunde, D. T. *Fundamentals of human sexuality.* New York: Holt, Rinehart & Winston, 1972.

Kilpatrick, W. The demythologizing of love. *Adolescence,* 1974, *9*(33), 25-30.

King, M., & Sobel, D. Sex on the college campus: Current attitudes and behavior. *Journal of College Student Personnel,* 1975, *16*(3), 205-209.

Kirkendall, L. A. Values and premarital intercourse—implications for parent education. *Marriage and Family Living,* 1960, *22*(4), 317-322.

Kirkendall, L. A., & Whitehurst, R. N. (Eds.). *The new sexual revolution.* New York: Donald W. Brown, 1971.

Kirkendall, L. A., & Anderson, P. B. Authentic selfhood: Basis for tomorrow's morality. In E. S. Morrison & V. Borosage (Eds.), *Human sexuality: Contemporary perspectives.* Palo Alto, Calif.: National Press, 1973.

Klemer, R. H. *Marriage and family relationships.* New York: Harper & Row, 1970.

Kolb, L. C. *Modern clinical psychiatry* (8th ed.). Philadelphia: Saunders, 1973.

Kornhausen, P., & Kornhausen, E. *The sexually responsive woman.* New York: Ballantine, 1965.

Krantzler, M. *Creative divorce: A new opportunity for personal growth.* New York: Evans, 1973.

Lesse, S. The current confusion over homosexuality. *American Journal of Psychotherapy,* 1973, *27*(2), 151-154.

Macklin, E. D. Going very steady. *Psychology Today,* 1974, *8*(6), 53-59.

Masters, W. H. & Johnson, V. E. *Human sexual inadequacy.* Boston: Little, Brown, 1970.

McCary, J. L. *Freedom and growth in marriage.* New York: Wiley, 1975.

Mead, M. Marriage in two steps. In H. Otto (Ed.), *The family in search of a future.* New York: Appleton-Century-Crofts, 1971.

Morris, D. *Intimate behavior.* New York: Random House, 1971.

Offer, D. Attitudes toward sexuality in a group of 1500 middle class teen-agers. *Journal of Youth and Adolescence,* 1972, *1*(1), 81-90.

O'Neill, N., & O'Neill, G. *Open marriage.* New York: Avon Books, 1972.

Otto, H. A. Man-woman relationships in the society of the future. *The Futurist,* 1973, *7*(2), 55-61.

Otto, S. J. *The new sexuality.* Palo Alto, Calif.: Science and Behavior Books, 1971.

Packard, V. *The sexual wilderness.* New York: Pocket Books, 1970.

Pomeroy, W. B. *Boys and sex.* New York: Delacorte, 1969.

Reiss, I. L. The scaling of premarital sexual permissiveness. *Journal of Marriage and the Family,* 1964, *26*(2), 188-199.

Reiss, I. L. Premarital sex codes: The old and the new. In D. L. Grummon & A. M. Barclay (Eds.), *Sexuality: A search for perspective.* New York: Van Nostrand, Reinhold, 1971.

Roberts, R. E. *The new communes.* Englewood Cliffs, N.J.: Prentice-Hall, 1971.

Rogers, C. R. *Becoming partners: Marriage and its alternatives.* New York: Dell, 1972.

Rogers, D. *The psychology of adolescence.* New York: Appleton-Century-Crofts, 1972.

Rubin, I. New sex findings: Some trends and implications. In H. A. Otto (Ed.), *The new sexuality.* Palo Alto, Calif.: Science and Behavior Books, 1971.

Rubin, Z. *Liking and loving.* New York: Holt, Rinehart & Winston, 1973.

Sex Information and Education Council of the United States (SIECUS). *Sexuality and man.* New York: Scribner's Sons, 1970.

Shulman, B. H. The uses and abuses of sex. *Journal of Religion and Health,* 1967, *6*(4), 317-325.

Simon, W., Berger, A. S., & Gagnon, J. H. Beyond anxiety and fantasy: The coital experiences of college youth. *Journal of Youth and Adolescence,* 1972, *1*(3), 203-222.

Sorensen, R. C. *Adolescent sexuality in contemporary America.* New York: World Publishing, 1973.

Sun-Times, Chicago: November 25, 1973.

Thorman, G. Cohabitation: A report on couples living together. *The Futurist,* 1973, *7*(6), 250-253.

Whitehurst, R. Alternative life-styles. *The Humanist,* 1975, *35*(3), 23-26.

Williamson, R. C. *Marriage and family relations* (2nd ed.). New York: Wiley, 1972.

Chapter 9

Living
in Our World

CHAPTER OUTLINE

This chapter examines groups whose purposes are to promote or to prevent changes within society and the relationship of such groups to the individual and to society. In addition, certain other critical social issues, such as consumerism, poverty, violence and war, territoriality, and overpopulation, will be reviewed. We will also explore the possibilities for creating desirable social conditions that encourage the actualization of individuals and groups. Finally, the chapter discusses who controls society (and to what purpose) and how we might attempt to change society.

FULFILLMENT THROUGH GROUP IDENTITY

Our society has developed a culture of its own—that is, beliefs, styles of living, and artistic and scientific tastes—that comprises smaller segments or groups of people who share certain interests, goals, or values. These groups are known as subcultures and often may be distinguished from one another on the basis of race, nationality, religion, sex, or age. It is entirely possible to belong to more than one subculture, although one subculture usually has a higher priority for an individual than the others; an Italian Catholic, for example, may be more Catholic than Italian or, in some cases, more Italian than Catholic.

Through participation in such groups, we often become more aware of issues that affect us directly. Groups seem to be more effective in getting things done and in solving problems than individuals (Shaw, 1971); groups can help to achieve a desired outcome by reinforcing desired behavior and by providing checks and balances for individual errors.

Ideally, groups should function to sustain their individual members and to fulfill the members' needs; however, group membership also requires conformity. Too much conformity stifles individual growth, just as the need for personal freedom may disrupt the stability of a group. Sometimes, however, nonconformists are able to move an entire group in a new direction.

When individuals strive toward common goals, a group cohesiveness forms, and members recognize their common identity. A reciprocal relationship begins; the group helps the individual to achieve his or her optimum growth, while the individual helps the group, an entity in its own right, to realize its potential.

241

Certain groups, however, may experience restriction, oppression, and exclusion. Our nation may have been founded to promote "equality and justice for all," but deeply rooted psychological, social, economic, and political forces are at work to separate these groups rather than to unite them in a common heritage. Groups such as American Indians, Mexican Americans, Puerto Ricans, Asian Americans, and blacks seek a determining voice in society as well as a share in the benefits of the larger society. It is possible for each such group to contribute from its own resources and to create a larger good through cooperation and sharing. As groups experience a sense of mutuality and interdependence with one another and as they receive recognition and acceptance from one another, there is less cause for any group to feel slighted, frustrated, or rejected and thereby to protest or to show hostile tendencies toward other groups. It is, then, at least theoretically possible for groups to achieve actualization and fulfillment in terms quite similar to those we have used in earlier chapters in discussing individual development.

STUDENT FRUSTRATION

Student protest, prominent in the late 1960s, ranged from intellectual and highly theoretical discussions to overt actions of dissent and even violence. Some observers of the campus scene regarded protesting students as maladjusted and society and the educational system as comparatively healthy institutions; others viewed student concern and anger as signs of emotional health and held society and the educational system culpable. Although neither position can account entirely for the dissident student actions of the late 60s and early 70s, recent assessments have tended to favor the latter view (Nikelly, 1971).

Its Causes and Challenges

The current college generation is better informed on social and political issues than previous generations, largely due to the mass media. Education, as well as the availability of facts, prepares students to criticize injustice and to work against evils in society, particularly those reflected in the crucial issues of ecology, poverty, and civil liberties.

Students tend to speak in terms of personal rights and the fulfillment of human needs, while the older generation tends to emphasize property rights and to assess individual growth in competitive terms of success and achievement.

What students want, in fact, is a realignment of these priorities. At a national level, more effort as well as more dollars, they feel, must be spent in the fight against poverty, illness, illiteracy, and unemployment. Students realize that they are becoming part of existing social institutions that are not truly responsive to the needs of all people. Rather than support such institutions, students are challenging them and insisting on change. Students react strongly against any kind of exploitation—either of man or of the environment—and seek to make love the bond that governs humankind rather than authority based on power or reward (Michener, 1973).

Much of the frustration of the youth culture is rooted in family experience.

Young people are urged to behave responsibly but often are given only token opportunities to participate in life. Consequent feelings of alienation force them to seek an identity that distinguishes them from their parents. Instead of gaining recognition through the family's social and economic position—a status aspired to in the past—young people today often attempt to live apart from their parents and without their financial support. Of course, a distance between the generations has always existed as adolescents and young adults seek to establish their independence and identity, but fast-changing attitudes of youth today make the matter one of increasing concern.

Is Education for the Individual or for the Society?

Our educational system, reflecting as it does the society at large, rewards the achiever, the "go-getter." The aggressive person is valued for his ability to "get things done," while the innovative thinker, the artist, or the sensitive person who is concerned about the needs of others may be overlooked. Many individuals are treated as "failures" because they could not or would not follow the aggressive, competitive pattern. Since this necessity for tangible results frequently dominates the need for inner satisfaction, students must often try to fit into an environment of which they essentially disapprove.

Although the educational process is theoretically based on democratic solutions to problems and on respect for humanity, the experiences of many students within an achievement-oriented educational environment run counter to these assumptions. How can students find their way when the educational system holds in principle that they must be considerate of the needs and rights of others and yet requires them to compete aggressively? The confusion that inevitably results affects students in detrimental ways. For many students, power and competitiveness begin to dominate their personal relationships as well as their educational experiences. It is little wonder that many sensitive students feel the educational system is as hypocritical as the political or military establishments (Clark, 1971).

Like the larger society of which it is a part, the educational system has often failed to help students develop meaningful lifestyles in which material things can be considered means to ends. When the "hippie" movement turned to an almost exclusive emphasis on love, it underscored the failure of the educational process to advance social feeling, empathy, and care. The ability to show affection, although natural and human, can be stifled by economic struggle and the social importance of material interests. In this respect, higher education has sometimes become part of the economic empire, even promoting the goals of large corporations or the Army, while giving only intellectualized treatment to the important values of social interest and self-exploration.

Young people who live within this superstructure discover that their need for intimacy and connectedness with others becomes buried, while efficiency, performance, production, and objectivity become the predominant life values. Their behavior is often characterized by unfulfilled social relationships, cynicism, loneliness, apathy, and the disavowal of one's real self—the much publicized concept of self-alienation (Collins, 1969). It is not surprising that many students feel

Figure 9-1. There is so much knowledge to be absorbed and stored that our minds cannot always process it without becoming confused and frustrated. Photo by Shirley Kontos.

programmed into a "functional" existence and view the "system" as imposing on them inauthentic roles. In addition, the feeling of helplessness fosters low self-esteem, which only intensifies feelings of apathy and ineffectuality.

Thus, some students, hungry for involvement and at the same time fearful of it, occupy themselves with ineffectual political causes or rely on instant pleasures (sex, drugs, alcohol) to overcome their alienation at least temporarily. Immediate gratification becomes an ethic for students who have merely established a cycle of temporary and superficial closeness.

Difficult as it is, it may be easier for students to work toward social change than for those in power to give in without struggle. Those in power may well be the real radicals; they may refuse to examine the fabric of our society and its institutions in an atmosphere of frankness, freedom, and equality and to provide democratic solutions (Klein, 1969). Students are often indicted for attempting to "destroy the system" when actually they are attempting to defend the traditional, humanistic values upon which our society was founded (Starr, 1974).

Where Do We Go from Here?

Educational reforms are urgently needed to change the mass programming and machine-like efficiency of colleges to more individual-oriented atmospheres in which students feel capable of making decisions and engaging in independent action (Smith, 1968).

To begin, universities can allow fuller student participation in academic affairs and encourage the airing of grievances in a democratic atmosphere. Students can be given more voice in the determination of course content and in the choice of instructional methods. Rational discussion can be centered around the definition and solution of the problems of society—discussions that encompass disagreement, respect for evidence, and healthy skepticism. Student advisory committees elected from the student body can give input into the academic committees that make decisions affecting the student body. Students can be encouraged to bring their own ideas and theories into the classroom and present them to all, students and faculty, in order to elicit response and criticism or comment. Learning can be on a student-to-student basis rather than a faculty-to-student basis as is mostly the case.

Is the Student Movement Over?

It seems that students are no longer in open rebellion against the system but have, for the most part, resigned themselves to the political and economic situation of our nation and the world (McNeil, 1973); idealistic notions are not as pronounced as they were several years ago. Although it is difficult to generalize, students today seem to be more willing to work from within the system instead of fighting it from the outside as they did in the late 60s and early 70s. There seems to be a renewed interest in academics and in career training. The pressures of the Vietnam war and the draft have subsided, and issues currently tend to be economic and ecological. Logically enough, students have become somewhat more conservative as they compete for graduate training and specialize in careers that will bring personal as well as economic fulfillment. However, students have become more liberal in their views toward homosexuality (and toward sex in general), tend to give little importance to patriotism, and continue to desire social reforms (Yankelovich, 1972). Just how much student values and attitudes have really changed is a moot question, for actions and choices do not always tell us what people really feel.

THE WOMEN'S MOVEMENT

Plato argued in the *Republic,* over 2000 years ago, that women function as men do and should receive the same type of education as men in order to share more fully in societal responsibilities to the ultimate benefit of both sexes.

Adler (1964) challenged discrimination against females as the source of maladjustment in both sexes over 60 years ago, stating that male superiority forces females to resent their femaleness and to feel victimized by males. Adler used the term *masculine protest* to show how each sex tries to compensate for its felt inferior position toward the other through unnecessary domination and undue ambition.

The male who doubts his masculinity strives to overcome his doubts, while the female who resents the inferior status artificially imposed on her by male-made cultural attitudes exhibits emancipatory strivings interpreted by males as "aggressive" and therefore unsuited to her stereotyped sexual role. Adler insisted that females need encouragement to achieve equal rights with males but that males also require psychological assistance in order to understand themselves. Only when men understand how they came to feel "superior" in the first place and what makes them feel threatened by a woman's equal participation in the affairs of society can they accept women as equals. And only through the perception of each other as equals, Adler maintained, can men and women achieve genuine love and fulfillment.

Karen Horney (1967) carried the argument forward as she protested against the exclusively male-dominated field of psychoanalysis. This situation, she insisted, deprived women of self-respect by inculcating absurd notions of females as more emotional and dependent than men, as inferior to them, and as incapable of assuming responsibility. She became an outspoken critic of Freud's notion that women suffer from "penis envy." Horney, instead, speculated that the conflict centered on male jealousy over the fact that only women can give birth to children. She protested against the social conditioning imposed on women by "superior" males and noted that, in her psychiatric practice, men had as many problems as women and that the problems were of the same nature. Horney pointed out that psychological problems exist among members of both sexes; anxiety, insecurity, loneliness, frustration, and compulsiveness can not be attributed to biological differences. Horney would not accept condescending views toward females, particularly from the psychiatric profession, and maintained that such views breed distrust and alienation—feelings that can hardly be growth-producing and actualizing.

What are some of the characteristics of women who are involved in the Women's Liberation Movement? One study (Worell & Worell, 1971) indicates that pro-liberation women have a greater desire for freedom from social constraints, a more democratic orientation toward life, greater self-sufficiency, and less authoritarian attitudes than have antiliberation women or college women in general. Pro-liberation males emerged as nonauthoritarian, resourceful, and thoughtful. Lott (1973) found feminist women to be less eager to have children than antiliberation women, noting that motherhood was probably rejected by these women because it may limit a woman's independence and perpetuate aspects of an inferior social status.

Women involved in the movement, contrary to popular assumptions, are generally not sexually frustrated, social failures, or man haters; neither are they verbally aggressive, hostile, competitive, or "castrating." A recent study (Stoloff, 1973) found that feminists generally came from the middle and upper-middle social classes and from politically liberal, urban families. They were closer to their mothers, who were described as articulate, active, assertive, and independent, than were the control subjects who were not members of the movement. The study also revealed that women activists were socially outgoing and self-expressive and tended to be politically gregarious and liberal. They prized personal autonomy as well as humanitarian values and were motivated to create conditions in which they could lead more productive and fulfilling lives. Stoloff concluded that, although for the time being the movement may encourage women to become more like men, it may ultimately "allow women and men to become more like themselves" (p. 340).

The Women's Movement is rooted in the fact that the dominant elements in our society, which are exclusively male, have defined the role of females with emphasis on inequality, exclusion, and exploitation (Millett, 1970). The biggest "foes" of women's liberation are often the "satisfied" women who prefer the security of their servitude over the risk of self-knowledge and potential self-fulfillment.

The Women's Movement also attempts to correct sexual myths about the passive and weak female. Since so many women have been dehumanized from childhood by being treated as a sexual object (that is, being treated on the basis of their physical appearance rather than on a basis of their feelings, emotions, sensitivities, and personal needs), a major priority of the Women's Movement is to attempt to redefine the female role in relation to the male's, so that each individual, regardless of sex, may reach full potential as a human being (Friedan, 1963). Sexual fulfillment depends on each partner's recognition of the other and of himself or herself as a total personality. The old ideas of the female who "gives" herself to the male are being replaced by an understanding of the mutuality of the sexual relationship in all its aspects (Beauvoir, 1949). Another aim of the movement is to encourage females and males to drop superficial defenses against each other, such as coyness in females or emotional indifference in males. Instead of playing games that keep them apart by reinforcing opposite behavior, men and women can learn to appreciate their similarities.

Women interested in liberation desire to be evaluated by the same criteria as men and have the same opportunities, while remaining women in their own right. It is a sad contradiction that women are offered inferior and confined positions in society and then labeled as "competitive" or "hostile" when they desire equality (Broverman, Vogel, Broverman, Clarkson, & Rosenkrantz, 1972). They merely want the freedom to determine their own futures rather than accepting a biological determinism. The male chauvinistic attitude that females, by their very nature, are dependent on men for personal protection and security inflates the male ego, but it does little to help foster an understanding of the female nature (Bardwick, 1971).

Naturally, the Women's Movement and the changes that have resulted thus far have caused anxiety in some men, although a surprising number of men seem at least intellectually willing to accept the changes. However, the true liberation of women will require understanding and desire for change equally from both men and women. The emotional and psychological adjustment to total equality must occur in the male as well as in the female. It is the insecure male who disparages the liberation movement and the insecure female whose protest and hostility is out of proportion to the real issues.

It seems unlikely that the movement alone has caused marital strife. It is true that the movement has made a qualitative difference in the way women think about themselves and their relationships with men—a difference that causes emotional and intellectual conflict and that is bound to confuse relationships, especially marriages, that were begun under quite different assumptions. However, women tend to view the new equality as ultimately capable of strengthening marriage and of making individual lives more fulfilling. Consciousness-raising groups have been formed to help women overcome their fear of achievement and abandon their reliance on passive roles. Males may need to be educated in a similar way (Mednick & Weissman, 1975).

Female students often experience great personal growth through participating in women's groups at school. Many women acquire greater confidence in themselves and feel more relaxed in their roles toward males. Instead of playing games with men, they are more willing to initiate honest relationships. They become more willing to assume independent and assertive roles, not for the purpose of competing with males but in order to share with them equally in life. College women no longer view career and marriage as incompatible, but as a necessary step toward growth and fulfillment (Gump, 1972). Idealistically speaking, the Women's Movement is not anti-masculine but pro-humanity; it is founded not on the basis of sex differences, but on the premise that everyone shares a common humanity. Finally, the liberation of women is not a new idea; rather, it is a practical application of principles of equality that have been espoused by rational, sensitive people for centuries.

THE BLACK STUDENT STRUGGLE

The myth that one race can be superior to another has been perpetuated throughout history and is, thus, difficult to eradicate. By no means is every American a racist now, but many hold underlying negative attitudes toward persons whose skin color is different from their own—attitudes that came from their parents and ancestors. Racism is, however, nourished by fear. Many whites view the black's rightful assertiveness and just demands as a threat to their own place in American society. On the other hand, feelings of inferiority can become a self-fulfilling prophecy—for instance, when blacks behave as they are sometimes treated.

People who are victims of discrimination and oppression usually develop in ways that will ensure their survival. They may become callous, aggressive, and lash out at those who oppress, or they may become meek, shy, or passive and avoid resisting their oppressors. Either route is a means for self-preservation. While immigrants from European nations faced some of the problems that blacks face today, these immigrants were often skilled and, despite linguistic and cultural differences, usually did not differ in color; they were therefore more easily assimilated into American culture. Further, the European immigrants came to this country willingly, seeking "the land of opportunity," but blacks were brought over in chains and segregated as inferior beings. These conditions fostered a specific subculture in which members demonstrated personality traits, attitudes, and expectations that differed from those held by members of the dominant culture.

Black students share in the struggle of all blacks but face, in addition, certain problems that are unique to their role as students. We must keep in mind that institutions of higher education were designed to meet the needs of white middle- and upper-class students. When black students won admission, they did not fully fit into this system, and many experienced academic problems because of inadequate academic preparation. Emotional barriers to learning as well as crippling social and economic disadvantages have prevented many blacks from performing on a level comparable to their white peers (Grier & Cobbs, 1971). Another dilemma among young blacks is the double message they receive about the benefits of a good education. The quality of education for blacks has improved dramatically during the past ten years (Brazziel, 1974). However, college education seems to promise success, and often this promise is not fulfilled. The system may have given black students the right to work for a degree but not the subsequent right to hold jobs for which they have been qualified. In addition, education may have alienated young blacks from their families without allowing them to identify with the goals of the dominant white society.

The self-image of black students will not change merely by talking about it, but it can be altered through improved interpersonal relationships and understanding. Blacks must be given equal opportunities to contribute to their school and society— that is, equal opportunities to develop a sense of personal significance and to build healthy self-images (Cobbs, 1970). Patronization, which is an all too common reaction of whites toward blacks today, only reinforces a self-image of weakness and inadequacy.

In conclusion, black students in college must cope with certain dilemmas that are not unlike the problems of the white student. But their skin color continues to interfere with their acceptance and integration, for traditional attitudes are not altered easily. Both blacks and nonblacks recognize what needs to be done; the task ahead is to do it. It is hoped that the new generation of blacks will mark the beginning of an era of acceptance and full understanding by all college members and by the society at large (Pettigrew, 1971).

The groups that we have discussed so far react to conditions imposed on them from the outside, from the larger society. We cannot fully understand group actions if we choose to ignore the economic, political, and social conditions to which they are reacting. Our task now will be to explore what happens in society at large.

MOVING INTO THE REAL WORLD

One of the most trying experiences we have to face when we leave college is adapting from the rather "unreal" college world to the "real" world, in which our roles are quite different. Two decisions a student must eventually make are where to live and how to make a living.

The World of Work

Work of any kind is closely connected with our sense of personal identity. Sometimes, especially when we are introduced to someone, it seems as if the question "What kind of work do you do?" actually defines who we are, what we think of ourselves, and how we should be regarded by others. Career choice is indeed a decision that affects our whole existence, for what we do becomes a part of what we are. Work can give us a sense of independence, but it can also control us and inhibit our feelings of creativity and freedom. Those who feel that work is a drudgery lead unfulfilled lives and may express their dissatisfaction against members of their families, their friends, and their fellow workers. On the other

Figure 9-2. For some people work is a habit and a compulsion—even a kind of therapy. Photo by Shirley Kontos.

hand, when our work provides self-esteem and when we feel wanted and appreciated, we tend to be happy and more productive.

Work, of course, does not have the same meaning for everyone. The author or painter may not look upon what he or she does as work in the same way as the salesperson, cook, or truck driver. Assembly-line workers, for example, look forward to going home to do something radically different from what they have been doing all day. They may find little connection between work and pleasure; rather, they work for money and for the pleasures and security that employment provides. Many people, however, find personal fulfillment in their jobs, especially when the work provides a sense of accomplishment and usefulness. When work is related to a product or service or when it directly connects us to other people, it can provide satisfactions and sustenance beyond the paycheck. When there is a separation between the worker and the service or product and very little association with other persons, however, work may become a chore or restriction, rather than a challenge that demonstrates our personal worth and tests our ability. For some persons, work is a habit, a compulsion. "Workaholics" cannot relax by doing something other than their work, and often they are trapped in thoughts of money and more money. For such persons, work is a kind of therapy; it may alleviate boredom and depression or provide escape from tension and anxiety that may stem from problems not connected with work.

College students often think about the possible careers available to them. Instead of fighting the system, as students did only a few years ago, there is a tendency among undergraduates now to strive for good grades, to enter graduate school, and to choose a career that offers economic stability. The work ethic seems to have returned to campus. Monetary remuneration and competitive attitudes have surfaced once again as student values have changed and as the job market has become increasingly restricted. Developing technical skills leading to vocational occupations is also the subject of renewed student interest. Students, as well as other people, are seriously considering the merits of second or alternate careers. Teachers or postmen may leave their professions and prepare for a career in real estate or insurance, either as a second career after retirement or as an alternate before then. Students seem to be seeking immediate security and income as well as providing for more interesting and challenging options later on.

The current educational tendencies in colleges and universities are toward developing knowledge and skills that can be applied to the needs of the job market. We note a trend away from introspection and self-searching activities and toward a greater appreciation of work that can bring fulfillment as well as meet the needs of society.

Life in the Cities

As cities have grown larger, the quality of life in cities—as seen in interpersonal relationships, how leisure time is used, and the role of the family—has changed. The intensity, pace, and variety of city life can provide so much stimuli, so many alternatives, that city dwellers may become confused about who they are or what they want. Some urbanites even "shut down" or limit their awareness for a while in order to recover from the excessive stimulation that city life has forced upon them; thus, they appear indifferent or "cold" to the average viewer. Due to the anonymity and social isolation of individuals in the city, their behavior often does not relate specifically to anyone else, and such persons tend to become self-bound. They tend to avoid emotional involvement, their feelings harden, and they tend to look away from suffering, crime, personal injury to others, and conditions of poverty. They may feel uneasy displaying their feelings, very possibly because they feel that keeping in their emotions can serve as a safety measure against injury, humiliation, or loss. Huge apartment complexes are designed on the basis of how many people can occupy the same space and how much profit will come to the developer rather than on principles of health, safety, aesthetics, and human need.

Although people continue to turn to the cities for employment, much as they did in the 19th century, inner-city areas are often considered too dangerous or too ugly to live in and are thus abandoned by those who can afford to leave. As a result, the deterioration of such areas is accelerated. Cities cannot maintain their important function as cultural centers in art, theater, and music if their patrons and audiences dwindle, move to suburbia, or fear to return to the center of the city at night.

The move to the suburbs may provide better living conditions for some, but often at the price of a provincial lifestyle, consumption of land and occupation of more space, time consuming transportation to and from the inner city where most

*Figure 9-3. Urban life has become more efficient, but it often lacks the
serenity and freshness of life close to nature. Photo by Shirley Kontos.*

of the jobs are located, and the inconvenience of having to travel distances to do the
necessary shopping. Furthermore, living in the suburbs does not seem to afford the
opportunity for one to learn from and experience other subcultures that are more
likely to be within the city. City planners have increasingly come to view the suburbs
as an expensive and ineffective solution to the problems of urban growth and aging.

One cause for the inadequate solutions to urban problems is the failure to
coordinate the professional efforts related to the rebuilding of cities. Architects,
sociologists, ecologists, psychologists, economists, health experts, and educators
have not combined their insight and knowledge to build the best setting for creative
and satisfying living.

What these experts have done up until now is to separately offer their ideas and plans for creating better living conditions in the cities rather than combining the ideas in a collective way so that each one's contributions may be coordinated with those of the others. For instance, the architect cannot be effective if the expertise of the city planner, economist, and ecologist are not taken into account. The lack of coordination through a central planning board that could pool the knowledge of the individual experts, perhaps due to political shortsights or due to lack of money and leadership, makes it difficult to combine the knowledge regarding the renovation and restructuring of our cities to make them more livable.

Ideally then, cities must be developed to encompass our psychological needs and encourage our aesthetic development as well as provide for our employment, safety, and health. Cities are made up of diverse people, with different experiences and needs, with dissimilar cultural and educational backgrounds, and with a variety of skills and expectations. Ethnic groups and little ghettos can enrich and unite city dwellers rather than polarize them. The development of a city need not produce a utopian city, but city planners must consider city dwellers as well as investors. Flux, variety, and change are part of a city's vitality, but stability, long-range planning, and an understanding of human needs on a human scale are equally important.

People who live in large cities do, however, seem to have certain personal characteristics that differ from those of rural dwellers. They are more tolerant of different languages, dress, and mannerisms, and they are acclimated to a wider range of food preferences, social styles, and leisure interests. Urbanites seem to require care for emotional problems more frequently than do rural residents, and more of them are admitted to hospitals for such care. Of course, cities offer more such facilities than do small towns, and the availability of services must necessarily govern their use (Kolb, 1973). On the whole, people in large cities appear to be more "on the go" and to stress success, both financial and social, more than rural individuals. These differences, however, may tend to fade as mass media have an increasing impact on unifying tastes, expectations, and even language.

CONTEMPORARY GLOBAL ISSUES

Modern technology has compressed global boundaries, and, in a sense, we have all become world citizens. We have come to realize that problems in other countries are similar to our own and that only common solutions can prove adequate. Population growth, expanding consumerism, and ecological abuses, for example, are of concern to all nations, regardless of whether they are highly industrialized or agrarian and regardless of the standard of living their citizens now enjoy, because Earth is a fragile planet, which cannot sustain endless utilization and exploitation.

Ecology

Ecology refers to the interrelationships of organisms. Humans have, to a considerable extent, manipulated and even created their own environment and now must find ways of surviving in a world where the natural balance of organisms has been destroyed. Pollution, overpopulation, and energy shortages are by-products of the technological security we have attempted to create, but they abuse nature's design and thus have the potential to destroy the world.

The underlying theme in ecology is interconnectedness. Water, sun, soil, animals, and plants are linked with one another for support, and this chain is essential for maintaining human life. To respond to the environment demands that we sense our part in a continuous chain. Our actions affect other people as well as the natural world, and a chain of actions and reactions takes place that links us together as social beings within both the natural and man-made environment.

Just as human beings need to get along well with each other, so must they learn to relate to the physical environment. Just as we can harm our interpersonal relationships through exploiting each other, so can we damage our environment through exploitation. Our desire for profits and material goods has produced unwanted by-products that cannot be reabsorbed by the environment. Unregulated industry and uncontrolled consumerism have depleted irreplaceable resources; yet, many people regard the loss of individual "rights" that government ecological controls would necessitate unfair and inconvenient. One such government control is the prosecution of violators for littering the environment or polluting air, lakes, or rivers.

The ecology movement is predicated on education that leads to action, but it may be that certain links in the natural chain can no longer be reforged. We may have gone too far in creating our own environment and in controlling and exploiting natural resources to return to a position of interconnectedness in the natural world.

Territoriality and Overpopulation

The problem of overcrowding is responsible for a growing interest in a relatively new field of study—*territoriality*. Ownership and exclusiveness of space, boundaries, and control are all aspects of territoriality, and the economic and political dimensions of the subject are of great importance. Emotions, however, also play a significant role in territoriality, as is evident when we consider space in relation to a parking lot, a classroom, or a cafeteria. We react emotionally with such spaces because we often feel they are a part of ourselves, that we possess them. Considerable research is now being done that explores how we adapt to closed spaces or limited territories and to people who claim these places.

Edney (1974) has suggested that we investigate whether we need space of our own in order to be happy or whether human beings can find fulfillment through togetherness, through sharing space with others. Related questions are concerned with whether people tend to secure more space than they really need if an opportunity presents itself and whether social distance or emotional space is essential to mental health or only a defensive maneuver to avoid involvement with others and possible hurt. Also, do inhabitants of large nations, with much open land, and those of small and congested countries seek to establish territorial boundaries with equal intent?

The National Institute of Mental Health (1969) has addressed itself to the problem of overcrowding by examining the behavior of animals in overcrowded conditions. Their findings indicate that overcrowding can produce stress; some of the animals failed to reproduce, and a few became ill and even died. While we cannot equate animal behavior with that of humans, this research suggests that it might be beneficial to study humans who live in overcrowded conditions or are restricted to space limitations.

About two-thirds of the world population live in economically underdeveloped areas (such as India, Java, Bangladesh), and world population is rapidly increasing despite the declining birth rate. Poverty is often associated with overpopulation, as are inadequate economic development, illiteracy, and sometimes political unrest. Education and greater personal awareness, particularly as it relates to birth control, seem to be among the best remedies for curbing overpopulation, but the dimensions of the problem are enormous and change through educational means can be a painfully slow process.

Consumerism

Money, as it accumulates in the hands of a few, brings power and independence. And money in the hands of the worker may compensate for feelings of alienation and dissatisfaction. Indeed, money can be used to purchase comforts and secure independence; sometimes it can even buy friends.

Consumerism encourages us to define our needs in terms of material possessions, and it may, through the creativity of advertisers, even produce new needs that only new products can satisfy. However, the amount a person buys or owns is not directly proportional to his or her happiness. Many American families today are blessed with material advantages and yet are poignantly aware that the "heart" has gone out of their home.

Poverty

Many persons in our society earn only marginal or temporary incomes, but not all of them are considered poor. Clergy, artists, and students, for example, often have meager earnings and may even live in substandard housing; yet they have not inherited the attitudes or point of view of the poor.

People whose families have been poor for generations—that is, people constantly subjected to the social preconditions that spawn the subculture of poverty (unemployment, low wages for unskilled persons, and individual worth based on material status)—develop distinct personality traits, such as mistrust, apathy, present- rather than future-oriented thinking, and deep feelings of inferiority and inadequacy.

Overcoming the psychology of poverty will require the redistribution of wealth, but the poor must also be encouraged to organize themselves, to train themselves for roles of leadership, and to acquire an education by which they may experience greater awareness of the world around them and begin to realize their potential for change. Simply providing jobs or placing the poor on welfare is not an effective and lasting solution, for such programs merely tend to keep the poor dependent and thereby perpetuate their feelings of inadequacy and powerlessness (Lewis, 1966). Overcoming the psychology of poverty will also require that research be focused on the rich, who favor the economic system as it is and are, therefore, partly responsible for the conditions of the economically deprived.

Violence and War

Violence (the use of force to cause injury or damage to persons or property) has existed since prehistoric times, and its weaponry has become increasingly powerful. Blunt instruments were replaced by gunpowder, which in turn has yielded to the sophistication of atomic weapons. Ironically, nearly all religions and philosophies have opposed violence, while governments have continued to support vast armies and encourage arms factories in the interests of preserving peace!

It may be difficult to determine when or if violence is justified. Certainly violence can bring about social change—as proven by the American, French, and Russian revolutions, the many labor riots, the racial violence of the 1960s, and the violent opposition to American intervention in Vietnam—but we can never be sure that other avenues of change might not have been as effective. For thousands of years, humans have been conditioned to believe that war is an inevitable reality and that violence solves conflicts, but slowly we have turned to the study of nonviolent means of solving conflict. If psychologists have been able to foster conflict resolution at the personal, family, and group level, why not at the international level?

Those who view the world as a hostile place in which to live—a human jungle where the strong live off of the weak—or those with deep-seated emotional instability and destructive attitudes may be particularly susceptible to the appeals of violence. For such persons, psychological help and intensive rehabilitation may help them to see that violent behavior is unproductive and harmful and that other patterns of growth-producing behavior are possible.

Although everyone is capable of expressing violent behavior, several factors working together are usually necessary to precipitate violence. The availability of weapons, motives of self-protection or revenge, overcrowded conditions in which tension is maximized, the prevalence of violence in the media, and the frustrating circumstances of poverty, unemployment, and discrimination are only a few of these factors. Violence also involves past learning based on family and childhood experiences and, to some extent, the emotional makeup of the individual. We have all witnessed circumstances in which one person becomes angry quickly and another "keeps his cool."

Psychologists and other investigators of human behavior do not hold that people have an innate tendency to wage wars and that, therefore, war is unavoidable.

Wars can, of course, be justified, just as individuals justify actions that are injurious to others. Thus, when a person feels that society or other persons have done him or her wrong, there can be retaliation for this wrong in the form of aggression. These wrongs are usually perceived and interpreted on a personal basis, and the retaliatory action is then rationalized. What often happens is that a very small and inconsequential injustice is noted, and an excuse is made because of it. The hostile behavior usually follows and is thus interpreted as an inevitable consequence of that minor injustice.

War can be accepted as an appropriate redress of national grievances, as an indication of commitment to principles, and as a provider of jobs and glory. It seems reasonable that psychologists and educators could apply their knowledge of behavior on an international scale to reduce conflict and to bring about greater understanding among nations. For example, Kagan and Madsen (1971) have found that when competitive persons interact with persons who tend to cooperate rather than fight, the latter begin to react competitively. The original competitors, however, fail to recognize their own role in bringing out aggressiveness in others. While we cannot generalize from this study, it at least suggests that nations that maintain vast and powerful armies and adopt a stance of selfish nationalism and moral superiority may cause other nations to retaliate in an aggressive fashion.

It is puzzling that we talk about the causes of war and its prevention, but we seldom explore the reasons for peace. It would seem logical that peace research might do as much to ensure lasting peace as continued efforts to investigate war.

LOOKING AT SOCIETY

Who Controls Society?

Ours is a class society based on earning power, which can secure comfort and independence, as well as on power over others. In such a society, competitiveness becomes a dominant motive, and many activities are shaped by the desire for profit or personal gain. Often our growth as persons is relegated to a position of secondary importance.

We are only beginning to understand what constitutes the best physical environment for us and how our actions toward the environment have made it what it is today. Our habits, attitudes, and values affect how we relate to our environment, which in turn affects us.

It has been demonstrated that large corporations can and often do manipulate the government to their advantage, for the sake of larger profits (Mintz & Cohen, 1971). Economic power can be and often is political power, and it may exceed the boundaries of the law as it exploits and manipulates natural and human resources. To some extent, free enterprise now controls the government and the society that gave it the freedom to do business in the first place. Only an informed and active citizenry can control its government as well as the corporate world of economic power.

It has recently been estimated that less than 30% of the world's population controls close to 70% of the wealth and that about 900 million people live on less than $75 a year income (*Newsweek,* 1975). In societies in which free enterprise flourishes, economic power tends to go to a select few, who often determine what course education and politics will take. In socialistic countries like China, this elite class may be eliminated altogether, and education, like wealth, is shared by all, with the aim of developing greater self-awareness and social cohesiveness (Freire, 1972).

Ideally, societies are expected to evolve and change into better societies, just as individuals grow and change into better persons as they mature and learn more from experience. However, those in the society who are economically and socially comfortable are not always interested in seeing societal conditions change for the better, and those who propose change often find it to be an enormous task. Actually, the emphasis of education should be on cultivating values that aim toward the welfare and care of all. Such attitudes are cultivated in other societies through education of the children.

Bronfenbrenner (1975), who has conducted psychological research both here and abroad, was astounded to find that the guiding principle for raising children in the People's Republic of China is "Serve the people"; similarly, in the Scandinavian countries, Eastern Europe, and Israel, the education of children stresses concern for others, cooperation, and care for those who cannot take care of themselves. In our society, the motto of the young tends to be "Do your own thing." We often struggle to achieve individuality, to find success alone, and to interpret happiness on a personal basis. We often forget that happiness requires the broader context of our bonds with others and our commitment to the whole human race.

Our society has become enmeshed with machines, which may sometimes cause us to feel that our lives are dominated by "nonhuman" factors and that we have lost touch with ourselves and each other. We find ourselves serving technology rather than using it for broader ends. On the other hand, technological developments have brought advantages—advances in medicine, agriculture, transportation—that help to prolong life and to bring people together. Technological progress does not necessarily require the exploitation and control of other human beings; neither does it require the selfish accumulation of wealth. Nevertheless, a dichotomy exists between those who are victimized by technology and those who control and who wish to retain the *status quo* for reasons of personal power and wealth. Only when society can ensure a more equitable status for all people will it be possible to check the unbridled abuses of technology and bend them to the service of all mankind instead of the few.

We may not always be effective in bringing about a desired change, but there is evidence that nonviolent protest gradually brings results. We criticize what we do not like, we rebel against injustices, we suggest reforms in society, we boycott unethical practices, we protest against war, we refuse to follow immoral conduct, we demonstrate against political oppression, and we strike against economic unfairness. Those of us who view society as static (unchanging) may have difficulty experiencing progress, while those of us who view society as dynamic (changing) will expect change and are therefore more likely to help to bring it about.

Although ours is an economically and politically free society when compared with other societies around the world, the government still exerts immense control over our lives through the power of the purse: taxes, social service funds, hiring policies, bank loans, and budgetary allowances for various urban and rural projects. As our society becomes larger, it poses a growing threat to our private lives and to our styles of living, through the influence of large corporations that control the economy for the sake of profit, the mass media, government bureaucracy, and so on. Therefore, we may begin to note a decline in our individual choices in life, ranging from what school we want to attend to where we want to live, what work we choose to do, and even what is most proper for us to eat and wear. Because of the threat of nuclear war, unemployment, pollution, inflation, and so on, the idealism and romanticism surrounding individualism has begun to wane; we realize that we are not as adaptable as we were a century ago. We have lost some of our ways to satisfy our need for privacy, our personal ambitions, and the spirit of free enterprise. We still have freedom, of course, but it is contained within the limits of what is best for society at large, instead of what is best for us as individuals.

Can We Change Society?

It is sometimes difficult to talk about social change in realistic terms. This is because those who control the society and those who have a vested interest to see that things do not change that may alter their advantageous position will react to anything that may spell out suggestions for social change. It will take action not only by those who are less privileged economically but also by those who have the power; those in power also must *want* change, even though it may not be entirely to their benefit. One view holds that if people are really free to choose, a fulfilling society will emerge automatically. If, for instance, a large and leaderless group were lost on an island and left to its own devices, it would, as a natural process, strive for the survival of the largest number. Another view suggests that a few, whether because of intellectual superiority, physical prowess, or social perception, would attempt to "make it" for themselves at the expense of others. This latter view may explain, in part, how our society has evolved.

Many social scientists believe that social change can be brought about by discussion and confrontation without violence or force. Education can serve to examine values and to foster those that seem in the best interests of a society. Educated persons often lean toward democratic values and actions that liberate the individual, but changes in the economic area do not seem to follow as a matter of course. When wealth, and thereby power, accumulate in the hands of a few, dissidence is often found in those who do not share in the power and wealth. Interest groups form, but they tend to fight among one another rather than joining together for the good of all. There are surprisingly few organized groups today that attempt to influence government and to change society that do not represent a special interest, be it race, profession, sex, or age.

Scientists, philosophers, and educators have much to say about social reforms. Fromm (1968), for example, has suggested establishing a nonpolitical council of 50 capable and morally outstanding persons that would be called the "Voice of the American Conscience." This council would offer suggestions to resolve major social issues—the defense budget, educational policy, unemployment, inflation. Locally, the council would be reinforced by "clubs" of from 25 to 300 persons who would also deal with the pressing problems in their areas—slums, schools, ecology. The clubs at the local level and the council at the national level would then attempt to influence and direct the federal government as well as to inform the citizenry on issues of crucial importance to the whole country.

Fromm maintains that through logical reasoning we can change society so that mutual human needs are fulfilled. We must learn "to be" instead of "to have." He feels that schools should define society as it should be and not as it is. Developing an awareness of the world and a sense of harmony and oneness with it should be the goal of education and of society.

Common Cause, a lobby that brings pressure on the government to respond more effectively to the people's best interests, follows Fromm's suggestions in a general way. The *Urban Coalition,* a group of concerned citizens and leaders who recommend policies of social and economic revitalization for our cities, is another such group. Working in a similar way is Ralph Nader, who tries to correct exploitation and malpractice. Nader's organization protects consumer interests and adopts an advocate role in the interest of individuals against the corporate giant.

Marcuse (1964), a professor of philosophy, holds that modern man is a slave to a grossly misused technology. Automation engages us in meaningless tasks that keep us apart from others and from the product we are producing. Although automation can give us more leisure time, it can also numb us to the joys of life; instead of speaking against the controlling conditions of life, we allow them to control us because of the efficiency, magnitude, and impersonality of technology. Marcuse believes that it is not those who are already economically comfortable who will bring about greater awareness and subsequent change but the students, the blacks, and the minorities—those who realize that we are not truly free—who will challenge our "moronizing" society.

Reich (1970), a lawyer, tackles similar problems from a different point of view. He holds that our social system will fail because disorder, alienation, and powerlessness are catching up with us. The younger generation feels betrayed by the American dream, and no society can survive the alienation of its youth. In his book, *The Greening of America,* Reich, like Marcuse, says that we must experience a new "consciousness" in our lives, a new view of the world, a new perception of reality. We must ask ourselves what we want from life, and we must try to find a common ground for all. We must learn to put the community ahead of personal need, for liberation is not found in personal aggrandizement. Reich advocates a kind of revolution, but it is a revolution of consciousness rather than one of economics or politics.

In the final analysis, we shape our own future whether we do nothing or whether we take action. Keniston (1965) argues that it is not an ability to reform society that is lacking but the conviction that we can really do something about social problems. Keniston believes that we have the talent, the creativity, and the resourcefulness to bring about change but that these qualities are stifled by the dazzle of science and the demands of industry, greed, and competition. Although we are not responsible for the world as it is today, we *are* responsible for ourselves and for our actions that can bring about change.

The Search for the Perfect Society

When we feel unfulfilled, we often imagine an ideal (*utopian*) society in which everyone has a job, money, education, and love. What is ideal for one person may not be ideal for another, of course, but the frameworks of utopian societies can be used as guides in creating social conditions that really do work.

In ancient Israel, prophets offered visionary promises of a better tomorrow, when wars would end, wealth would be distributed, evil would perish, and the desert lands would bloom as paradise. Jesus and his followers declared that joy, peace, and justice would one day come to the poor and the oppressed. Similarly, Plato, when he was disenchanted with conditions in Athens, developed an ideal state in his *Republic.* And, during the Renaissance in Europe, a general pessimism against the injustices of the social order grew, and two Englishmen, Sir Thomas More and Francis Bacon, described their respective versions of the ideal society. More described a communistic society, while Bacon described a scientific society ruled by an elite who worked to improve the quality of human life for all.

Karl Marx (1818-1883), a socialist and journalist, theorized that a major force in society is the economic struggle among the classes, which fosters the attitudes of personal gain and individual survival instead of nourishing community feeling and social interest. His vision of a classless society was predicated on the fact that people must control their work, produce what they need, and share in the outcome of their work (Brown, 1974). As the struggle among classes decreased, increasing energy could be given to create a free society in which work was shared by everyone.

Skinner (1971) asserts that we can assure ourselves of a secure future if our behavior is controlled scientifically through systematic schedules of reinforcement. Through rewards and conditioning, children can learn to behave in ways that are advantageous to them and to others. We can thereby produce the personalities that an ideal society requires. In the schools and in the family, behavior can be shaped so that it benefits the larger society.

Fromm's (1955) perfect society, which he labels "humanistic communitarian socialism," reflects Adler's notion of social feeling. Fromm's ideal society is based on the mutual caring of its citizens, who are free to be themselves, who are involved, productive, creative, and interdependent, and who think rationally and lead effective and fulfilling lives. Such a society encourages personal freedom as well as strengthens brotherly solidarity.

Maslow (1965) conceived of an ideal society in which people were in a psychological state of harmony with each other and with nature and in which they developed their potential, cooperated for mutual benefit, cared for one another genuinely, and were able to fulfill personal needs without denying those of others. He called this ideal state an *eupsychian* society, a term loosely translated as "well-spirited."

Glimpsing the Future

Alvin Toffler (1974), a social critic, journalist, and educator, maintains that our educational system is geared to the past and to the present and offers only a glimpse of the future. He contends that education needs more "action learning"— that is, greater involvement in the world, which is constantly changing. To a large extent personal growth depends on how we fit ourselves into the future; if the future is unclear to us, our mental and emotional growth may be stunted.

Buchen (1974) postulates that society must create a "collectivised" individual, a world citizen, a community-oriented person who sees himself in others and allies himself with the good of all. Such a citizen thinks beyond national boundaries and views life in terms of a world-wide perspective.

Toffler (1970) insists that we cannot keep up with the rapid changes that are taking place in our lives. He believes that we can improve our ability to cope with rapid change by studying the future more carefully. Since rapid change requires that we make choices, Toffler suggests that the counseling professions may help us to focus more on the future and to make choices.

SUMMARY

The philosophy of democratic living stresses equal rights and privileges for all persons and groups within our country; it emphasizes inclusion rather than polarization to the end that input from different groups can contribute to the welfare of all. But staid elements in the social structure continue to maintain a monolithic stance toward various subgroups, failing to grant them the opportunity to participate in the decision-making processes that affect them directly. When a group as a whole is actualized, its individual members also find fulfillment; when the group is suppressed and treated with prejudice and discrimination, the negative repercussions affect its individual members as well. Three major subcultures were discussed in regard to past and present discrimination and potential actualization: the college student, the female, and the black student.

Because of their antagonistic behavior, youth are sometimes considered to be maladjusted, while the larger society is viewed as relatively stable and healthy. The overwhelming evidence, however, supports the view that dissenting students are intelligent, sensitive, and well-adjusted, while many of the values that society espouses—competition, aggression, acquisition—do not seem conducive to individual fulfillment. Student dissension represents an attempt to correct injustices in society, ranging from problems of ecology to those of war, poverty, and parental attitudes. The educational system has also come under attack by the student protest movement, for schools tend to represent the interests of the larger society rather than those of individuals.

The Women's Liberation Movement shares some of the goals of the student movement. Oppression and discrimination have made the female resentful of a family life and a society controlled by males. Not only do women seek equal rights and equal participation but a deeper understanding of human nature—both male and female. The pervasive notion of male superiority has damaged the male as well as the female, and the movement is a corrective, therapeutic force for both sexes. That the movement can pose a threat to those who disapprove of it for personal reasons is understandable; but the essential idea is that the Women's Movement aims to promote fulfillment and actualization on a broader scale, regardless of sexual barriers.

The plight of blacks has important parallels with the repression of self and the denial of individual fulfillment that we have found to characterize the situation of women and students. Along with other institutions, the educational system has become implicated in repression and must change if fulfillment and self-realization are to be found by all who seek higher education. Although education allows the black person to interact more freely with whites, this association may bring out differences and hostilities that went unobserved when segregation was in effect. The black experience in higher education has helped us to realize that social and educational reforms, as well as equal opportunity, are imperative if the strengthening of black identity and consequent self-realization are to be achieved.

It is not merely with *rights*—women's rights, student rights, black rights—that we are concerned, but with the rich benefits to all that actualized minorities contribute. Indeed, the clamor for rights has a harsh and strident sound compared to the ideal of self-actualization through belonging. In the final analysis, our life extends from ourselves to the family, to the group, to the city, to the state, to the nation, and beyond to the whole planet. Society comprises groups that are affected by and interact with the conditions of living, and our survival depends on them. When a person is ill, we must treat the whole person as well as seek to change the conditions that brought on the illness. So, by the same analogy, must we take a look at society and how it operates. The way that some individuals and groups behave tells us something about the society in which they are embedded.

We are only beginning to examine what values and styles of living will save our natural environment and perhaps our species. We need to belong to and to interact with groups, but we also need to belong to the world. We cannot reach higher levels on the stepladder of actualization when we are still struggling with the lower needs: fighting to survive, dealing with shortages of resources, living in bleak and alienating cities, and contending with unemployment, insecurity, and violence. Groups, social institutions, and the physical environment all nourish and sustain us, and we need to preserve and to improve these sources for growth and fulfillment. The constant interplay among person, group, and society at large creates an organic whole on which we depend and which, in turn, relies on us. To a large degree our behavior is determined by the society in which we live and by the natural environment; only recently, however, have we begun to appreciate how considerably we, in turn, direct that society and alter that environment.

QUESTIONS TO THINK ABOUT

1. How do you feel about student involvement in educational planning? Do you think this is a realistic goal for young people, or do you feel that experienced adults know "best" about career preparation and course requirements?
2. As a student, how willing are you to become deeply involved in social reforms? What sacrifices might be required of you?
3. Do you think the Women's Liberation Movement can help you as a female? As a male? Are there aspects of it with which you disagree? If so, what are these aspects?
4. Do you believe that a changing role for women dooms the family as a significant institution in our culture? What impact on the rearing of children might women's liberation have?
5. What are some of the changes you wish to see at your college or university? What can you do to help implement these reforms?
6. Have you had any close association with races or subcultures very different from your own? Did you find these persons as close to the stereotype of that subculture as you had expected? Explain.
7. Are you sensitive to situations that seem to be sexist or racist? How do you usually react to them? What alternate or improved ways of behaving in such situations have you learned from this chapter?
8. Do you think that the desires and wishes of the various subcultures are basically the same as those of the dominant culture? Defend your answer.
9. Would the assimilation of subcultures be a blessing to American life or a significant loss? Explain your position.

10. Do you think that those in government really understand the plight of the poor in our country? Document your answer.
11. Have you taken part in any activities that have to do with ecology or population control? If so, what contributions did you make?
12. Have you had any experience with living space in your home, at work, in school, or in other public places? What are your feelings about needing space of your own? Do you need as much as others do? What are your reasons?
13. Do you feel that we must prevent overpopulation through birth control? How do you react and with what arguments toward people who are against it?
14. Do you think that war will be abolished in our lifetime despite the heavy investment in the arms industry? Are there alternatives to war?
15. Have you noticed significant changes in societal attitudes and values during the last decade? If so, what are these?

REFERENCES

Adler, A. *Problems of neurosis* (1929). New York: Harper & Row, 1964.
Bardwick, J. M. *Psychology of women.* New York: Harper & Row, 1971.
Beauvoir, S. de *The second sex.* New York: Knopf, 1949.
Brazziel, W. F. *Quality education for all Americans.* Washington, D.C.: Howard University Press, 1974.
Bronfenbrenner, U. Alienation and the American psychologist. *APA Monitor,* 1975, *6*(9 & 10), 2.
Broverman, I. K., Vogel, S., Broverman, D., Clarkson, F., & Rosenkrantz, P. Sex-role stereotypes: A current appraisal. *Journal of Social Issues,* 1972, *28*(2), 59-78.
Brown, P. *Toward a Marxist psychology.* New York: Harper & Row, 1974.
Buchen, I. H. Humanism and futurism: Enemies or allies? In A. Toffler (Ed.), *Learning for tomorrow.* New York: Random House, 1974.
Clark, K. B. The pathos of power: A psychological perspective. *American Psychologist,* 1971, 26(12), 1047-1057.
Cobbs, P. M. White mis-education of the black experience. *The Counseling Psychologist,* 1970, *2*(1), 23-27.
Collins, C. C. *College orientation: Education for relevance.* Boston: Holbrook Press, 1969.
Edney, J. J. Human territoriality. *Psychological Bulletin,* 1974, *81*(12), 959-975.
Freire, P. *Pedagogy of the oppressed.* New York: Herder & Herder, 1972.
Friedan, B. *The feminine mystique.* New York: Norton, 1963.
Fromm, E. *The sane society.* New York: Rinehart, 1955.
Fromm, E. *The revolution of hope.* New York: Harper & Row, 1968.
Grier, W. H., & Cobbs, P. M. *The Jesus bag.* New York: McGraw-Hill, 1971.
Gump, J. P. Sex-role attitudes and psychological well-being. *Journal of Social Issues,* 1972, *28*(2), 79-92.
Horney, K. *Feminine psychology.* New York: Norton, 1967.
Kagan, S., & Madsen, M. C. Cooperation and competition of Mexican, Mexican-American and Anglo-American children of two ages under four instructional sets. *Developmental Psychology,* 1971, *5*(1), 32-39.
Keniston, K. *The uncommitted.* New York: Harcourt, Brace, Jovanovich, 1965.

Klein, A. (Ed.). *Natural enemies? Youth and the clash of generations.* Philadelphia: Lippincott, 1969.

Kolb, L. C. *Modern clinical psychiatry* (8th ed.). Philadelphia: Saunders, 1973.

Lewis, O. The culture of poverty. *Scientific American,* 1966, *215*(4), 19-25.

Lott, B. E. Who wants the children? *American Psychologist,* 1973, *28*(7), 573-582.

Marcuse, H. *One-dimensional man.* Boston: Beacon, 1964.

Maslow, A. H. *Eupsychian management: A journal.* Homewood, Ill.: Irwin-Dorsey, 1965.

McNeil, E. B. *Being human: The psychological experience.* New York: Harper & Row, 1973.

Mednick, M. S., & Weissman, H. J. The psychology of women—Selected topics. *Annual Review of Psychology,* 1975, *26*, 1-8.

Michener, J. A. What's good about today's youth. *U.S. News & World Report,* December 10, 1973, 48-55.

Millett, K. *Sexual politics.* Garden City, N.Y.: Doubleday, 1970.

Mintz, M., & Cohen, H. S. *America, Inc.* New York: Dial Press, 1971.

National Institute of Mental Health. *The mental health of urban America.* Washington, D.C.: U.S. Government Printing Office, 1969.

Newsweek. To have and have not. September 15, 1975, 37-45.

Nikelly, A. G. Ethical issues in research on student protest. *American Psychologist,* 1971, *26*(5), 475-478.

Pettigrew, T. F. The role of whites in the black college of the future. *Daedalus,* 1971, *100*(3), 813-832.

Plato, *Republic* (Translated by F.M. Cornford.). New York: Oxford University Press, 1945.

Reich, C. A. *The greening of America.* New York: Random House, 1970.

Shaw, M. E. *Group dynamics.* New York: McGraw-Hill, 1971.

Skinner, B. F. *Beyond freedom and dignity.* New York: Knopf, 1971.

Smith, G. K. (Ed.). *Stress and campus response.* San Francisco: Jossey-Bass, 1968.

Starr, J. M. The peace and love generation: Changing attitudes toward sex and violence among college youth. *The Journal of Social Issues,* 1974, *30*(2), 73-106.

Stoloff, C. Who joins the women's liberation? *Psychiatry,* 1973, *36*(3), 325-340.

Toffler, A. *Future shock.* New York: Random House, 1970.

Toffler, A. *Learning for tomorrow.* New York: Random House, 1974.

Worell, J., & Worell, L. Supporters and opposers of women's liberation: Some personality correlates. In L. Worell (Cm.), *Women's liberation: Equality, legality, and personality.* Symposium presented at the annual meeting of the American Psychological Association, Washington, D.C., September 1971.

Yankelovich, D. *The changing values on campus: Political and personal attitudes on campus.* New York: Washington Square Press, 1972.

Chapter 10

Intervention for Growth

CHAPTER OUTLINE

Where to go and what to do when problems overwhelm us is the subject of this last chapter. When we feel limited, or when our own coping resources have been exhausted, we must be willing to seek help to acquire alternative behaviors and to discover opportunities for further growth.

FROM WHOM DO WE SEEK HELP?

The immediate family or, perhaps, a close friend, relative, clergyperson, physician, or teacher can usually provide solace and guidance in times of personal distress. However, with the increased complexity of society and the consequent specialization of professional services, we have come to recognize at least five major specialists who deal with people and their problems of adjustment and fulfillment: the psychiatrist, the clinical psychologist, the counseling psychologist, the psychiatric social worker, and the psychoanalyst.

The *psychiatrist* has been trained in general medicine and has earned an M.D. degree. He or she then specializes in psychiatry, which may require another five years of professional training; the first three years may be devoted to special training in emotional disturbances under direct supervision in an accredited institution, and the last two years may be devoted to treating psychiatric clients. He or she is then eligible for candidacy to the American Board of Psychiatry and Neurology by passing an oral and written examination that certifies him or her as a specialist in psychiatry. Such a person is then qualified to administer medical and drug therapies (electroshock, psychotropic drugs, neurological examinations).

If a client's emotional condition is suspected of having an organic cause, a psychiatrist or a neurologist (a specialist in neurological problems that normally do not have overlapping emotional conditions) is consulted. If the emotional condition is due to organic causes, then medical treatment is followed. However, if no organic factors are found, psychotherapy is initiated in order to uncover the nature of the emotional problems. Because of their medical background, psychiatrists can dispense medicine for a variety of emotional conditions, such as anxiety and depression. They are also well equipped to look for possible physical conditions that may aggravate emotional states—alcoholism, drug addiction, neurological impairment—as well as to assess the client from a psychiatric point of view. Many psychiatrists work in hospitals and clinics in which psychiatric consultations are often requested, while others maintain a private practice with hospital privileges for those patients who require them. Although psychiatrists usually concentrate on the physical aspects of their client's program, they also engage in individual and group psychotherapy, and, in this respect, their functions often overlap with those of the

269

psychologist, counselor, and psychiatric social worker. It is particularly in those cases that require medical intervention and hospitalization that the psychiatrist's role is unique.

Clinical psychologists constitute almost 1/3 of all the psychologists. Although clinical psychologists' training is in research methods and in the scientific approach to the study of human behavior, they also work directly with clients to correct maladaptive behavior. They generally contend that emotional symptoms are not medical problems but are problems that have developed because of a person's inability to maintain satisfying relationships with others. The clinical psychologist, then, is a researcher as well as a professional practitioner.

Clinical psychologists earn a Doctor of Philosophy degree in clinical psychology and spend an additional year in supervised training as an intern in a hospital or clinic. They also receive special training in the administration of psychological tests that may contribute to a better understanding of the client. After practicing in the field and gaining five years of acceptable qualifying experience, they are eligible to become a Diplomate in clinical psychology, a title awarded by the American Board of Examiners in Professional Psychology after the candidate has passed stringent examinations. Some psychologists terminate their training at the M.A. level and accept more limited professional responsibilities.

Clinical psychologists in the academic setting often teach courses on personal adjustment and supervise graduate students in training. Frequently, they consult faculty members and administrators (with their client's permission) regarding academic or social problems related to the student's general well-being. They may be asked to participate in the planning and evaluation of academic programs that foster optimum learning. They may also serve as a liaison with community agencies or other medical and educational institutions regarding students who must leave college for psychological reasons.

The *counseling psychologist* undergoes training similar to that of the clinical psychologist. Counseling psychologists are concerned primarily with helping their clients to resolve immediate problems and to plan for the future; they attempt, when necessary, to promote skills in social effectiveness and personality modification. The goal of the counseling psychologist is to assist persons through interview sessions (individual or group), and occasionally through psychological tests, to understand their problems better and to solve them more effectively through a greater understanding of personal strengths and weaknesses. The counseling psychologist usually deals with persons whose personalities do not require drastic change, although he or she may also help the emotionally and physically handicapped adjust to the community or shift to more suitable occupations.

Nearly all academic institutions have counseling centers where students can seek guidance concerning their academic or personal difficulties. Problems such as vocational indecision, emotional apathy, dissatisfaction in school, and confusion about life goals are dealt with, as counseling psychologists try to build confidence in their clients by promoting the skills necessary to cope with the ordinary problems of living. These centers also offer career counseling and usually maintain libraries with information on careers and occupations. Counseling centers may offer special training such as remedial reading or drug education, and vocational placement services are sometimes included.

Some counseling psychologists specialize in *vocational guidance* and *career counseling,* which involves the administration of tests and questionnaires to evaluate an individual's personality and abilities and to help clients choose occupations suited to their aptitudes, interests, and lifestyles. Vocational and guidance counselors can detect academic deficiencies and strengths based on their interpretation of such tests and can recommend special preparatory courses or remedial programs when necessary. Vocational guidance is an important area in high school and college counseling, and students who have not given serious thought to career choices may find it beneficial to consult with a counseling psychologist.

The terms *counseling* and *psychotherapy* are often used loosely and somewhat synonymously, as are the terms *counselor* and *psychologist.* Some institutions and clinics coin their own titles: vocational counselor, psychiatric counselor, school counselor, rehabilitation counselor, college counselor, family counselor. The educational backgrounds of these professionals may vary from their having a B.A. to their having a Ph.D., with emphases in psychology, sociology, or education. Their training may or may not include an internship or period of supervised training. The important distinction is that counselors try to help us cope with an *immediate* situation without attempting to change our basic personality pattern.

The *psychiatric social worker* may assist clients directly to overcome a variety of social and personal problems, but he or she is specifically trained to assess their problems through collateral interviews—that is, through conducting sessions with persons other than the client in order to gather relevant and objective information. Interviews with the client's parents, relatives, co-workers, roommates, and instructors are often held; they are, however, always held with the client's permission, unless his condition is so severe that he is considered potentially dangerous to himself or others.

The psychiatric social worker usually has an undergraduate degree in psychology, sociology, or social science, at least two additional years of graduate work, and a supervised internship in order to earn the Master's of Social Work degree (M.S.W.). He or she may specialize within this profession, such as the caseworker who works primarily with marital problems, broken homes, delinquency, probation, poor housing, or unemployment. Obviously psychiatric social workers perform many of the same services as others in the psychiatric field, but they do not prescribe medication or administer psychological tests.

The *psychoanalyst* is usually a physician who is trained in psychoanalysis, a method of therapy based on Freud's theory of personality. Psychoanalysis concentrates on unconscious processes, dream analysis, free association, and the impact of childhood experiences. Some psychoanalysts are not medically trained and are known as lay analysts. After completing internship, psychiatric residency, and training at a special psychoanalytic training institute, psychoanalysts are expected to undergo analysis themselves, although they may at the same time function as analysts for others. Clients undergoing psychoanalysis are expected to attend sessions several times a week, and therapy may last for several years. One general reason for the lengthy psychoanalysis process is that patients have to work through feelings and thoughts originating in their childhood and reconstruct their whole lifestyle in a different and more effective way. Stated loosely, the personality is taken apart (analysis) and then put together again in a more mature way (synthesis). There have been attempts recently to shorten the length of psychoanalysis while maintaining its effectiveness. There are relatively few psychoanalysts compared with other types of therapists, because their training is lengthy and expensive, as is the therapy they provide. For most clients short-term psychotherapy is a less expensive and less time-consuming solution.

Many other types of therapists are trained to assist people in supportive ways to achieve competence, adjustment, and actualization. The *occupational therapist,* for example, teaches special skills to emotionally or physically disabled persons. Through special training in an area of aptitude and interest, such persons may become independent and productive citizens as they gain confidence, self-esteem, and identity. The *recreational therapist* offers training in various creative and educational activities designed to remotivate and resocialize persons who may have physical handicaps as well as emotional problems. These activities are considered to be therapeutic and may vary from arts and crafts to dancing, writing, and singing. Self-expression is an important therapeutic goal, for it is imperative that the handicapped or disturbed person learn that he can give of himself by being creative and of use to others. Both recreational and occupational therapists complete a B.A. degree, and may also have had graduate training as well as served a supervised internship. Therapists typically work in mental hospitals, clinics, and educational and correctional institutions. It should also be mentioned here that clergy members, teachers, probation officers, volunteer workers, and various types of supervisors all play a significant role in helping the disadvantaged, the handicapped, and the disturbed gain self-esteem and personal fulfillment.

PSYCHOTHERAPY: AN OVERVIEW

Psychotherapy is a process by which undesirable patterns of behavior are molded into desirable forms through the implementation of certain psychological techniques (Patterson, 1973). These techniques may range from advice and persuasion to an exploration of the client's motives or self-analysis; there are no set alternatives for changing undesirable behavior. Not all persons react the same way to distress, and the severity of a problem as well as a reasonable solution depend on the "eye of the behaver." Some people tend to dramatize the notion of psychotherapy, lending it an aura of mystique, but more often than not therapists relate to their clients as they do to a close friend (Schofield, 1964). Certainly therapists use learned skills, but they also rely on intuition and their own personalities (Reisman, 1971).

Although counseling and psychotherapy are often used synonymously, counseling is usually shorter and focuses on more immediate problems. It tends to focus realistically on ongoing or impending problems and to encourage decisions made on the basis of consequences, without extensive self-probing or the prolonged analysis of past experiences. Psychotherapy, on the other hand, looks at the whole personality of the client and dwells on the analysis and resynthesizing of his or her experience. Theoretically, the client is then able to form a better perspective toward life based on deeper self-understanding and on improved insight about his or her own behavior. In both types of intervention, encouragement from the therapist is very important; interpretation, feedback, empathy, acceptance, respect, nonpossessiveness, honesty, and confidentiality are characteristics that should be found in all psychotherapy situations and applicable to all types of therapists (Martin, 1971).

The goal of many therapists is to restore the client's functioning within the shortest period of time. While some therapists still respect the arduous and time-consuming techniques of Freud, many rely on more practical techniques to reduce the client's symptoms and to help him cope more efficiently with his problems.

The Therapeutic Relationship

Regardless of their orientation, all therapists attempt to create a situation in which the client does not hesitate to express himself. Therapists must also be honest about their own feelings. In short, therapy allows the client to experience a satisfying, genuine interpersonal experience. Commitment on the part of a therapist helps the client *want* to change, encourages him to improve, and enables him to develop respect for himself. Specifically, the therapist identifies the problem, helps the client to formulate alternate patterns of behavior, and encourages the client to act—all through informal discussion *with* the client in an atmosphere of equality, warmth, and freedom. The therapist does not aim to eliminate problems entirely but to reduce their size or importance so that the client can handle them.

Individuals enter therapy for a variety of reasons—to enable them to satisfy basic needs, to learn to adjust to society's values, to develop and sustain fulfilling interpersonal relationships. They may seek help in overcoming a specific problem, or they may be interested in self-exploration leading to fuller self-understanding and possible changes in personality and functioning. The basic orientation of therapists, however, is to promote conditions for personal growth so that the client can rely on his own power to effect changes in himself and the environment; they assume that every person has the potential to change for the better and the disposition to actualize himself under his own motivation (Rogers, 1961). Therapy encourages the client to take a critical look at himself and to challenge the negative value judgments that he often holds. Through therapy, the client is often liberated from social pressures to conform and is able to adopt a realistic, present goal toward which to move (Culbert, Clark, & Bobele, 1968).

In the therapy situation, clients ideally become neither totally dependent on others for support nor strongly independent of them; rather, they become both sensitive to the needs and expectations of others and self-directed as they discover the lifestyle that is most meaningful to them. In essence, they begin to overcome the artificial differences between self and others.

Needless to say, therapists should have a positive attitude about themselves. They should remain open minded, flexible, and able to communicate with their clients, because, through their own behavior, they help to set the mood for the relationship. Perhaps the single most important trait in helping a client to improve is the genuine regard and esteem in which the therapist holds the client (Truax, Wargo, Frank, Imber, Battle, Hoehn-Saric, Nash, & Stone, 1966.) This trait is not always learned in books (Bergin & Jasper, 1969), although intellectual qualities are obviously necessary for mastering the conceptual tools required in therapy. It is nevertheless encouraging to discover that knowledge alone is not sufficient to help others; how we feel about them and what we come to mean to them may also prove to be critical determining factors in successful therapy. Carkhuff (1969) maintains

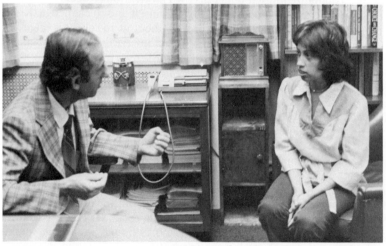

Figure 10-1. Psychotherapy involves two persons being open to each other in an atmosphere of mutual respect, candor, acceptance, and equality. Photos by Jody Ellyne.

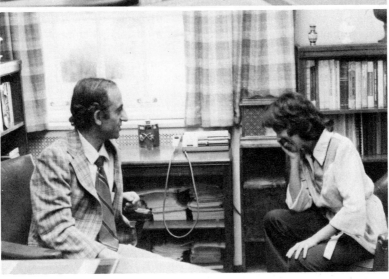

that trained therapists are not the only persons who can offer valid help to someone in need of counseling. Indeed, he proposes that psychologists could also train lay persons (or "paraprofessionals"), or at least select those who are already actualized, to aid those who are in need of help.

Burton (1972) draws several conclusions from the autobiographies of 12 prominent and successful therapists. In spite of their respect for scientific objectivity, these men were all warmly human and involved persons. Interestingly enough, all 12 had suffered from some kind of physical problem in childhood, had come from rather mobile families, and had experienced no significant degree of sexual conflict in their early lives; in fact, early sexual experiences seemed to have had very little effect on their later lives. These therapists felt that their personal growth and the authenticity of their identity had been stimulated by working with their clients in intimate, personal relationships rather than by study or personal analysis. An intuitive sensitivity to the inner needs of their clients seems to have helped them to understand their clients better as well as to develop their own personalities. Often these therapists went through deep and meaningful experiences with their clients. Each of the 12 therapists had experienced despair, depression, and even rejection in their lives and were thereby able to empathize readily with their clients. Finally, these 12 men all seemed to want to know the truth about what makes people function and seemed to feel considerable concern over social as well as individual problems. They experienced growth in themselves through the intense, personal experiences with their clients; they found fulfillment not through their intellectual pursuits but through their emotional commitments to their clients.

Humanistically-oriented therapists have tended to abandon the doctor-patient relationship, since it is predicated on a passive and "sick" person at the mercy of an all-knowing person. They believe that such a relationship may stifle and limit the possibility for honest communication between client and therapist. The humanistic therapist prefers the term *encounter,* which implies a dialogue between two equals in a relaxed and open atmosphere. The therapist places his or her whole self into the encounter and, unlike the physician who tends to be neutral or authoritarian, believes that the client must be the architect for his or her own actualization. The client must initiate the directions that the therapist then attempts to follow in an empathic way.

Consider the recollections of this young man when asked why he had sought therapy. Perhaps his remarks will clarify the therapeutic relationship in terms of client as well as therapist.

Incident

I was upset over some things and went in to talk to a psychologist. I didn't want to burden my friends with my problems—things they probably wouldn't understand. The guy was really nice; nothing like the guys you see in the movies who stare and attempt to analyze everything you do. He was warm and interested in what I had to say. He talked *with* me like I was his friend. I felt relaxed talking with him, and I could have stayed there more than the time allowed for our session. I really felt he was on *my* side.

He made me realize some things I hadn't been fully aware of. He helped me to uncover more of the *real* me, you might say. He made me see that, although my life may not always go along just right, I nevertheless belong here. I can use my problems to grow and change. The fact that I can behave this way—to notice things and to make changes—should be a source of satisfaction. He made me realize that I have many strengths despite my own knowledge about my weak spots and that I can use these strengths to my advantage insofar as I am willing to accept myself. In a nutshell, you might say, I began to realize that I have potential; I can change my life for the better, and my actions do matter to other people.

Therapeutic Orientations

Psychoanalysis aims to reveal the unconscious mind to the client through free association (the client says whatever comes to mind and the therapist interprets the content of what was said) and dream interpretation. Childhood experiences, particularly relationships with the mother, are often considered indices of current maladjustment. The therapist attempts to reconstruct the childhood feelings, bring out the unconscious segment of these feelings, and help the client become more aware of himself. Therapists also try to work out unresolved, infantile conflicts as they emerge in the client's transference relationship with them. Transference refers to a positive or negative feeling or attitude toward the therapist that is normally directed toward other important persons in the client's life—very often the parents.

In *client-centered* therapy, the therapist, by providing an atmosphere of candor and acceptance, creates conditions under which the client wants to change. Accurate empathy, positive regard, and honesty toward the client are important therapist traits. As the therapist accepts the client, the client also learns to accept himself and to hazard even more of himself in an attempt to live more fully and to actualize himself (Rogers, 1961). Because it is based on equality between therapist and client, client-centered therapy is very popular in our country. It stresses the client's ability to grow on his or her own power; the relationship with the therapist, which is warm, accepting, and free of threat, fosters personal growth.

Adlerian psychotherapy focuses on understanding the client's behavior in terms of his goals, his intentions, and his lifestyle. It attempts to interpret the client to himself, to strengthen his social feeling, to help him formulate realistic goals based on logical consequences, and to aid him in practicing skills that will become viable means of attaining fulfillment. The emphasis is on the present and the future rather than on the past and on interpreting life through immediate experience. Personal significance is developed through fostering a sense of social usefulness and a community feeling; that is, when a client is at home with himself, he can become at home with the world (Ansbacher & Ansbacher, 1956).

Rational-emotive therapy is based on the assumption that maladjustment occurs because a person's emotions and actions are controlled by the attitudes and opinions he or she learned during childhood. If these beliefs are negative, self-defeating, and unrealistic, they affect the person's emotions and actions negatively. The client is shown by the therapist that these false ideas control his behavior and that he suffers because of them. If the therapist can render these ideas ineffective and inoperative for a particular client, hopefully the client will abandon them for more realistic and workable ideas (Ellis, 1962).

Psychodrama refers to a client's acting out, in a group, the interpersonal situations that cause him problems. The client assumes a role within this dramatic representation of his conflict and learns from his actions and from the group's actions and reactions how to cope with a similar real-life situation.

Gestalt therapy attempts to integrate the fragments of a client's thoughts, perceptions, and emotions into organized total patterns. By helping clients to form "whole" experiences, Gestalt therapy brings them closer to reality and strengthens their competence to cope with it. The client comes to understand the interplay between person and environment and the apparent functions of his or her life that have been overlooked. Gestalt therapy focuses on eliminating the obstacles that stand in the way of actualization.

Existential therapy is intended to help the client achieve spontaneity, an authentic sense of identity, and a natural way of relating with others. The client is encouraged to act freely in making choices, in examining his values, and in deciding for himself what life should mean to him. Existential therapy emphasizes the discovery of meaning in life and the importance of values in determining behavior; it emphasizes the here and the now, the subjectivity of experience, and the necessity for becoming more fully aware of one's feelings, attitudes, values, and goals (May, Angel, & Ellenberger, 1958). The therapist often becomes involved in the client's world and serves as a model for him.

Transactional analysis is based on the assumption that our interactions and communications spring from three aspects of our personality: the child, the adult, and the parent. The client is made aware which of these aspects of himself has become more dominant in his actions and is helped to alter or replace it with a more viable and realistic one (Berne, 1961). The aim of this type of therapy is to liberate and strengthen the adult way of behaving so that the client may be more able to freely choose options and be responsible for these choices.

Behavior therapy is based on the idea that maladjustment consists of self-defeating learned patterns of behavior that the client acquired at an earlier age in an attempt to cope with anxiety. By applying principles of learning theory, the client is helped to unlearn inadequate patterns of coping behavior and to condition himself against the negative attitudes that fostered these inadequate responses (Dollard & Miller, 1950). Behavior therapy, or behavior modification, is a special kind of learning theory therapy, and, because of its recent popularity, it will be described more fully later on in this chapter.

Directive therapy assumes that the client is not able to conduct himself in a responsible manner and deal effectively with choices, values, and goals. The therapist, therefore, assumes some of this responsibility as he guides and directs his client or even intervenes in certain of his problems. He nudges his client into constructive directions. As the client learns that the techniques he is being taught actually help him to cope more effectively, he assumes increased responsibility for his own behavior (Thorne, 1950). In general, the therapist assumes an active role and relies on suggestion, persuasion, and re-education in altering client behavior.

Integrity group therapy stresses honesty and openness. It is an experience similar to "confessing," and it is followed by acknowledging responsibility for our actions. Integrity therapy is based on the premise that many emotional problems are the outgrowth of an omission or commission of behavior that violates moral standards, and, hence, the person needs to make amends and even to feel contrition over such behavior. The person must share openly with others; then, the tension or depression that stems from the behavior will lessen.

There are also a variety of *marital* therapies, which deal with the conflicts between spouses when they seek help as a couple. Similarly, there are several types of *family* therapies through which the whole family learns to recognize its difficulties and to find more desirable, alternate behaviors (Harper, 1975).

These approaches all share a common goal—to help people decrease their need for help. Each approach attempts to establish relationships built on respect and openness. There is an effort on the part of the helper to understand the problem presented, to identify the pertinent factors related to it, and to explore possible solutions. There is an emphasis on pointing out positive and growth-enhancing behaviors and in discovering ways to lessen undesirable behavior. There is an expectation that the helper will facilitate change in the client through a corrective interaction. When the outcome of therapy is successful, clients become more reality-oriented, confident, accepting of themselves, and capable of coping with problems.

Therapy in Action

In this section excerpts will be offered from therapy sessions to show how the therapeutic orientations differ from one another in actual practice. In these brief descriptions of six of the ten orientations discussed in the previous section, no attempt will be made to show how problems are solved. Rather, the descriptions will demonstrate how a client-therapist dialogue goes and what techniques may be used. Bear in mind, of course, that not all practitioners of a particular school will function exactly as presented here, since there is always considerable variation in individual styles even when therapists belong to the same school.

Adlerian therapy

Student: I don't seem to be able to stop blowing my stack. It gets me into trouble. People get turned off; I almost lost my job.

Therapist: How long have you been doing this sort of thing?

Student: I don't know. Even when I was a kid, I got into fights with my parents.

Therapist: Who would usually win?

Student: I won most of the time.

Therapist: Through anger you get your way, it seems.

Student: Yeah, it seems like it, doesn't it?

Therapist: Try and think for a moment as far back as you can. Try to recall an important event, an incident from your childhood, your earliest memory.

Student: I remember going to this drug store. I wanted ice cream, but my mother wouldn't buy me any. I raised hell, and she gave in.

Therapist: What do you make of that?

Student: Yeah, I see what you're getting at—the payoff. You mean I learned to get my way by raising hell.

Therapist: What position do you have in the family?

Student: Oh, I'm the youngest and my mother's favorite, too. My father was strict, so I avoided him.

Therapist: He is less of a challenge to you?

Student: By golly, I can see it now. It's with people I see as softies that I get so aggressive, not with strong people.

Rational-emotive therapy

Student: I don't seem to be able to stop blowing my stack. It gets me into trouble. People get turned off; I almost lost my job.

Therapist: What goes through your mind when you act this way? Is there anything you're telling yourself when you get mad like that?

Student: Well, for one thing, people listen to you more if you raise your voice and get mad. You get through to others when you're emotional; they pay attention, and they notice you.

Therapist: Well, then, if this gimmick of yours works, why are you here? What do you want from talking to me?

Student: Sometimes this "gimmick," as you say, doesn't work. But I feel that when you're soft and sweet, people think you're weak. They'll step all over you.

Therapist: How did you arrive at this conclusion?

Student: I don't know, I just did.

Therapist: I can't see where it's justified or valid.

Student: Yeah, but that's the way I think.

Therapist: But what if the thinking on which you base this action is entirely false?

Student: Well, I never thought of that.

Gestalt therapy

Student: I don't seem to be able to stop blowing my stack. It gets me into trouble. People get turned off; I almost lost my job.

Therapist: How do you feel being here with me right now?

Student: Kinda scared, I'd say. Sort of ill-at-ease right now.

Therapist: And what is going through your mind right now as you tell me that you're scared?

Student: Well, I wonder what you think of me. You might get angry at me or criticize me for getting mad easily. You might tell me to cut it out and shape up. It's just an uncomfortable feeling all over.

Therapist: Is this how you feel with other people? I mean, is this real for you in life in general? Do you always think people are going to let you have it?

Student: Yeah, I've got to be on guard most of the time—be on my toes, ready for action; otherwise, people are going to step all over me.

Therapist: It is the same in your daydreams or your fantasies?

Student: I daydream a lot, as a matter of fact, that I have authority over people; that is, they fight me with words and arguments, but I always win like a good debater. I'm always right.

Therapist: And when you dream in your sleep what kind of things go on?

Student: Well, sometimes I dream that I'm walking with another person in the dark, and I get lost. Then I get mad; I holler and scream my lungs out and finally someone rescues me.

Therapist: Do you see any connections between your feelings with me here and your feelings in your daydreams and dreams at night? Do you think there is any basic theme at work here?

Student: When I'm frightened, I attack. Get them before they get me, I guess.

Transactional analysis

Student: I don't seem to be able to stop blowing my stack. It gets me into trouble. People get turned off; I almost lost my job.

Therapist: When exactly does this happen and with whom mostly?

Student: It happens with people older than me—in fact, much older people. I don't feel that way with other students or even people in their thirties.

Therapist: Do you think older people somehow encourage you to behave more like a child?

Student: Yeah, I do seem to react to older people as if they were my parents.

Therapist: If you had to act like an adult toward them, like an equal, how would you do it? Do you have any idea? Think, for example, of how other adults relate to one another.

Student: Well, they talk more straightforward to one another. Maybe I still look at myself as a child, so I guess I act like a child. But how do I change all this?

Therapist: It seems to me that you've got the answer already; begin to see yourself as an adult like them and see what happens.

Student: But I don't necessarily feel like an adult because people seem to put me down. They make me feel young or inept.

Therapist: Maybe you're giving off vibes that tell them you feel like a child. So naturally they go on and treat you like one.

Student: There's some truth in that. And I guess there'd be no harm in trying to act older. After all, I'm not a kid.

Directive therapy

Student: I don't seem to be able to stop blowing my stack. It gets me into trouble. People get turned off; I almost lost my job.

Therapist: I suggest that you count to ten before you start talking in these situations, or else try to say nothing; then go to another room and holler at the four walls. But, if you are at work, holler quietly!

Student: Do you think that'll work? It sounds crazy.

Therapist: You'll have to try it and see if it works. Otherwise you have to realize that you are an impulsive, emotional person who must learn to control himself. The fact that letting out your emotions is getting you into trouble is a good enough reason to stop it. Obviously you're not gaining anything by this behavior.

Student: You mean I'll have to make the effort myself?

Therapist: Yes, you can practice exerting some force on yourself. Try and keep the lid down the minute you sense this rage coming up to the surface. If you do it once, it may be easier the next time.

Client-centered therapy

Student: I don't seem to be able to stop blowing my stack. It gets me into trouble. People get turned off; I almost lost my job.

Therapist: You should take an honest look at yourself and make some changes; you don't like the way you are, it seems.

Student: Yeah, I've got to stop this nonsense; I always regret it afterwards, and it bothers me a lot. I wish I could stop it.

Therapist: You're concerned over the results of your behavior.

Student: It's not getting me anywhere, and I just can't go on like this.

Therapist: You seem unhappy with what you're doing, and you want to change.

Student: Well, of course.

Therapist: By letting me get to know you better, you think we can work out an understanding of this thing you do. You think the answer lies in our exploring your feelings together.

Student: I can't spill this out to just anyone—someone I don't trust or who doesn't understand me.

Therapist: You feel you can trust me, then, and that by opening up to me you can see exactly what and why you're doing what you are doing.

Student: Yeah, you just said it; I find it easy to talk to you.

Group Psychotherapy

Group psychotherapy, a relatively recent phenomenon, has become increasingly popular. The obvious advantage of this type of therapy is that several persons may be helped simultaneously. But group psychotherapy has a more important rationale; since people develop personal problems through interaction with others, only a therapy based on interaction will help to clarify and resolve these problems. In group therapy, then, others act as stand-ins for the persons with whom one originally developed the problems. For example, if a male student who believes all females are unstable can be allowed to express his feelings to the females of the group and then feed on the reaction he receives from them, such information can serve as a corrective experience with regard to his erroneous thinking about women. Difficulties in relating with the opposite sex, unresolved conflicts with siblings, lack of trust in others, poor self-esteem, and inadequate self-identity are typical of the problems that are often overcome through group psychotherapy (Yalom, 1970). Often one client learns from another who has been able to cope successfully with a similar situation. Finally, the security and acceptance a client finds within the group will hopefully transfer to his interactions with persons outside the group.

Group therapy allows each of its members to experience the corrective input of others. As members work through their conflicts with others, they gain insight into what they are doing and why; they begin to understand how they come across to others and why others react to them as they do. Insight is generally produced by the interpretations offered by the other members, by their reactions to what the person is saying, and sometimes through their experiences in coping with similar situations, conflicts, ideas, feelings, and so on. Their probing into the person's behavior and nudging the person into seeing things in a different light can also lead to increased insight. This new knowledge enables them to behave differently and more effectively so that they may receive a more positive reaction from others. Because

Figure 10-2. A group experience can provide the freedom for us to learn from one another and to become less isolated socially. Photo by Shirley Kontos.

group therapy requires interpersonal interactions, people invariably show the undesirable aspects of their lifestyles, which are often the source of their problems. Rapid change is, therefore, often possible (Gazda, 1968).

The therapist or leader acts as a catalyst for all those present. He does not control the group; the group leads itself and makes its own decisions. Each member expresses his or her real feelings and concerns, and the therapist promotes exchange and interaction. One group member described the therapist's role as "kind of an electrician who connects the wires and causes the room to light up."

Social mobility, industrialization, the weakening of family ties—all these have increased alienation, boredom, and loneliness in people and have often made them feel powerless in large communities. Functioning within a small group helps them to cope with individual anxieties and encourages openness and contact rather than guardedness and defensiveness. Thus, group therapy has attained wide popularity in recent years and continues to attract the attention of both professional workers and clients in colleges, clinics, schools, industry, and community organizations. Learning how others feel and letting others know how you feel—even confronting someone you dislike—helps to resolve interpersonal differences. Groups encourage active involvement and reciprocal helping relationships, sharpen the ability to communicate and to interpret cues properly, and provide an understanding of how others communicate with us. Group psychotherapy emphasizes individuality as well as responsibility, and such experiences close the gap between merely intellectualizing a situation and comprehending it through our own actions and reactions with others (Jacobs & Spradlin, 1973). The study of human behavior has relied on philosophical theories as well as on biological explanations, but people are social animals, and it is perhaps within the social context that their personalities can be most fully understood.

Each group is unique because of the individuality of its members and because of each member's reasons for joining the group; thus every group progresses at its own speed. The basic function of the group process is feedback—for each member to give his or her impressions of others and to receive, in return, their impressions and reactions. Everyone does not make a major contribution at every meeting, but feelings, both positive and negative, are shared. Some group members listen, others confront; some soothe, others antagonize; but members can learn to recognize themselves in others and to gain insight into their own interactions.

Encounter groups. The term *encounter* has been applied to many diverse groups—such as human-relations groups, marathon groups, sensory-awareness groups, and sensitivity-training groups. Perhaps the most prevalent type of group is the T-group, or training group, which tends to be composed of reasonably adjusted persons who want to improve their interpersonal relationships and to become better functioning individuals (Appley & Winder, 1973). Their "leaders" may have had considerable experience or merely a short course in group processes.

Although these groups employ different methods, they are similar in many ways: they rely on nonverbal communication; they tend to be unstructured (their leaders are not always professionally trained); and their members are searching for a new experience rather than basic personality change (Yalom, 1970). Social facades theoretically dissolve as members accept one another as they are. Interpersonal honesty is encouraged and rewarded, while the "games" often relied upon by society at large to maintain a desirable social image are discouraged. Groups thrive on mutual feedback, on self-disclosure, and on the re-evaluation of beliefs and attitudes.

The competitive and mechanistic nature of our society has promoted an alienation and psychological distance among people that is at odds with the human need for physical closeness and emotional intimacy. Many individuals who have sacrificed intimacy to avoid exposure have become emotionally pent-up and are searching for emotional outlets that are safe and ego strengthening. Sensitivity training is a new medium of communication that is designed not to solve specific problems but to allow individuals to gain new insight and an emotional awareness of themselves. Sensitivity training within group encounter sessions often emphasizes physical or sensory communication, such as holding hands, embracing, touching feet, rubbing cheeks, or nude bathing, rather than verbal discussion. Self-hypnosis, physical exercises, and massage are also used.

Encounter groups may have certain disadvantages and even dangers. Their leaders do not always possess the qualifications of the trained clinician, and sponsors, in their enthusiasm, do not always fully examine the qualifications of the leaders they hire. Further, such groups may provide only a temporary boost to the egos of their members instead of a lasting improvement in their interpersonal relationships beyond the training group. In fact, when Lieberman, Yalom, and Miles (1973) surveyed college students who had participated in various types of encounter groups, they found that about one in every three had made positive and lasting changes, while one in ten had suffered psychological setbacks.

In the structured setting of these groups, however, members are afforded the opportunity to "let go," to take risks without fear of being hurt. The more frequently participants "open up" within the group, the greater the likelihood that they will be able to sustain their spontaneity outside the group. Distressful situations carried from the past may create tense feelings in a person's present, but when these situations are re-evaluated in the light of group feedback, the person may become more accepting of his or her feelings and more capable of constructive action. Sensitivity training may stimulate the senses so that individuals learn to be more aware of the feelings of others as well as of their own. They may also become more comfortable with and accepting of their own bodies and thereby less vulnerable when faced with emotional intimacy.

Industry, churches, schools, and community agencies are increasingly offering encounter groups to help people become more effective in their interpersonal relationships and more competent to cope with pressures.

People seeking a beneficial group situation should determine whether the purposes and goals of the group are consistent with their own and whether the therapist is competent; also, attendance should be on a voluntary basis. A person experiencing acute problems or a crisis situation can begin by talking to a private counselor; together they may reach a decision regarding the most suitable type of group therapy. Not everyone benefits from sensitivity training, and the person who is already in therapy of any sort should consult his or her counselor before joining such groups.

Effects of group therapy. Gibb (1970) reviewed over 250 studies of encounter groups and observed that, in general, the group members' attitudes toward themselves and others changed in a positive direction, that the members became more aware of their own feelings and those of others, and that they became more spontaneous and open in their relationships with others. Participants also reported a greater agreement between their feelings and their behavior. Other positive effects were the ability to identify with others, to cooperate with them, to experience a feeling of commitment, and to develop a sense of self-direction with less need for control and structure from others. Group participants tended to feel more comfortable about themselves; they participated with greater ease in social situations and were more able to accept people as individuals. Research, then, confirms that positive changes do occur in group settings, with enduring effects outside the group situation.

On the basis of his research and personal experiences with groups, Gibb (1968) points out that group experiences serve to validate a person's positive feelings about himself and others, thereby unfolding previously inert creative potential. Gibb maintains that such potential is not actualized through lectures, reading, or introspection: it emerges in an intimate, interpersonal experience involving informal dialogue, emotional feedback, and validating consensual reactions.

Gibb also points out that the ability to deeply enjoy a particular moment with another person, without being distracted by the past and the future and without being corrective, introspective, or competitive toward that person, is a highly significant factor in personal fulfillment. The experiences of genuine self-regard and love for others are not mutually exclusive but interdependent, and groups foster an atmosphere wherein people feel they *can* love others freely without fear or defensive behavior. Pretense is so prevalent in our society today that genuine feelings are often buried under fears of various sorts, and individuals often lose themselves in various socially prescribed roles that are stifling and dehumanizing. In a group setting, feelings emerge that often enable an individual to understand the essentials of his or her identity. Role playing diminishes in group situations, and, as we become accessible to others, the inner, inhibiting tensions of fears and doubts tend to diminish. Neither complete autonomy nor total dependency should be the product of group experience, but through sharing with others and responding honestly to them we may achieve personal integration and self-realization.

Gibb also comments on the importance of verbal communication in group experiences. The verbal messages we give can be misinterpreted; and ambiguity, to say nothing of misunderstanding, creates fear and distance, especially if the message is sensed as negative. Through experience, groups learn to clarify their words so that individuals are able to come across to others as they really are. Verbal clarity generates trust and opens new opportunities for intimate experiences and greater freedom and closeness with others.

The point has been made by Marin (1975) that some group therapies overemphasize self-reliance and tend to grant exaggerated importance to the individual at the expense of the general society. Another danger is implicit in the notion that we are responsible for our own behavior. Such an attitude can foster a callous turning away from the world that we may justify with a philosophy of "that's the way things are." Certain kinds of group therapy, then, seem to legitimize the belief that the world is absurd and confused; they justify a selfish turning inward. Thus, these group therapies fail to foster community feeling, reciprocity, and collective responsibility when it is important to recognize that our survival depends on our commitment to the world. In the final analysis, what is "out there" is nothing more than a reflection of what we ourselves are.

HELPING OURSELVES CHANGE

This section includes some beneficial techniques that, for the most part, we can do on ourselves (with a minimal amount of intervention from a therapist). The main objective of these techniques is to eliminate or lessen bothersome symptoms (anxiety, fear, lack of concentration for study) and to increase physical and mental relaxation. A primary technique is behavior modification, which will be the first technique that we will discuss.

Behavior Modification

The theory of behavior modification assumes that maladjustment is the result of unfavorable learning experiences and that behavior can, therefore, be modified by providing favorable or corrective learning experiences. In effect, an individual may unlearn certain patterns of behavior. Behavior modification refers to the relatively short-term treatment of various types of symptoms and specific maladaptive behavior, including phobias, poor social adjustment, unsatisfactory interpersonal relationships, and various destructive habits. In general, behavior-modification techniques assume that a person's problems result either from ineffective habits or from unnecessary, learned anxiety (Ullmann & Krasner, 1969).

Behavior therapy uses principles of learning to alter persistent and unsuitable habits brought on by anxiety-producing situations that interfere with the ability to function. Anxiety is created by a painful or unpleasant stimulus or situation, but it may become associated with many other stimuli or situations that have little obvious connection with its original source. A student, for instance, who nearly drowned in a swimming pool and was pulled out amid the stares of curious onlookers may become anxious in large crowds or be afraid to ask questions in the classroom because he dislikes being stared at. Neither situation at first glance seems related to the near-drowning incident; yet, the chain of association may persist strongly. Techniques of counter-conditioning or deconditioning can serve to desensitize him to these stimuli or situations.

Behavior therapy requires good rapport between therapist and client and the participation of both in the assessment of the problem. As the client experiences a lessening of symptoms, he realizes that these changes have occurred in part because of his own participation in the treatment. The client, consequently, learns to influence his own behavior in the direction of his desired intentions. In a sense, he becomes his own therapist as he forces his behavior to move in a chosen direction. Obviously such a process can only happen over a period of time, and, in the initial stages, the therapist is usually highly directive.

A number of technical terms are employed in behavior therapy. *Aversive conditioning* refers to "punishment" following undesirable behavior, such as a blast of unpleasant noise after a client's self-depreciating comment. *Positive reinforcement* involves the use of a pleasant stimulus (reward) following the behavior and thereby strengthening it. For example, if you earn excellent grades by studying hard and if the grades will assure you a scholarship, then your studying behavior will most likely be strengthened because of the favorable reward. *Extinction methods* are used to eliminate what might be a "pay off" for undesirable behavior. In such a situation, rewards such as affection and care are denied to the person who exhibits undesirable behavior. *Conditioned avoidance* pairs an unpleasant stimulus with a pleasant but detrimental behavior; for example, an emetic may be given to an alcoholic every time he drinks so that alcohol becomes associated with something unpleasant.

Progressive relaxation involves the tensing followed by the slackening of all the body muscles. While the client is in a state of complete relaxation, the unpleasant stimulus to be extinguished is introduced. As the anxiety reappears, the stimulus is removed, and the client is helped to relax again. The disturbing stimulus is then reintroduced. This procedure is repeated until the client feels comfortable with the unpleasant situation. This is a simple description of *desensitization;* the person is conditioned to relax with situations that previously made him anxious.

Behavior-modification therapy can be used for eliminating specific unwanted behaviors such as enuresis, nail biting, overeating, or other detrimental habits. However, therapists are in disagreement regarding the permanency of such "cures."

Many believe that the mere elimination of symptoms does not create a permanently improved condition, for the person may well develop the same or different symptoms if he is placed again in a stressful situation. These techniques, however, have had considerable success, and college and university psychologists and counselors increasingly rely on them. For some students, the idea of eliminating undesirable behavior by a strictly mechanistic procedure, without trying to understand why the symptom is expressed in the first place, is appealing. Another reason for the popularity of such techniques is that many mental-health workers maintain that behavior modification is at least a first step in resolving deeper, personal conflicts. If symptoms are relieved, an individual may well be in a stronger position to go on to resolve his deep-seated problems.

We will now consider more specific situations of behavior-modification theory and how certain modification techniques can be applied to bring about relearning.

Conditioning. Operant conditioning is a learning situation in which the correct response is reinforced and consequently is more likely to happen again. The person thus learns to respond in a way that brings about the desired results. If you become sick after smoking a cigar, you probably will not smoke another, and, if a cup of tea gives you a lift, then you are apt to continue drinking tea. A great deal of our behavior to succeed in society is learned behavior based on operant conditioning, as we learn to make responses that fulfill our needs and help us reach our goals. Food, comfort, and freedom from pain are *primary* reinforcers, while money, esteem, academic grades, and material possessions are examples of *acquired* reinforcers. More specifically, primary reinforcers are generally related to our survival and to our more basic needs in life, whereas secondary reinforcers are more socially determined, more apt to be affected by the environment and culture in which we live. It is obvious, then, that we can extinguish some undesirable behavior by arranging for it to occur in conjunction with an unpleasurable result. Conversely, we can strengthen desired behavior by following it with something pleasurable.

Krasner and Ullmann (1973) refer to *shaping* as guiding behavior to a desired goal by providing reinforcements in stages as a client gradually moves toward the goal. The boy who wishes to become an astronomer, for example, may require reinforcement to get through his grade school math. However, he will need different levels of reinforcement for his high school math and college algebra.

Fading is a technique by which something we initially depended on is gradually minimized until, finally, we are self-reliant. As the talkative person, for example, reduces his or her verbal output, the shy person, who may have been depending on others to maintain the conversation, may gradually begin to talk more.

Since emotions are triggered by the nervous system, they, just as actions, may also be influenced by conditioning. For example, when an unpleasant situation (darkness) is paired with a normally neutral condition (being alone), the pair (being alone and in the dark) can, through conditioning, become strongly associated. It is possible, then, for a person who finds himself alone in any situation to experience fear—even when there is nothing to be fearful about. Thus, many unpleasant feelings can be conditioned with relatively neutral persons or situations without the person's full awareness as to when and how this association was made. For example, if you are generally comfortable with people but uneasy, say, with tall persons who are also blond, it is quite possible that some kind of conditioning took place earlier in your life that you do not remember. You must now recondition yourself to tall and blond persons so that they no longer evoke unpleasant emotions. *Progressive desensitization* involves situations in which stimuli that once elicited unpleasant reactions have been re-evaluated so that they now produce emotional reactions that are pleasant or at least tolerable.

An important condition for desensitization is that the annoying or unpleasant situation be paired with relaxation—that is, the opposite of anxiety. The person who, for example, is afraid of water, might begin by relaxing and imagining he is in a pool with water up to his knees—a situation evoking little anxiety. As he relaxes, he imagines a more frightening situation—perhaps where half of his body is submerged. As he proceeds, the fear of water is gradually replaced by relaxation. Fear of cars, heights, or animals and test anxiety are examples of specific situational anxieties that can often be alleviated through progressive desensitization.

It is important to the success of the desensitization process that the situations introduced only gradually approach the real, fear-producing situation and that every step toward the desensitizing goal be reinforced positively. Progressive desensitization often requires the help of a trained professional, although deep muscle relaxation can be self-taught and is a relatively easy process once you have experienced its desirable effects (Paul, 1966).

The motivation to change is vital if behavior-modification techniques are to be effective. A relatively simple example of one technique in behavior modification is illustrated below.

Incident

A recent graduate about to assume a teaching position complained of nausea, heart palpitation, nervousness, and profuse perspiring at the thought of speaking to a large group. He had experienced these symptoms in a more limited way in his graduate classes, and he could not accept the thought of finding himself in such a psychological state for the rest of his life. He had no other significant personality or social difficulties; it seemed obvious that his main problem was anxiety associated with talking to groups.

The psychologist whom he consulted devised a procedural schedule to desensitize him to speaking before large groups of people. In an effort to train his client to be more relaxed, the therapist had him close his eyes and imagine that he was talking to someone in the room. He progressively increased the number of persons to be imagined but made certain that a state of relaxation was maintained. At the same time he switched from imagined persons to real persons in the room and gradually increased the number present. When the symptoms appeared, he would reduce the number of persons present and repeat the procedure. When the student became less sensitive about talking to a group of persons, he was able to assume a teaching career with very few interfering symptoms.

Reinforcement. When actions are followed by a new and pleasant experience, these actions are said to be positively reinforced; that is, through desirable consequences, the repetition of beneficial actions is encouraged. Money, prestige, grades, affection, respect—all these are examples of *positive reinforcement.*

Another way to change behavior or to reach a desired effect is to introduce an unpleasant experience that is discontinued when the undesirable behavior ceases; this is known as *negative reinforcement*. If a friend frowns at what you are doing and makes you feel uncomfortable and if the frown disappears when you stop, negative reinforcement occurs. If your friend slaps you when you say something unpleasant, it is *punishment*. When nothing takes place after you behave in a certain way, the *extinction* of that behavior occurs. For example, if we express love for someone who gives us neither positive nor negative reinforcement, we would tend to give up or lose interest in that love. Positive reinforcement is usually thought to be more effective than negative reinforcement or punishment. Punishment is the least effective method of changing behavior. as it does not provide an opportunity for the person to learn new and more effective ways of behaving.

Much interpersonal behavior is based on cues and responses of which we are often unaware. We act and react on the basis of cues we get from others, and we give out cues as well. A good illustration of this delicate network of messages may be seen in the behavior of a married couple. Through continuous interaction they have developed a complex system of cues and responses—verbal and nonverbal—that other persons may not always perceive clearly and are not expected to respond to. The tone of voice, the expressions in the eyes, the way the hands rest, the manner in which words are phrased—all are stimuli that may become reinforced because of the consequences that have followed these cues. Such cues tell us when and when not to act. More importantly, they may indicate the most desirable way to behave. For instance, if the cue is anger, it may be unwise to counteract with anger, as the results, from experience, may be unpleasant for both persons involved.

Using and arranging the reinforcers that you already have available can help greatly to eliminate undesirable behavior. Genuinely caring for others, showing interest in their lives, being supportive of them—all these can be positive reinforcers for one who feels lonely or unwanted, especially when the frequency and intensity of these outgoing behaviors gradually increase. Of course, individuals should select their own reinforcers and rank them according to the personal influence they have. Listening to Brahms may be a satisfactory reinforcer for one person, while drinking beer may serve the same purpose for someone else. It is not difficult to align behaviors that we do not want with behaviors that we desire if we make sure that the latter come first. If a student, for instance, spends fifty minutes daydreaming for every ten minutes he studies, he may begin by studying for ten minutes and then allowing himself to daydream for the rest of the hour. As long as the first ten minutes of study is mandatory to daydreaming, he can begin gradually increasing his study time and decreasing his daydreaming time so that he can end up spending fifty minutes studying and ten minutes daydreaming.

Self-change through reinforcement also demands that you be concerned enough with a problem to want to solve it, that you know the particular situations in which the unwanted behavior occurs, and that you identify the undesirable behavior accurately through careful observation. For example, if you want to eliminate shyness, you must determine under what conditions or in what situations you feel shy. One person may be shy with wealthy persons and quite comfortable with poor people; another person may be shy with the opposite sex but comfortable or even a social leader with members of his or her own sex. Also, shyness may be the wrong label for what is actually fear or need for approval. Examining the chain of events and noting precisely when the undesirable behavior occurs can help you decide where the change is to be made. You should take account of what happens before undesirable behavior and what happens afterward because only when you have isolated the undesirable behavior can you try to increase those behaviors that are productive and to decrease those that are destructive.

Self-change is based on learning new, more effective behaviors and unlearning ineffective ones; we reinforce what we desire to learn and try to eliminate behaviors that we do not want. To do this we must identify the specific behavior we want to eliminate or change and note how frequently it occurs, what triggers it, and what follows after it. Only then can we break the sequence by manipulating the situation so that the behavior will not occur again.

Positive reinforcement is probably the most widely used method of fostering desirable behavior and eliminating unwanted actions. If you want to strengthen a certain behavior, you can arrange for that behavior to be followed immediately by something you desire. For example, if you tend to study for only one out of every three quizzes, you can reinforce yourself every time you *do* study by following the study behavior with something you like—eating pizza, going to the movies, playing racquetball. These reinforcers, however, must immediately follow the behavior that you want to strengthen. Reinforcing a behavior that is not in harmony or agreement with an undesirable behavior can also help to lessen the latter. If you want to stop drinking alcohol, for example, you might drink a nonalcoholic beverage and increase its consumption through positive reinforcement (a delicious meal). Here you are extinguishing an undesirable habit by nourishing a desirable one.

Another effective way to eliminate undesirable behavior is to manipulate the events that occur just prior to the undesirable behavior. One way to halt an antecedent event (a person or a situation) that leads to undesirable behavior is to avoid that event entirely and to strengthen the avoidance response through positive reinforcement. If you wish to stop drinking beer every evening, begin by staying away from situations where beer is served. Then strengthen this behavior with a reinforcer (playing basketball, taking guitar lessons) that means something to you just as drinking beer did. Undesirable interpersonal behavior can be handled in a similar way. If you tend to quarrel with someone because you feel he makes negative or hostile remarks, you can learn to pause before you respond to such remarks and to reinforce positively any pleasant comments he makes. In this manner, you may actually "train" him to be more pleasant toward you without his knowing it.

Breaking up the usual chain of events leading to undesirable behavior is also helpful. The beer drinker noted above might observe what he routinely does prior to drinking beer. Does he watch TV, eat, read, or talk? Then he might make a conscious substitution or re-arrangement. He might listen to a record or go for a walk instead; that is, he might do things in a different order and in combination with new activities to break the chain.

Finally, it is also helpful to do something you find difficult, but desirable, under only the most favorable situations. If you are shy, for example, but find that after a vigorous swim you are relaxed and able to talk with someone at the poolside, you can reinforce this social success within that particular situation. Then by gaining confidence in one such situation, you can more easily begin the same behavior in similar situations, as, for example, talking to someone on the bus or in a class.

However, the behavior involved in this spreading effect, known as *generalization,* must begin within a favorable setting and then be extended to less optimal circumstances.

Modeling. Imitation or *modeling* refers to adopting behavior by observing how others have successfully achieved their goals. If we examine such a process more closely, we discover that most of our behavior since childhood has been learned by watching others. Indeed, imitation or modeling is a widely used way of learning new behavior—whether it be language, baseball, singing, or writing. By observing others, we may eventually incorporate their behavior as part of ourselves, provided, of course, that this behavior is reinforced (Bandura, 1969). Modeling behavior is not so much "copying" as it is a process of self-discovery, of learning what responses are appreciated and valued by others and at the same time acceptable and natural to ourselves. Only through experimentation can we learn this.

Relaxation. Students can learn to use relaxation techniques—a first step in inducing a mild form of self-hypnosis—to alleviate anxiety and tension (Jacobson, 1970). One such technique is to focus attention on a single object or to concentrate on a pleasurable past experience for several minutes at a time. The idea is to recapture a pleasant mood that will allow you to block out annoying stimuli or thoughts. Another technique is to press hard on your knees for several minutes. As you sit forward in a chair, place the palms of your hands on your knees with all the pressure focused downwards. Squeeze as tightly as possible for as long as you can. Then, reduce the pressure. If you deliberately produce muscle tension that cannot be physiologically maintained, the tension will ultimately be released and general relaxation will follow.

Sex can be used as a "tranquilizer" since it relieves tension states. Some tense persons rely on pills to "calm down," others need a few martinis in the evening to "loosen up," and still others depend on marijuana to relax. Exercising for a certain period each day has an enormously tranquilizing effect on the person who is likely to become tense in a sedentary position during most of the day. A hot bath or shower, massage, or meditation are other effective ways to relax. Too often people in our psychologically sophisticated culture react to tension as evidence of "neurosis" and indicative of the need for therapy; instead, proper physical activity and a different outlook on life may be the only prescription required.

Teachers of physical education have long advocated exercise and physical fitness as a means of lowering anxiety states, and there is some evidence that athletes are generally likely to experience less anxiety than nonathletes. One study, for example, suggests that exercise reduced neuromuscular tension more efficiently than simple relaxation (de Vries, 1966). Studies on the effects of physical activity in lowering anxiety have not been unanimous, perhaps because of the many different types of anxiety, but a recent survey (Martens, 1972) concluded that prolonged physical activity generally tends to lower anxiety and tension. More research in this area is needed, however, to demonstrate the specific relationship between reduced anxiety and physical activity.

Some people avoid emotional outbursts because they fear that losing their "cool" will brand them as unstable individuals. Well-adjusted and intellectually competent people, however, accept that part of themselves that wants to express itself in feeling and emotion. Weeping, joy, excitement, anger, and laughter help to express pent-up feelings and promote relaxation. Finally, confiding in a close and trusted friend and being more outspoken and less sensitive to the opinions of others also helps to reduce tension.

An individual's emotional condition can make his body tense and strained. A desire for perfection, undue ambition, excessive concern over details and deadlines, the fatigue associated with studying, and strained interpersonal relationships can create and maintain tension. The student, for example, who is rigid in his thinking and actions and who behaves in a compulsive manner often finds that he is unable to relax. A reexamination of his philosophy toward life may offer him new perspectives; he can learn to reorder his priorities in order to reduce strain. Learning to do one thing at a time and with proper intervals of rest and recreation is often an effective formula. Confiding in someone he trusts can also relieve tension. He can also relax parts of the body by applying muscle tension—by stretching the muscles and making them rigid—and by gradually releasing this tension.

Transpersonal Psychology

The human being gains pleasure from altering the senses, the feelings, and the mind; we naturally desire to lessen what is dull and boring and to heighten the pleasant and unusual. In fact, all of us have an enormous capacity to alter our levels of consciousness (awareness of ourselves and of things around us). Psychedelic experiences, meditation, visions, dreams, intuition, trances, and hypnosis are examples of varying levels and depths of consciousness. Some of these altered states of awareness are brought about by mind-altering drugs (such as LSD or peyote) and, also, by alcohol and marijuana. Some persons experience a deep awareness through prayer, listening to music, reading, being alone in nature, or living through moments of intense love for someone. There is a wide range of possibility, and each of us experiences levels of awareness in very individual ways. The exploration of levels of awareness is sometimes loosely referred to as *transpersonal* psychology.

These new and innovative techniques for behavior change often involve unique inner experiences and mind and body control. The aim of transpersonal psychology is to expand our personal boundaries and to get in touch with our inner selves. While humanistic psychology stresses the development of social conditions for personal growth, transpersonal psychology has more to do with developing our inner lives, with understanding our feelings, and hopefully with exerting control over them. By exploring the deepest folds within ourselves, transpersonal psychology aims to uncover realms of consciousness that usually remain undetected by others. A few of the more common techniques are described in the next sections.

Transcendental meditation. Another way to promote fulfillment and personal well being in our competitive and stressful lives is through the transcendental-meditation technique, which originated in India and was brought to this country by the Maharishi Mahesh Yogi in the late 60s. Transcendental meditation seems to be an answer for some to the tensions and pressures of contemporary life, for it helps one achieve tranquility and personal contentment. This technique advocates that the individual sit quietly with closed eyes and repeat a *mantra,* or specially selected series of Sanskrit syllables, for 20 minutes twice every day. Theoretically, this procedure enables individuals to shut out everyday distractions, to concentrate on themselves and their own bodies, and to thus get in touch with the deeper layers of the mind. This technique, however, does not involve hypnosis, suggestion, or any other form of mental control. It is merely allowing thoughts to come and go freely, without control.

In the tradition of humanistic psychology, transcendental meditation is based on the idea that all of us have the ability, with proper training, to cause and direct change in ourselves, to initiate greater personal efficiency, and to discover new possibilities for fulfillment. Further, it is based on the premise that we improve society as we enhance our individual lives.

One study examining the effects of transcendental meditation on personality shows that students who engaged in regular meditation sessions for two months developed greater self-regard and self-acceptance, became more emotionally spontaneous, and showed greater capacity for intimate contact with others than did a control group (Seeman, Nidich, & Banta, 1972). These authors note that the psychological changes they found in these students are very close to the personality characteristics of actualized persons. Another research study indicates that people in a meditation session become deeply rested and, afterwards, mentally alert and apparently refreshed. Their heart rate, oxygen consumption, and degree of anxiety decrease during their "session"—clear indicators of a deep state of restfulness (Wallace, 1970). Reaction time, physical performance, clear thinking, emotional stability, ability to recover from stress, and ability to learn better also seem to increase as a result of transcendental meditation. The meditator often becomes more spontaneous and creative and behaves with greater freedom (International Meditation Society, 1972). Research also indicates that persons who practice transcendental meditation are less apt to use stimulants, tranquilizers, or anti-depressants to lessen their symptoms and improve their general feelings of well being.

Alpha biofeedback. Alpha biofeedback is the name given to the experimental process that assesses our physiological processes during relaxation. By relying on this technique, a person can learn to induce relaxation.

The brain constantly emits various electrical waves. One of these waves is the *alpha*-wave, which increases when a person is relaxed and rested, although awake, or when a person has closed his or her mind to outside distractions. If individuals receive feedback on the state of their alpha waves, they can learn to increase them voluntarily through further relaxation. In other words, through the use of electronic devices, they can monitor what is happening within them and, with training, can change or control these inner states. With one type of biofeedback machine, electrodes are applied to the subject's head and are attached to the machine, which emits a tone when alpha waves are being produced. From another room the subject is instructed by microphone on how to relax. When the tone appears, the subject recognizes that the state of alpha waves has increased, and he learns to associate this tone with the feeling of restfulness and relaxation that produced it. Later, he can learn to reproduce these feelings on his own without the use of a machine. Mastering this feedback technique may require about 20 one-hour sessions for most people (Roche Report, 1974).

The theory behind biofeedback implies that the mind can be trained to control the bodily processes. Such control is not merely conditioning, as we generally know it; and, although we do not know the exact factors involved, we do know that when we receive feedback on bodily changes with the help of a machine, we are able to influence the feelings and thoughts that are associated with the bodily changes that reflect relaxation and restfulness. At present, relatively few well-controlled studies on the effects of biofeedback techniques exist; but researchers seem to find this a promising area for future investigation, and complex and sophisticated equipment is being used experimentally to examine ways by which relaxation can be induced by the person himself.

Asthma, sleeplessness, high blood pressure, epilepsy, irregular heartbeat, headaches, fears, and anxiety have been lessened through alpha biofeedback (Birk, 1973). In at least one respect, this technique is not a radical departure from other therapeutic techniques we have discussed, for it too emphasizes the individual responsibility each of us must accept for creating and maintaining our own well-being. By getting in touch with ourselves and by bringing previously involuntary bodily functions under voluntary control through alpha biofeedback, we may come close to a mind-cure approach that can lessen many of our physical symptoms—a view held for many years but only recently verified through modern electronic techniques.

Yoga. Yoga is an Asian-oriented technique based on the assumption that our bodies must be rested before our minds can become serene. The practice of yoga is becoming popular in our culture and is used successfully as a form of relaxation against tension and anxiety (Iyengar, 1966). Yoga aims to make the body free of tension so that we can psychologically become more in touch with our bodies and our environment. While yoga was originally devised to help people withstand the harsh physical living conditions in the East, in our times yoga is used to help the practitioner attain greater relaxation, a healthier muscle tone, and a greater awareness of the mind and body.

The tightening and relaxing of muscles and the various controlled postures and breathing exercises of yoga may appear rigid and ineffective to many Westerners, who are more accustomed to rigorous exercise and sports for relaxation. The theory behind yoga, however, is that since our bodies maintain one usual posture during the waking hours of the day, some parts do not receive an adequate supply of blood. By assuming bodily positions different from ordinary ones and tilting our body away from the center of gravity, we increase the blood flow into those areas and thereby help the functioning of the hormones and the glands. These changes make us more aware of our bodily processes and result in relaxation.

The "Body" Psychotherapies

The body-psychotherapy approach toward self-actualization emphasizes the wisdom of the body and urges us to become more in touch with its functions and changes. Instead of calming and tranquilizing the body in order to block out interfering anxiety, these approaches attempt to excite the senses in order to bring about a fuller appreciation of sensory processes and their use in a creative, constructive way. The main idea here is to attain psychological well-being through our bodies. Some therapists, however, feel that these therapies are quite superficial because they do not really define essential problems.

Reichian therapy. Wilhelm Reich (1949) maintains that our creative energy is numbed by seven rings of protective muscular armor, which can be broken up by direct bodily manipulation of a given area. This manipulation allows negative emotions to be released. These "rings" start from the top of the head and end at the lower part of the spine. For Reich, the term armor means the stiff, tensed-up muscles that protect a person from experiencing feelings and sensations that he finds painful and generally unpleasant and that block his creative energy and freedom. From the manner in which a person behaves, the Reichian therapist can determine which "ring" is blocked and can then help the client by performing certain prescribed exercises on that area. Reich, at times, appears to treat the human body as if it were a "bundle of stiff muscles," but many clients have found help in this procedure.

Bio-energetic therapy. Alexander Lowen (1967) adopted certain Reichian principles in dealing with emotional problems through body psychotherapy. Lowen, like Reich, attempts to remove external muscular blocks by unstiffening the muscles so that body energy can circulate more freely. In this manner repressed emotions are released through, for example, yelling or even kicking something, as these actions can release pent-up negative feelings. Lowen pays less attention to direct body contact and muscular manipulation than does Reich, stressing instead methods by which the client can let go of the emotions through verbalizations and self-directed exercises.

Primal therapy. Arthur Janov (1970), the originator of primal therapy, postulates that we experience pain and tension when our needs for food, comfort, warmth, love, privacy, and the like are not met. This tension and pain lie buried and, according to Janov, need to be relived by the client so that he or she may associate the original experience with his or her present life. We all have experienced critical episodes in our lives that have hurt us; these Janov calls primal scenes. The pain ("scream") from the unpleasant experience has been kept out of our awareness, laid away unexpressed in the unconscious portion of our personality. Janov's theory implies that, if we are able to live through that scene again, we are no longer burdened with the fear connected with it and may live fuller and more creative lives. Since we did not consciously experience the pain of the primal scene in the first place, we cannot change until we relive the experience and feel it intensely at a conscious level. This theory seems valid; however, careful research is needed to establish whether these methods are effective over a long period of time.

Other body therapies may include creative dance or body movements, which may consist of unrehearsed and spontaneous movements and uninhibited physical expressions. Once the body can "let go," it may pave the way for the feelings and the thoughts inside the person to come out in a freer manner. Body massage, known for centuries for its soothing effects on the human body, is another technique that is based on the therapeutic benefits of muscle tension relief. Even sauna baths, steam baths, or whirlpool baths may be included here, as these have similar effects on some persons.

RESOURCES FOR GROWTH

There are many activities, programs, and projects in any community that foster actualization and self-fulfillment. "No man is an island," and growth usually begins within a group of some sort—through relationships with others in meaningful work, in educational situations, and in creative endeavors.

One way toward fulfillment is to find satisfaction in our work. Ultimately, most of us spend much of our lives working; thus, it is imperative that our work be satisfying and meaningful to us. If our work is boring and unchallenging, we often become unhappy with other aspects of our lives, for work may not only support us materially but also give us a feeling of accomplishment and a source of enrichment.

Sometimes personal circumstances have prevented us from discovering what it is we can best do with ourselves. Besides job skills, we need to broaden our capacity to feel, to hope, to wonder, to care, to understand, to love, and to be at home with ourselves. Indeed, it sometimes seems that we are more concerned with "what people will say" than with what it is we ourselves wish to say. In short, each life is a personal statement, and the work you choose to do is a critical declaration.

Growing with a college education and participating in recreational activities are other ways we can fulfill ourselves. Interacting with peers and instructors helps you to evaluate yourself, assess where you are, and predict in which direction you might best move.

Offering your services for the benefit of others also has a fulfilling effect on your personality and expands your outlook on life. Seeing changes in others as the result of your own intervention demonstrates that you have some control over life and that you are an effective agent of action worthy of the respect and affection of others.

Like other kinds of group membership, participation in religious activities can foster personal growth and self-discovery as well as forge new bonds of human connectedness. In religious experience, one may find the comfort and the understanding that our materialistic and competitive society often fails to provide.

SUMMARY

Every person has the potential to find fulfillment and to actualize himself or herself through interpersonal intimacy, commitment to worthwhile goals, and meaningful social relationships. When these outlets fail, we can seek professional help, which may range from career counseling to in-depth psychoanalysis. We may seek this help from a variety of sources: from the psychiatrist who holds a medical degree and can use medication for emotional conditions, from the psychologist trained in the scientific understanding of human behavior, from the counselor who deals with the management of more immediate problem situations, from the

Figure 10-3. Growth is understanding how we came to be what we are and how we can change from what we are into what we want to be. Photo by Shirley Kontos.

psychiatric social worker who may manipulate the environment to help the client find better adjustment, or from the psychoanalyst who uses Freudian techniques to give us insight for constructive action. There is an enormous overlap in the duties and responsibilities of these workers; they share the goal of helping clients to become better functioning and more fulfilled persons, just as they share the personality characteristics of warmth, empathy, genuineness of feelings, and intuitive understanding.

In general, psychotherapy is a process whereby therapist and client, through verbal communication, create an interaction that is designed to clarify certain factors associated with a particular difficulty and to effect a subsequent change in the client's behavior that enables him to cope with difficulties more effectively. Through the identification of the problem and a re-evaluation of the client's reaction to it, the client gains insight into his behavior; through encouragement in an atmosphere of honesty and acceptance, he considers new alternatives in behavior and begins to function in a more competent manner. Counseling, on the other hand, refers to the solution of rather immediate problems, particularly to the clarifying of vocational goals. Psychotherapy and counseling, however, can take place on a group basis with much the same principles of interaction.

Several group processes are used in therapy, depending on the goals to be achieved. Some concentrate on personal effectiveness, while others focus on self-analysis and personality change. Sensitivity training and behavior-modification techniques are innovative new approaches that are proving helpful in the attainment of self-actualization. Although there is considerable overlap between encounter groups and group psychotherapy, the former concentrates more on nonverbal communication and immediate social relationships and is entered into by "normal" persons, while the latter encourages personality change through the intense intervention of professional workers.

Just as there is a variety of trained professionals knowledgeable in the techniques of group and individual interaction, so is there an increasing number of interventions by such professionals. There seems, however, to be a trend to rely on group methods to achieve individual actualization. Although the psychotherapeutic techniques of all these methods vary considerably, they share the goal of offering the client valid human relationships and providing him with a setting in which he may grow and change in order to become a fully functioning person.

Personal fulfillment, however, is not a trained specialist's "gift" to a seeking client. Indeed, most of us achieve actualization and self-realization on our own. Through our own family we can find fulfillment, as we can in our careers, in religious activities, in community projects, in creative endeavors, and in a host of other broadly educational programs. Giving of ourselves to others through volunteer participation, taking an active part in sports and recreational activities, or joining self-help groups for particular problems are other ways of achieving personal growth on our own. It is not only the kind of persons we are that determines the happiness we find in life, but also the knowledge that we have about ourselves and the world around us that determines how effective our response to life will be.

QUESTIONS TO THINK ABOUT

1. Have you had experience with any of the "helpers" discussed in this chapter? What were your expectations? Did you find the assistance you received to be worthwhile and lasting?
2. Have you ever experienced a helpful relationship with a friend, relative, or other person who was not psychologically trained? Did this person have qualities similar to those given as characteristic of trained therapists? Did this person have something else that trained therapists may not necessarily have?
3. Can you think of a problem that might be resolved through behavior

modification? Could you set up a program for yourself through which you could eliminate this problem, say by desensitization or reinforcement? Explain the nature of the problem and the program you propose to eliminate it.
4. Would you tend to seek group therapy or individual help? Explain. Would the nature of your problem govern your choice?
5. Has this chapter helped you to find better ways to actualize yourself? Explain.

REFERENCES

Ansbacher, H. L., & Ansbacher, R. E. (Eds.). *The individual psychology of Alfred Adler.* New York: Basic Books, 1956.

Appley, D. G., & Winder, A. E. *T-groups and therapy groups in a changing society.* San Francisco: Jossey-Bass, 1973.

Bandura, A. *Principles of behavior modification.* New York: Holt, Rinehart & Winston, 1969.

Bergin, A. E., & Jasper, L. G. Correlates of empathy in psychotherapy: A replication. *Journal of Abnormal Psychology,* 1969, *74*(4), 477-481.

Berne, E. *Transactional analysis in psychotherapy.* New York: Grove, 1961.

Birk, L. (Ed.). *Biofeedback: Behavioral medicine.* New York: Grune & Stratton, 1973.

Burton, A. *Twelve therapists: How they live and actualize themselves.* San Francisco: Jossey-Bass, 1972.

Carkhuff, R. R. *Helping and human relations* (Vols. I & II). New York: Holt, Rinehart & Winston, 1969.

Culbert, S. A., Clark, J. V., & Bobele, H. K. Measures of change toward self-actualization in two sensitivity training groups. *Journal of Counseling Psychology,* 1968, *15*(1), 53-57.

de Vries, H. A. *Physiology of exercise for physical education athletes.* Dubuque, Iowa: W.C. Brown, 1966.

Dollard, J., & Miller, N. E. *Personality and Psychotherapy.* New York: McGraw-Hill, 1950.

Ellis, A. *Reason and emotion in psychotherapy.* New York: Lyle Stuart, 1962.

Gazda, G. M. (Ed.). *Basic approaches to group psychotherapy and group counseling.* Springfield, Ill.: Thomas, 1968.

Gibb, J. R. Group experiences and human potentialities. In H. A. Otto (Ed.), *Human potentialities.* St. Louis, Mo.: Warren H. Green, 1968.

Gibb, J. R. The effects of human relations training. In A. E. Bergin & S. L. Garfield (Eds.), *Handbook of psychotherapy and behavior change.* New York: Wiley, 1970.

Harper, R. A. *The new psychotherapies.* Englewood Cliffs, N.J.: Prentice-Hall, 1975.

International Meditation Society. *Scientific Research on Transcendental Meditation.* Los Angeles: Maharishi International University, 1972.

Iyengar, B. K. S. *Light on yoga.* New York: Schocken Books, 1966.

Jacobs, A., & Spradlin, W. (Eds.). *The group as agent of change.* New York: Behavioral Publications, 1973.

Jacobson, E. *Modern treatment of tense patients.* Springfield, Ill.: Thomas, 1970.

Janov, A. *The primal scream.* New York: Putnam, 1970.

Krasner, L., & Ullmann, L. P. *Behavior influence and personality.* New York: Holt, Rinehart & Winston, 1973.

Lieberman, M. A., Yalom, I. D., & Miles, M. B. *Encounter groups: First facts.* New York: Basic Books, 1973.

Lowen, A. *The betrayal of the body.* New York: Macmillan, 1967.

Marin, P. The new narcissism. *Harper's Magazine,* October 1975, 49-56.

Martens, R. Trait and state anxiety. In W. P. Morgan (Ed.), *Ergogenic aids and muscular performance.* New York: Academic Press, 1972.

Martin, D. G. *Introduction to psychotherapy.* Belmont, Calif.: Brooks/Cole, 1971.

May, R., Angel, E., & Ellenberger, H. F. (Eds.), *Existence.* New York: Basic Books, 1958.

Patterson, C. H. *Theories of counseling and psychotherapy* (2nd ed.). New York: Harper & Row, 1973.

Paul, G. L. *Insight vs. desensitization in psychotherapy.* Stanford, Calif.: Stanford University Press, 1966.

Reich, W. *Character analysis.* New York: Farrar, Straus & Giroux, 1949.

Reisman, J. M. *Toward the integration of psychotherapy.* New York: Wiley, 1971.

Roche Report. Alpha biofeedback: Makes waves in self-treatment. *Frontiers of Psychiatry,* 1974, *4*(1), 1-2.

Rogers, C. R. *On becoming a person.* Boston: Houghton, Mifflin, 1961.

Royce, J. E. *Personality and mental health.* Milwaukee: Bruce, 1964.

Schofield, W. *Psychotherapy, the purchase of friendship.* Englewood Cliffs, N.J.: Prentice-Hall, 1964.

Seeman, W., Nidich, S., & Banta, T. Influence of transcendental meditation on a measure of self-actualization. *Journal of Counseling Psychology,* 1972, *19*(3), 184-187.

Thorne, F. *Principles of personality counseling.* Brandon, Vt.: Journal of Clinical Psychology, 1950.

Truax, C., Wargo, D., Frank, J., Imber, S., Battle, C., Hoehn-Saric, R., Nash, E., & Stone, A. Therapist empathy, genuineness, and warmth and patient therapeutic outcome. *Journal of Consulting Psychology,* 1966, *30*(5), 395-401.

Ullmann, L. P., & Krasner, L. *A psychological approach to abnormal behavior.* Englewood Cliffs, N.J.: Prentice-Hall, 1969.

Wallace, R. K. Physiological effects of transcendental meditation. *Science,* 1970, *167*(3926), 1751-1754.

Yalom, I. D. *The theory and practice of group psychotherapy.* New York: Basic Books, 1970.

Name Index

Subject Index

Adjustment, 115-116
 during adolescence, 185-189
Adlerian therapy, 277, 279-280
Aggressiveness, 64-65
Alcohol abuse, 204-205
Alienation, 193-196
Alpha biofeedback, 294-295
Ambivalence, 55
Anxiety, 117-120
 basic, 19
Assertiveness, 63-64
Attitude, 69-70
 changes in, 168
Autonomic nervous system, 53, 123
Avoidance, conditioned, 287

Behavior modification, 5, 278, 286-294
Behaviorism, 5, 14-15, 23
Beliefs, mistaken, 108-110
Bio-energetic therapy, 296
Birth trauma, 35
Black students' struggle, 248-249
Blocking, 170
Body language, 177
Body psychotherapies, 295-297

Career development, 102-104
Changes during college years, 190-191
Childrearing, 52
City living, 251-253
Client-centered therapy, 277, 281-282
Clinical psychologist, 270
Cognition, 91-92
Cohabitation, 229-232
College, adjustment to, 183-189
Common Cause, 259
Communal living, 229
Communication, 174-178
 improvement of, 176-177
 levels of, 174-176
 nonverbal, 177-178
 verbal, 44, 174-176
Compensation, 128-129
Competence, 20-21
 for coping, 163-165
 interpersonal, 43-46
Concession, 167
Conditioning, 287-292
Conformity, social, 67
Conscience, 68-69
Consummerism, 255
Coping, 161-176
 definition of, 161-163
 developing competence for, 163-165
 ways of, 165-174

Counseling psychologist, 270-271
Creative self, 13
Crying, 172

Dating, 220-221
Daydreaming, 138-139
Defense mechanisms, 128-141
Deficiency motivation, 84-85
Deliriants, 201
Denial, 140-141
Dependency, 62-63
Depressants, 200
Depression, 120-123
Desensitization, 287
Devaluation, 140
Directive therapy, 278, 281
Disengagement, 169
Disorders, personality, 145-147
Displacement, 136
Divorce, 232-233
Drives, 84-86
Drug abuse, 200-204

Ecology, 253-254
Educational goals, 243-245
Efficacy, feeling of, 21
Ego, 10-11, 95-97
Emotions, 87-91
 communicating, 44
 dealing with, 89-91
 stages of emotional growth, 88-89
Encounter groups, 284-285
Ethnocentrism, 70-71
Exhibitionism, 146
Existential psychology, 5, 15, 23
Existential therapy, 278
Extinction, 290

Fading, 288
Fallacious thinking, 160
Family climate, 60-61
Family structure, 59-62
 changes in, 61-62
Family therapy, 279
Fetishism, 147
Flight into activity, 171
Free association, 22
Freedom, 6
Fulfillment, 3, 31-46
 drive toward, 31-32
 paths to, 32-46

Gestalt therapy, 278, 280-281
Group affiliation, 72-74
Group identity, 241-242

306